# THROUGH THE HOWLING WILDERNESS

# THROUGH THE HOWLING WILDERNESS

The 1864 Red River Campaign and Union Failure in the West

## Gary D. Joiner

With a Foreword by Edwin C. Bearss

The University of Tennessee Press / Knoxville

Sections of chapters 2, 3, 4, and 6 draw on material first set out in Gary D. Joiner and
Charles E. Vetter, "The Union Naval Expedition on the Red River, March 12–May 22, 1864,"
*Civil War Regiments* 4, no. 2 (1994): 26–67.

In parallel with the work for this volume, the author produced a shorter study of the military
campaigns for the general reader, published as *One Damn Blunder from Beginning to End:
The Red River Campaign of 1864* (Wilmington, DE: Scholarly Resources, 2003). Sections of
chapters 3–7 appear in a shorter summary form there, along with a more detailed account of
the Confederate defenses in the Red River Valley, particularly those in and near Shreveport,
and some of the maps used in this volume and created by the author.

This book is printed on acid-free paper.

Library of Congress Cataloging-in-Publication Data

Joiner, Gary D.
   Through the howling wilderness : the 1864 Red River Campaign and Union failure in the
West / Gary D. Joiner ; foreword by Edwin C. Bearss. — 1st ed.
      p. cm.
Includes bibliographical references and index.

ISBN-13: 978-1-57233-544-8 (hardcover : alk. paper)
ISBN-10: 1-57233-544-0 (hardcover : alk. paper)

   1. Red River Expedition, 1864.
   2. Louisiana—History—Civil War, 1861–1865—Campaigns.
   3. Arkansas—History—Civil War, 1861–1865—Campaigns.
   4. United States—History—Civil War, 1861–1865—Campaigns.
   5. United States—History—Civil War, 1861–1865—Riverine operations.
   6. United States. Army—History—Civil War, 1861–1865.
   7. United States. Navy—History—Civil War, 1861–1865.
   8. Strategy—History—19th century.
   I. Title.

E476.33.J66 2006
973.7'36—dc22            2006011466

To Edwin Cole Bearss, chief historian emeritus of the National Park Service and the nation's preeminent Civil War scholar, who taught the author, at age twelve, what it means to be a historian.

**The value of initiative cannot be overestimated.**

—General Richard Taylor

# CONTENTS

# ILLUSTRATIONS

## Figures

## Maps

# FOREWORD

For too long the 1864 Red River Campaign, certainly by most criteria an important military operation with far-reaching political and economic ramifications, has been slighted by historians and a reading public fascinated by the Civil War in the East and, particularly, by the two great armies that battled there. Thankfully, in the years since the Civil War Centennial, but especially beginning with the books by Thomas L. Connelly, Wiley Sword, Albert Castel, Richard McMurry, and others, the war in America's heartland now commands due recognition.

Ludwell H. Johnson's well-received *Red River Campaign: Politics and Cotton in the Civil War*, published in 1958, sounded a corresponding drumbeat, but it was little heeded until the 1990s, when it called forth a similar upsurge of interest in the war's largest, and arguably most significant, amphibious campaign. In the years since I became involved as a member of the congressionally mandated Civil War Sites Advisory Commission (CWSAC) and in heritage tourism, the Red River Campaign has begun to command the attention it merits. Sites associated with the Red River battle actions, both on land and water, as well as the marches and engagements associated with General Frederick Steele's Camden Expedition, have been identified and evaluated as nationally significant.

My association with CWSAC, preservation groups, and heritage tourism required me to become familiar with the Red River Campaign and its sites. In October 1994, at a three-day meeting of Jerry Russell's Civil War Round Table Associates in Alexandria, I met Gary D. Joiner. I was already familiar with his scholarship and interest in Union naval operations, having prepared the foreword for a collection of monographs on the Red River Campaign published first in the journal *Civil War Regiments* and later by Parabellum Press. The article Gary coauthored with Charles E. Vetter was titled, "The Union Naval Expedition on the Red River, March 12–May 22, 1864." Vetter, sadly, died some four months before the conference, but when Joiner addressed the associates, they were as impressed as I by his knowledge and by his responses in the ensuing question-and-answer session.

Since then, Joiner's and my travels have crossed a number of times as resource people for *Delta Queen* cruises up the Red River, for land-based expeditions for

History America and Blue & Gray Education Society, and for other tour groups whose participants delight in walking in the footsteps of history.

For me, these tours were also a learning experience. They underscored the fact that, within a decade, Joiner's research and writing skills had made him an unsurpassed font of information on naval and amphibious warfare in the Red River basin. In 2003 he published his anxiously awaited and critically hailed *One Damn Blunder from Beginning to End: The Red River Campaign of 1864.* Here, Joiner not only provides an excellent overview of General Nathaniel Banks's failed campaign but also pulls no punches in his evaluations of Union plans and their leaders. Nor does General E. Kirby Smith escape the author's ire. What sets this book apart is Joiner's recognition that the Red River Campaign was an amphibious operation and that its success or failure was dependent on the cooperation of the Union army and navy and their leaders and on the vagaries of the Red River and its former channels. Joiner's study of the paper trail, reinforced by his knowledge of the region's geography, enabled him to solve problems that eluded Admiral David D. Porter then and historians until today—that is, to explain why the Red River's annual rise did not occur in the spring of 1864. What had been heretofore attributed to weather conditions was part of a brilliant scheme by Confederate engineers that diverted much of the Red's water into a former channel. Joiner's assessment of the Confederates' use of hydraulics—and other important features of technology, including submarines—and their knowledge of geography to first check and then turn back the Federal advance on Shreveport is enlightening.

Having said this, I was honored when Joiner and the editors of the University of Tennessee Press invited me to read the manuscript and to prepare the foreword for *Through the Howling Wilderness: The 1864 Red River Campaign and Union Failure in the West.* I was honored because Joiner's latest is a tour de force. Whereas in his 2003 publication he gave us an excellent overview of the battles fought by Banks's people in Louisiana and Steele's in Arkansas, this time he goes into greater detail. He gives more attention to the Union's unsuccessful efforts to carry the war into Texas following the capture of Vicksburg and Port Hudson. His chapter on the hearings before the Joint Committee on the Conduct of the War makes clear why, in the next century, Senator Harry S. Truman studied the records of those proceedings when he chaired the Senate Committee Investigating the National Defense Program. This enabled Truman to identify pitfalls he should avoid in conducting such hearings.

Joiner also returns to his first love, the navy. He provides the rationale for why Admiral Porter cannibalized his Mississippi Squadron to take it up Red River, an inappropriate armada that included timberclads, river monitors, most of the Eads City series ironclads, and tinclads. Particularly unnecessary was the giant ironclad *Eastport,* which proved to be a Jonah.

A number of informative appendixes are included and are relevant to understanding the scope of the navy's commitment to the expeditions. The many computer-generated maps are invaluable, along with the illustrations. *Through the Howling Wilderness* goes that "extra mile" in giving us a better appreciation of the significance of the war in the Trans-Mississippi and how not to conduct an amphibious campaign. It will appeal to a broad audience. Defeat on the Red River had major and far-reaching repercussions on how the Confederate and Union leaders employed their resources during the Atlanta Campaign, and it probably prolonged the war.

*Edwin C. Bearss*
*Historian Emeritus*
*National Park Service*

# Acknowledgments

No author creates a work alone. This is particularly true of historians. Research is often a labyrinthine process and colleagues often open doors to new areas of investigation. I want to thank those who have assisted in my efforts, either directly or indirectly in projects that resulted in this volume. For those I don't mention, please forgive me.

Archivists are the historian's best ally. They collect and organize primary source material that is vital for study. I have been fortunate to work with some of the best, particularly DeAnne Blanton, at the National Archives and Records Administration in Washington, D.C.; Sherry Pugh, at Jackson Barracks in New Orleans; and Laura Connerly, now retired from Louisiana State University in Shreveport. This book would not have been possible without them. I also want to thank the other archivists of Louisiana State University in Shreveport; Hill Memorial Library at Louisiana State University in Baton Rouge; the Howard Tilton Library at Tulane University in New Orleans; Wilson Library at the University of North Carolina, Chapel Hill; the U.S. Army Military History Institute at Carlisle Barracks Pennsylvania; the U.S. Navy Historical Center at the Washington Navy Yard in Washington, D.C.; the University of Texas in Austin; Hamilton County Library in Cincinnati, Ohio; and the Cayuga County Museum in Auburn, New York.

I have been privileged to know and work with some of the best researchers and writers working on the history of the Mississippi Valley and the region to its west. I consider them my friends as well as colleagues: Ed Bearss, chief historian emeritus of the National Park Service; Anne Bailey, professor of history at the Georgia College and State University, Milledgeville; Arthur Bergeron, archivist at the U.S. Army Military History Institute at Carlisle Barracks, Pennsylvania; Jeffrey Prushankin, professor of history at Pennsylvania State University, Abington; Lieutenant Colonel Dana Mangham, professor of history at the U.S. Army Military Academy at West Point; Richard Lowe, professor of history at the University of North Texas at Denton; Terry Jones, professor of history at University of Louisiana, Monroe; Steven Woodworth, professor of history at Texas Christian University in Fort Worth, Texas; Steve Bounds, manager of the Mansfield State Historic Site in Louisiana; Scott Dearman, interpretive ranger at Mansfield State Historic Site; and Steve Mayeux of Avoyelles Parish, Louisiana. All of these people in various ways have made this work a better one.

Two historians influenced me more than others. The first is Dr. Ludwell Johnson, professor emeritus of the College of William and Mary. Professor Johnson's *Red River Campaign: Politics and Cotton in the Civil War* is the seminal work in the area of the 1864 Red River Campaign. All other books begin with this seminal work. Dr. Johnson's classic, originally published in 1958, has weathered the test of time and revisionists.

The second historian is the late Charles Edmund "Eddie" Vetter. Eddie was the chair of the Department of Sociology at Centenary College in Shreveport, Louisiana. In 1992 Eddie approached me with the idea of coauthoring an article on the Red River Campaign. It was published in *Civil War Regiments* two years later. That article, "The Union Naval Expedition on the Red River," became the kernel of my Ph.D. dissertation, "One Damn Blunder from Beginning to End: The Red River Campaign of 1864," and this book. Eddie and I had planned on a full-length collaboration and were working on the early stages of research when he died unexpectedly. This book is the culmination of that early effort. Eddie encouraged me to follow my instincts and concentrate on the inland navy and its role in the war. His guidance rekindled in me the desire to pursue a Ph.D.

I will be forever grateful to my wife, Marilyn Segura Joiner, who played a key role in the completion of this work. She spent countless hours editing the manuscript and serving as its initial proofreader. Her support largely made this journey possible. I also want to thank Terry Winschel, National Park Service historian at Vicksburg National Military Park and longtime friend, for reading the manuscript with a careful eye. His vast knowledge of the Civil War in its many aspects is a most valuable tool indeed.

Two outstanding historians of the Civil War who helped hone this work during the academic process under which it was crafted are Dr. Alan Farmer and Dr. Robert Poole of St. Martin's College, Lancaster, England. Their guidance was thoughtful and indispensable.

Lastly, although great care has been taken to eliminate them, any errors in the research and writing are solely the author's.

*Gary D. Joiner*
*Shreveport, Louisiana*
*June 2005*

# INTRODUCTION

The Red River Campaign of 1864 in the Civil War was an overly ambitious attempt to send large Union army and navy forces deep into the interior of Louisiana, seize the Rebel capital of the state, and defeat the Confederate army guarding the region, enabling uninhibited access to Texas to the west. The campaign was important to both the Union army and navy in the course of the war and afterward. It altered the political landscape in the fall presidential elections in 1864 by removing a major challenger to Abraham Lincoln at the Republican convention. It redirected ten thousand veteran troops of Major General William T. Sherman's command from operating in Tennessee and Georgia during the pivotal Atlanta Campaign, thus delaying the end of the war by weeks or months. The campaign forced the navy to refocus its inland, or "brown water," naval tactics and to reassess how its vessels should be used. Profound consequences included legal, political, and sociological issues that surfaced in congressional hearings as a result of the Union defeat. These issues lie at the roots of the New South and remain points of contention today.

During the warm, humid spring of 1864, deep in the interior of the pine barrens and along the sinewy streams of the Red River Valley in northern Louisiana, a drama unfolded that briefly lifted the veil of obscurity from that region west of the Mississippi River. The Union army initiated a bold attempt to capture the Confederate capital of Louisiana at Shreveport. The campaign was considered a high priority by President Lincoln, Sherman, and others in the highest circles of the United States government and military. It featured one of the largest joint army and navy operations of the war. The navy and the army quartermasters took 104 vessels up a narrow, winding, unforgiving river. The army assembled more than forty-two thousand men operating in three pincers. The expedition was characterized by technological innovations, such as the first use of the periscope in battle and complex dam systems. Twelve Medals of Honor were awarded for heroism in the campaign. The operation taught the army and navy lessons in the critical importance of expanded cooperation between the armed services and demonstrated other scenarios that were unlikely to produce success. And while the Union had tactical and numerical advantages, the campaign proved that overwhelming power is not necessarily a guarantee of victory. The potent combination of politics and forceful personalities also influence military outcomes, often in counterproductive ways.

With the tremendous display of men and firepower sent into northern Louisiana, how could the Union effort end in disgrace and near disaster? The answer to this over-arching question concerning the Red River Campaign cannot be simplified in a single response. This book will respond by identifying significant themes and resolving the central questions at their core.

The primary target of the campaign was the Confederate capital of Louisiana. Why was it important? The Union commanders undertook the campaign with a tremendous air of arrogance. Why did they have an almost total disregard for their opponents? Politics and perceived economic gain overshadowed military necessity in planning the operation. Did political interference doom the expedition before it began? The army and navy were obsessed by the prospect of valuable cotton vulner-able and ripe for military grabbing at certain points during the campaign. Did this affect the planning and ultimately contribute to the defeat of their forces? Follow-ing the campaign, Congress placed most of the blame for the expedition's failure on Major General Nathaniel P. Banks. Was this deserved or was Banks a scapegoat for an ill conceived, as some historians have contended, cotton raid? The army's com-munication among the three prongs was all but impossible. Could the plan have been simplified to create less confusion? With some notable exceptions, army and navy commanders did not trust each other. There were also regional rivalries among the Union troops. Did this discord seriously hamper the operation? The navy entered the campaign with reckless abandon, bringing many vessels to the missions that were unsuitable for the river in which they were to operate. What was the proper mix of boats, and could the naval plan have been altered to achieve success? Both the army and navy entered the mission with a lack of intelligence capability that made them almost blind to local geographic conditions. What role did this play in the campaign? The Confederates worked feverishly for a year preparing for such an invasion. Were their efforts in vain? The Rebels responded to rapidly changing Union plans with some confusion but more often with speed and efficiency.

Was this reaction enough to disrupt Union plans or did the Union commanders bring the debacle upon themselves largely unaided? The failed campaign had several results. The expedition was the last combined operation in the Civil War on con-stricted waters deep within Rebel-held territory. The navy continued joint operations, but in waters more suitable for the craft committed to those missions. Union Major General Nathaniel Prentiss Banks's political aspirations were ruined, and he was not a threat to Lincoln in the 1864 presidential elections. The campaign was the subject of high profile hearings before the Joint Committee on the Conduct of the War. They ele-vated Rear Admiral David Dixon Porter to new heights of fame, excoriated Lincoln's policies, and placed the overwhelming blame squarely on Banks.

Historians and the general public seem to have an insatiable appetite for the Civil War. Over 140 years have passed since the cannon last roared in anger, yet books and articles continue to be written each year reporting nuances of the war not covered previously and reexamining the issues. This war tugs at Americans like no other event in United States history. Perhaps it is the very "civil" nature of the war that fascinates each generation—the intense memory of enemy against enemy as brother against brother.

Events in the Civil War fought west of the Mississippi River—particularly those in 1864—have received comparatively little scrutiny. Why? The eastern theater in Virginia grabbed the headlines of newspapers in that day and still commands a large percentage of bookshelf space today. It is not surprising that Virginia received the bulk of the coverage. The great armies fighting in the eastern theater, the Army of the Potomac and the Army of Northern Virginia, were known for their dashing heroes, their hard-fought battles, and for clashes in which the participants came from some of the most populated areas of the young country.

The capitals of both the United States and the Confederacy were not only in the eastern theater; they were exactly one hundred air miles from one another. Rapid coverage of events easily circulated within the capitals and to the nearby areas, most of which had adequate rail and telegraph services. Adding to the poignancy of stories about clashes between brothers was the site of the capital seat of the rebellion in what had been a leading state of the United States and home to many of the nation's founding fathers. As the war progressed, Union victories mounted, leading politicians and residents of the United States to believe that victory was near at hand. Although early Confederate victories and stalemated battles received widespread coverage in both the North and South, by late 1863 northern newspapers were reporting war-related events as an ever-growing cavalcade of Federal victories. The northern press rallied to the cause of the Union, almost as a propaganda arm of the government, enhancing the hope of a weary nation for the war's end and vigorously reporting anything that appeared to be advances by their forces.[1]

The Red River Campaign was a resounding victory for their opponents. Newspaper reports during the first half of the campaign were plentiful and optimistic. As it continued, filed reports exhibited brevity and restraint. Perhaps another reason for neglect of the Red River Campaign is the fact that it is the victor who traditionally writes the history.

The State of Louisiana was an integral part of the Confederacy, and her greatest city was New Orleans, the largest city in the South. The state and city have been synonymous with each other since the founding of the city in a crescent bend of the Mississippi River in 1722. At the beginning of the Civil War, New Orleans was the heart of culture and commerce of the entire Mississippi River Valley and the Gulf Coast of the United States, just as it had been under previous Spanish and French ownership. The city's wealth was apparent in the architecture of its public buildings and homes and its grand commercial ventures. New Orleans was the largest port in the South, serving as a point of embarkation and debarkation for passengers and goods flowing along the river.

New Orleans and the surrounding marshy areas area reflected a diversity of ethnicity, marked by a population of Creoles of French and Spanish descent, Italians, Acadians who fled Canada, Irish, slaves, and free men of color, as well as Jews and

Indians. Aside from the Jews and Indians, the area was overwhelmingly Roman Catholic, providing a common link.

New Orleans was the queen city of Louisiana, but it was not representative of the entire state. Just seventy-five miles upstream was the capital city of the state, Baton Rouge. It was at this point that Louisiana began a transition, both geographically and culturally.

North of Baton Rouge, the mouth of the Red River poured into both the Atchafalaya River and the Mississippi. The Red River Valley and its northernmost city, Shreveport, differed greatly from the marshy lands surrounding New Orleans. Hills and pine forests were characteristic of the landscape approaching Shreveport. Because the Red River Valley was unsuitable for the sugarcane plantations that formed the basis of wealth in the southern parts of the state, cotton was the valley's principal crop. The wealth brought by cotton became the economic engine driving the economy of the northern part of the state.

Union forces captured New Orleans with relative ease in 1862. The leaders of the great city feared destruction of their homes and businesses in a lengthy battle.[2] The city surrendered without a shot being fired. On the other hand, Shreveport, New Orleans's younger and less refined sister, took a different attitude. The citizens of the state's second city had no imposing buildings, no great works of architecture or business empires to defend against enemy fire. They were, however, determined to confront any invader who would rob them of their livelihood and threaten their homes and families.

By 1864 the war in the West moved northward to Tennessee, and Union Major General U. S. Grant was well known throughout the country following his victory at Vicksburg in July 1863. The war west of the Mississippi River, however, seemed just a sideshow to the larger events of the war occurring in the East during those pivotal years. The relative obscurity of the war in the West reversed for a few months after the fall of Vicksburg. In March 1864 Federal forces invaded northwestern Louisiana with much fanfare. Unlike the glittering triumphs the Union was securing on other fronts, the Red River Campaign was a colossal failure. It was an embarrassment for the military, and that embarrassment heightened when, late in 1864, Congress began an investigation to determine what went wrong. The campaign was a joint effort between the Union army and navy. Although much larger field armies operated in other theaters, particularly in the East, the combined force that ascended the Red River was unusually large for an effort west of the Mississippi River.

Most modern scholarship of the Civil War ignores the Red River Campaign or gives it only passing mention in narratives. There are several reasons for this. Nineteenth-century sources of the campaign, including autobiographies, diaries by participants, published letters, accounts of battles, later reminiscences, speeches before veterans' groups, and early scholarly works, were overwhelmingly from Union participants. Perhaps 90 percent of the Confederate records of the Trans-Mississippi Department were lost or destroyed by the end of the war. Union participants, of course, only gave congressional testimony following the campaign; therefore, no Confederate voices were heard in the proceedings. Most important, the campaign was waged west of the Mississippi River after the fall of Vicksburg. The war in the West moved to Tennessee and Georgia and with it went most of the reporters. Reporters assigned to cover the campaign were hampered by the harsh conditions of such a deep foray. Few reports were filed after the Battle of Mansfield, the Union defeat that doomed the expedition. The campaign was a large Union failure when other armies were gaining victories and adding to their fame. The Union leadership wanted to ignore its role in the campaign and the Confederates had no way to capitalize on it. All of these reasons combined to bury the campaign in the dustbin of history until the late 1950s. Since then there has been little light focused on it.

The foundation for all documentary study of the Red River Campaign is found in Union and surviving Confederate orders and letters in *The War of the Rebellion: A Compilation of the Official Records of the Union and Confederate Armies*, the *Official Records of the Union and Confederate Navies in the War of the Rebellion*, and congressional testimony and analysis found in the *Report of the Joint Committee on the Conduct of the War: The Red River Expedition*.[3] There are few official Confederate sources that have survived outside the *Official Records*.

Compared to campaigns fought east of the Mississippi River, historical accounts of substance covering the campaign are rare. The first scholarly attempt to chronicle the campaign was first published in 1958. *The Red River Campaign: Politics and Cotton in the Civil War* was initially the doctoral dissertation of Professor Ludwell Johnson at Johns Hopkins University. Kent State University Press reprinted the volume in 1993.[4] It is the best examination of the relationship between economic and political factors as the primary reasons for the campaign. William Riley Brooksher's *War along the Bayous: The 1864 Red River Campaign in Louisiana* was another view of the subject along the lines of Professor Johnson.[5] The most recent published account of the campaign is by the author of this book, and in 2005 with the A. M. Pate, Jr., Award for excellence in historical research and writing on the Civil War in the Trans-Mississippi. *One Damn Blunder from Beginning to End: The Red River Campaign of 1864* was published in 2003.[6] Aside from covering the campaign in Louisiana and Arkansas, it describes in detail the Confederate efforts to defend the region. This book was honored in 2004 with the Albert Castel Prize for best historical book on the western theater and in 2005 with the A. M. Pate, Jr., Award for excellence in historical research and writing on the Civil War in the Trans-Mississippi. *One Damn Blunder* was intended for a broad audience, with limited citations.

This volume, of necessity, draws upon that manuscript but expands its scope to include events prior to the campaign and to the congressional hearings following the operation. This volume also sheds new light on the campaign that the previous work could not present due to space and time limitations. This new forum discusses the Confederate defenses in greater depth, delves into the reasoning behind the actions of leaders on both sides, and, most important, discovers the reason why Admiral David Dixon Porter brought the largely inappropriate mix of firepower and large-hulled gunboats up the narrow, treacherous, and ever-winding Red River.

# CHAPTER 1

## The Campaign in Context

The Red River Campaign was one of several significant combined operations between the Union army and navy during the Civil War. The expedition up the Red River in the spring of 1864 utilized the greatest concentration of inland naval vessels operating in concert during the entire conflict.

Following the fall of Vicksburg and Port Hudson in July 1863, the U.S. Navy's Mississippi Squadron, commanded by Rear Admiral David Dixon Porter, patrolled the Mississippi River with a vast array of heavily armed vessels. Porter's hold on the Mississippi and its tributaries was absolute, with the exception of the Red River. He consolidated Union control of the Mississippi River as U. S. Grant moved into Tennessee and raised the siege of Chattanooga. Grant, in March 1864, was promoted to lieutenant general and general in chief of the army and moved his headquarters to Virginia. The Mississippi Squadron continued to patrol the waters of the Mississippi Valley until it was called upon to assist Major General Nathaniel Banks in an attack on Shreveport.

As the Red River Campaign was being proffered as an operation in early 1864, Sherman wanted to lead the expedition and Porter jumped at the chance to work with his old friend. When Sherman was forced to bow out to command the Atlanta Campaign, Porter was stuck. He expected to work with his old comrade, but his enthusiasm cooled when he found that he would be cooperating with Banks. Despite his concerns, he was a naval officer who had signed on to the mission, and he needed to carry through with it. Porter did not trust Banks. Both Grant and Sherman disliked the political general, and Porter was well aware of his lack of success through both personal contact and the communications with the admiral's foster brother, Admiral Farragut.[1] The air of mistrust emanating from Porter, Grant, and Sherman extended up and down the chain of command. Their opinions sowed the seeds of discord during the campaign. Sherman's men were western veterans, and their views were typically those of their leader. They held little regard for political generals. The same attitudes were present in naval officers.

Economic and political considerations played a key role in planning campaigns after the fall of Vicksburg, and this was particularly true for operations in the Trans-Mississippi. Cotton was not simply an economic boon to the Confederacy; it was a great economic attraction for the North as well, particularly the textile mills of New England that were starving for the raw material of their businesses. The existence of tremendous amounts of quality Red River Valley cotton was without a doubt the key factor in Shreveport's being added to the Union high command's target list.

In 1864 Shreveport's local economy was much healthier than its small population in 1860 might have indicated, and its importance as a war center had become assured. The town's location near the northern limits of navigable waters on the Red River made it a safe haven for those fleeing the war. In late 1863 Union military planners were prosecuting the war in Tennessee and Virginia, planning to move into Georgia, and the concept of an attack on Texas via the Red River Valley in Louisiana was being formed.

A major reason Shreveport was chosen was the presence of a field army that had been largely unchallenged. A Rebel state capital was located in the town, and two Confederate capitals in exile were nearby and unmolested (Missouri's at Marshall, Texas, and Arkansas's at Old Washington, both within sixty miles of Shreveport.) But the overriding reason for the campaign was the existence of cotton.

The Confederates termed the area west of the Mississippi River the Department of the Trans-Mississippi. This department extended westward to the present border between California and Arizona and northward to the Kansas Territory. Shreveport was its headquarters. The town also served as the capital of Confederate Louisiana and as the nexus for the rudimentary military-industrial complex west of the Mississippi. In addition, it was the primary cotton exporting and trans-shipment point north of New Orleans. Shreveport was the most important trading center in the Red River Valley.

The lower Red River Valley served as a dividing line between Catholic southern Louisiana and Protestant northern Louisiana. Settlers migrating from the east with Scottish, Irish, and English heritage populated the river valley.[2] Shreveport was situated near the northwest corner of the state. It had been incorporated for less than thirty years. As such, it was still developing its own culture and identity. One thing was certain, though. Its location on the Red River and its proximity to Texas and Arkansas made it the economic center of a region that encompassed northwest Louisiana, northeast Texas, and southwest Arkansas.

The town was the northernmost point on the Red River open to navigation. Its location placed it at the head of the Texas Trail, the cattle and immigrant road that led livestock and migrating pioneers to south and west Texas. The trail was the major route of goods and supplies coming from Mexico. Prior to the annexation of Texas into the Union in 1845, the towns of Shreveport, Greenwood, and Logansport had been the westernmost in the United States. Shreveport occupied a diamond-shaped plateau, a remnant of a Pleistocene river terrace, approximately one square mile. With the exception of Grand Ecore in Natchitoches Parish, about sixty miles downstream, the Shreveport hill terraces on the west side of the river were the last high ground on the Red River before it emptied into the Mississippi River, some 230 river miles downstream.[3]

The first European settlers had arrived at the site in the 1820s and established a trading post on the east bank of the river.[4] The site was the southernmost place to

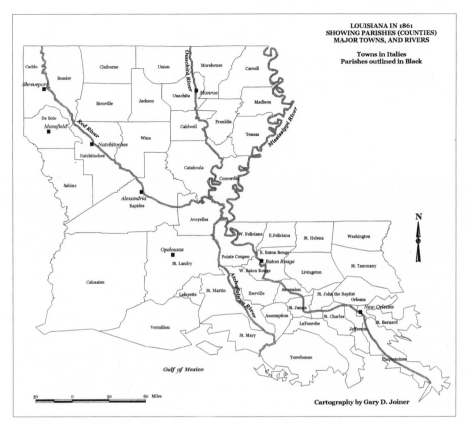

*Louisiana on the eve of the Civil War, 1861.*

cross the Red River and then enter Texas without navigating through the Sabine River swamp. However, the site was not an ideal crossing point due to navigation problems on the river. In the early 1830s, Captain Henry Miller Shreve was awarded a contract from the United States government to remove a giant logjam on the river above and below the trading post. Shreve derived his title from being a steamboat captain, but he also held the highest position within the U.S. Army Corps of Engineers west of the Appalachian Mountains: superintendent of the western waters. He used the confluence of Cross Bayou and the Red River as his base of operations for removal of "the Great Raft."[5] Soon after the logs were removed, the trading post became a major ferry operation. The owners of the trading post and a ferry had facilities on both banks of the river and on both sides of Cross Bayou, attracting settlers to the site.[6]

The raft was cleared by the early 1840s and, despite a constant problem of trees snagging and re-forming the logjam, the Red River was open for commerce. The most important implication of the removal of the raft was the opening of the rich alluvial valley to cotton production. During this period, cotton plantations were established throughout the flat sandy plain near Shreveport. It is not surprising that Shreveport became the home of cotton factors, intermediary cotton traders, and the machinery to process the fiber. Cotton gins and presses were built throughout the area to take the cotton from its raw form as bolls and turn it into large transportable rectangular blocks called "bales." As lands were opened for farming, cultivation increased and the five-hundred-pound bales could be efficiently moved to market in New Orleans. After a decade of commerce, authors writing about Shreveport in 1850 described "a picturesque, dangerous, disease ridden, unruly, rapidly expanding frontier river town."[7]

The cotton industry almost immediately spawned businesses to support the growing population. The owners of the trading company entered into a partnership with Shreve and other local men to form the Shreve Town Company. The main thoroughfare was named Texas Street, being the head of the Texas Trail, which began at the river. The "Texas" name does not reflect only geographic proximity but also its frontier attitudes, commerce, and settlers.

As the cotton industry grew, it attracted other businesses. In addition to the normal grocery and mercantile stores, there were several saloons, brothels, and gaming rooms. One man, arriving in 1849, said Shreveport was "a typical 'wide open' frontier town," with the general lawlessness and recklessness intensified by the presence of riverboat men, raft cutters, and other frontiersmen.[8] Most men carried weapons when in public.[9] Shreveport was slow to acquire refinements, but within twelve years of its charter there were signs of respectability that grew up alongside less genteel institutions with the building of Methodist, Baptist, and Presbyterian churches.[10] Between 1850 and 1864, Shreveport transformed itself into a thriving economic center. It developed a central business area intermixed with homes as the town expanded on its western side into the valley leading to the first of several parallel ridges. The valley, formerly a swamp created by Cross Bayou, was called "St. Paul's Bottoms" after St. Paul's Methodist Church located there. To the south of the town and across Silver Lake was another plateau of high land consisting of rolling hills. These eventually turned into the flat fields bordering the Wallace Bayou swamp.[11] The ridges, the plateau, and the rolling hills formed the basis for the town's defensive system during the war. In 1863 a British officer, on his way to observe the operations of the Army of Northern Virginia, recorded in his diary that "Shreveport is a rather decent-looking place on the Red River."[12]

In the late 1860s Albert Harris Leonard wrote in his *Memoirs* of how his hometown had changed in the almost twenty years he had lived there: "From the earliest settlement to the close of our Civil War, two social systems struggled for supremacy in Caddo Parish. The Spirit of the frontier and the Civilization of the South. The first predominated during about two decades but all the time the second became more and more potent, and about the year 1860 was predominant, though largely modified by the manners and customs of the frontier."[13]

What Leonard termed "the Civilization of the South" was found in areas widely planted in cotton and sugarcane and was rooted in slavery as an economic machine. In the mid-nineteenth-century South, slavery was the driving force behind the agricultural economy. It was thought at the time that slaves were required to operate large cotton and sugarcane plantations as well as large row-crop plantations and farmsteads. (Row crops were any commercially viable crops that required planting in organized and often slightly elevated parallel rows.)

The 1850 decennial census illustrated that Shreveport and the surrounding parishes and counties were becoming more civilized. The census counted a population of about one thousand people in Shreveport. These included twenty attorneys and eighteen physicians.[14] Slaves within the town were not counted as a separate category from those in the parish in the 1850 census. Some of Shreveport's business owners did not fit the stereotype of middle-class Southerners. Among the inhabitants were twenty-one free blacks, at the time called "free men of color" (as nonslave African Americans were then called). One businessman, Norman Davis, a fifty-year-old mulatto from Virginia, was listed in the census as a barber.[15] He acquired ten acres on and near the main street in 1849 and soon began to subdivide the property and sell lots.[16] According to published accounts of the period, Davis was readily accepted into the white community and was treated with dignity and respect.[17]

The 1850 census revealed a population of 8,884 in Caddo Parish, of whom 5,208 were slaves. The population of Bossier Parish was 6,962, of whom 4,455 were slaves.[18] The census listed 42 free people of color in Caddo Parish.[19] Although the census listed no free people of color in Bossier Parish, local conveyance records listed fourteen free people of color in 1853 and eleven in 1858.[20] During the decade of the 1850s, the number of free persons of color declined throughout the South.

With the exception of house servants, very few slaves lived within the city limits of Shreveport. Many of these house servants were purchased to satisfy a demand for conspicuous personal consumption.[21] Slaves were also useful in public works projects such as building levees and maintaining roads. Generally slaves were not needed as manual laborers within the town since foreign immigrant workers provided the heavy lifting labor of longshoremen and warehousemen.[22]

Caddo and Bossier were atypical of most parishes of Louisiana and counties in the South because they had more than the average number of slaves and slaveholders.[23] In the 1860s the ratio of slaves to white people in Bossier Parish was four to one, making this the highest slave/white ratio on a per capita basis of any county in the United States.[24]

In 1860 the population of Shreveport had been just 2,190.[25] But, by 1864 this number had swollen to more than 12,000 as war refugees flooded in from southern Louisiana, Arkansas, and Missouri.[26] Many of the refugees were family members of men serving in the area; others were from places nearer the front lines.[27] Although some of these people found work in war-related industries, many were destitute and required aid from the military and local government.[28] Those who found jobs did so because Shreveport and Caddo Parish had become a very important trading center. It was the primary transshipment complex for north Louisiana and east Texas cotton. Situated at the end of the Texas Trail, it was a shipping point for cattle being sent downriver. In 1860 Caddo Parish was fourth in the state of Louisiana in the total number of business establishments and second in the state in the annual value of products manufactured (on a per-parish basis), giving even more opportunities.[29] The economic vitality of the area and Shreveport's location at a crossroads for trade and navigation made it an ideal center for a military complex.

Shreveport was far removed from the fields of military action, so why was it considered an important target? Surely, if the major Confederate field commands east of the Mississippi River could be neutralized and the large urban centers on and near the river were brought under Federal control, any forces west of the great river would simply shrivel up and die. It seems the adage of "kill the head of the snake and the body will follow" should apply here. Actually, this argument was brought forth in the Union high command, but it was almost completely ignored before the Red River Campaign was under way.[30]

The Red River Valley in Louisiana, southwest Arkansas, and deep east Texas had taken the nickname the "Upper Cotton Kingdom" with good reason. This was the greatest cotton-producing area in the Confederacy. The rich, deep, sandy alluvial soil of the Red River was one of the most perfect in North America for growing cotton. The weather in 1863 had been kind, rainy at the beginning of the growing season but not too wet. It cleared as the cotton plants matured for harvest, and the dry spell ensured a bumper crop.[31] By late winter of 1863–64, tens of thousands of cotton bales, "white gold," had been harvested by the cotton plantation slaves and processed into bales at hundreds of gins in the region. The bales were then moved by wagons to steamboat landings and were sitting on the banks of the Red River and its associated streams ready for shipment southward. Late cotton crops were still growing and had not yet been harvested.[32]

Beginning in March 1863 Shreveport became the focal point for a vast array of defenses on and near the Red River. The town was the hub of a vital war industry with a naval yard, factories, foundries, arsenals, powder mills, and other facilities that reached into other states. The outlying facilities directed from Shreveport were located at Houston, Tyler, Marshall, and Jefferson, all in Texas. Confederate military units in Louisiana, Texas, Arkansas, the Indian Territories of Oklahoma, New Mexico, and Arizona all answered to Shreveport. The war-related industries at these locations armed, clothed, and sustained all Confederate forces west of the Mississippi River. Shreveport was well fortified with a series of forts, walls, and artillery emplacements. Near the mouth of Cross Bayou was a construction yard for a fledgling riverine naval force, the nexus of a thriving small-scale military-industrial complex.[33]

Shreveport's position at the head of the Texas Trail and its status as a military, political, and economic center ensured this position. However, it became an important military target almost by accident. Union military planners conceived the Red River Campaign from political pressure. Military necessity played a secondary role. Once the primary target was chosen and the principal military units were identified, preparations for the expedition proceeded rapidly. Union commanders allocated huge numbers of men and boats to the mission, but from the beginning they used flawed logic.

Most military campaigns begin with solid planning, establishing strict sets of goals and objectives. Contingency plans are made in the event that conditions in the

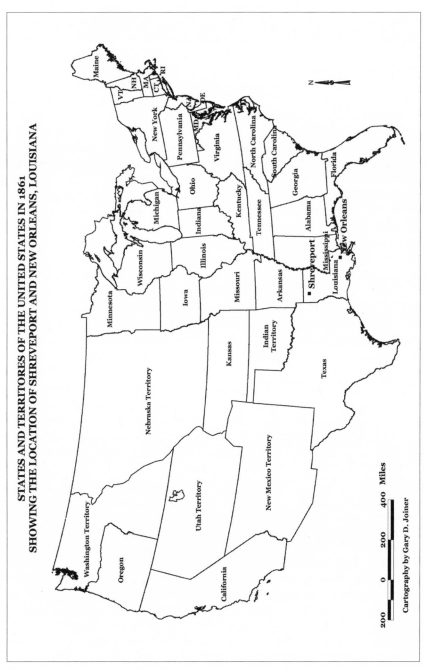

STATES AND TERRITORIES OF THE UNITED STATES IN 1861
SHOWING THE LOCATION OF SHREVEPORT AND NEW ORLEANS, LOUISIANA

*States and territories of the United States, 1861.*

field alter the master plan, but the basic ideas remain the same: define the primary and secondary objectives, determine the best method to accomplish the tasks, gather the appropriate assets to conduct the mission, perform the assigned tasks, complete the primary and secondary goals, and, finally, extricate the forces. If a target is to be captured and held, less capable garrison forces can be brought in to relieve the front line troops.

Sometimes, campaigns are attempted that do not follow this regimen. They rarely succeed and are often spectacular failures. The Red River Campaign's origins were intertwined in political needs and economic desires and had very little to do with military necessity. Several points of view and conflicting opinions surfaced once the military signed on to the campaign.

The year before the Red River Campaign began brought many changes in the course of the Civil War. During the first half of 1863, the Confederates maintained their viability as a nation, though they were pressured militarily. The Union army had suffered several failures or costly tactical ties in major battles by the middle of the year. Then the tide of war began to change on both the eastern and western fronts. Union successes following the great twin victories in July 1863 at Vicksburg and Gettysburg fueled a common opinion that the end of the war was near. The South was not ready to admit defeat, but Union pessimism turned into an air of overconfidence. On January 17, 1864, the Union general in chief, Major General Henry Halleck, wrote to his protégé, and soon-to-be general in chief, Major General Ulysses S. Grant that "people . . . are acting in the mistaken supposition that the war is nearly ended, and that we shall hereafter have to contend only with fragments of broken and demoralized rebel armies. Such is the tone of the public press and the debates in Congress."[34]

The northern press carried this optimism to their readers. The *Atlantic Monthly* proudly proclaimed in its January issue that the new year of 1864 was "The Beginning of the End."[35] *Harper's Weekly* and *Frank Leslie's Illustrated Journal* brought forth a plethora of stories and illustrations describing the seemingly endless Union advances and victories.[36] In these accounts, the navy was portrayed as formidable and its primary inland fleet, the Mississippi Squadron, as almost unstoppable. The accounts of the Vicksburg Campaign of the previous year paid homage to the navy's ability to carry its forces to the heart of the enemy, wherever he may be hiding.[37] The northern press lionized Union army commanders and reported their exploits with great attention to detail.[38]

During January, Union strategists were riding this wave of optimism and were comforted by a rapidly expanding industrial base. At their disposal was a war machine that was battle tested and becoming larger by the day. Northern factories were producing war materiel at ever-increasing rates, and these vital supplies were reaching the giant supply depots for field use in preparation for new campaigns. Use of railroads and troop transports allowed great numbers of troops to be dispatched with relatively short notice. Troops could be moved from one theater to another in a matter of days.

On the other side, the Confederacy was hard pressed but still possessed strong field armies, though they were shrinking due to attrition. The vital supply lines from Texas and Louisiana with their huge quantities of cattle, grain, and that most important trading commodity, cotton, were severed after the fall of Fortress Vicksburg and Port Hudson. The grandiose-sounding Confederate Department of the Trans-Mississippi was cut off from the east and the Mississippi River came fully under Union control. The Union navy heavily patrolled the great river, allowing only limited contact between Confederate forces on either side. Guns, powder, and other items necessary to keep armies running were either manufactured in northwest Louisiana and east Texas or smuggled up from Mexico, but they could not be shipped across the Mississippi River to assist the eastern armies.

Manpower was a constant concern for the South, and the relative sizes of field armies illustrate this. In January 1864 Robert E. Lee and his once magnificent Army of Northern Virginia fielded approximately thirty-eight thousand effectives against a tenacious Army of the Potomac with seventy-three thousand men.[39] The Confederate Army of Tennessee faced two-to-one odds after being pushed from its sanctuaries at Chattanooga by Major General Ulysses S. Grant and his army group.[40] Grant's forces consisted of the armies of the Tennessee, Ohio, Cumberland, and portions of the Potomac. Confederate troops west of the Mississippi River were scattered across northern Louisiana, southwest Arkansas, and throughout east Texas. On paper the number of Confederate cavalry available, particularly in Texas cavalry regiments, appeared huge. In fact, most of these western units were dismounted and fought as infantry. Confederate troops were spread so thinly on both banks of the Mississippi River that only guerrilla raiders operated against the vastly numerically superior Union forces in hit-and-run attacks. Union Major General William T. Sherman, posing an obvious threat and taunting the Confederates, marched his forces out of Vicksburg and crossed the state to attack Meridian near the Alabama border. He met almost no opposition on his march.

It was at this point in the dichotomy of fortunes of the Union and the Confederacy that the Union high command planned the coming year's campaigns. In their view, the number of targets worth taking occupied a very short list. In order of importance, they were Richmond, Atlanta, Mobile, and Shreveport.[41] Charleston, as the seat of the rebellion, should have been included on this list, but Charleston probably could not be taken until Atlanta was secured. The navy had laid siege to the city and was ineffective in reducing its defenses. At this point in the war, Richmond and Atlanta were obviously the most important targets. Attacks on these cities were designed to draw the two largest Confederate field armies into battle and, it was hoped, lead to their destruction. Concurrent attacks on these sites would split Confederate resources and effectively strangle major urban areas east of the Appalachians remaining under Rebel control. Charleston was already under siege from the U.S. Navy, and landward pressure from a fallen Atlanta would seal its fate. Mobile, the last deepwater port on the Gulf of Mexico in Confederate hands, was also a major prize. It was a constant worry to Union strategists since it was well fortified and protected by torpedoes (mines) and the large ironclad CSS *Tennessee*. Mobile offered the Confederates the potential of disrupting vital Union supply lines to New Orleans by possibly breaking the blockade or endangering operations to the north once the drive for Atlanta began. Mobile figured prominently in the Union plans, not so much for what it was but for what it could do. The last target on the list was Shreveport, the capital of Confederate Louisiana, and headquarters of the Army of the Trans-Mississippi. Economic conditions were to move Shreveport higher up the priority list of the major targets.

Cotton, particularly the lack of it in New England mills, played a key role in the early planning of the Red River Campaign. The Union invasion of the Lower Mississippi in 1862 had several objectives. The closing of the Mississippi River to the Confederates and the capture of New Orleans, the largest city in the South, were certainly priorities, but the chance to capture a huge supply of cotton and bring the New England mills back on line offered tremendous political and economic opportunities.[42] Lincoln needed New England for the 1864 elections. Benjamin Butler and Nathaniel Prentiss Banks were the senior-ranking field officers in the Union army and both were politically ambitious and well aware of the needs of their textile mill benefactors.

Lincoln realized he had to keep New England pacified, alleviate the cotton shortage, and carry on the business of ending the rebellion. The primary source for cotton to operate the textile mills was the South, and the war had cut off this source. The textile industry was a major component of the New England economy, and the lack of cotton had created massive layoffs. Before the war, almost five million spindles operated in the mills in New England.[43] In 1862 only 25 percent were operating.[44] The capture of New Orleans had yielded only twenty-seven thousand bales, a drastic reduction from the two million bales processed by the port before the invasion.[45] New Orleans was the receiving point, not the producing center, for cotton from the Mississippi Valley and its tributaries. The lack of cotton available at the port of New Orleans came as a tremendous shock to the Union strategists. Cotton must be obtained, and the general who procured it would reap tremendous political rewards.

The seeds of the Red River Campaign were planted even before the New Orleans expedition of Massachusetts Major General Benjamin F. Butler. He was the commanding general of the Department of New England, headquartered in Boston. Butler was politically astute and held high aspirations. He received career assistance from benefactors including the New England senators and congressmen of the Radical Republican wing. Butler was an opportunist and was constantly looking for methods to enhance his career. As the cotton sources dried up in 1861, New England politicians were clamoring to the president for relief. It is not surprising that Butler rose to the top of Lincoln's list of generals who might help him and the New England textile magnates.

President Lincoln had been led to believe—incorrectly, as was demonstrated by later events—that the German immigrant farmers of the hill country of Texas were pro-Union and would stage a revolt against their Confederate leaders if the opportunity arose.[46] New England needed cotton desperately, and bankers and mill owners were lobbying hard for relief. Liberating cotton-producing areas and bringing them back into the Union fold could achieve this. Butler suggested an amphibious invasion at some point along the Texas coast, at which point the anticipated counterrevolution by the German patriots would occur in the Texas hill country.[47]

Butler did not know that others had similar ideas. Some of Lincoln's cabinet members had been promoting this as a way of shoring up the faltering support of the

New England power brokers. At the lead in these discussions were Secretary of State William H. Seward, Secretary of War Edwin M. Stanton, and Secretary of the Treasury Salmon P. Chase. In August 1861 Major General George B. McClellan submitted for President Lincoln's review a memorandum outlining his opinions on the campaigns that should be conducted by the Union army and navy in the future. Among these, McClellan commented on a project that, in his words, "has often been suggested and which always recommended itself to my judgement . . . a movement . . . up Red River and Western Texas for the purpose of protecting and developing the latent Union and free-state sentiment well-known to predominate in Western Texas."[48]

Butler also did not know that on November 12, 1861, naval Commander David Dixon Porter had submitted to Secretary of the Navy Gideon Welles, a detailed plan for the rapid capture of New Orleans.[49] This plan was presented to President Lincoln just a few days later and then submitted to General McClellan with Lincoln's hearty endorsement. A schedule was slated for the following January to carry Porter's plan to fruition. McClellan at this time was mired down in his own actions in Virginia.[50] Butler took his idea to Secretary of War Stanton on January 15, 1862, and, a few days later, Stanton asked McClellan for his opinion. McClellan turned the idea down, most likely due to his desire to lead it himself.

Learning of this apparent betrayal, Butler circumvented McClellan and secured the proper authorizations. He proposed that instead of landing in Texas, the expedition would strike at the heart of the Confederacy by denying them the use of the Mississippi River and capturing the great prize of New Orleans.[51] Butler changed his aspirations from the relatively easy invasion of open Texas coastal areas to a much more difficult Mississippi River attack.

Porter's plan was selected with Butler to lead the land forces. Flag Officer David G. Farragut was to command the naval forces, with the brash Porter leading the fleet of mortar schooners. As these vessels approached New Orleans, they pounded the forts below the city, forcing the metropolis into submission and neutralizing the lower defenses. New Orleans fell with ease on April 25, 1862. The late historian Charles Dufour described the fall of the Crescent City as "the night the war was lost."[52] This bold stroke severed the bread bowl of the Confederacy west of the Mississippi River from the main action east of the river. The war would last another three years, but the beginning of the end was achieved with the fall of the Crescent City.

Butler showed his dictatorial side in dealing with the citizens of New Orleans at the very time Lincoln hoped Louisiana would be the first Southern state to be repatriated. Lincoln could not fire him, for he was too politically powerful. Butler so infuriated New Orleans's residents, though, that he was removed and given a field command in Virginia.

Butler was replaced with yet another political general. President Lincoln realized his opportunity for an easy reconstruction of Louisiana had been compromised by Butler's infantile tantrums, particularly his overreaction to the women of New Orleans in his General Order 28, pronouncing all women not properly escorted in the city to be prostitutes.[53] In *The Civil War in Louisiana*, John D. Winters states that the order fomented violent opposition within the city, across the South, and abroad.[54]

Lincoln was challenged to find a successor who would follow his ideas and not be a temperamental maverick. He chose the new commander for practical reasons.

Major General Nathaniel Prentiss Banks was identified as the replacement. Banks was rakishly handsome, a fastidious dresser, and a political heavyweight. He was honest but authoritarian, with no tolerance for those questioning his ideas, even career military officers. To his discredit, he was vain and at times showed exquisitely timed poor judgment.[55] Like Butler before him, Banks came from Massachusetts and clearly understood New England politics. From humble beginnings, Banks became a self-made man (if there is such a thing in politics), serving as a three-term governor of Massachusetts and also in Congress, rising to the position of Speaker of the House of Representatives. He had aspirations of running against Abraham Lincoln in the 1864 presidential elections and was arguably the most popular military figure from New England. The northeastern press loved him and curried his favor. In a region in which Abraham Lincoln was at best distrusted, Banks offered his backers an alluring alternative. In return, Banks always gave preferential treatment and access to cotton brokers or factors, even to the point of allowing them to accompany him on campaigns.

Banks was battle-tested. He had showed some panache in his second test of battle against the legendary Stonewall Jackson at the battle of Cedar Mountain, but he was trapped and then rescued from capture by the timely arrival of reinforcements.[56] He then was given the assignment of commander of the defenses of Washington.

Banks's replacement of Butler provided several apparent solutions for the president. First, Lincoln could put someone in Louisiana who understood politics, could quell a volatile situation, and perhaps rejuvenate the reconstruction process in New Orleans. Second, Banks could do a better job of cooperating with Grant in taking the Mississippi into Federal hands. Third, Banks would be able to calm down the New England mill owners and, Lincoln hoped, increase the amount of cotton sent to the mills. Fourth, and perhaps most politically expedient, Banks would be far removed from his New England political support and would be less of a threat to Lincoln in the upcoming elections just over a year away. Grant had hoped that Banks would use troops from the Department of the Gulf to assist him in reducing Vicksburg. Banks cooperated by investing Port Hudson in siege. Port Hudson surrendered to Banks after the fall of Vicksburg on July 4, 1863, denying him the battlefield victory he so desperately needed.

Pressure was placed on Banks, as it was on his predecessor, to plant the flag in Texas, and now events outside the control of Washington or New Orleans began to spin affairs in a new direction.[57] Even before Vicksburg fell, French troops landed in Mexico and quickly installed Maximilian as the emperor of Mexico on June 7, 1863. There were renewed fears in Washington that the French and perhaps the British would enter into open cooperation with and perhaps even formal recognition of the Confederacy.[58] Planting the U.S. flag on Texas soil became a political necessity, not simply a presidential wish. Once the Mississippi River was open to Federal navigation, Banks was given orders to move forward. Banks received his orders through letters from President Lincoln and communiqués from General in Chief Henry Halleck.

Halleck was a master at delivering orders that could be read several different ways. If the recipient succeeded, Halleck would share in the glory; if he failed, the recipient would bear the sole blame. No one was better at delivering these masterpieces than Halleck.[59]

Banks agreed with Grant at this point that Mobile was a much more important target than Shreveport and later said that Halleck had pressured him instead into pursuing an attack on Texas on several occasions.[60] Halleck had proposed an attack up Red River, but Banks countered that an attack on Sabine Pass at the mouth of the Sabine River that formed the boundary between Louisiana and Texas would serve as a better base to attack Houston, and from there to advance into the hill country of deep east Texas.[61] On August 31, 1863, Banks ordered Major General William Buel Franklin to load one brigade from the First Division of the 19th Corps (troops that had accompanied Banks to Louisiana) onto transports, and, with the accompaniment of naval gunboats, land and secure Sabine Pass.[62] The small fleet arrived at the pass on September 7 and was met by a force of some fifty men with five guns dug in at a mud fort. The little force neutralized two of the gunboats, and the remainder were forced to retire. The transports never had a chance to disgorge their soldiers on the mud flats, and the entire expeditionary force was compelled to return to New Orleans.[63] Banks blamed the fiasco on the navy.[64] Neither the army nor the navy was blameless. Neither invested adequate time in planning this foray. Banks's very vocal blame of the navy

*Major General Nathaniel Prentiss Banks and his staff in 1864. From Francis Trevelyan Miller et al., eds.,* The Photographic History of the Civil War in Ten Volumes *(New York: Review of Reviews Co., 1912),*

caused a rift between him and Farragut and Porter. The distrust created here would only increase in the following months.

In late October, Banks sent Franklin on another invasion attempt, this one even less thoroughly planned than the first. His idea was a march overland through the Bayou Teche country and into the prairies of southwest Louisiana to a point somewhere on the Sabine River, where the expedition could ford or otherwise cross into Texas. Franklin picked his way across south-central Louisiana, at that time very sparsely populated. The region supplied almost no ability to forage for needed supplies. The column made it to just west of Opelousas in St. Landry Parish, moved up to Alexandria, and then turned around, unsure of what to do.[65]

Simultaneously with Franklin's expedition, other actions were taken as well. During this trek the navy sent units up the Ouachita and Red rivers to divert attention from Franklin's column. The gunboats did little damage. Action was also seen in southern Louisiana in St. Mary Parish. In conjunction with these disparate movements, an amphibious force landed at several points along the lower Texas coast. Banks reported to his superiors that "the flag of the Union floated over Texas to-day at meridian precisely" when it was planted into the sand dunes at Brazos Santiago.[66] Landings or attacks were also successful at Brownsville, Matagorda Bay, Aransas Pass, and at Rio Grande City.[67] In reality, the flag of the Union flew over mostly uninhabited sand dunes on barrier islands. The total effect on the Confederate State of Texas was inconsequential, but the commander of the Department of the Gulf was very pleased with himself.[68]

Banks's actions did not receive universal acclaim from his superiors. He had not informed Halleck of these actions before the campaign began and Halleck was not happy to hear of the "success."[69] Halleck had indicated that Banks should attack up the Red River. Banks had ignored the general in chief's orders (or perhaps found them characteristically unclear). Halleck was the ranking officer in the Union army and was headquartered in Washington, where he could influence policy and planning. He was Machiavellian at times, and he now used his considerable political skills in order to get what he wanted.

Halleck fired off letters to Banks on December 7, 1863, detailing his displeasure, thus forcing Banks to reevaluate his position.[70] He then wrote letters to Sherman, who at the time was engaged in wreaking havoc in eastern Mississippi, and Major General Frederick Steele, the newly appointed commander of the Department of Arkansas, to solicit their opinions about a Red River expedition.[71] Steele's department adjoined the target area and Sherman was very enthusiastic. Sherman wanted to command the force personally and operated for a time under the assumption that he would do so. Sherman had spent some eighteen months prior to the hostilities as the superintendent of the Louisiana Seminary of Learning and Military Institute in Pineville, across the Red River from Alexandria.[72] Of all the officers involved in the campaign, Sherman knew more about the area than anyone else and provided much valuable information, particularly to the navy.

Once these opinions were solicited, Halleck approached Grant, flushed with victory at Chattanooga.[73] Grant and Banks at this time were both in favor of a move on

Mobile and Grant was formulating what would become Sherman's campaign against Atlanta. Banks foresaw what the capture of a city of Mobile's stature would do for his presidential hopes. Halleck's letter to Grant was forceful in explaining that President Lincoln believed a Red River expedition was more politically important than the capture of Mobile. He also implied that Banks's coastal positions in Texas were part of the grand scheme to recover Texas. President Lincoln wrote Banks a congratulatory letter on Christmas Eve, 1863, perhaps at the urging of Halleck.[74] Grant tried to lobby for the Mobile campaign over a Red River expedition by circumventing Halleck, but he failed to secure support.[75]

Grant could clearly see several uses for a Mobile campaign. It would protect his right flank and deny the Confederates the use of the deepwater port. It would free naval resources that could be used elsewhere. Once the troops needed for this campaign were free for further action, the distance required to join Sherman would be relatively short. He could also clearly see the negative side of a Red River campaign. The troops would be heading in the opposite direction of his plans for attack. If the campaign became mired, he would lose their usefulness in the east, where he needed them most. Sherman wanted to command the Red River expedition, but Grant wanted Sherman to rip up Georgia. Even if the campaign were a success, the troops would be hard-pressed to join their parent units in time for the Atlanta Campaign. Last, Grant could not help but see a major drawback to this Louisiana foray. What was the goal? If the expedition reached Shreveport and the Confederates did not come out and fight, where would the climax come? If the Rebels decided to fight in the pine hills of Texas east of the Sabine River, how would the army pursue them? How would the lines of supply be configured? Where would supply bases be established and would they be safe? What if tens of thousands of men were strung out deep in enemy territory and were cut off? Where would the blame be leveled?

These were questions that should have been asked at the cabinet level and in the general staff. However, Grant did not want to create a deep divide with Halleck and acquiesced to his pressure. Banks also came on board when he was made aware of versions of the correspondence among the other generals.[76] Finally, Banks received several letters from Lincoln urging him to bring about elections in the free part of the state.[77] Lincoln wanted a congressional delegation loyal to him from Louisiana in the next elections. Banks could see that a successful campaign under his command up the Red River would be more helpful to him in the upcoming election than it would be to Lincoln. He conceived a grandiose but overly complex scheme, and by the third week of January 1864 the bobbin-boy-now-general turned his boundless enthusiasm to accomplishing Lincoln's wishes for a new Louisiana political order, a rejuvenation of the New England textile industry, and preparation for his bid for the presidency.

# Chapter 2

## Confederate Preparations

From March 1863 until the campaign began in March 1864, the Confederate commanders in the Department of the Trans-Mississippi worked at a feverish pace to prepare for an anticipated invasion up the Red River. Their efforts were astounding considering the limitations of time and manpower. At the same time events in the war moved farther away from this theater, but political and economic needs of the New England states and the politicians wooing them forced the Union focus back to the Rebel territory west of the great river. The preparations for the campaign by both the Union and Confederacy illustrate a scene of fragmented purposes, conflicting strategic and tactical goals, and vastly differing levels of experience and command style. The efforts made by the Confederates also show remarkable ingenuity.

The Confederate government reorganized its western military districts early in 1863. The areas under its control west of the Mississippi River were placed under a separate command or department. During the twelve months between March 1863 and March 1864, the new command made impressive progress in preparing for a possible invasion of the Red River Valley. The command was hampered, though, by conflicting ideas among the leaders as to the best means of defending the region, and it was particularly concerned about the rapidly deteriorating Confederate positions east of the Mississippi River. The fall of Vicksburg on July 4, 1863, almost completely halted the movement of supplies flowing from Louisiana and Texas to the armies in the east. Even before Vicksburg's fall the Confederate command west of the Mississippi River began repositioning forces to counter an ever-increasing Union threat. The Rebel commanders were not in agreement as to how this was to be done.

Lieutenant General Edmund Kirby Smith, commanding general of the Confederate Department of the Trans-Mississippi, and Major General Richard Taylor, head of the District of Western Louisiana, kept a close watch on Union movements in late 1863 and early 1864. Taylor's spies in New Orleans and Confederate reports elsewhere led both men to believe that either Union major generals William T. Sherman or Nathaniel P. Banks would make a thrust up the Red River when the spring rains made the river rise.[1]

Taylor and Smith were constantly at odds, and their frustration at each other's style is evident in reports at the time and in postwar correspondence. In his memoir *Destruction and Reconstruction,* Taylor referred to Kirby Smith and his large headquarters staff as the "Hydrocephalus at Shreveport."[2] Taylor, following in the manner of his training under General Thomas J. "Stonewall" Jackson, wanted fast-paced movement and a measure of finesse to meet the enemy. He was experienced in masking his movements to keep his opponent off balance. Smith wanted elaborate plans using strong points to defend his department.

After the summer of 1863 the Confederacy west of the Mississippi River was almost completely isolated. The Union navy heavily patrolled the great river, severing all but limited contact to the east. Union forces also held strategic positions in the west. New Orleans had been occupied since April 1862, and Union forces held north and central Arkansas with forces headquartered in Little Rock. In Louisiana the Union Department of the Gulf was located in New Orleans with the Union army controlling Baton Rouge and the bayou country as well as prairies in southwest Louisiana. The Confederates controlled all of Texas (except some barrier islands), most of the Indian Territory in what is today the state of Oklahoma, southern Arkansas, and north and central Louisiana.

An understanding of the geography of the region is essential to an understanding of the defensive strategy chosen by the Confederate command. From upstream, Shreveport was the last high ground on the river that was large enough to support a town-sized population. The town was bordered on the east by the Red River, on the north by Cross Bayou, on the south by a shallow river overflow remnant called Silver Lake, and on the west by several parallel rows of ridges running in a north-to-south orientation.[3] These ridges were almost the height of the plateau and were separated by valleys filled with pine forests or boggy stream bottoms. The northern portions of the ridges stopped abruptly at the narrow flood plain of Cross Bayou. To the south of the town and across Silver Lake was another plateau of high land that consisted of rolling hills that eventually turned into the flat fields bordering the Wallace Bayou swamp.

Just below Shreveport was located the headwaters of Bayou Pierre, a major distributary stream of the Red River. This bayou flowed out of the Red River and roughly paralleled it until its water reentered the river just above Grand Ecore. A giant logjam called "the Great Raft" created Bayou Pierre, like most of the other water bodies in the Red River Valley. The raft was created by the river's sinuosity and the sandy composition of its banks.[4] As trees collapsed into the stream from the unstable riverbanks, the current carried them along until they collected on bars or snagged into the bed, forming an interlaced tangle of islands. As time passed, other trees landed on these islands, colonizing them and creating new areas for the accumulation of debris.[5] As the raft grew, the water coming down the stream did not diminish; thus parallel streams and lakes were formed. Among these were Caddo Lake, Cross Lake, Lake Bistineau, Bayou Pierre, Cross Bayou, Twelve Mile Bayou, Cane River, Flat River, Willow Chute, and Red Chute. Captain Henry Miller Shreve received a contract from the United States in the early 1830s to clear the raft, which at times exceeded one hundred miles in length. He had removed most of it by the 1840s, but the tendency of the river was (and still

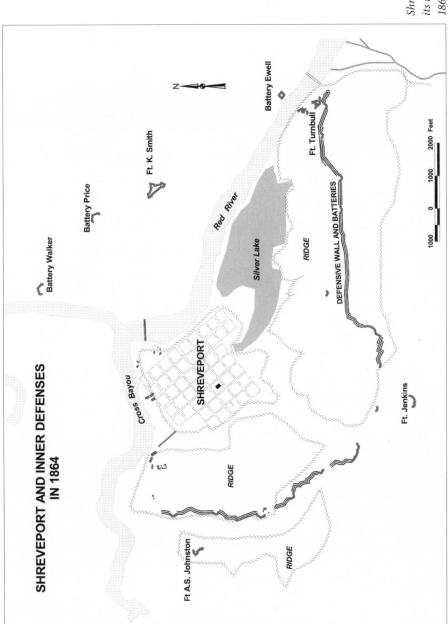

*Shreveport and its inner defenses, 1864.*

SHREVEPORT AND INNER DEFENSES IN 1864

Battery Walker

Battery Price

Ft. K. Smith

N

Battery Ewell

Cross Bayou

Red River

Silver Lake

SHREVEPORT

RIDGE

Ft. Turnbull

DEFENSIVE WALL AND BATTERIES

RIDGE

Ft. Jenkins

Ft A.S. Johnston

RIDGE

RIDGE

1000    0    1000    2000  Feet

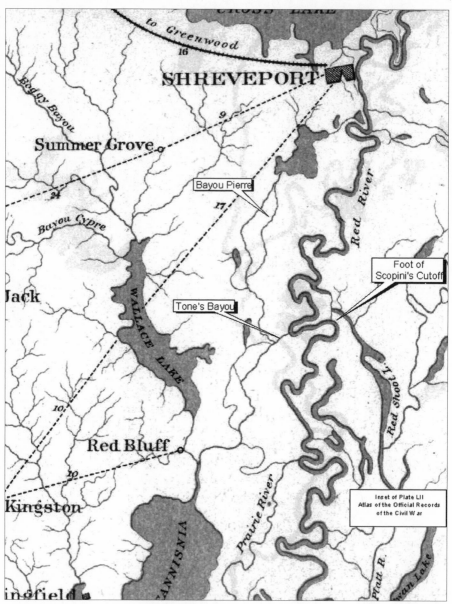

*Red River below Shreveport, including Tones Bayou, the wreck site of the* New Falls City *at the foot of Scopini's cutoff, and Bayou Pierre. This map is a portion of folio Plate LII from the original atlas to accompany the* Official Records of the War of the Rebellion. *Original in collection of the author. Additional cartography by Gary D. Joiner.*

remains) to rebuild the raft. This monumental project opened Red River for navigation and was considered to be of great military importance to open lines of communication and supply.

Approximately nineteen miles south of the original site of Shreveport was located a man-made water channel, which is today called Tones Bayou. This feature was approximately thirty-one miles south of the town, by river, in 1864. James Gilmer, a wealthy planter who was hostile toward Shreveport, created it in 1851.[6] In 1850 he brought several construction slaves called "mechanics" from another of his plantations to build a town he wanted to call Red Bluff. The town was never built, but the means to starve Shreveport of commercial traffic was.[7] The channel he constructed was a shunt between Red River and Bayou Pierre extending some 5,100 feet. It was created from an ancient crossover channel, which had been blocked by Henry Miller Shreve in 1843.[8] The fall in elevation from the east end to the west end was seven to eight feet.[9] It had assumed the name of a local resident, Antoine Pourier's Bayou or Tones (a shortened form of Antoine's) Bayou, and it drew off 75 percent of the flow from Red River.[10] This new channel would later be a cornerstone of the Confederate defenses protecting Shreveport.

In 1860 the State of Louisiana enacted legislation to remove the problem of Tones Bayou. It proposed to purchase a riparian (river) right-of-way at Scopini's Plantation northeast of the bayou and to remove a long elliptical loop from the river.[11] The resulting work begun in 1859 created Scopini Island.[12] Construction problems and military necessities dictated that it was not used until 1862.[13] The parallel streams, the man-made shunt, and the raft lakes provided opportunities for navigation which would both aid and worry the Confederates in their efforts to defend the Red River Valley.

By the spring of 1864 Shreveport had a thriving war-based industry.[14] With little or no help coming from east of the Mississippi River, it had to be self-sufficient. Fortunately, the region's ample natural resources and antebellum infrastructure allowed this to happen. Outlying military installations, including several in east Texas, were also directly linked to the army command in Shreveport. Arsenals, foundries, a powder mill, and magazine were created in Marshall, Texas, and a powder house and warehouses in Jefferson, Texas. Tyler, Texas, housed an ammunition factory and ordnance works were found in Houston and San Antonio.[15] Shreveport was the location of at least one foundry, a powder house, an arsenal, two sawmills, and corn storage sheds, all of which were located along the south bank of Cross Bayou near its mouth.[16]

This industrial base served two purposes. First, of course, was to support the Confederate army in the region. The second was to support the naval construction and repair yard in Block 66 of the original plat of the town of Shreveport.[17] The Confederates built the ironclad CSS *Missouri* here. They also repaired the high-speed ram CSS *William S. Webb* after its capture of the USS *Indianola*. It was from this yard that the *Webb* would begin its famous dash down the Red and Mississippi rivers near the end of the war. The yard was also the home of the tender *Mary T.*, which was also sometimes called the *J. A. Cotton* or the *Cotton II*.[18] Also based in Shreveport until it accidentally burned and sank in September 1863 was the large tinclad *Grand Duke*.

The *Missouri* would be the last Confederate ironclad to surrender in home waters.[19] The man in charge of the construction of the *Missouri,* and who later served as its captain, was Lieutenant Jonathon Carter, CSN.[20] The iron armor for the *Missouri* was obtained by ripping up the rails from a segment of the prewar Southern Pacific Railroad tracks, which had been laid west of Shreveport.[21]

These tracks were owned by the Vicksburg, Shreveport and Texas Railroad. The rail bed had been laid from Shreveport to the Texas line.[22] Five miles of rail had been laid to link Shreveport with the east Texas segments.[23] The railroad owned six locomotives, and the twenty-ton engine *Ben Johnson* operated out of Shreveport.[24] The rail bed had been cleared all the way to Monroe. The track had been completed between Monroe and the village of DeSoto opposite Vicksburg on the Mississippi River. The unfinished rail bed offered both promises and problems for the Confederates. Completed portions of the line offered swift transit of men and materiel. The railroad right-of-way also offered a tempting avenue of approach for Federal forces in Arkansas and at Vicksburg after the fall of that city in July 1863.

The Union navy had limited knowledge of the naval facilities and of some of the vessels built and stationed there. The primary questions concern the extent of their knowledge and when and how this information was discovered. The most secret operation at the Shreveport navy yard was the construction of five submarines for the defense of the Red River. The subs were never used in battle, but the Union navy certainly knew about them from naval and army correspondence and orders issued during 1864–65.[25] It is certain that Union spies operated in Shreveport from January 1864 and periodically thereafter to the end of hostilities. They often had great difficulties in sending their information across the battle lines. It is uncertain whether the U.S. navy knew about the submarines prior to the campaign.

A remarkable report was made by Union Major A. M. Jackson of the 10th Colored Heavy Artillery on March 13, 1865. The account is a synopsis of a spy report from Shreveport. Although there is at least one glaring error, the description of the vessels within the report are CSS *Hunley* class submarines:

HDQRS. MILITARY DIVISION OF WEST MISSISSIPPI,
*office of the chief signal officer,*
*New Orleans, La., March 13, 1865*[26]

COLONEL: I have the honor to submit to your consideration the following report of information received at this office this 13th day of March, 1865:
In a letter from Captain Collins, Confederate scout, to a person in this city, he states that he expects a visit about this time from one Ike Hutchinson, from Lavaca, Tex., who has charge of the torpedoes in Red River. This, taken in connection with Mr. Hunnicutt's report of the designs of Jones (also from Lavaca), who was at Houston, Tex., January 12, to destroy the ironclad Tennessee and other gunboats at the mouth of Red River, leads me to believe that there is some such plan on foot, of which the commanders of gunboats should be notified. The following is a description of the torpedo boats, one of

which is at Houston and four at Shreveport: The boat is 40 feet long, 48 inches deep, and 40 inches wide, built entirely of iron, and shaped similar to a steam boiler. The ends are sharp pointed. On the sides are two iron flanges (called fins), for the purpose of raising or lowering the boat in the water. The boat is propelled at the rate of 4 miles an hour by means of a crank, worked by two men. The wheel is on the propeller principle. The boat is usually worked 7 feet under water and has four dead lights for the purpose of steering or taking observations. Each boat carries two torpedoes, one at the bow, attached to a pole 20 feet long; one on the stern, fastened on a plank 10 or 12 feet long. The explosion of the missile on the bow is caused by coming in contact with the object intended to be destroyed. The one at the stern, on the plank, is intended to explode when the plank strikes the vessel. The air arrangements are so constructed as to retain sufficient air for four men at work and four idle two or three hours. The torpedoes are made of sheet iron three-sixteenths of an inch thick, and contain 40 pounds of powder. The shape is something after the pattern of a wooden churn, and about 28 inches long. Jones, the originator and constructor of these boats, also constructed the one which attempted to destroy the New Ironsides in Charleston, S.C. . . .

> I have the honor to be,
> Very respectfully, your obedient servant,
>
> > A.M. JACKSON,
> > *Major, Tenth U.S. Colored Heavy Artillery*
> > *(in absence of Captain S. M. Eaton).*
> > Lieutenant-Colonel C. T. CHRISTENSEN,
> > *Assistant Adjutant-General,*
> > *Military Division of West Mississippi*

This report offers a tremendous amount of information, not only about the vessels but also about the manner in which the information was obtained and also the team developing the submarines. The information was gathered apparently from a captured letter and the report of a Union operative. The Mr. Hunnicutt mentioned was most certainly a Union spy operating in Shreveport. The men working on the submarines were members of the Singer Submarine Corporation, which made both submarines and mines (torpedoes). Ike Hutchinson was most probably J. R. Hutchinson, a private in the 8th Texas Cavalry Regiment, who worked at Shreveport with the Singer Submarine Corporation from May 20, 1864.[27] The Jones mentioned was James Jones, of the Singer Submarine Corporation, known to be in Shreveport at the time.[28]

Although it is the most detailed account, this was not the first mention of the submarines in official Union correspondence. Shortly after the Red River Campaign, Admiral David Dixon Porter sent an order to one of his captains regarding measures to deny the submarines an exit from the river. The message was likely to have originated from a spy and was generated within a month of the campaign's close, if not before.

MOUND CITY, June 25, 1864.[29]

SIR: The rebels are fitting out at Shreveport four torpedo boats. They will be ready in two months.

You will at once prepare a chain to extend across the mouth of Red River on floats, and so fitted that it can be opened to permit vessels to go in and out.

By keeping the chain constantly on the stretch and a small gunboat lying close to it at the mouth of the river guarding it, no torpedo boats can get out.

Obtain all the information you can about this and do not be caught napping.

Do not forget that Old River is also open at times.

Very respectfully, your obedient servant,

DAVID D. PORTER,
*Rear-Admiral.*
Lieutenant-Commander F. M. RAMSAY,
*Commanding [USS] Choctaw and 3d*
*Dist. Miss. Squadron.*

Knowledge of the Confederate naval assets on the Red River, when combined with other intelligence information, assisted Admiral Porter in determining which vessels he would assign to the Red River Campaign. Another document has recently been identified as a source of tremendous influence on Porter's decision. This odd item is a death certificate dated February 14, 1864. The deceased was James O'Leary, a Landsman in the U.S. Navy attached to the USS *Black Hawk* at Mound City.[30] Only the first page exists, and the paper has received significant water and oil stain damage, but it is largely intact.

The important item, other than O'Leary's demise, is the date of his death, February 14, 1864. Admiral Porter was at Mound City, preparing for the Red River Campaign. In less than four weeks, his assembled flotilla would be at the mouth of the Red River preparing to enter. Drawn on the back of the unfortunate O'Leary's death certificate is a map of Shreveport. In some respects it is very detailed, but not in every area of the town. The map focuses on the southern portion of the Confederate defenses and extends to the plateau where the core of the town was located. It includes information on both banks of the river, location of mills, artillery batteries, roads, military camps and comments about potential pro-Union local citizens and recent developments in armaments. Regiments guarding Shreveport are listed. Some items are listed incorrectly. Fort Kirby Smith is shown on the west bank of the river, but it was located somewhat inland near the eastern bank.

An armored vessel is shown with the label "Rebel Ram the Webb going down to Alexandria." The vessel drawn closely resembles the CSS *Missouri,* including the centerline paddlewheel. The *Webb* was a side-wheel ram. The mention of the *Webb* was very important news. The Union navy had been looking for the dangerous and agile ram since it participated in the capture of the USS *Indianola* the previous year. The

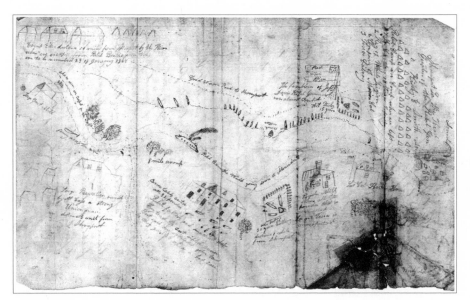

*Spy map drawn on the reverse of James O'Leary's death certificate. Collection of Louisiana State Museum.*

navy had sent vessels searching for the *Webb* down the Atchafalaya River, where it was believed to be hiding. News of the ram being in Shreveport and operating openly on the Red River would be important information. Admiral Porter had a healthy respect for the vessel. He also had knowledge of the *Missouri,* which had been described as a small *Arkansas* or *Tennessee* ironclad.[31]

According to the map the western bank of the Red River bristled with guns, and a large water battery, located one mile south of Shreveport, is shown on the eastern bank. The author of the map listed the battery as servicing thirty guns. This gauntlet, if it existed, would be reminiscent of the water batteries and guns along and atop the ridges of Vicksburg.

A road is clearly defined near and paralleling the western bank of the river. It is labeled "Good Wagon Road to Shreveport." The road on this map is the Winter Road, near Louisiana Highway 1 today. The spy drew in the locations of buildings in downtown Shreveport, but not Cross Bayou, the naval yard, or three of the great forts and none of the artillery batteries and connecting walls.

This map was perhaps the greatest influence on Admiral Porter's decision of which vessels should be included in the expedition. Although there are no records of it in his writings or correspondence with General Sherman and other confidantes, the map must have carried great weight. The number and location of guns, the vivid drawing of an ironclad similar in configuration to the *Arkansas,* and the site location of forts and military camps would have changed the calculus of the force composition Admiral Porter was planning. Whether or not the admiral had knowledge of the submarines in February, this map certainly contained enough information to convince him to bring deep draft river ironclads and monitors up Red River.

The author of the map was either a spy or an escaped military prisoner. The map is unsigned, but there is a note added to the lower left (southwest) corner of the map. It reads "Camp Eden[?] a distance of 10 miles from Shreveport by the River when we escaped from Rebel Bondage on the ever to be remembered 23 of January 1864." There was a parole camp on the bluffs overlooking Bayou Pierre, about 10 miles south of Shreveport, near the present intersection of Flournoy Lucas Road and Ellerbe Road. This camp appears on a Confederate defense map of Caddo Parish.[32]

Shreveport was considered to be a viable target by Union planners. To be near the military command structure and the Confederate state government of Louisiana, the state government in exile from Missouri was located first in Shreveport and then in Marshall, Texas, forty miles to the west. The Confederate capital of Arkansas was located in Washington, Arkansas, seventy-five miles by road to the north. Shreveport was the only Confederate administrative center worth striking west of the Mississippi River. In fact, by late 1863 the Union High Command felt that there were only four targets of any consequence left in the entire Confederacy: Richmond, Atlanta, Mobile, and Shreveport.[33]

On March 7, 1863, Smith arrived in Alexandria, about 112 miles downstream from Shreveport, and took over formal command of the Confederate Trans-Mississippi Department.[34] The location of the headquarters in Alexandria soon proved to be untenable, and it was moved to Shreveport in May 1863, when General Banks threatened Alexandria.[35] The move was reasonable since Shreveport's remote location provided a longer distance from a Union invasion from the south; however, it would also provide for shorter response time in the event that a Union operation originated at Little Rock. Richard Taylor had suggested Shreveport as a suitable site from the beginning of his tenure in Louisiana, but General Smith had opposed it, preferring the central location of Alexandria.[36]

Kirby Smith brought Brigadier General William R. Boggs with him as chief of staff. Boggs was a graduate, fourth in his class, of the United States Military Academy at West Point, Class of 1853. Of his classmates, James B. McPherson, Philip H. Sheridan, and John M. Schofield all became Union generals. John Bell Hood became the highest-ranking Confederate general from the class. As an interesting aside, while at West Point, Boggs befriended a lower classmate who later gained fame as an artist, James McNeill Whistler.[37]

One of Boggs's mentors was Dennis Hart Mahan, professor of Military and Civil Engineering. All cadets who attended the academy after 1833 and before the war studied under Mahan, and his textbook was the bible of field fortifications.[38] Boggs spent the war as a staff officer and was never given a field command.[39] In Louisiana he became General Kirby Smith's chief of staff.[40]

Once in Louisiana, Smith gave Boggs the task of creating a defense of the Red River Valley and its tributaries, especially the Ouachita and its lower portions, known as the Black River. He made an inspection trip to determine possible positions and methods of defense. With Boggs's evident support, Smith began to consider bringing slave labor both into public works projects and into the army as early as September 1863.[41]

Boggs determined that several measures should be undertaken. With the brief scare of a thrust up the Red and Ouachita rivers in the late spring of 1863 as a major distraction, he began to lay out his ideas. To protect the Ouachita he built a fort at Trinity near Harrisonburg. This emplacement was known as Fort Beauregard. He also began the entrenchment and fortifications of the high bluffs at the village of Grand Ecore, which served as the port town of Natchitoches, four miles to the southwest.[42]

After much discussion and bickering between Kirby Smith and Richard Taylor, Boggs selected a position near the town of Marksville in Avoyelles Parish for a lower Red River fortification. This was named Fort DeRussy for Colonel L. G. DeRussy, the engineer who constructed it. The Confederates had previously begun work at this location, but had abandoned the effort.

*The engineers of the Trans-Mississippi Department who served under General Boggs. Standing, left to right: David French Boyd, major of engineers; D. C. Proctor, First Louisiana Engineers; unidentified; and William Freret. Seated, left to right: Richard M. Venable, chief topographic engineer; H. T. Douglas, colonel of engineers; and Octave Hopkins, First Louisiana Engineers. From Francis Trevelyan Miller et al., eds.,* The Photographic History of the Civil War in Ten Volumes *(New York: Review of Reviews Co., 1912), 1:105.*

Taylor agreed with Smith that Fort DeRussy should be strengthened in some manner to counter any naval invading force.[43] The site was located on a hairpin turn in the river, and, if properly armed and manned, it could thwart gunboats. Boggs designed the fort with forty-foot-thick walls of packed earth that stood twelve feet high, with the entire structure surrounded by a deep, wide ditch.[44] This fort and its outlying works became the southern anchor of the Confederate defenses on the Red River. The fortification was to be augmented with a division of infantry consisting of three to five thousand men who were to operate in the vicinity but not to be garrisoned at the site.[45]

Smith hoped that a suitable site could be picked just below this location at or below the confluence of the Ouachita/Black with the Red.[46] No suitable site was located for a large structure here, but Boggs did find sites for four small forward defensive positions close to the town of Simmesport near the mouth of the Red River. The largest of these was named Fort Humbug and known to the Union soldiers as Fort Scurry, after one of the Texas Division brigade commanders, Brigadier General William R. "Dirty Shirt" Scurry. These small defensive positions are known collectively as the Yellow Bayou forts. As early as April 22, 1863, Boggs reported to Taylor that Smith believed Fort DeRussy could not be defended against the combined Union army and navy expedition without adequate garrisoning of troops. He was adamant that it not be abandoned unless absolutely necessary.[47]

Taylor wanted to build an obstruction that would allow the Great Raft, the giant logjam on the Red River, to re-create itself. He hoped to build this structure near Fort DeRussy, thinking that only a complete jamming of the river would stop the Union Navy. He believed the obstruction was of greater importance than the fort and did not want the fort to be finished. Taylor's method of operations was movement. He disliked field fortifications and, he believed, large-scale river obstructions would protect his flanks from the Union navy in the event of an incursion up the Red River. He disliked the idea of Fort DeRussy or any other device that could become a trap for his own men. A Union boat's captain who later viewed the fort noted in his memoirs that the fort's casemate batteries had been strengthened with railroad iron.[48] Taylor indicated that the fort's final armament consisted of eight heavy siege guns and two field pieces.[49]

Throughout 1863 and the first half of 1864, Taylor openly disagreed with Kirby Smith over defensive strategy. Later he would contemptuously call the fort "our Red River Gibraltar."[50] Taylor's dissatisfaction with the fort was evident in his refusal to man the structure fully, although he had a full division of Texas troops in the vicinity.

Taylor had problems with conflicting orders from Smith and with engineering officers he believed were incompetent. One he felt capable was Captain David French Boyd, the engineer in charge at Fort DeRussy who was a loyal ally of Taylor. Major Henry T. Douglas, the new chief engineer for the department after Boggs had assumed the chief of staff duties, and clearly in the camp of Kirby Smith, displayed his disdain for Taylor. Boyd, a loyal follower of Boggs and Taylor's engineer at the fort was more even-handed and knew he must work with his department commander.

Taylor ordered Boggs to build the obstruction below the fort in the fall of 1863, and it appeared to be very formidable. It was built of heavy wooden pilings created from trees felled from around the site and driven into the streambed completely across

*Brigadier General William R. Boggs. From Francis Trevelyan Miller et al., eds.,* The Photographic History of the Civil War in Ten Volumes *(New York: Review of Reviews Co., 1912), 10:265.*

the river.[51] To these was added a second line constructed shorter in height. These two lines were braced together and strengthened with cross-banded ties. Attached to this structure was a raft of trees and timber, which rested on the floor of the stream.[52] In addition, the Confederates had cut down "a forest of trees" upstream and allowed them to pile up above the structure. They also drove pilings into the riverbed downstream from this dam, extending two hundred yards at what appeared to be close but random intervals.[53]

The diary of a Shreveport man who worked on the barrier gives perhaps the only Confederate account of the structure. We learn from him that the location of the barrier was six river miles below the fort.[54] Work on the barrier was feverish. Thomas Pope Fullilove wrote to his wife Elizabeth (Lizzie) on December 15, 1863: "There is getting to be too much confusion and hurry to do much here. I fear our object will not be accomplished and the scarcity of tools add confusion."[55] Fullilove states that the barrier was erected in a straight section of the river that allowed the current to hinder its construction.[56]

Fullilove wrote three days later that the water had been rising and the weather was bad. He had been detailed to work on the embankment connecting the fort to the river battery casemate.[57] In a letter dated January 31, 1864, he wrote:

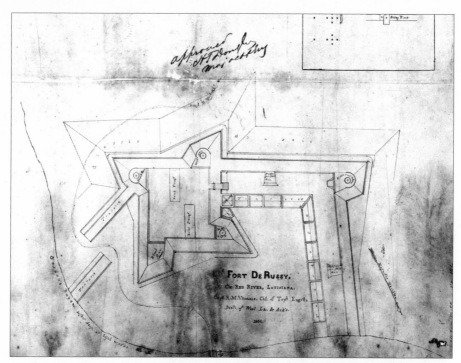

*Portion of Map 196, Confederate Engineers' sketch of Fort DeRussy by Confederate Major Richard Venable, 1864. Note the approval of the plans by H. T. Douglas. Jeremy Francis Gilmer Papers, Southern Historical Collection, University of North Carolina, Chapel Hill.*

The piling will be complete in about one week but the sinking timber, I think, never. Our raft is in part of the river nearly straight, the piling certainly cannot stand and we can never get logs enough in the river to block it up in high water. We haul a log way 175 ft. long and 15 ft. wide on our side and 75 ft. long on the other but the current carries them off so badly that it is doubtful in my mind whether they will meet. Every night we lose almost as much as we gain in the day at the ends and it is sinking down in the middle so that it is somewhat dangerous to work on it. A negro was drowned the day before yesterday at the piling about 50 ft. above our log way, the body could not be found, however no effort was made until today. We are hard run down I assure you. Yesterday we worked about half the day in the rain and 1/2 of the negroes are nearly naked and nearly all of them with shoes not fit to wear. Often the mud is so deep & so stiff that their shoes get pulled in pieces. A good many, some 25 or 30 are sick and coming in everyday, and mud and water every where it rains & only 110 hands at work. The piling is driven in at an angle of 45 across the 5 in a cluster 15 ft. apart in one row & a second row behind them ten ft. & single & cut off 3 ft. above the water & a plate pinned on the top, then the clusters are brought (rolled) together at the top 15 ft. higher than the plate & braces from the plate to the top of the clusters & cross pieces from plate on a level to the clusters. The clusters are driven after this manner:

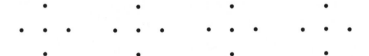

... A great many of the piling have come up without any cause. One whole cluster came up at one time after being fastened together. No floating has yet been put in but tomorrow a floating raft will be begun to lodge against the pilings made of logs pinned together.[58]

Adding to the confusion, Boyd was kidnapped by Jayhawkers in early February and was not released until just after the Red River Campaign began.[59] By February 10 the barrier had a gap of only forty feet, and he then felt that it would take another three weeks to finish the job.[60] The obstruction was completed within days of the Union navy's entry into the river.

With Fort DeRussy and the obstruction near completion, Boggs focused on the defenses upstream by scouting and preparing positions. There were no defensible positions between Fort DeRussy and north of Alexandria. In fact, no fortifications were prepared in Alexandria until after the 1864 expedition. Boggs gambled on Fort DeRussy and ample land forces under General Taylor to save the central Louisiana town. His primary mission, of course, was to protect Shreveport.

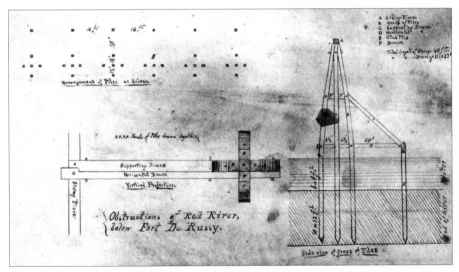

Portion of Map 196, Confederate Engineers' sketch of the obstruction as part of Fort DeRussy by Confederate Major Richard Venable, 1864. Jeremy Francis Gilmer Papers, Southern Historical Collection, University of North Carolina, Chapel Hill.

The first truly high ground encountered coming up the river from Alexandria was the high bluff at Grand Ecore. Boggs was not the first military engineer to see the value of this site. The hill and bluff complex had been the site of a military camp and fortification during the Mexican War. It had been one emplacement in a vital line of fortifications both guarding the Red River from the Mexicans in Texas and serving as a marshalling point for the forces of General Zachary Taylor (the future president of the United States and father of General Richard Taylor). A portion of the hill structure was used for Fort Salubrity during that war. Among the young officers who had served in the complex was Ulysses S. Grant.[61]

The bluffs at Grand Ecore were 120 feet high. Boggs began fortifying the hills and bluffs with his usual vigor, an action Smith supported.[62] Taylor, however, did not like the idea of having his forces hemmed into the hill complex with no room to maneuver. He wanted the river to be obstructed when needed at the narrows near the bluffs and another location to be fortified, Plaisance. Taylor complained to Smith, and in September 1863 Smith replied that Boggs was at Grand Ecore examining the progress of the entrenchments. He enclosed a copy of the orders to Major H. T. Douglas (then chief engineer of the department) to cease any major expansion of the works. He also agreed to the fortification at Plaisance, across the river and downstream, if it could be constructed with current manpower.[63] At this time the Confederates had already placed heavy artillery at the bluffs.[64] Smith suggested to Taylor that one of the nine-inch guns (there were two located at the site) could be left at Grand Ecore.[65] On October 5, Smith ordered Boggs to remove the two nine-inch guns, take them to Shreveport, and cease any further works on the river below the bluffs.[66] As late as January 1864, Taylor sent a dispatch to Boggs complaining about some of the engineering officers, their abilities, and their desire to carry out orders at both Grand Ecore and Fort DeRussy. Fortification work had continued against the orders of General Smith. Taylor blamed Major Douglas for the problems.[67] The bluff structure would be critical to both the Union army and navy during the campaign.

North of Grand Ecore and extending upstream to the bluffs south of Shreveport, the river narrowed and the currents were swifter. At various points the banks were elevated from the surrounding land, but there was no place to create a commanding fortified position using elevation as the central feature. The Red River Valley, with its great looping meanders, obscured parallel channels, distributaries, and ox-bow lakes, would become the next segment in Boggs's master plan.

James Gilmer's plan to starve Shreveport in 1851 offered General Boggs the opportunity to lay an elegant trap. Gilmer's project and the remedy created by the state of Louisiana bore great difficulties for the Confederates. There are few records that detail Boggs's efforts. A large percentage of the dispatches, orders, and general correspondence from the Trans-Mississippi Department are missing and assumed destroyed at the time of the capture of Shreveport.[68] To reconstruct Boggs's next defensive plan, sources other than *the Official Records of the Union and Confederate Armies in the War of the Rebellion* must be used. Since the Union fleet and army units did not pass by some of these structures until the surrender of Shreveport, and indeed may never

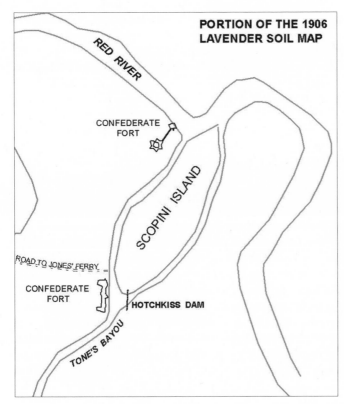

**PORTION OF THE 1906 LAVENDER SOIL MAP**

RED RIVER

CONFEDERATE FORT

SCOPINI ISLAND

ROAD TO JONES' FERRY

CONFEDERATE FORT

HOTCHKISS DAM

TONE'S BAYOU

*Tones Bayou, based on the Lavender Soil Survey map of 1906. Original in Archives and Special Collections, Noel Memorial Library, Louisiana State University, Shreveport. Additional cartography by Gary D. Joiner.*

have passed them, there is no official correspondence from the Union side describing them. They were perhaps, Boggs's most ingenious achievement.

To understand how Boggs's plan worked, one must remember what James Gilmer did. Bayou Pierre is an ancient raft channel of the Red River. It exits the river just below Coates's Bluff in what is today the city of Shreveport and roughly parallels the river, sometimes making great arcing meanders until it rejoins the river just north of Grand Ecore. When Gilmer cut the shunt channel to make Tones Bayou, the majority of the river flow dumped into Bayou Pierre in the same manner that Henry Miller Shreve had created his islands in the Red River in the 1820s and 1830s. Gilmer let the force and direction of the Red River's current create the hydrodynamics for him. The Confederates observed that when in operation it removed almost all of the water into the bayou.[69]

To remedy the effects of the channel diversion, the state of Louisiana created a cutoff, referred to as a ditch, across the eastern end of Scopini Plantation. The cut off was not the ideal they had hoped for. In fact, at times the "ditch," as it was referred to, was almost impassable.[70]

In the April 22, 1863, dispatch to Boggs concerning Fort DeRussy, Taylor suggested an obstruction upriver between Tones Bayou and Coushatta Chute (Bayou

Coushatta where it joins the Red River near the town of Coushatta.)[71] To this venture Smith gave his endorsement. He was concerned, however, with the effect an obstruction at the narrows would have on his line of communications.

Boggs also reported to Taylor that he did not believe that permanent obstructions in the Red River were a good idea. He also told him that "Lieutenant-General Smith has directed that the obstructions in the mouth of Tones Bayou be removed, and steps be taken to stop the cut-off. This will take nearly all the water from Red River above Grand Ecore, and, owing to the scarcity of wagons, will make it difficult to supply your army from this region."[72]

Captain Thomas P. Hotchkiss was ordered by the CSA secretary of war (certainly at the urging of Kirby Smith) to close the bayou.[73] He did this by building a dam that bore his name.[74] The dam did not, as one might think, close Scopini's cutoff.

It was located near the southernmost bend of Scopini Island, the piece of ground formed between Scopini's cutoff and Tones Bayou. To guard this vital dam, Boggs built two fortifications, one on either end of Scopini Island.[75] The southern structure is a long artillery battery. It overlooked the Hotchkiss dam and had clear field of fire across open ground to the next downstream meander of the Red River. The battery was approximately 570 feet in length and shaped like a giant, elongated "E." The northern anchor is a pond that may have been a borrow pit or a gun emplacement.[76] Lying behind this emplacement was a large infantry camp, Camp Morgan, designed to provide garrison for the forts.[77] The northern structure was a square star fort with a causeway and apparently a water battery. It resembled Fort DeRussy in design, though perhaps not in scale.[78] This emplacement guarded Scopini's cutoff and was designed to provide enfilade fire for the southern battery. The winding river would allow either fortification to assist the other with covering fire. With Bayou Pierre on one side and the Red River on the other, a landing force encountering fire from either battery would have disembarked troops and headed over land. Due to the level of the ground and the cut-in bank nature of the old river surrounding Scopini Island, the troops would have marched up to an all but impenetrable river with a swift current and into the face of heavy artillery and infantry fire. The open field objective, the narrow marching front and almost nonexistent flanking opportunities are reminiscent of the Rodriguez Canal, which was the fortification line for General Andrew Jackson at the Battle of Chalmette (New Orleans) in the War of 1812. If the Union army had followed the Winter Road up the west bank of the Red River instead of invading inland, Taylor would have had the opportunity to marshal his forces behind this line. A portion of the artillery from the defenses in Shreveport as well as all his field artillery would have been available to him.

Although there is no direct on-the-ground evidence, there was an additional obstruction at Scopini's cutoff near the northern fortification to make this scenario work. The dam would have no impact on the river's flow if the Scopini cutoff was functioning normally. The obstruction consisted of a raftlike dam. One source states that when the blockage was blown, it drained the Red River "like pulling the plug out of a bathtub."[79] The obstruction was blown between March 18 and April 5, 1864, and the river was not returned to its main channel course until 1873.[80] In the summer following the 1864 Red River Expedition a Texas cavalry unit, the W. P. Lane Rangers, came to the site and crossed Bayou Pierre in short order, but it took them half a day to cross Tones Bayou.[81]

Boggs was not satisfied with having the Tones Bayou defensive system stand alone. His intent was to first slow down the fleet. He knew that if the river level dropped significantly the Union navy could not bring its deeper draft ships up through the narrows. (He was correct, as the history of the 1864 campaign was played out.) He asked for and received permission to sink one of the Confederate defense fleet vessels below Tones Bayou. The vessel was the *New Falls City,* which was at anchor in or near the mouth of Coushatta Chute. *Ways Packet Directory* lists it as being an 880-ton sidewheel packet with a wooden hull, having a length of 301.3 feet and a beam of 39.7 feet with a draft of 7.6 feet.[82] It was possibly the largest vessel to navigate the Red River up until that time. Not only was it to be sunk, it was to be wedged across the stream, creating a sandbar beneath it. This would halt the Union warships until the vessel could be removed. Kirby Smith, through Boggs's suggestion, ordered it to be taken from Coushatta Chute (Bayou Coushatta) and placed at the foot of Scopini's cutoff.[83]

There are only two sources that describe or directly mention the Tones Bayou complex. David French Boyd, while in captivity at Grand Ecore during the campaign, tried to smuggle a letter to Taylor. He told his commander to "Move heaven and earth to close up Scopini's Cut-Off!" to remove the remainder of the river.[84] The second is the Lavender Soil Survey map of 1906, which portrays the forts and dam.[85]

Boggs also deployed a chain across the Red River at some point near his trap above the wreck of the *New Falls City.* The chain was forged at a plantation near Loggy Bayou on the Bossier Parish side of the river.[86] This complex of forts, dams, chains, and a steamboat became the most important part of the Confederate defenses on the river during the campaign, although the Union naval force had firsthand information only about the *New Falls City.*

General Boggs was also commanded to create an extensive defensive complex to protect Shreveport directly. Union spies were certainly aware of these works as early as January 1864:

OFFICE OF THE CHIEF ENGINEER, DEPT. OF THE GULF,
New Orleans, La., January 22, 1864.
Major-General BANKS,
*Commanding Department of the Gulf:*

GENERAL,: I have the honor to submit the following information concerning the routes from the Mississippi River to the interior of Texas:... Suppose it is determined to concentrate the forces near Shreveport, preliminary to a movement into Texas. This point is the principal depot of the enemy west of the Mississippi. There are some machine-shops and dock-yards there and the place is fortified by a line of works with a radius of 2 or 3 miles. The position is a strong one, being on a bluff and commanding the eastern bank. The point suggests itself at once as a proper one for such a concentration.

D.C. HOUSTON,
*Major, A. D.C., and Chief Engineer, Dept. of the Gulf.*[87]


The works described by Major Houston were indeed impressive based on the amount of time it took to construct them, the amount of labor available, and the fact that their designer was also working on various other major fortification projects at various points all along the Red River, even several hundred river miles away.

Boggs chose the highest hills, ridges, and bluffs as anchor points for the defensive system.[88] The complex extended across the Red River to cover the eastern approaches in Bossier Parish. On the Caddo Parish side, the anchor forts were linked by defensive parapets that resembled levees.[89] At hill, ridge, and bluff tops too small for large fortifications, Boggs placed artillery batteries. The large forts were combinations of construction types typical of Dennis Hart Mahan's textbook.[90] They made full use of the hill lines and interior routes of communication.[91] Boggs did not build his line on the central plateau of the town itself. He extended his defenses to adjacent ridges. There were three large anchor forts on the Caddo side and one on the Bossier side.

Beginning at the eastern anchor on the Caddo side, Boggs established a large fort on the first high ground north of Grand Ecore, known as Coates's Bluff. This fort was named Fort Turnbull, but the local name, attributed to Major General John Magruder, was Fort Humbug. He called it a "humbug" due to the use of Quaker guns (tree trunks blackened to look like cannon and mounted on wagon wheels). These were interspersed with real ordnance to give the impression of an impregnable position. The river in 1864 came up to the foot of the bluffs on which the fort was built. It was a large complex and covered several interior bluff lines. Radiating from this fort were several artillery batteries. To the north was a battery that was to provide crossfire for Battery Ewell across the river.[92] Due south of Fort Turnbull was Battery I, located on the southernmost rise of the bluff structure. West and somewhat north of this was Battery II, located on the west side of the bluff complex. Next in line were batteries III and IV. Battery III was located on an extension of the bluff and was positioned so that it could cover the area to the south of the defensive line or be turned to the north to fire at targets in the river. Battery IV was placed very close to the Confederate hospital, on the high ground above it. These batteries would most likely have been under the direct control of Fort Turnbull.

Battery V was located on a high hill behind the defensive line where it could offer fire to either the south or be turned to the east and cover targets in the river. Battery VI and two unnumbered batteries faced south and were to provide support for the next anchor fort, Fort Jenkins. This fort was positioned outside the defensive ring and occupied the highest topographic elevation in Caddo Parish. The line then proceeded westward to Battery VII, located at the southwest corner of the ridge line extending westward from the river at Coates Bluff. Between this bluff and the town of Shreveport

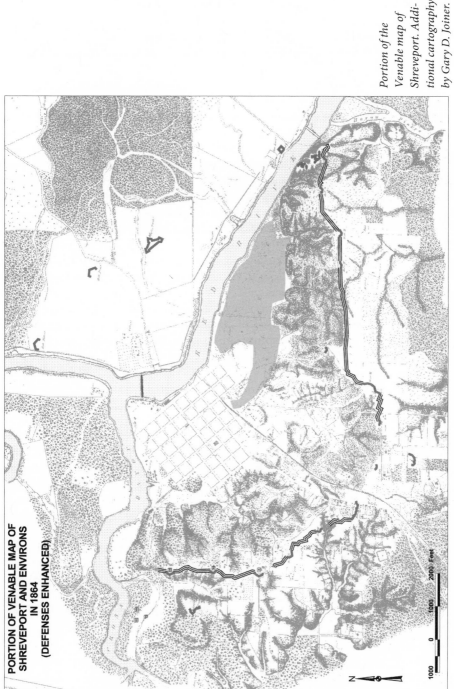

*Portion of the Venable map of Shreveport. Additional cartography by Gary D. Joiner.*

lay Silver Lake, a shallow bog overflow from the Red River. Only one road entered the town from the south, and Fort Jenkins provided a frowning battlement to guard it.

From Battery 7th the defensive line extended to the northwest. Connecting to another ridge, this one aligned north to south. Behind this ridge lay the marsh and the Bottoms. Batteries VIII, IX, X, XI, and XII were all located on this ridge. Battery XII was located on the extreme northern tip of this ridge. Behind it and to the east was a spectacular view of the town; to the north lay Cross Bayou. Any attempt to ford the stream below this point would have been difficult at best due the stream's depth and open position.

On the ridge running parallel and west to the one just discussed, Boggs built Fort Albert Sidney Johnston. This was a long fort designed to cover Cross Bayou to its north and to prevent any attempt to attack Shreveport from the west. Any skirmish line formed west of this ridge would have met with fire from the fort. Attackers from the west would have been forced to cross an opposing parallel ridge line and then descend into a densely wooded stream bottom before rising to the fort's ramparts atop a high ridge.

To cover the Confederate capital from the east, General Boggs designed a series of four fortifications with one being an anchor. This was a triangular star fort named in honor of Kirby Smith. It was aligned to protect from an attack to the east, north, or southeast. South of this was Battery Ewell, a smaller square fort. Northwest of Fort Kirby Smith lay Battery Price formed as a large lunette facing northeast. To the west-northwest of Battery Price lay another large lunette, Battery Walker, located on the river and facing north. The three northernmost Bossier side emplacements could provide enfilade fire for each other. The southern fort, Battery Ewell, was designed to protect Fort Kirby Smith, provide fire coverage against riverine targets, and offer enfilade fire for Fort Turnbull and its north battery.

This entire line radiates out like the rim of a wheel from the town of Shreveport, extending from one to three miles in a broad arc. Inside this defensive line lay the center for the military industrial complex of the Trans-Mississippi west, the naval yard, a major infantry compound, and the Confederate government of Louisiana. Forces in place within Shreveport or in the defensive works could have reached where they were needed the most within a minimum amount of time. This would include crossing troops from the Shreveport/Caddo side to the Bossier side. This was facilitated by a pontoon bridge, located near the mouth of Cross Bayou.[93]

Boggs and his engineers created a final significant structure on the Red River just below Shreveport and guarded by Fort Turnbull and Battery Ewell. This structure appears on the Venable map of the defenses of Shreveport as a thick line labeled "Raft."[94] Two Confederate engineers' drawings exist that explain the significance of this structure. They are from a set of maps, surveys, and drawings prepared by Confederate Major Richard Venable and the only copies that exist are those that were sent to Richmond. These were spirited away at the end of the war and are now a portion of the Southern Historical Collection at the University of North Carolina at Chapel Hill.

The plan of the raft shows an ingeniously constructed floating dam made of wood. It spans the river and is held in place by ship anchors. Both sides are secured by heavy supports that appear to be tower bases. The distance below water from the base of the structure to the bed of the river channel is approximately twenty feet. This would allow the submarines to leave the safety of the harbor and move downstream undetected. The vessels could foray under the raft, and prying eyes would have great difficulty seeing them. In the center of the dam and directly over the flow channel of the river was located a very large trapezoidal-shaped plug. This device was held in place by the current of the river. It could be pulled back upstream and to the side when vessels needed to either enter the Shreveport safe harbor or be deployed to the south. The flow of the river was unimpeded by the raft whether the plug was open or closed. The second engineering drawing describes the system by which the plug was opened and returned to the closed position. The raft was placed near Fort Turnbull, the largest of the defensive positions, for obvious reasons. Battery Ewell, slightly upstream and on the eastern bank of the river, would be in position to provide enfilade fire. Additionally, the north battery of Fort Turnbull and Battery III could provide additional covering fire if needed. The thick construction of the raft would have made ramming difficult at best, and covering fire provided by the elevated fort and batteries on the west bank and the river level battery on the eastern bank would have made an attack by river or land an extraordinarily complex maneuver.

As the winter of 1863–64 progressed, news arrived of Sherman's Meridian expedition, and Smith and Taylor began to think that perhaps Mobile was the next

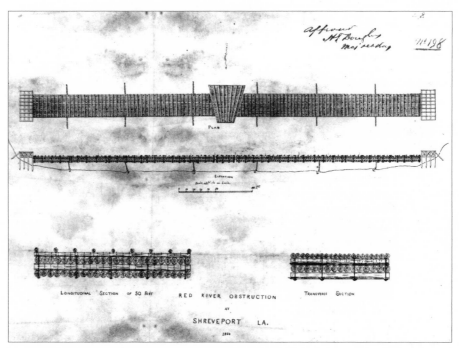

*Confederate Engineers' drawing of the raft at Shreveport. Jeremy Francis Gilmer Papers, Southern Historical Collection, Wilson Library, University of North Carolina, Chapel Hill.*

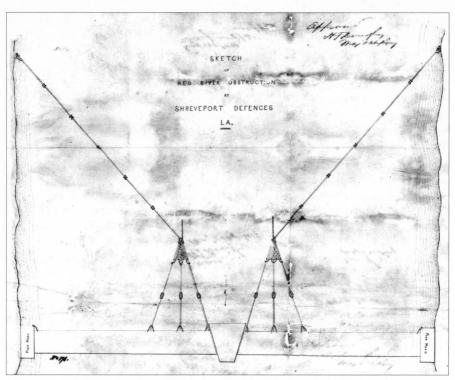

*Confederate Engineers' drawing of the raft at Shreveport showing the operating mechanism. Jeremy Francis Gilmer Papers, Southern Historical Collection, Wilson Library, University of North Carolina, Chapel Hill.*

target, but Banks's men were still poised in New Orleans. Taylor believed Banks would not move from the Bayou Teche area without Sherman's support.[95] All hopes of a reprieve seemed to evaporate as news came in from reliable sources in New Orleans and Vicksburg of a huge naval build-up at Vicksburg and massing of infantry and support troops at Vicksburg and near New Orleans.[96] Smith ordered his widely scattered troops into new concentration areas in early March.

As usual his orders were carried out with varied degrees of urgency, with Major General John Magruder's Texas-based troops the last to be released to Louisiana soil.[97] Smith ordered these units, consisting primarily of cavalry regiments, to gather in Alexandria.[98] He also ordered Taylor to reposition his forces. The brigade of Texans under Camille Armand Jules Marie de Polignac, a French prince and Confederate brigadier general, was ordered from Trinity, near Harrisonburg on the Ouachita River, to join the brigade of Louisiana troops led by Colonel Henry Gray at Alexandria. Major General John G. Walker's Division of Texans was to operate in the prairie near the mouth of the Red River.[99] This area between Marksville and Simmesport offered good maneuvering room, assuming the troops did not find themselves trapped in the winding courses of Bayou de Glaize and other streams. The bayous and streams that sliced through the region made organized marches all but impossible without the constant assistance of engineers.[100] At this stage of planning, only Louisiana and Texas troops were repositioned.

Considering the short time available to the Confederate engineers, the defenses in the Red River Valley were well planned and superbly placed. In less than twelve months from the time they began construction, the fortifications of the Trans-Mississippi Department were almost complete. The fortifications created by Boggs and his engineers were very sophisticated and relied heavily on the use of regional geography and existing engineering features such as the Tones Bayou channel. Boggs's endeavors were certainly elaborate and delivered defense in depth. Given greater opportunity they would have been even more formidable. However, in light of the amount of time available to prepare for an invasion, were these measures adequate? Was the Confederate defensive strategy sensible? Finally, what was the human component of the strategy and was it sufficient to defend the valley?

Adequacy of defenses can only be ascertained if they successfully defend against a determined foe. Boggs's defensive works at Fort DeRussy were incomplete at the time they were attacked. Plans called for a strengthening of the rear casemate, but this was not done.[101] The bastion was an antinaval fortification designed to stop warships from passing its location. Its weakness was on the west or landward side. The Confederate engineers never believed that it could be attacked from the direction of Marksville. Most of the proposed infantry detachment would certainly have been deployed to the rear of the fort, but the walls were inherently weak. The lack of defensive measures from Fort DeRussy to Grand Ecore, near Natchitoches, was created by a lack of time and poorly defensible terrain. The extensive works at Grand Ecore were abandoned before the invasion in on an ongoing dispute between Kirby Smith and Richard Taylor. The time and effort used in fortifying the great bluff could have been more effectively applied elsewhere. The siege guns located at Grand Ecore were removed to Shreveport. The defensive positions throughout the Red River Valley were inadequate in that they generally suffered from a lack of artillery pieces and sufficient manpower to deter an attacking force.

Boggs's great triumph lay in his series of defenses in and around Shreveport, particularly at Tones Bayou. By trapping the water into a parallel stream, Shreveport would still be served by a full depth of water in the Red River channel while denying an enemy fleet the water it needed for navigation. This offered the possibility of either capturing or destroying an invading naval force, something that was recognized not only by the engineers who built the trap, but also by both Smith and Taylor.

Rebel naval construction and the accompanying raft architecture must be considered as a great milestone. The Confederate naval yard, positioned close to the downtown area of Shreveport and yet largely hidden by naturally terraced banks, saw the building of the ironclad *Missouri,* the repair of the *Webb,* and the secret construction of five *Hunley*-class submarines. All of this was accomplished in less than a twelve-month period.

Confederate defensive strategy in late 1863 and early 1864 appeared to be schizophrenic. Smith commanded Boggs to create or strengthen defenses in as many places in the valley as possible, given available resources and a short time line. Boggs was in the unenviable position of being forced to serve two masters who were constantly at odds. Theoretically, his immediate superior was Taylor, whose disdain for static fortifications was well known. Taylor's preference for using mobile field forces operating freely in the countryside rendered the need for strong field fortifications as non sequitur. Smith was Boggs's department commander and he answered directly to both men. Examples of problems created by the two divergent philosophies were the buildup and then abandonment of Grand Ecore, the reconstruction of Fort DeRussy rather than a stronger obstruction in the river below the fort, and creation of some of the massive fortifications at Shreveport without adequate artillery pieces in them. The one instance in which both Smith and Taylor agreed was in the construction of the Tones Bayou trap. Open animosity between Smith and Taylor created problems for the Confederate engineers, even to the details of design and the allocation of ordnance pieces.

The human component—in other words, the personalities of the Confederate commanders—led to problems in achieving the defensive goals. The Trans-Mississippi Department, headquartered in Shreveport, consisted of three districts: the District of Western Louisiana, commanded by Taylor; the District of Arkansas and Missouri, commanded by Sterling Price; and the District of Texas, commanded by John Magruder. All three men were major generals. They reported to Smith, the department commander, who was promoted to the rank of full general in February 1864. The personalities of these four men directly influenced the campaign from the beginning. Smith had a difficult time reining in each of these men. All strongly believed that their style of command was superior to the others, and each had a tenuous relationship with Smith.

Smith's overreliance on static field fortifications would have doomed the Confederates when confronted with a William T. Sherman style of warfare. Union troops who had operated under Sherman at Meridian would have bypassed the strongholds, cutting them off until they surrendered. The Confederate commander's reliance on field fortifications was very similar to Confederate general John Pemberton's defense of Vicksburg in spring and summer of 1863. If followed, the result would most probably have yielded similar results, a smashing Union victory.

Taylor's style of maneuver, learned under the tutelage of Stonewall Jackson in the Shenandoah Valley of Virginia, would work if he were able to concentrate enough forces at a place of his choosing to halt and perhaps destroy his enemy. The two philosophies could be mutually exclusive. The Red River defenses saw both coexisting, although not harmoniously.

Magruder, known to his favorites and detractors as "Prince John," hoarded his forces for use in Texas and did not want them dispatched to Louisiana or Arkansas. The majority of the Confederate cavalry west of the Mississippi River was under his direct control. He would not permit all of his cavalry units to be equipped with mounts or arms until he was ready. He delayed the dispatch of his horsemen into Louisiana until it was almost too late and many of his units were forced to fight as infantry. He refused to lead his units into battle outside Texas.[102]

Sterling Price, known as "Old Pap," was a former governor of Missouri. His attentions were always aimed north, and not to his department headquarters in Shreveport. He was subservient to Kirby Smith when it suited him. Price was a mediocre field commander at best.[103]

The Confederate commanders achieved some remarkable goals. In twelve months from taking command, Kirby Smith and his talented chief of staff, General Boggs, created a number of sophisticated fortifications that spanned the length of the Red River in Louisiana and some of its tributaries. Plans were prepared to divert almost all water from the river into a parallel stream to deprive the river of its water to protect Shreveport and yet trap an invading naval flotilla. Plans were made to bring forces from the three districts in the command to bear on a threat from the south, or any other direction as needed.

There were inadequacies in the plan. Some of these were born in the differing styles of command of Smith and Taylor. No direct line of mobilization was created to send troops between districts until a request was made, which would have to originate in Shreveport, not from the field. Taylor's disregard for fortifications delayed the construction of Fort DeRussy. Smith's low opinion of Taylor caused him to interfere with the latter's operational plan. The independent streaks in the Arkansas and Texas commanders made their quick response in time of need a tenuous hope at best. Smith exerted control in matters that interested him, especially fortifications. His inattention to pre-positioning major units, particularly cavalry, almost caused his command's defeat.

# CHAPTER 3

# Union Plans

While the Confederates worked on their defensive strategies for slightly more than a year before the campaign began, the Union commander, Major General Nathaniel Prentiss Banks, had just a few months to prepare his plan. While Taylor's ideas were bold in the manner of Thomas J. "Stonewall" Jackson and Kirby Smith's plans were rooted in the solid military foundations taught at West Point, Banks brought little of this acumen to Union planning procedures.

Prior to the war, Nathaniel Banks was a rising political figure in both New England and national politics. He was born in Waltham, Massachusetts, near Boston, on January 30, 1816. Banks shared a similar background with Abraham Lincoln in several respects. Both men came from modest backgrounds and were self-taught. Both were pragmatic and had mastered the art of compromise. Finally, both overcame their humble beginnings to achieve national prominence.

The differences between the two men were significant. Lincoln was awkward in appearance and seemed rustic. Banks was always fastidious in his dress and speech, honed as an actor while still a teenager. Lincoln spoke conversationally, even before large groups, while Banks's public speaking style was marked by theatrical flourishes.[1] Banks's most recent biographer, James Hollandsworth, points out that the major difference between the two men was the reason each aspired to a life in politics. Lincoln's political life focused on the ideals upon which America was founded, while Banks used politics for personal promotion and to further business interests of his friends and supporters.[2]

During the 1840s and 1850s, Banks's pragmatism positioned him against the Whigs and pushed him into the arms of the Democrats. As the Whigs disintegrated over the slavery issue, Banks became a moderate Democrat. He was a nationalist and not an abolitionist. An example of this was his vote as a member of the House of Representatives to not oppose statehood to Texas in 1845, although it increased the number of slaveholding states.[3]

Banks understood the link between his native New England and the South from working as a child in the textile mill managed by his father. This job earned him the nickname of "the Bobbin Boy." New England became increasingly abolitionist during the 1850s, but it relied on Southern cotton to run its major industry, processing textiles. His position as a moderate Democrat allowed him to steer the middle course in his political career.

Banks began to depart from his centrist Democratic allies in the 1850s when Charles Sumner, a staunch abolitionist, was elected as the U.S. senator from Massachusetts. Although he detested him, Banks backed Sumner. This move demonstrated his ability to put personal goals ahead of principles.[4] As a member of the U.S. House of Representatives in 1854, he voted against the Kansas-Nebraska bill that allowed either territory to vote itself in as a state choosing slaveholding or free-soil. Although this was against his convictions, it was very popular in his district. His position on the bill forced him to leave the Democrats in favor of the new American, or "Know Nothing," Party.[5] Returning to a second term in the U.S. House of Representatives in 1855, Banks was elected Speaker of the House.[6] He became one of the best Speakers in its history.[7] Banks did such a good job that Northerners and Southerners credited him with being the best Speaker since Henry Clay.[8] The American Party split along the same lines as the Whigs, and Banks then turned to the antislavery Republican Party. Since his district was at the forefront of the abolitionist movement, Banks knew he

*Major General Nathaniel P. Banks. From Francis Trevelyan Miller et al., eds.,* The Photographic History of the Civil War in Ten Volumes *(New York: Review of Reviews Co., 1912), 10:177.*

had to follow the sentiment if he wanted to keep his political position and run for the presidency. In 1858 Banks ran for governor in Massachusetts. He was successful and was reelected in 1859 and in 1860.

The Republicans believed that they had no chance of electing a New Englander in the 1860 presidential elections, and Banks was forced to put his ambitions on hold.[9] Banks was not radical enough for the Republicans, and he was passed over again later that year. In January 1861 Banks left politics when he took a job as resident director of the Illinois Central Railroad, a job recently vacated by George B. McClellan.[10] Just as Banks began the new post, Fort Sumter was fired upon and Abraham Lincoln, now president, offered Banks a commission as a major general of the United States Volunteers. He was commissioned on May 16, 1861.[11] This early appointment as major general made Banks the fourth senior ranking and most senior army commander west of the Appalachian Mountains once he took over the Department of the Gulf. Despite his lacking formal military experience he was placed in command of the District of Annapolis, Maryland. His orders were inconsistent and his discipline of officers and enlisted men was erratic.[12]

General McClellan, one of only three army commanders superior to Banks, ordered him to take a force into Virginia's Shenandoah Valley to help remove the Rebels operating there and to guard the rear approaches of Washington. Banks appreciated the need for glory on the battlefield to assist him in a run for the presidency. He gladly accepted the assignment.

Fame on the field of battle eluded Banks in the Shenandoah Valley, where he was matched against the South's best tactical commander, Stonewall Jackson. Jackson's rapid movements and feints kept Banks guessing at the location of the main body of the Rebel troops. On May 24, 1862, Banks and his force were nearly cut off at Strasburg, Virginia, by the Louisiana Brigade. These Southerners were led by Brigadier General Richard Taylor, whom he would meet again on several battlefields. The Federal retreat turned into a rout as civilians joined the throng of soldiers. Wagons, buggies, and cargo carts littered the road, abandoned as the Louisiana Tigers neared. The vehicles slowed both the Union troops and the pursuing Rebels but allowed Banks and his men to escape to Winchester.[13] The scene would be repeated in Louisiana.

Banks did not realize that Jackson and his entire force were not only in pursuit but also preparing an encirclement of Winchester. Banks placed his men and artillery on the highest hill in the area. Taylor stormed the hill but Banks's men immediately fled. This swift flight was the only reason they survived. Banks was personally courageous and tried to stem the tide. He shouted to his men as he tried to reform their ranks, "My God, men, don't you love your country?" One of them responded, "Yes, and I am trying to get to it as fast as I can."[14] Jackson took Winchester, and Banks fled, leaving behind nine thousand small arms, two pieces of artillery, herds of sheep and cattle, tons of food, and medical supplies. Here he gained another nom-de-guerre: "Commissary Banks."[15]

At the Battle of Cedar Mountain in August, Banks's men fought well but barely escaped capture from the determined attacks of Jackson. Banks deployed his units piecemeal, resulting in at least one unit, the 10th Maine Infantry regiment, receiving

40 percent casualties in a matter of minutes.[16] Trying to rescue an artillery battery and cover the retreat of the 10th Maine, Banks ordered a squadron of the 1st Pennsylvania Cavalry to charge the Confederate line. They were decimated, with only 71 of 164 troopers present for duty the following day.[17] President Lincoln decided to pull Banks from frontline duty and ordered him to organize the defenses of Washington.[18] The general went to work with his usual enthusiasm and created formidable defenses with his newly created forces. These soldiers were to form the crux of the 19th Corps in Louisiana in September 1863.[19] Because he managed to rehabilitate himself in a major command, Banks was sent by Lincoln in December 1862 to replace Benjamin Butler in Louisiana.[20]

Once in Louisiana, Banks participated in the Vicksburg Campaign (although Banks would argue that this was a separate campaign) with operations culminating in the siege of Port Hudson. The Confederate bastion was located just upriver from Baton Rouge. Although Banks made several spirited attacks, the Rebels held out until after the fall of Vicksburg, denying him his great battlefield victory, although he certainly won the contest.[21]

Lincoln next directed Banks to invade Texas to accomplish two goals. The immediate need was to thwart the ambitions of the French puppet ruler of Mexico, Maximilian of Austria. The president believed that Napoleon III of France wanted Mexico to regain its former holdings, including Texas. Aid to the South from both England and France was still an issue at that time, and goods were pouring across the Texas-Mexico border. The other goal was to bring Texas back into the Union by creating an area of pro-Union sentiment.[22] This was a continuation of the president's reconstruction policy begun with the taking of New Orleans the previous year. Lincoln trusted Banks to do this. Although he was a potential rival, Lincoln believed he was the ideal man for the job.[23]

Banks's attempt to invade Texas was poorly conceived and resulted in a botched attempt to land forces at the mouth of the Sabine River on the Louisiana-Texas border.[24] Shortly after this failure, Banks sent his newly formed 19th Corps across southern Louisiana in a move to invade Texas. Banks's nemesis in the Shenandoah Valley, Richard Taylor, newly promoted to the rank of major general, had arrived in Louisiana in late summer of 1862 as the commander of the District of Western Louisiana. He fought the Federal forces at Bisland in St. Mary Parish in what has been called the Teche Campaign. Union Major General William Buel Franklin, commander of the 19th Corps, had been given no clear orders as to how he should invade Texas or what he should do once he arrived. He turned his men around in south-central Louisiana, reaching no farther than Opelousas in October 1863.[25]

Banks's military career to this point provides insight into the general's character, successes, and failures. Although a major political rival of Lincoln's, Banks was loyal to the president's administration and he exhibited characteristics of a capable administrator. Lincoln held the Massachusetts general in high regard, although not as a military commander, and he appreciated Banks's adherence to the administration's plans for reconstruction. Banks was personally courageous, but he did not inspire loyalty among his soldiers. He trusted his staff implicitly, even when they were obviously giving him bad advice. Finally, his total lack of military training derailed his attempts to gain glory on the battlefield at almost every turn.

From late 1863 through January 1864, Banks changed his opinion about the best line of attack into Texas and pursued a new venture of an attack up Red River with his usual boundless enthusiasm.[26] He solicited advice from Major General Henry Halleck, the army's general in chief, who wanted this expedition to begin. Halleck wrote letters to show his support of a Red River expedition and to outline his intentions to Lincoln, Grant, Sherman, and other officers.[27] Halleck told these commanders that the president wanted Texas invaded via the Red River and that he (Halleck) intended to support the effort in every possible manner.[28] Banks described his plans to his allies in New England, telling them of the possibilities of reopening their textile mills with newly acquired Louisiana cotton from the Red River Valley. They consequently made offers of support in securing cotton if the expedition was undertaken.[29] Banks also corresponded with Sherman, Grant, Porter, and Frederick Steele, his counterpart in Little Rock, Arkansas.[30] His letters and telegrams to each individual varied according to what he wanted and what he expected from them.

The political landscape was changing in Washington. For at least eighteen months, President Lincoln had wanted the Union to mount a campaign to plant the flag on Texas soil. With Banks in Louisiana, Lincoln thought he had removed his most visible Republican rival for the 1864 election from the politically charged air of Washington. Banks's friends, New England bankers and textile mill owners, would be all too happy to put pressure on their congressional delegations to support the expedition. President Lincoln needed them if he was to succeed in his run for reelection in the fall.

Grant, Sherman, and Porter were all close friends and allies. Their cooperation in large-scale projects proved successful in several operations, particularly at Vicksburg. Sherman had a burning desire to lead an expedition up Red River since he had lived at Pineville, on the river opposite Alexandria, before the war. He lobbied Grant to put him in charge of the campaign. His friend and superior was reluctant even to consider the operation, but Halleck was pushing for it to begin and the president desperately needed it.[31] At that time Grant was in the early process of planning the capture of Mobile. He certainly felt that he could not spare Sherman from these plans. Grant, however, lacked the authority to countermand Halleck's orders and thinly veiled suggestions. He acquiesced, therefore, in the use of a portion of Sherman's troops but not Sherman himself.[32]

By the end of January, Sherman had begun his Meridian Campaign, limiting the time he could contribute to the planning of the Red River Campaign. Halleck was writing to Sherman directly and intimating that both he and Banks would lead the expedition when he was finished tearing up Meridian. Grant was kept out of this loop and was not told what troops, if any, from east of the Mississippi would be used. Porter had offered his full support to Sherman if the expedition were carried out. No doubt he thought that Sherman would lead the campaign and that it would be a great opportunity to work with his friend.[33]

Still thinking that Halleck might order him to be the expedition's senior field commander, Sherman agreed to meet with Banks in New Orleans.[34] He arrived in New Orleans on March 2 and found Banks in a whirl of activity, but not—in Sherman's opinion—activities to support the pressing problems at hand.[35] Although he had completed his planning for the upcoming campaign, Banks could not devote much time to explain his ideas to Sherman. Banks urged Sherman to remain in the city for an extra two days to attend the grand inauguration of the new Union governor of Louisiana, Michael Hahn. Sherman was disgusted and later wrote in his memoirs that Banks wanted him to participate in the ceremonies and festivities of the great occasion. "General Banks urged me [Sherman] to remain over the 4th of March to participate in the ceremonies, which he explained would include the performance of the 'Anvil Chorus' by all the bands of his army and during the performance, church-bells were to be rung, and cannons were to be fired by electricity. I regarded all such ceremonies as out of place at a time when it seemed to me every hour and minute were due to the war."[36]

Banks told the great field commander that he, not Sherman, would be the overall field commander.[37] This was so much hyperbole since Halleck had not and never would give Banks sole authority over the expedition. Halleck confided to Sherman in April, "General Banks is not competent, and there are so many political objections in superseding him by Steele that it would be useless to ask the President to do it."[38] Sherman wrote to his wife, "I wanted to go up Red River, but as Banks was to command in person I thought it best not to go."[39] Since Banks was inducted into the army with the rank of major general, he and his predecessor, Benjamin Butler, outranked not only Sherman but also Grant and every officer serving in the field at that stage of the war.[40] Banks's rank forced Halleck and Grant to treat him differently from any of their field commanders. This had been evident in the Vicksburg Campaign and carried through now.

Sherman, after conferring with Grant, backed out of personally leading troops up the Red River. He also realized that Porter's fleet would be in jeopardy if Banks impulsively left them at some point without protection. Porter had already committed himself to the campaign. Sherman, with his typical insightfulness, loaned Porter ten thousand of his most trusted veterans under the very capable Brigadier General Andrew Jackson Smith.[41] The troops were an independent command added to assist Banks but not under his direct control. They had their own transport vessels and were to accompany the fleet.

Sherman placed some severe limits on their use and the extent of their cooperation. They could operate directly with Banks, but at no time during the campaign were they to abandon the fleet entirely for land operations. A. J. Smith and his men were to accompany Porter, not Banks. They were not to be used in a thrust further than Shreveport, and, most important, due to Grant's upcoming projects, they were to be returned to Vicksburg no later than April 15.[42]

In March, Grant was promoted to lieutenant general and Halleck suggested that Grant be made general in chief. Grant was given superior rank and operated in the field, leaving Halleck to deal with politics.[43] In *Combined Operations in the Civil War*, Rowena Reed contends that Halleck was demoted and that the Red River Campaign carried his indelible stamp.[44] This was not the case. Grant did not want to play Washington politics. The two men needed each other at this stage of the war.

Halleck was maneuvering for troops other than those assigned to Banks to be used in the campaign. Grant protested and told Sherman that if he did not personally lead his Western troops, they would probably be lost permanently from his command.[45] By March 10, the day Grant was made general in chief, the forces were moving into position. Grant made no attempt to halt the operation.

These limitations irritated Banks, as did the qualities of the troops loaned to him. They were Westerners, veterans, and hard fighters, to be sure, but they disregarded proper military behavior such as keeping their uniforms neat and clean. Banks felt they were too unruly and unkempt, and he displayed open disdain for them, calling them gorillas. His Easterners of the 19th Corps were more to his liking, cutting fine figures in parades and showing proper discipline on the march. Most of them were not battle-tested, nearly to the extent of the troops from Sherman's command, but they looked like soldiers should look and that meant a great deal to Banks.[46]

The regional differences between the two groups of soldiers were stark. The United States had existed for less than one hundred years, but the attitudes of its inhabitants east of the Appalachian Mountains were generally more refined. These descendants of the early colonists who remained between the mountains and the Atlantic Ocean believed they were more civilized than their western counterparts. The western troops believed they were tougher than the Easterners and derided them. Brigadier General A. J. Smith, commander of Sherman's contingent, added to this by often criticizing Banks and his staff.[47] One of Smith's men referred to the Easterners as "undependable holiday soldiers, paper collar and white glove gents, who could neither shoot nor forage."[48] An Easterner responded that Smith's men were "gorillas, coarse, uncouth, ill-dressed braggarts and chicken thieves."[49]

Banks also chafed against Sherman's requirement that the troops accompany the navy, but at least this meant he would not have to put up with them. He was also bothered by the fact that March had arrived and Sherman had ordered the return of these unruly Westerners by the middle of April. Banks often repeated to anyone who would listen that he believed the Rebels would not fight him before Shreveport, if then. He believed he would fight his big battle in Texas, and by that time he wouldn't need Sherman's men.[50]

Sherman left New Orleans on March 3, wanting to get away from Banks and the vision of a looming fiasco. He wrote to Porter, Grant, Halleck, and others, telling them of his decisions and warning Porter to be careful.[51]

Union Major General Frederick Steele had recently been placed in command of the District of Arkansas, based in Little Rock. Steele was reluctant to participate in the Louisiana campaign and was wary of the concept of the plan. He attempted to separate his forces from the proposed operation in all planning discussions. If any major Union commander in the Red River expedition was a reluctant pawn, it was Steele. He tried to commit to only a feint or demonstration to draw the Confederates away from Banks, citing, among other things, the need to monitor elections in Little Rock.[52] All of Steele's protests were cast aside, and when Grant became general in chief of the army he ordered Steele to participate fully in the operation. On March 15 Grant telegraphed Steele in Little Rock, "Move your force in full cooperation with General N. P. Banks' attack on Shreveport," adding that "a mere demonstration will not be sufficient."[53]

Banks fired off several questions to Halleck concerning overall command of the operation.[54] He wanted a clear decision from the president and the general staff as to his own authority.[55] Halleck played the part of concertmaster, writing all senior commanders who would have a part in the operation, asking the extent of their intended cooperation, while Banks was conducting his letter-writing campaign. Halleck also informed Lincoln of the communications between himself and Banks, slanted of course, to Halleck's point of view.[56] Other than his misgivings about Banks, Halleck faced the almost impossible task of assigning an overall commander for the expedition since the component units spanned three departments (Gulf, Arkansas, and the Army of the Tennessee in Mississippi), the U.S. Navy's Mississippi Squadron, the army's Quartermaster Corps's transport boats, and the independent Marine Brigade.[57] Halleck's answer to this Gordian knot of independent command structures was not to assign an overall commander, and he moved mountains to get the campaign organized.

On paper, the campaign appeared to be a sure-fire proposition. It combined overwhelming numerical superiority of infantry and cavalry, a huge naval contingent, more than adequate logistical support, plus the blessings of the president, the cabinet, and the chief of staff of the army. The expedition would consist of three pincer movements. The two southern legs would meet at Alexandria, a major road and river junction in the center of the state. Union navy vessels had reconnoitered the river as far as that town the previous year. The combined force would then proceed north to Shreveport. The northern leg was to sweep down from Little Rock and approach Shreveport from the north. This plan effectively forced a battle or siege with no clear route of escape, with the possible exception of flight to the west for the Confederate army and the hapless civilians caught in the trap.

The first group was to travel via navy and army vessels up the Red River to Alexandria. Porter, commanding the Mississippi Squadron, was to bring almost all of his naval assets into the Red River. This was a precursor to modern force projection theory to supply overwhelming fire support for infantry attacking a series of fortifications located on a river or shore. Porter boasted that he would strip the inland fleet of available hulls and guns for the expedition and the total of 210 large ordnance pieces loaded on Porter's flotilla lent credence to his word. He had promised his old friend Sherman that he would ascend the Red River "with every ironclad vessel in the fleet."[58]

The spy map Porter had seen at Mound City must have been the deciding factor in choosing which vessels to bring up Red River. With the information being so recent, Porter's promise to Sherman became almost a literal reality. The only vessels which did not participate were those under repair, such as *Tuscumbia* and a very small number of tinclads which patrolled the Mississippi River. The admiral's decision to send relatively deep draft vessels up the Red River was a grave error that almost cost him his fleet. The combination of information on the Shreveport defenses and the potential of a heavily armed and armored naval foe tipped the balance from prudence to brute firepower.

The fleet Porter took up the river was a powerful mixture of ironclads, monitors, tinclads, a timberclad, several high-speed rams, and supply vessels. Ironclads were covered with at least two and one-half inches of armor plating. Tinclads were lightly armored and were at least partially covered with one-quarter to one-half inch of iron plating. Monitors were hybrid vessels created during the Civil War. They were technically ironclads but were outfitted with rotating turrets. Monitors had decks that barely cleared the water when fully loaded with ammunition and supplies, and they had very shallow drafts, making them ideal to work in rivers. Timberclads were created at the beginning of the war. They relied on thick laminated wooden beams for armor. Rams had little or no armor but contained massive amounts of laminated wood at the bow to support an iron ram. The iron beak was attached directly to the keel timber, and the wood laminate acted as a shock absorber when the vessel rammed an opponent.

These were the vessels that had engaged the Confederates time after time on the Mississippi, Arkansas, and Tennessee rivers, and many had gained fame in the Vicksburg Campaign. James Buchanan Eads, perhaps the greatest American engineer of the nineteenth century, designed several of the boats. The fleet included the ironclads *Benton, Essex, Choctaw, Eastport, Lafayette, Carondelet, Louisville, Mound City, Pittsburg,* and *Chillicothe;* the large river monitors *Neosho* and *Osage;* the lesser river monitor *Ozark;* the large tinclads *Black Hawk* and *Ouachita;* the timberclad *Lexington;* and the tinclads *Covington, Fort Hindman, Gazelle, Cricket, Juliet, Forest Rose, Signal, St. Clair,* and *Tallahatchie.* Also included were the ram *General Sterling Price* and support vessels that included dispatch boats, tenders, tugs, and supply vessels.[59] The Army Quartermaster Corps had its own transport and supply vessels.

These were to accommodate the ten thousand men from two divisions of the 16th Corps and one division from the 17th Corps under A. J. Smith.[60] Also accompanying the fleet were the vessels of the independent Mississippi Marine Brigade with their rams, support vessels, and a hospital boat. This force carried approximately one thousand marines.[61] In all, the fleet consisted of 104 vessels, one of the largest congregations of inland warfare craft in the Civil War.[62] The most impressive was the *Eastport,* a behemoth 280 feet long and 43 feet wide (beam) with a draft (depth below water line) of six feet three inches. It carried two 100-pounder rifled cannon, four 9-inch smooth bore, and two 50-pounder rifled cannon.[63]

The *Eastport* and several of its ironclad sisters were sent on this expedition because Porter had been warned of the Confederate naval presence in Shreveport, particularly the existence of ironclads and probably submarines.[64] The memory of what the CSS *Arkansas* had done to the fleet at Vicksburg remained vivid in his mind. Spies or informants had described the CSS *Missouri* as a smaller *Tennessee* or *Arkansas.* The spies told him two of the iron monsters were completed in Shreveport and three were under construction.[65] This was an exaggerated report from an intelligence operative, but it was, perhaps, the greatest influence on his thinking. Porter wanted to take no chances of getting caught with inadequate firepower in a narrow river; thus he would lead each leg of the journey with his largest (and most cumbersome) vessel,

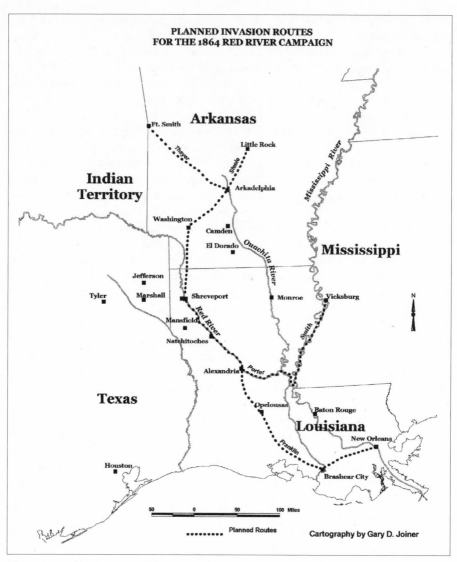

PLANNED INVASION ROUTES
FOR THE 1864 RED RIVER CAMPAIGN

*The invasion plan as conceived by General Banks.*

the *Eastport.* Its two heaviest guns, the 100-pounder rifles, were located in the twin forward gun positions, where they were designed to be ironclad killers.

The second major group was to travel overland. This pincer consisted of 19,000 infantry and cavalry from the Department of the Gulf. They included two divisions from the 13th Corps, two from the 19th Corps, and Brigadier General Albert Lee's cavalry division of 5,000 men.[66] Some 2,500 men of the U.S. Colored Troops, the Corps d'Afrique, were scheduled to arrive after the main column reached Alexandria. Banks's engineers and logistics troops would move north with 32,500 combat troops (including A. J. Smith's 10,000 and the 1,000 marines) and 90 artillery pieces.[67] This huge column was to travel across the bayou country of southern Louisiana from their bases near Brashear City and New Orleans and head west to the main north-south road at Opelousas. From there it would move to Alexandria and join Porter's fleet. The combined forces were then to proceed north along the most practicable route to Shreveport, with Porter's vessels providing protection and succor for the joined forces.

The third group was to sweep southwest from Little Rock and south from Fort Smith, both in Arkansas. It was to leave its base later than the other two, giving them adequate time to approach Shreveport. The particular route was left to Steele. His first intention was to proceed southward to the Ouachita River and then descend to Monroe, Louisiana. From there he would follow the bed of the prewar-proposed Southern Pacific Railroad that cut across north Louisiana from east to west. Only the bed was prepared westward to Shreveport. This segment ran almost directly due west for 110 miles, and it was a very straightforward approach.[68]

Steele decided against this avenue of attack and opted for a lengthier approach through Arkadelphia and the Confederate capital of Arkansas at Washington.[69] This may have been an attempt to seize the entire Confederate governmental structure in Arkansas as an additional benefit. In either case, Steele would be forced to cross the Red River either at Shreveport or north of the town, and this was no small feat. The Red River was over one thousand feet wide at the ferry landing from the Bossier Parish side to its terminus at the wharves in Shreveport.[70] In fact, this was one of the widest points in the entire length of the river. In spring the current typically flowed at least as fast as the Mississippi River. Steele would have known this, and it may have been a factor in preparing for a line of attack from the north rather than the east. Also, given Steele's reluctant participation in the campaign, he may have favored an approach to the Red River, which would have allowed him to support operations but not directly engage in heavy fighting.

Steele's force would consist of two columns. One column of 3,600 men of the Frontier Division, based at Fort Smith on the Indian Territory border, was to march 170 miles to the town of Arkadelphia.[71] Steele would lead the main body of troops from Little Rock and join the Fort Smith column. This force of 6,800 consisted of the Third Division, 7th Corps, and two cavalry brigades.[72] Steele's force added 10,400 men to Banks's force converging on Shreveport, making the total effective force approximately 42,900, excluding sailors and support personnel such as teamsters and garrison troops.

This grand combination of overwhelming land and naval power appeared to be an unstoppable force. Yet, the very seeds of disaster lay in the initial plans. Timing was critical. All three prongs or pincers must arrive at specific points at predetermined dates for the campaign to remain on schedule. The troop deadline loomed large. On April 15, ten thousand of the best troops would be returned to Sherman. The three groups would be advancing independently from the others. Communications were negligible since the distance between Steele and Banks was over four hundred miles by the shortest method of travel. No one would know if even the initial logistics would succeed. The fleet and its attached infantry would not be able to count on Banks until they all met at Alexandria. If any of the columns or the fleet were delayed, the entire plan was in jeopardy. Added to all of these factors was the open distrust and skepticism of the leaders of each pincer for the other commanders. Of the three separate groups, Porter and his loaned infantry commander, A. J. Smith, were the only two leading officers who displayed mutual respect and were operating in their combined interest.

The operation began with each group having faith that their counterparts were acting according to schedules developed in the planning process, but none had the means to verify the actions of the others. Even worse, Banks's commanders viewed him as a lightweight and a political climber who did not have the soldiers' best interest in mind. Banks's extreme overconfidence in his own abilities and an almost total lack of understanding of the Confederate forces in the region plagued the operation from the beginning. It would soon be evident that the lack of an overall commander would lead to the problems that Sherman foresaw.

If ever there was a campaign in the Civil War that began with strong political overtones, had major support at the highest levels in Washington, and was given more than adequate resources to make it a success, the Red River Campaign of 1864 was that operation. Conversely, if there was a campaign in which the planning factors were bound to ensure confusion among the participants, animosity among the various major components, and a high potential for failure, the Red River Campaign also fit that bill.

# CHAPTER 4

## The Union Advance

The Union forces arrayed against the Confederate defenders were numerically superior. Their forces displayed overwhelming firepower on both land and water. The Federals committed such a huge force that, on paper at least, it appeared unstoppable. The seeds of disaster were sown on the very sheets of paper upon which the orders were written. Timetables and commitments were difficult to follow, geography was not taken into account, and individual personalities and desires of the senior commanders played the greatest role in the conduct of the campaign.

Banks's plan called for the two southern pincers of the operation to join at Alexandria. The first was Sherman's men, who were to assemble at Vicksburg and travel via transport vessels to the mouth of the Red River, where they would meet Porter. The second was Banks's forces from the Department of the Gulf, who were to travel overland to join them. The full complement of 32,500 effectives and support troops were to encamp in and near Alexandria.[1] Once all had gathered in Alexandria, Banks would decide the best avenue of approach to Shreveport. The combined land and naval force appeared to be all that was needed for a sure victory. Artillery support was plentiful. The navy's armed men-of-war and the army's Quartermaster Corps transports together totaled 104 vessels.[2] Porter's boats mounted 210 heavy guns, and Banks's own artillery added another 90 field pieces.[3] Banks would later tell a Joint Congressional Committee on the Conduct of the War that everything seemed in place, "One bound to Alexandria, one bound to Shreveport, one bound to the Gulf."[4] He believed it would be an easy three-step operation. Yet it was plagued by numerous problems.

Union commanders experienced delays and took actions that would affect negatively on their success. The army's senior commanders failed to follow timetables. Troop transports left Vicksburg late, which delayed the 16th and 17th Corps's rendezvous with the fleet at the mouth of Red River. The 13th and 19th Corps began their overland trek several days after the schedule required. Once under way, Union forces advanced with ease, and this lulled them into believing that the Confederates were neither prepared nor willing to give battle. Naval intelligence was limited and that which was available was faulty. Admiral Porter placed his faith in reports that the Rebels had amassed a fleet of ironclads at Shreveport, a significant error. He did nothing to corroborate this information. This clouded his judgment in the selection of vessels and the order in which they would proceed up the river. The squadron's overwhelming firepower and the huge number of heavily armored gunboats lulled him into believing that once a location was secured, the vessels could hold it with relative ease. Porter soon noticed that the Red River's depth was fluctuating and he did not know why. He did nothing to investigate the cause.

Porter and his men were distracted by the sight of thousands of bales of cotton along the riverbanks. The navy was allowed to procure cotton under the Naval Prize Law, and with the price of the "white gold" extraordinarily high, the lure of undefended, high-priced, and easily accessible cotton appealed to their sense of greed.

The operation was plagued from the beginning by President Lincoln's failure to appoint an overall commander. Banks, who relished that role, was not a suitable choice since he was more concerned with his presidential aspirations and political duties than his position as the senior army commander in the campaign. He gave little attention to schedules and appeared detached from the daily activities of his forces. Neither he nor Porter addressed the problem of tensions caused by regional differences among their troops. Banks openly favored the eastern troops of the 19th Corps and the western troops of the 13th Corps, while Porter and Sherman's commander, A. J. Smith, openly supported the western troops.

The campaign began on March 10 with the departure from Vicksburg of twenty-one Union steamboats packed as tightly as possible with Sherman's ten thousand men and equipment. The departure date was already three days delayed from the original timetable, creating tension.[5] Brig. Gen. A. J. Smith led Sherman's troops. Army transports with Sherman's veterans proceeded down the Mississippi River to the mouth of the Red River, arriving on the evening of March 11. Porter, the Mississippi Squadron, and the Mississippi Marine Brigade met them.[6] With the entire fleet gathered at the rendezvous point, Porter and Smith confronted their first problem—how to enter the river and find the main channel. Porter had navigated the lower reaches of the stream the previous year, but the channel changed constantly. The marshy overgrown appearance made it difficult to determine which opening was the mouth of the river. The problem was compounded by a sandbar at its mouth, which diverted much of its water into the Atchafalaya River. This jumble of ancient stream confluences set the physical tableau for the beginning of the campaign.[7]

Porter and Smith decided to establish their toehold near the mouth of Red River. Porter was worried about Confederate ironclads on the Red. He led his fleet into the river with the squadron's largest ironclad, the *Eastport,* which grounded on the sandbar at the mouth of the river. The *Eastport*'s captain, Lieutenant Commander Seth Ledyard Phelps, managed to wrestle the huge ironclad over the sandbar. Once over, the *Eastport* was followed by the other ironclads for support in the event that Confederates awaited them. A. J. Smith immediately brought his transports into Old River, an ancient arm of the Mississippi. Smith's men disembarked at Simmesport, just west of the mouth of the Red, which was to be his staging point for the attack on Fort DeRussy. Porter sent some of the ironclads up the Ouachita River to neutralize a

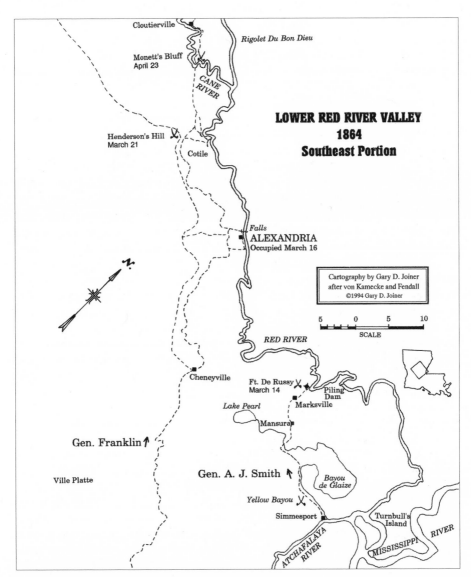

*Lower portion of the Red River Campaign in Louisiana.*

Rebel fortification at Trinity.[8] However, most of the fleet was to proceed up the Red to address the massive water batteries guarding Fort DeRussy and "amuse the Fort until the army could land."[9] The plan was for A. J. Smith's men to march on the fort from the rear while Porter distracted them at the front.

Smith's veterans successfully foraged in Simmesport, completing the next day by torching a house. This was an overture to what would become their penchant for incendiary retribution.[10] "Total War" as a concept was first practiced by A. J. Smith's men in the Meridian Campaign in eastern Mississippi that February and then perfected in the backwaters of central Louisiana.

Confederate Major General John Walker was the first Confederate commander to hear about the thrust into his territory, and he immediately sent a dispatch to Richard Taylor warning him of the incursion. The first reports he received estimated fifteen thousand to seventeen thousand Union troops and thirty to forty guns.[11] This perhaps can be attributed to some green troops among his scouts "seeing the elephant" (seeing battle or confronting the enemy for the first time). Walker, who had only thirty-eight hundred combat troops and twelve artillery pieces, was inclined to believe them.[12] He sent Brigadier General William R. Scurry's Brigade forward to occupy four hastily constructed forts near Yellow Bayou, one named for its commander. Some of Scurry's pickets had been in Simmesport, and they were the first Confederate troops in the Red River Valley to meet the Union thrust. The pickets either fell back in disarray or were captured.

Walker evacuated the forts and removed his men from the Bayou de Glaize area, fearing encirclement.[13] His three companies of cavalry were immediately cut off with Smith's capture of Simmesport. Walker had no way of knowing the size of the Union force.[14] This premature withdrawal doomed Fort DeRussy. Conversely, it saved a Confederate division and its artillery for later use.

Union Brigadier General Thomas Kilby Smith, who commanded the Provisional Division of the 17th Corps, began probing for Walker. He sent a reconnaissance patrol on the only road to Fort Scurry. The Union troops captured some Confederates who were surprised by their quick approach. When the patrol reported back to A. J. Smith, he ordered his transport vessels to unload all of his gear and return to Porter and rejoin the fleet. He began a quick march on the Marksville road to take Fort DeRussy.[15]

Fort DeRussy, A. J. Smith's target, was often referred to by the Confederate staff in Shreveport as the "Confederate Gibraltar." Like its namesake, its primary ordnance faced the water. Although the rear of the unfinished fort was fortified, it was not sufficiently strengthened to withstand a large attack.

On March 13 A. J. Smith decided to form two brigades of the 16th Corps led by Brigadier General Joseph A. Mower in line of battle on either side of the Marksville–Fort DeRussy Road.[16] As his men waited for the order to attack, artillery in the fort began pouring fire into their ranks as they maneuvered into position.[17] Adding to the cacophony, and certainly disconcerting the Union troops, the *Eastport, Osage, Fort Hindman,* and *Cricket* arrived in front of the fort, and the *Eastport* fired one of its 100-pound rifle shells at the water batteries.[18] The shell burst over the heads of the Confederates within the casemates, and they abandoned the water battery.[19]

At 6 P.M. the order was given for Mower to charge his brigades into the breastworks. The fort was defended by a skeleton garrison and fewer than three hundred men were overwhelmed in short order. Union casualties were thirty-eight killed and wounded.[20] Although it was in truth a glorified skirmish, the Union reports made the affair sound like a full-scale battle.[21]

Accounts disagree as to the number of rounds fired by the warships. Marine Lieutenant Frank Church, commanding Porter's 24-man bodyguard aboard the *Black Hawk,* reported two shells fired from the gunboats and then the barrage was halted.[22] The vessels that arrived for support had been delayed for several hours when they encountered Taylor's obstruction, or "raft," downstream at a sharp bend in the river the maps called the "bend of the Rappiones."[23] Porter was challenged to devise a way to destroy it and a "forest of trees" that the Confederates had impaled in the channel.[24] Porter ordered Phelps to "clear that away!"[25] Phelps ordered the *Fort Hindman* to have the obstacles ripped out by alternately ramming or attaching the timbers to the boat's hawsers via ropes.[26] Shortly after this, the *Eastport* and its escorts steamed upstream, and the naval crews watched the finale of Mower's brigades attack on the fort. The action had great significance to the campaign because it solidified the Union position and protected their rear areas.

Mower and his men boarded the transports to accompany the fleet to Alexandria.[27] Porter left the *Benton* and the *Essex* at the fort for three days as the troops of A. J. Smith with T. Kilby Smith tried to destroy the works.[28] The *Benton* and *Essex* fired at point-blank range to destroy the water battery casemate and were unable to do so despite their powerful guns.[29] The *Benton* and the *Essex* never ascended farther up the river to assist the fleet during the expedition. Instead, they performed picket duty guarding the navy's rear from some undetermined Confederate threat. The delays at Fort DeRussy did not bother Porter. He wanted his arrival at Alexandria to coincide with Banks's according to schedule.

*Brigadier General Joseph A. Mower. From Francis Trevelyan Miller et al., eds.,* The Photographic History of the Civil War in Ten Volumes *(New York: Review of Reviews Co., 1912), 10:191.*

Porter sent his heavy monitor *Osage* to accompany Mower's transports as they prepared to take Alexandria. Lieutenant Commander Thomas O. Selfridge Jr. commanded the warship. The *Osage* arrived in Alexandria on the afternoon of Tuesday, March 15, and received the town's surrender without firing a shot.[30] Selfridge sent word back for Porter to hurry because he feared the citizens of Alexandria might realize that their population outnumbered his crew and might attempt to capture his boat.[31] Mower's five thousands troops landed a few hours later.

Porter had hoped to catch Confederate boats unawares at the Alexandria wharves, but he had missed his opportunity by hours. The Confederates did not station heavily armed vessels at Alexandria at that time, but they did have transports and perhaps small gunboats. When word came of the attack on Fort DeRussy, Richard Taylor ordered Alexandria evacuated by both vessels and army units. One vessel grounded on the rocks forming the "falls," or rapids, and was burned. In the haste to depart, three artillery pieces were left behind and captured.[32] Porter brought the bulk of his fleet to Alexandria, let his men enjoy the town, monitored the slowly falling water, and waited for Banks.

While Porter had no idea of Banks's location, the Confederate cavalry operating deep in southern Louisiana did.[33] Unfortunately for the Rebels, they were not in contact with the main body of their forces and could not share the valuable information. Cavalry acted as the eyes and ears of the army in the Civil War, and Taylor was moving blindly. His Louisiana cavalry was operating far behind enemy lines between Brashear City (Morgan City), at the mouth of the Atchafalaya River, and Opelousas. Communication with them was difficult at best.

Taylor had no qualms about leaving Alexandria to Union forces. He was going to pick his battlefield, and the deep cotton fields of the Red River Valley in central Louisiana did not appeal to him. He sought to find a place closer to Shreveport. It is evident from his correspondence with Kirby Smith's chief of staff and engineer, General Boggs, that both men thought the Federal forces would ascend the river and could be trapped in the narrows between Natchitoches and Shreveport.[34] Taylor's plan seems to have been to draw Banks north from Natchitoches along the river road to a point of his choosing.[35] There is no way to conclusively prove this, but it can be inferred through the correspondence between Taylor and Boggs.[36]

Taylor had ordered supply depots pre-positioned at several points on the roads traversing the pine barrens of the Kisatchie Hills between the Sabine and Red rivers and also between Alexandria and Shreveport.[37] The depots were strategically placed on back roads and on the properties of landowners who were loyal to the Confederacy. He had ordered his far-flung brigades to meet at predetermined places, all near supply depots. The brigade of Texans under Prince de Polignac had been ordered to march from Trinity on the Ouachita River to join the brigade of Louisiana troops led by Colonel Henry Gray operating near Alexandria. Gray and Polignac joined about twenty-five miles south of Alexandria, where they were met by Taylor. The general formed the two brigades into a small division commanded by one of his favorite lieutenants, Brigadier General Alfred Mouton of Lafayette, Louisiana.[38]

Taylor announced his intention to gather his forces at Natchitoches, and he sent word for General Walker to join him. Walker had been waiting for orders to withdraw from his position on Bayou du Lac between Marksville and Cheneyville.[39] While making preparations to move his force around the unknowing Union troops, Taylor received word from his Louisiana cavalry units that Banks's main column was moving north from Franklin.[40] Taylor needed the cavalry to keep an eye on A. J. Smith's column at Alexandria. He ordered the cavalry led by Colonel William Vincent to leave the Bayou Teche area and join Mouton. The Louisiana and Texas infantry divisions combined gave Taylor seven thousand combat effectives.[41] For a short period, Taylor outmanned the Union forces, but he did not want to fight at Alexandria.

Vincent's orders to join Mouton could not be acted upon immediately due to the distance involved. Vincent arrived on March 21, six days after the orders were given. The District of Texas commander had not yet released his Texas cavalry under Brigadier General Tom Green. Prior to Vincent's arrival, the Confederate army had no effective reconnaissance arm.

Taylor had no viable way of keeping track of the Union troops in Alexandria. He took his army to Carroll Jones's place near Hinestown, one of the prepared foraging depots in western Rapides Parish, located about twenty-eight miles northwest of Alexandria.[42] Upon their arrival Taylor immediately sent the 2nd Louisiana Cavalry Regiment north to Bayou Rapides, about twelve miles north of his location and some twenty-two miles north of Alexandria at the village of Cotile.[43] Their mission was to keep Taylor informed, to skirmish with the lead elements of A. J. Smith's column, and to try to slow the Union column's progress while Taylor and his two divisions proceeded north to Natchitoches.

Taylor's relief at seeing his cavalry was short-lived. They arrived on the night of March 21 after riding hard or skirmishing for six days with little sleep. They encamped at Henderson's Hill, a toe-shaped ridge that rose above the confluence of Bayou Rapides and Bayou Cotile. The weather turned ugly and cold and they were pelted by rain and hail. Trying to keep dry, Vincent's pickets were not vigilant.[44]

Mower led a Union force of approximately one thousand men, including a light artillery battery and the lead elements of Banks's column belonging to Brigadier General Albert Lee's cavalry division as he hunted for the Rebel cavalry. Rapidly marching twenty-five miles in seven and a half hours, Mower and his men ended their march in "knee-deep mud."[45] They captured several Confederates, including officers, and obtained the password used that night by Vincent's cavalry detachment encamped on the hill. Mower "borrowed" a Confederate officer's coat and took his regiments to the hill, led by the veteran 8th Wisconsin Volunteer Infantry Regiment. Mower, dressed in the officer's coat over his uniform, gave the password during the driving storm. Just before dawn, the exhausted cavalrymen were surprised to see a thousand rifles aimed at them. Mower captured 350 cavalrymen, four cannon, and four hundred horses while suffering no losses.[46] After the action one Union soldier had his upper teeth shot out by an irate Rebel officer.[47] Taylor once more was without his eyes and ears.

Mower's raid was unknown to Banks, for the commander was not with his troops. Banks reveled in orchestrating details, supremely confident that he was in control. Ensuring that his new governor of Louisiana, Michael Hahn, was seen as having overwhelming support, he put his all into the festivities.[48] His military activities were therefore delayed a few days. He knew he could catch up and beat Porter to

Alexandria.[49] Banks exuded so much confidence and moral certainty that he made his peers in the army shake their heads in dismay. His superiors in Washington viewed him warily, but his confidence made his 19th Corps proud of him.

Hahn's inauguration was held on March 5 and, according to at least one soldier who witnessed it, the pageantry was magnificent.[50] Banks wrote to Halleck that the inauguration was such a spectacle that it was "impossible to describe it with truth."[51] His reports from the field in the upcoming campaign were to have a similar ring.

Beginning in New Orleans and traveling eighty miles by railroad and then another twenty-five miles by steamboat transports, the 19th Corps arrived at the assembly point for their overland trek.[52] After a day of final preparations, Banks ordered General Lee at the head of his cavalry division to lead the great column on the roads that would take them to Alexandria.[53] Moving from various outlying bases, the 19th Corps assembled at Franklin in St. Mary Parish and followed Bayou Teche, one of the most beautiful streams in the South.[54] The column was so long, at times stretching twenty miles, that the last units would sometimes be more than a day's march behind the lead elements. Banks's plan never considered using lines of parallel approach, because this was difficult if not impossible in the swamps of southern Louisiana. Here, roads were built on the natural levees of the streams. The 13th and 19th Corps continued this practice as the column marched into the wider alluvial plains farther north, never bothering to examine the possibility of shortening the column or rearranging the train's components.[55] This illustrated a lack of military training on the part of Banks (whose orders were strictly followed) and the 19th Corps commander, who should have altered the column order to fit the terrain.

General Albert Lee was Banks's chief of cavalry for the Department of the Gulf. Lee commanded 4,653 officers and troopers, excluding 350 men detailed to guard and garrison duties.[56] Interspersed with his veteran cavalrymen were recently mounted infantry operating more like dragoons than cavalry. They were new to riding and had trouble handling and tending to their horses. Lee was forced to train them on the march, a difficult task at best. When he was exasperated, Lee referred to them as his amateur equestrians.

After the lead elements of the cavalry division left Franklin on the morning of March 13, they finally rode into Alexandria at nine on Sunday morning, March 20. They had traversed 175 miles.[57] After a short day's rest, Colonel Nathan A. M. Dudley and his First Brigade of cavalry accompanied Mower to Henderson's Hill.

Banks had his trusted deputy and commander of the 19th Corps lead the infantry in the campaign. This was Major General William Buel Franklin. Banks had sent Franklin across southern Louisiana the previous year with negligible success; therefore, he was familiar with the area his fifteen thousand infantry were now traversing. He began his second campaign into the interior of Louisiana with three thousand infantry from New Orleans; the remainder had been stripped from outposts on the barrier islands of Texas. They traveled with their equipment by ship to Berwick Bay, south of Franklin, Louisiana.[58] As the roads along Bayou Teche (the planned route) dried up, the column averaged seventeen miles a day.[59] The roads had been well torn up by the cavalry's passing, so there was no way the infantry could get lost.

*Major General William Buel Franklin. From Francis Trevelyan Miller et al., eds., The Photographic History of the Civil War in Ten Volumes (New York: Review of Reviews Co., 1912), 10:183.*

The column crossed over Bayou Courtableau and passed through Grand Coteau, Opelousas, and Washington. They had now traversed a corner of the Attakapa Prairie. From there the column entered the low pine hill country before reaching the Red River Valley and the rich, red, sandy alluvial plan that produced huge amounts of cotton. Here the road led them north to Alexandria, near the geographic center of the state.[60] The column was seven days behind schedule on March 25.[61]

Banks had not endured the hazards and deprivations of the march with his infantry. He had floated into Alexandria the day before on a transport named *Black Hawk*.[62] The vessel was filled with reporters and cotton speculators and Porter was not amused. He considered Banks's choice of conveyance an insult. The admiral's flagship, a large tinclad also named *Black Hawk*, was his pride and joy.[63] The perceived insult was not lost on the admiral or his favored captains.

Porter and his forces had arrived at Alexandria on March 15 and 16. With the city's surrender in hand and no sign of Banks and his legions, he quickly became bored. His demeanor was similar to that of his friend and colleague Sherman. He could not bear inactivity. Though he was, perhaps, more calm and contemplative than Sherman, idleness was not part of his persona.

Since he had time on his hands, Porter was not averse to procuring cotton. Speculators aside, he had naval tradition and, more important, the Naval Prize Law on his side. Federal law allowed the navy to seize war prizes from the property of a belligerent nation, turn them into an admiralty court, and then have the proceeds divided up by the captors on a predetermined basis.[64] The admiralty court was located at Springfield, Illinois. In the wording of the law at the time, war prizes were to be sold by the court and the proceeds divided by percentage. The naval personnel presenting prizes to the court received 50 percent of the total value of the captured property. Admiral Porter received 5 percent of the 50 percent. The remaining 50 percent was paid into a fund, administered by the navy, for disabled seamen.[65] There was no such mechanism for the army to gain benefit from spoils of war, and this caused immediate animosity between the two services. Porter testified before Congress and later reported his efforts in his two postwar books. Commander Selfridge later wrote in his memoirs that the "incentive of prize money naturally influenced the navy to be especially active (in obtaining cotton)."[66]

Porter wrote the U.S. district judge in Springfield, Illinois, on March 24, requesting the adjudication of 2,129 bales of cotton, 28 barrels of molasses, and 18 bales of wool. He was very specific that this was all captured from the Confederate government. He listed twenty vessels that should share in "the prize." These included all his ironclads and monitors, as well as most of his tinclads. The list included both the *Benton* and *Essex,* which were relegated to duty near the mouth of the river, but excluded

*The Mississippi Squadron at Alexandria shortly before the completion of Bailey's dam. The ironclad on the left is the* Louisville *with its armor plating removed. The monitor with cotton on deck is the* Neosho. *The vessel with tall smokestacks is the* Lexington. *Rare Book, Manuscript, and Special Collections Library, Duke University, Durham, NC.*

all vessels of the Mississippi Marine Brigade and the army's Quartermaster Corps.[67] The only photograph of the ironclads and monitors at Alexandria shows the *Neosho* with bales of cotton stacked on its deck, for they were too large to fit in the holds.[68] The navy gathered more than 3,000 bales of cotton in and around Alexandria.[69] The true number may never be known—nor will the total number of bales burned by the Confederates in retaliation.

In apparent response to the wholesale theft of cotton within a few miles of Alexandria, Taylor had his soldiers burn thousands of bales to keep them out of Union hands and pocketbooks. Wellington W. Withenbury, a steamboat pilot acting as a local expert and riverboat pilot for Admiral Porter and later General Banks, stated in testimony before Congress in March 1865, "I have no notion that a single person in that vicinity burned their own cotton. There was a great effort made to induce General Dick Taylor to rescind the order to burn cotton. He said, 'Don't ask me; General Banks is coming with his army of occupation; make your peace with him. If he respects your rights, I certainly shall.' General Taylor and his forces retired apparently with the determination not to burn cotton."[70] According to Withenbury, a source who should know, Taylor would not have incinerated millions of dollars of cotton unless there was wholesale seizure by Banks or Porter.[71]

When Franklin entered Alexandria at the head of the infantry column, and over a week later than scheduled, Admiral Porter remarked on how fine they looked, even after a grueling march:

> It was as fine a body of troops as were ever seen in the Southwest. Notwithstanding a march of twenty-one miles, they came in quite fresh and full of spirits.
>
> But more than a week of valuable time had been lost since the 17th instant, the day on which General Banks promised to meet the Navy at Alexandria, and the conclusion arrived at was that the General did not possess the military virtue of punctuality which the Navy had recognized in Generals Grant, Sherman, A.J. Smith, and other officers with whom they had hitherto cooperated.[72]

Franklin's 19th Corps came in on the same road, strung out fifteen to twenty miles.[73] It took the better part of two days to get them in and bivouacked. The last regiment marched in on March 26, eight days behind schedule.[74]

It is evident from Porter's later writings that Franklin's troops were in fit condition and that Banks and Franklin had not wanted them to appear shabby when they entered Alexandria as the conquering heroes. Porter intimates that they looked too good. Perhaps that was the reason they had taken so long to come to the appointed meeting place. He strongly contrasts the way the Eastern troops of the 19th Corps looked and behaved compared to his more favored western troops of A. J. Smith's command.[75] According to Porter, when Banks first saw Smith's men, he exclaimed, "What, in the name of Heaven did Sherman send me these ragged guerrillas for?"[76] His eastern troops began calling the westerners "gorillas."[77]

Banks finally arrived and was dismayed by what he saw in Alexandria. The navy was carrying on a bustling business in gathering, processing, and transshipping cotton—all legally.[78] Banks's cotton-broker friends were angry at the navy's efficiency in procuring cotton. Banks saw his grand scheme to be the savior of the New England textile mills floating down the river or burned by the Confederates at nearly all points on the horizon.[79] On April 2 Banks wrote orders allowing civilians who wanted to sell their cotton to prevent it from being burned, to bring it to the quartermaster's office for shipment to New Orleans and sale.[80] This policy was too little, too late. Politicians and cotton brokers appealed to Banks personally, attempting to cut deals, although it appeared that he showed no favoritism.[81] He concentrated on organizing local elections and tried to placate the people bombarding him with requests and demands.[82] Most of the demands were local but not all.

In the middle of all this business and political activity, Banks became troubled not by his personal interests but by a letter which arrived on March 26 from Grant. Grant was now lieutenant general and general in chief of the U.S. Army, meaning that Banks was no longer Grant's superior by date of commission. Grant had been named to the post on March 10. This promotion made him Banks's superior and Halleck had assumed the post of chief of staff.

In the letter, Grant, who had never been enthusiastic about the campaign but was never in a position to stop it, gave Banks his minimal expectations. He outlined a general schedule and demanded that Banks follow it. Grant, of course, had no way of knowing that Banks had already created delays and that the troops had suffered additional weather-related delays. Had he known of the delays, he would likely have had little sympathy. Grant told Banks that the expedition was important because it would reduce the number of Union troops needed to secure the open navigation of the Mississippi River. He added, "It is also important that Shreveport should be taken as soon as possible."[83]

The letter included a caveat that disturbed Banks. Regardless if there was any reason for a delay in taking Shreveport by the end of April, Banks had to return A. J. Smith's command to Sherman by the middle of that month. Grant was emphatic about this, saying it must be done, "even if it leads to the abandonment of the main object of your expedition."[84] If he could manage to capture Shreveport, Banks was instructed to garrison it and retain enough troops to keep the Red River open to navigation and to return with the balance of his forces to New Orleans to prepare for operations against Mobile.[85] He was not to chase the Rebels into Texas.

Banks's idea of a leisurely movement to Shreveport, such as he had undertaken to Alexandria, had now evaporated like the pillars of smoke from burning cotton. He also realized that anything short of taking the Confederate capital of Louisiana would bring him political ruin denying his presidential aspirations. This letter changed Banks's demeanor and attitude. He became obsessed by time schedules and orders of march, yet the political considerations to reconstruct Louisiana given him by Lincoln remained with him as well. Not one to shrink from a challenge, Banks now prepared to take Shreveport. He was ready. The Red River was not.

Porter had been monitoring the river levels since the day he arrived, and he did not like what he saw. Sherman, who had earlier lived across the river from Alexandria, explained to him that the Red River rose every spring and that this was the only time the fleet, particularly the deep-draft gunboats, could get to Shreveport.[86] Porter watched for the anticipated rise. But instead, he saw the river falling, sometimes an inch a day, sometimes an inch per hour.[87] Porter became apprehensive, at least according to Banks. The general said later in congressional testimony that he appealed to Porter's lust for cotton, for surely in Shreveport there were huge storehouses filled with the white gold.[88]

Porter again and again told any interested party who would listen that he could take his fleet, and he meant *his* fleet, "wherever the sand was damp."[89] Banks still had a difficult time in convincing the admiral that he needed his help, knowing that his supporters in Washington fully expected Porter's assistance on the expedition. Banks was finally successful and Porter, with his usual braggadocio, told the general that he would accompany him even if "I should lose all my boats."[90] He almost did.

Porter realized he could wait no longer and prepared to move upstream. He sent light draft vessels forward to check the channel depth at various places in and above Alexandria. He secured the services of a very experienced river pilot, Wellington W. Withenbury, who advised him to take only his light draft ironclads, monitors, and tinclads and the army transports. Withenbury told Porter about the falls, which were well known to steamboat men. The falls at Alexandria consisted of sandstone boulders, which in high water were never seen and were deep enough to cause no harm. In normal conditions in spring, the boulders could be navigated using care, their positions marked by swirls and eddies. When water was particularly low, the boulders were easily seen and this meant that the water levels were just a few feet above the channel floor.[91] The twisting course through the boulders was called "the chute." It was this swiftly flowing water that formed rapids around the sandstone, giving the parish in which Alexandria was located its French name of Rapides.

Porter listened to Withenbury's counsel and then did a curious thing. He told Withenbury, against the latter's protests, to take the *Eastport* over the falls.[92] Withenbury protested but Porter once again emphatically ordered him to follow his instructions. Withenbury then suggested taking the lighter draft vessels over first. Porter again ordered him to take the *Eastport* first.[93] Two questions are vital to the remainder of the naval portion of the campaign, and they both come into focus at this point in time. First, why was Admiral Porter adamant about leading with his largest and most cumbersome ironclad? Second, why was the river behaving as it was?

Porter was brilliant, seasoned, extraordinarily self-confident, and certainly no stranger to command. He was also egocentric and bullheaded. As the most powerful and knowledgeable admiral on the inland waters of the United States, why would he make such a rash judgment? He saw the river falling and monitored its depth several times daily. The *Eastport* was the pride of his fleet, but it was also a liability in this situation. Perhaps he knew or suspected what lay ahead on the river.

The *Eastport* was his ironclad killer and it had an excellent chance of disabling or sinking a well-armored foe at longer distances than his monitors or even his "Pook Turtles," the *Louisville* and her sisters. It had a huge ram and could deal a knockout punch at close quarters if the opportunity arose.[94] Porter's intelligence sources had informed him of multiple powerful ironclads and other combatant vessels at Shreveport. The idea of a squadron of up to five ironclads similar to the CSS *Arkansas* blinded him to the obvious limitations of the giant *Eastport*.

And the river, usually full and fast in the spring, what was its mystery? The Confederates had set their defense plans in motion beginning March 18. The intricate series of defensive works that General Boggs created in mid-1863 now became critical sites. Kirby Smith ordered several things to occur in sequence as he and his staff anticipated the Union navy's ascent to Shreveport. He ordered the *New Falls City* brought up from its hiding place in Coushatta Chute (Bayou Coushatta).[95] It was placed at the foot of Scopini's cut-off, one meander bend south of Tones Bayou.[96] The engineers then wedged it cross-wise in the channel, so tightly in fact that its bow and stern ran up on the banks fifteen feet on each side and a sandbar began to build upstream. The engineers then poured mud into its hold and cracked its keel, transforming it into an instant dam.[97] There is some conjecture about its placement, with Loggy Bayou being the southern-most possible location; however, Boggs and Smith intended for the vessel to be placed at Scopini's cut-off. This action may have been executed as late as April 5.

After the placement of the *New Falls City,* other Confederate engineers used black powder to blow up the Hotchkiss dam, built the previous year. The river water exited its channel into the old Tones Bayou channel and thence flowed directly into Bayou Pierre, just as planned. The bayou flowed back into the Red River a few miles above Grand Ecore, but just before this occurred the bayou's flood plain opened into a nineteen-mile-diameter bowl, and this is where most of the river water collected.[98] The admiral watched the river fall for several days followed by a brief rise. This rise was the small portion of the flow exiting Bayou Pierre and coming back into the river. The rise gave him the encouragement to begin sending the fleet north.

Following Porter's refusal to keep the *Eastport* in deeper water, Withenbury piloted the huge ironclad toward the falls.[99] The experienced pilot's concern was proven cor-

*The* Eastport, *perhaps on Red River. Note the extremely low water and mudflats in the foreground. Archives of the Mansfield State Historic Site, Mansfield, LA.*

rect. The boat's draft was too deep and it grounded in the chute. It was wedged among the boulders, and despite the efforts of tugs and the lighter draft gunboats pulling and tugging at it, there it stayed.[100] Eventually the water level rose enough to float the vessel, and it finally traversed the falls.[101]

Porter decided to leave some of his heavy ironclads at Alexandria, but not the *Eastport*. Although the *Eastport* was grounded, Porter managed to move some of the light-draft gunboats past it by sending them in relatively shallow water outside the chute. Among them were the ironclads *Louisville, Pittsburg, Mound City, Carondelet,* and *Chillicothe;* the monitors *Osage, Neosho,* and *Ozark,* the timberclad *Lexington,* and the tinclads *Cricket, Juliet,* and *Fort Hindman.*[102] The *Eastport's* bulk displaced enough water on either side to help facilitate the passage of the lighter boats.

Withenbury asked Porter's permission to go to Grand Ecore aboard the *Black Hawk,* Banks's headquarters boat, and the admiral agreed. He later reported to Congress that they passed the *Eastport* on the way up the river and it was grounded again.[103] The fleet required four days to travel one hundred river miles to Grand Ecore. The slow progress, as Withenbury pointed out, was due to the lighter draft gunboats waiting for the heavier ones.[104] Porter's fears of a potential Confederate fleet waiting for him around each bend of the twisting river forced him to keep the vessels concentrated. He could not afford to have his light-draft vessels move too far forward of the heavy ironclads.

Among the most destructive troops in the Union contingent were the members of the Mississippi Marine Brigade, who were ostensibly under the command of A. J. Smith. They were actually an independent command, neither army nor navy, and there was no direct line of authority over them. They had looted and burned their way up the river, and neither Banks nor Porter knew what to do with them. Not only were they a problem with discipline, several were infected with smallpox. There were also persistent rumors that the brigade was planning a mutiny because their actions were constrained.[105] After the brigade's fast rams and support vessels moved past the falls, their hospital boat, the *Woodford,* grounded. Its hull pierced, it sank and had to be burned.[106] Banks and Porter were pleased to receive orders that arrived aboard the naval tug *Alf Cutting.* Major General James McPherson, commanding at Vicksburg, needed the Marine Brigade and its vessels to patrol the Mississippi River because the Mississippi Squadron was not available for that duty.[107] The brigade commander and his marauders left Alexandria on March 27. With no one to rein them in, they stopped at every village and plantation on their way to the mouth of the river, burning and looting each.[108] Banks and Porter were relieved to see them leave, but their departure removed 1,000 combat soldiers from Banks's legions.[109] This loss was offset by the arrival of a brigade of the Corps d'Afrique, adding 1,535 men and bringing the total of U.S. Colored Troops (USCT) to 2,500.[110]

While waiting for Porter to move more of the fleet over the falls, Banks ordered new elections and held them April 1.[111] Again he neglected his military duties in Alexandria and cajoled locals who wanted to sell their cotton, jayhawkers, and pro-Union refugees into voting. Porter called the election a farce and a humbug, gratuitously adding in his congressional testimony, "We are sailors, not politicians."[112] Banks also continued enjoying showing off his 19th Corps soldiers. Marine Lieutenant Frank Church, commander of Porter's marine guard detachment, wrote in his diary on March 27: "Saw the dress parade of the New York Volunteers. They were reviewed by General Banks and staff. Their bayonet exercises and charge were splendid. At 8 p.m. the Admiral was serenaded by Banks. While the band was playing 'Mocking Bird' ['Listen to the Mocking Bird'] a shed fell on them badly injuring a major and two men."[113]

Banks allowed Franklin to manage the army while he played politics and decided to ascend the river to Grand Ecore after the election on April 1. The order of march was set, with A. J. Smith's veterans at the rear of the column. Lee's cavalry left Alexandria and passed Henderson's Hill on March 26. A. J. Smith's men left on the evening of the twenty-seventh and the morning of the twenty-eighth. The length of the column at times extended more than twenty-five miles. Smith's men marched to the steamboat landing at Cotile, about twenty-two miles north of Alexandria near Henderson's Hill. There they boarded the army quartermaster transports to accompany the war fleet.[114]

Just before Banks boarded his headquarters boat *Black Hawk* on April 2 and headed for Grand Ecore, he wrote General Halleck one of many messages that caused concern for the War Department in Washington. Banks was confident that Rebels would not confront him before Shreveport, if then, and he anticipated being in Shreveport by April 10. He told Halleck that he would then "pursue the enemy into the interior of Texas, for the sole purpose of dispersing or destroying his forces."[115] Banks reminded the chief of staff that he was well aware that Smith's troops must be returned, obviously to placate U. S. Grant. Banks was skating on thin ice here. He was attempting to show Halleck that he was confident the original plan would work, yet he was skirting close to the edge of what Grant had ordered him to do, and that was not to invade Texas. Halleck shared the message with President Lincoln, who understood his staff officer's fears. Lincoln commented, "I am sorry to see this tone of confidence; the next news we shall hear from there will be of a defeat."[116] Lincoln was prescient.

March and April in northern Louisiana are transitional months. The moist air streaming up from the Gulf of Mexico meets the drier air of the continental United States, and storms of violent intensity are common. The air becomes muggy and a relative humidity of 80 percent or higher is common. The heat quickly dries out the Red River Valley's sand and the red clay of the nearby hills. Thus the roads marched on by the Union forces alternated between dustbins and a muddy soup. General Franklin marched his troops along the river road within sight of the gunboats, just as the campaign had anticipated. Union diarists described the land changing as they neared Natchitoches. For the first time they saw rocks beside the road and hills in the near distance. Viewing the Red River, they remarked that it was appropriately named.[117] A. J. Smith's men were greeted by slaves waving and singing at some of the riverside plantations. One diarist wrote that he heard the slaves singing that it was a great day "when the Linkum gunboats come."[118]

Lee's cavalry division reached Natchitoches on March 30 and took the town simply by riding in. Franklin arrived on April 1 after marching eighty miles in four days.[119] The column set up bivouac between Natchitoches and the small village of Grand Ecore, four miles farther north on the Red River.

The village acted as a port for Natchitoches. The channel of the Red River, once fronting Natchitoches, had moved, creating the Cane River, actually a long lake. Grand Ecore was the place on the west bank of the Red River where the old Spanish Royal Road, the *El Camino Real*, began its long trek to Mexico City.[120] Located on the high bluffs at Grand Ecore were the old forts of Seldon and Salubrity, where Grant had been stationed in the days proceeding the outbreak of the Mexican War.[121] The Confederates had fortified and then abandoned the place as the Union forces came up the river. Porter anchored the fleet in a sheltered bend in the river immediately downstream from the bluffs. He was joined by A. J. Smith's men and their transports. Banks floated into Grand Ecore late in the evening of April 3, delayed once more by assisting the *Eastport*, which had grounded again.[122] Now it was time for Banks to determine the best route for the final bound to Shreveport.

The Union forces opened the campaign with enormous advantages, which they squandered. Despite having overwhelming resources in men, artillery, cavalry, and naval firepower, they failed to communicate. They also paid little attention to predetermined schedules. Admiral Porter's insistence on using inappropriate vessels, particularly the *Eastport*, led to a series of delays. As the navy became distracted with the abundance of cotton to seize, the army had its own problems due to Banks's lack of leadership. He failed his troops miserably while attending to his own political ambitions. This allowed the undermanned Confederate forces to gather strength and gain an advantage over what were clearly superior Union numbers. The most important factor, though no one realized it at the time, was that Banks's tardiness and lack of military training had already doomed the campaign. If he personally led his forces and reached Alexandria on time, the Confederates' diversion of the river may have had a lesser effect on the navy.

Banks's progress to Grand Ecore had been relatively easy, though time consuming. He arrived on April 3, and in twelve days A. J. Smith's ten thousand men were scheduled to depart from his command. The army faced a major problem in its approach to Shreveport, and Banks had to make a decision quickly. The maps carried by Banks's staff and the river pilots were different. Some showed roads missing from others. Banks's primary map showed distances between towns and villages, but not necessarily the roads connecting them.[123] The same was true for lakes, villages, and town locations. Streams were shown flowing in different directions, their true size varied, and often a stream might have several different names.[124] Brigadier General Charles P. Stone, Banks's chief of staff, consulted with Withenbury, the river pilot who had taken on the additional role as an adjunct adviser to Banks.

Withenbury later testified before Congress that he had examined Stone's maps and gave him copies of his own, showing where towns and roads were located.[125] The map the army used was the LaTourette's Map of Louisiana published in 1853. This map portrayed the entire state of Louisiana on a single large sheet and displayed little detail.[126] Union topographic engineers, under Colonel John S. Clark, Banks's aide-de-camp and topographic engineer, altered the map to identify features as they saw them.[127] Clark was adept at making maps that Banks could understand, since the general was untrained in military mapmaking. Banks and his staff relied upon the

LaTourette Map as gospel, but the map was not as reliable as it should have been, and it was not a substitute for field intelligence provided by cavalry. The National Archives holds two maps, dated 1864, by Major D. C. Houston of Clark's staff, which portray two additional roads drawn in as single lines closely following the Red River, one on the east bank (locally known as the Summer Road) and the other on the west bank (locally known as the Winter Road).[128] These maps were obviously drawn either at the close of the campaign or soon afterward. This is the route that Richard Taylor and William Boggs expected the Union forces to take. Certainly Porter, and probably Banks, would have tried the river route and discovered a serviceable road if not for the convincing recommendations of the riverboat pilot.

Withenbury was a twenty-year veteran pilot on the Red River. He had made numerous trips up and down the river and had seen every feature on and near the river. He also had a financial interest in cotton grown on the river near Alexandria and near Shreveport for which he had collected $4,413.73 from the Confederate government.[129] Although he proudly proclaimed himself to Porter, Banks, and members of Congress to be "a Union man" from Connecticut, he was in fact a businessman dealing in the most lucrative commodity of the South. He also claimed to be an informant for the Union army, and this places him in position to be a spy in Shreveport passing information to the Federal authorities in New Orleans.[130] After the campaign he was listed as a claimant to some of the cotton confiscated by the navy.[131] He did not want to see his cotton captured by Union forces. He also did not want to see the Confederates destroy his baled cotton if the Union forces came close to capturing his holdings. The Rebels burned cotton and ravaged plantations to keep Federal forces from gaining the staple for sale. Susan Dollar asserts that in the northern Red River Valley, particularly in Natchitoches Parish, the destruction wrought by both sides constituted "equal opportunity" destruction regardless of political affiliation, social status, gender, or color.[132] This perhaps explains what Withenbury did next.

When asked about the roads leading to Shreveport, Withenbury pointed to and described in great detail the two road networks shown on the LaTourette map. These two roads both bow far away from the river, forming an irregular parenthesis. The road on the east bank of the river, the Fort Towson Road, was an old military road that led from Campti, a few miles upstream from Grand Ecore, then inland to the town of Minden.[133] The LaTourette map ends the road there. In fact, the road went to Fort Towson in the Indian Territory. This old fort monitored the Union forces at Fort Smith.[134] The river pilot told Congress: "I pointed out on the [LaTourette] map precisely all the roads."[135]

Withenbury knew that Banks would not use this road after he was asked about the eastern road. The pilot told the general it would take three extra days to move around the lakes on that side. If Banks would have chosen the Fort Towson road, his approach on Shreveport would have led him to making an assault from the eastern bank of the river, and this presented the problems of an amphibious assault. Withenbury explained to Banks that the roads would be better on the east, but he was much more specific about the roads to the west.[136]

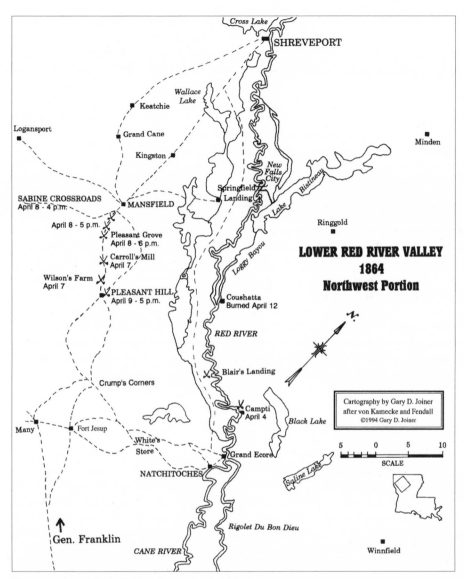

*Upper portion of the Red River Campaign in Louisiana.*

When questioned about the western inland road, Withenbury testified before Congress that he told Banks the Pleasant Hill to Mansfield road would take the army away from the river and the protection of the navy until they reached Shreveport.[137] Withenbury knew Banks was on a tight schedule so he could also expect his cotton to be safe if the army did not ascend the river with the navy. He knew from his long experience on the river that the two roads Houston would later sketch did, in fact, exist. Porter pleaded with Banks to let him make a reconnaissance upriver for two or three days, but the general refused. He was watching the calendar and thought the delay was a waste of time. Banks decided to move his army west and take the inland road. Porter, of course, had to take the river route.

Once Porter began his move toward Shreveport, he wrote his friend Sherman that he saw the road and the fields filled with corn and herds of cattle grazing near the west bank of the river. Porter wrote: "It struck me very forcibly that this would have been the route for the army, where they could have travelled without all that immense train, the country supporting them as they proceeded along. The roads are good, wide fields on all sides, a river protecting the right flank of the army, and gun-boats in company."[138]

Withenbury changed the course of the campaign in a single night. Banks, eager to take Shreveport and claim his glory, trusted the river pilot as a parishioner would a priest. The pilot denied the Union army the support of the great guns on the warships and gave it a sense of false security. If there were no roads for Banks to ascend to Shreveport beside the river, the Confederates could not flank him through the piney wilderness that he saw from the heights of Grand Ecore. Withenbury saved his cotton and, except perhaps in Porter's eyes, was still a good Union man.

Banks seems to have been totally satisfied with Withenbury's information. The general wrote his wife the next day that "the enemy retreats before us and will not fight a battle this side of Shreveport, if then."[139] Based on the meager information at hand and his belief that there were only two roads, Banks made the correct choice between the alternatives. However, even considering the severe time limitation placed upon him by Grant, his refusal of either a naval or cavalry reconnaissance of the area to his north and west is unforgivable.

Clark reported to Franklin his estimates of enemy strength based on intelligence reports and the interrogation of captured Confederate soldiers. He estimated that Confederate forces to their front included as many as 5,000 infantry and cavalry from General Magruder, the district commander in Texas, 5,000 from Price in Arkansas, and an additional 10,000 troops already positioned in Louisiana. He estimated the total number of effectives to their front to be 20,175 and seventy-six artillery pieces. He also reported to Franklin that the Union forces would consist of 15,000 to 18,000 infantry and cavalry since the Mississippi Marine Brigade had been released to other areas of operation.[140] Franklin was handling his day-to-day affairs of the army while Banks made himself busy organizing another election at Grand Ecore and bribing the villagers by vowing protection of their cotton from Confederate destruction.[141] But politics were not his only interest here. Other tasks also occupied him as well.

Although Banks would later blame Franklin in testimony before Congress, he spent a considerable amount of time making sure the wagons of his supply trains were fully stocked with provisions for the march. His supply train included three hundred wagons for Lee's cavalry division, seven hundred wagons for Franklin's infantry, and at least another fifty for the artillery and A. J. Smith's men.[142] The train carried just ten days' supplies for the column of more than 30,000 men and was considered to be abnormally large for the time. The Army of the Potomac, during the same month of April, had more than five thousand wagons while engaged in the Wilderness Campaign. At this time, that army consisted of 120,000 men. At its largest extent, the number was seven thousand wagons.[143] Although the numbers of wagons appear to be in proportion, the Army of the Potomac's wagons typically carried supplies for field operations of extended duration.

Banks and Porter agreed to meet at a point opposite Springfield Landing in northern DeSoto Parish on April 10.[144] Springfield Landing was located four miles from the Red River on Bayou Pierre on a narrow channel connecting Bayou Pierre Lake and Lake Cannisnia.[145] The landing was about sixty miles by road and more than one hundred miles by river from Grand Ecore.[146] According to the plan Banks was to leave Grand Ecore on April 6 and Porter was to leave on April 7.[147] At Springfield Landing or near it, Porter's fleet and the army transports would replenish Banks's supply trains and the two groups would make the final approach to Shreveport. Withenbury did not accompany Porter upriver, and the admiral had only been as far upstream as Alexandria in 1863. Grand Ecore was at that point, Porter's deepest penetration into the Red River Valley. Porter would not know where he was when he reached Springfield Landing. He also had to consider which vessels were best suited for the river above his base of operations in Natchitoches Parish.

The *Eastport* was now such a liability that Porter decided to leave it at Grand Ecore. All the maps showed the river between Grand Ecore and Shreveport to be winding and contorted. This stretch was in fact called the narrows by river pilots. Porter correctly assumed that if the *Eastport* grounded in a tight bend, he might not be able to get it out. He decided to constitute his final assault force with the lightest-draft gunboats. He chose six vessels, the monitors *Osage* and *Neosho*, the timberclad

*The* Neosho. *From Francis Trevelyan Miller et al., eds.,* The Photographic History of the Civil War in Ten Volumes *(New York: Review of Reviews Co., 1912), 6:228.*

*Lexington,* the tinclads *Cricket* and *Fort Hindman,* and the sidewheel ironclad *Chilli-cothe.*[148] The admiral made the *Cricket* his flagship. The gunboats accompanied twenty transports loaded with supplies and T. Kilby Smith's small division of about 2,300 men from the 17th Corps for protection.[149] Porter had his portion of the force defined and hoped that the army was using as much forethought.

Banks established the order of march just the way he wanted it. The cavalry would begin to form up and ride out on the morning of April 6. It would take well over a day for the entire column to be under way. Lee's cavalry was followed immediately by its three hundred wagons at Franklin's insistence so as not to delay his own supply train.[150] The wagons of the column were protected by 2,500 U.S. Colored Troops of the Corps d'Afrique. Some were with Lee but most were with the infantry wagons. Immediately following the cavalry's wagons and the train's guards were the fifteen thousand infantry under Franklin. Banks and Franklin rode at the head of this contingent. The infantry marched in the order of the two divisions of the 13th Corps, then one division of the 19th Corps. The men were unable to march more than four abreast because of the narrow roads.

Behind this long line of infantry were the seven hundred wagons of their supply train.[151] When Banks had taken such care in defining the marching order, he neglected to note that three hundred wagons to the front of the main infantry column and another seven hundred wagons to their rear would box them in. The infantry would have difficulty assisting the cavalry to their front and would not easily be able to fall out or retreat with such a huge train behind them. Banks's use of only one road set the stage for disaster. In his defense, he trusted his advisors to be correct in their assessment of the terrain ahead, and they showed him only one road on their maps. The fact that he did not allow his cavalry to fan out ahead and seek other routes qualifies his actions as one of the greatest blunders in the Civil War. Following the seven hundred wagons of the supply train were A. J. Smith's 7,500 men of the 16th Corps. Relegated to eat the dust of the column, they did not leave Grand Ecore until the next day.[152] The column's only flankers were a single brigade of cavalry under Colonel Oliver Gooding. This brigade never fanned out ahead as a screen but covered the column's rear and, when possible, its left flank.[153] Artillery was dedicated to each of the infantry components and traveled with them.

The great column traveled the single road, which some days was dusty and on others a muddy ditch. This column of men and materiel resembled a giant accordion, stretching out at some points, squeezing impossibly tight in others, and at times not moving at all. The wagon teams slowed the column down and effectively set the pace. The cavalry was not allowed to move far ahead and conduct its mission. Lee was repeatedly told to protect his own wagons and was not allowed to place them with the infantry's train. Banks's "bound" had become a creep. Frustration was rampant and the terrain they entered did little to ease the men's attitudes.

The column marched westward and found the relatively easy traveling in the river valleys was behind them. Red sand was replaced by red clay. Hard when dry, when wet it was slick and stuck to everything. When wet, the clay made movement tiring, and it made footing treacherous. The giant fields of cotton-bearing land that the troops

*Brigadier General Albert Lindley Lee, Banks's chief of cavalry. From Francis Trevelyan Miller et al., eds., The Photographic History of the Civil War in Ten Volumes (New York: Review of Reviews Co., 1912), 10:293.*

had grown accustomed to seeing were gone, replaced by yellow pine trees that grew so thick in places that there was no undergrowth. At times the road appeared as a long green cathedral with the road the only aisle. A Union cavalryman called the area a "howling wilderness."[154]

After a torrential downpour on April 7, a reporter for the *Philadelphia Press* remarked that the narrow road appeared "more like a broad, deep, red-colored ditch than anything else."[155] He added that he had "ridden for fifty miles into the heart of this pine country, and from the beginning to the end of the journey there was nothing but a dense, impenetrable, interminable forest, traversed by a few narrow roads, with no signs of life or civilization beyond occasional log-houses and half-cleared plantations." Later he added, "Such a thing as subsisting an army in a country like this could only be achieved when men and horses can be induced to live on pine trees and resin."[156] The forest became oppressive with a terrible sameness. The men found very little water that was not falling from the sky. Once it hit the earth, the rainwater became as bright red as the ditch they were marching in and equally unappealing.[157] As the rain pelted down, the column stretched out even more and tempers flared toward the rear. The pace had slowed to a crawl and the western soldiers thought it was the easterners' inability to march and conduct a campaign that was the problem.[158]

As the Federal soldiers picked their way west then north, Taylor finally began receiving some much-needed reinforcements, although not all that he needed and requested. About the time Lee felt the first raindrops, Brigadier General Tom Green was crossing the Sabine River into Louisiana at Logansport in DeSoto Parish. Leading several regiments of Texas cavalry, the fearless Green was coming to Taylor's aid, having finally been allowed to leave Texas soil.[159] His cavalrymen and mounted infantry were famous for their individuality and the variety of their weapons and gear. Their regimental leaders were Bagby, Buchel, Debray, Hardeman, Likens, Major, Terrell, and Woods.[160] After a short rest at the village and college campus at Keachi, they joined Taylor at Pleasant Hill and then rode ahead to find the location and activities of the Union forces.

Green's arrival was critically important to Taylor. The aggressive Texan cavalrymen would perform the true task of cavalry—reconnaissance and intimidation. Without them, Taylor had little chance of slowing the Union column until he was prepared to meet them. He could not readily identify which units he would be fighting without the cavalry's assistance. It was Green's cavalry who confirmed Banks was using only one line of approach and that he had stupidly hindered his own cavalry by forcing them to stay with their train.

Perhaps the most unusual of these commanders was Colonel August Buchel, late of the Prussian army. He commanded a regiment of cavalry raised from the Texas hill country in and near New Braunfels. Because the German immigrants felt they were fighting for their new homeland, they were particularly enthusiastic fellows. Their presence made Lincoln's hope of a German-Texas counterrevolution ring hollow.[161]

Taylor requested as many regiments as possible to be sent to him from Arkansas. Kirby Smith vacillated. He knew that Frederick Steele was coming down from Little

*General Edmund Kirby Smith. From Francis Trevelyan Miller et al., eds.,* The Photographic History of the Civil War in Ten Volumes *(New York: Review of Reviews Co., 1912), 10:243.*

Rock. At the same time, he knew that Banks posed by far the greatest threat. Smith ordered most of his Arkansas infantry under Major General Sterling Price to come to Shreveport so that they could be sent out in any direction as needed. These forces were the small divisions operating under the command of Brigadier General Mosby M. Parsons and Brigadier General Thomas J. Churchill. Taylor expected both Parsons and Churchill to join him south of Shreveport in DeSoto Parish. Smith delayed them while they waited for their ammunition.[162] He was apprehensive and wanted to fight Banks farther south. Without adequate forces he could not make his move. Taylor bitterly blamed his reinforcement and supply problems on Kirby Smith in Shreveport. He would continue to blame Smith for all the logistical and remote command failings of the campaign to the day he died. Taylor referred to Smith as a "pompous potentate presiding arbitrarily over an empty empire."[163] Some officers and civilians in Shreveport loyal to Taylor reported to him that reinforcements were being delayed to make Kirby Smith look good by saving Taylor if the latter got into trouble fighting Banks. Taylor, with his usual abruptness, confronted Kirby Smith in heated correspondence.[164]

According to Boggs, Smith wanted to take most of the army, including Taylor and his growing number of infantry and cavalry regiments, against Steele first even though Banks at the time was closer.[165] Kirby Smith met Taylor at Mansfield on April 6 and during a heated meeting in which Taylor objected to every plan variation Smith recommended, nothing was decided and the commanding general gave Taylor no specific orders. During the meeting Smith suggested that they go against Steele, or that they gather all their forces behind the defenses in Shreveport. He even suggested they perhaps should evacuate Louisiana and Arkansas and fight it out in east Texas. Taylor was appalled.[166] When Smith left the meeting providing no specific orders of action, Taylor was free to do what he wanted, or so he thought.

On April 8 instructions arrived for Taylor from Shreveport that were so obscure as to be almost unintelligible. Smith wanted Taylor to fight a battle in a place that could be easily supplied. He was told not to fight on that day, as it had been declared a National Day of Prayer.[167] Smith withheld the Arkansas and Missouri troops for a time and would have looked the conquering hero if Taylor had been hard-pressed against Banks.[168] Smith's letter arrived too late to have any effect on events and Taylor probably would have ignored it if he had the opportunity. While the Confederates were gathering, the Union columns were feeling their way first west and then north.

Lee led the column westward from Natchitoches through the rolling red clay hills on the old Spanish Royal Road. About twelve miles west of Natchitoches they passed near the old Spanish capital of Texas at Los Adaes and then turned away to the north from the old road to Mexico City at a stagecoach road intersection.[169] Lee pushed up the road to another store at Crump's Corners where four days before his men had encountered Confederate cavalry.[170] Lee halted there for the night. Refugees whom the column met on the road told Union officers that the Rebels were massing at Sabine Cross Roads and that it "was the point where the rebels said they were going 'to begin to bury the Yankees.'" The officers laughed the information off as so much braggadocio.[171] The next day was April 7 and the Confederates had not shown any interest in doing anything but light skirmishing.

Colonel John Clark rode at the head of the column with Lee and observed the advance that morning.[172] Lee had set out early with three of his four brigades; Gooding was still occupied with flanking duties. The road ran north for about twelve miles with very few curves and almost no homesteads. At noon Lee reached the village of Pleasant Hill. He had ten regiments of cavalry, half of which were mounted infantry, not accomplished horsemen.[173] Most had been untested in battle. Clark reported that the cavalry, with its wagon train in tow, left Pleasant Hill and three miles north of the village ran into four regiments of Green's cavalry at Wilson's farm.[174] Green chose to change his tactics and charged the Union cavalry. Lee could not accurately estimate their numbers. He formed his men on both sides of the road and set up his mountain howitzers to provide support.

Green charged and forced the Union right back several yards, the Rebels attacking with their customary wild yells. The first brigade of mounted infantry came up and fired a volley into the Confederate ranks, which then fell back into the field. Trees on Lee's right still contained an unknown number of Rebels keeping up a withering fire. There was no way to charge them in the dense woods. The Confederates fell back and Lee had held his ground.[175] His cavalrymen had not folded and had behaved well in the face of a forceful attack. Union casualties were seventy killed and wounded in an action that lasted half an hour.[176] While the fight was unfolding, the column ground to a halt. Franklin and Banks were well to the rear and did not ride forward since neither expected organized opposition.

Although the battle was small compared to other actions during the campaign, it was very important to the Confederates. Green forced the Union cavalry into a new mind set. From this point, Lee was leery of every rise of ground and turn in the road. The Union cavalry became overly cautious. Green effectively slowed the Union column to a crawl, giving Taylor enough time to prepare his forces for the next day. He identified which Union units were in the lead of the column and how they would fight. While gaining this information he intimidated his opponents, making them apprehensive.

Both Lee and Clark tried to explain to Franklin what had happened and how things had changed, Lee by messages and Clark in person. Lee was concerned that for the first time the Rebels were operating differently. They had not been seen as ghostly riders far in the distance. This time they had massed and were waiting in an area of their choosing. The men to their front were cavalry and no infantry were seen. That meant that this was perhaps just the first of their positions on this road. Lee requested that his wagons be moved back with the infantry's train and infantry, perhaps a division, be brought forward to assist him.[177]

Franklin denied him out of hand and then Clark tried to intercede since he had seen the skirmish. Clark was in agreement with Lee. Franklin refused the repositioning of the train and the reinforcements, telling Clark that "he must fight them alone—that was what he was there for. It might require the sacrifice of men, but in war men must be sacrificed."[178] Clark tried to placate both generals and told Franklin he would go back to Lee and tell him to press forward. Franklin then assured Clark that Lee would get infantry support if he really needed it, and Franklin would decide if he needed it. Franklin then told Clark to inform Lee to "keep your train well up" as he fully expected to reach Mansfield the next day.[179]

Clark then went to Banks to plead his case. Banks ordered a single brigade of infantry to be moved up ahead of the wagon train to support the cavalry. The brigade was under the command of Brigadier General Thomas E. G. Ransom, who commanded the 13th Corps component of the expedition. His mistake was not to send the entire 13th Corps detachment forward with the brigade. Ransom was unsure what was expected of him, and he chose to follow the order to the letter and sent only Colonel William J. Landram, commanding the Fourth Division of the 13th Corps, and Colonel Frank Emerson's First Brigade of the Fourth Division, consisting of only about 1,200 men.[180]

Clark rode back to Lee and told him what Franklin wanted and gave him the news that he could expect infantry support. The brigade was meant to salve what Banks and Franklin thought were Albert Lee's jittery nerves. Neither expected any opposition for days. Only the cavalry leader and the cartographer saw what happened at Wilson's Farm, and both knew that Franklin and Banks were detached, stubborn, and almost immovable in their plans—now that they had plans. Lee later told Congress that he was laughed at for insisting that they would have a fight before they got to Shreveport.[181] The cavalry rode ahead tentatively.

Taylor now had good cavalry and in sufficient numbers to perform the tasks for which they were designed. Green's orders were not to bring on a battle, but to delay

*Brigadier General Thomas E. G. Ransom. From Francis Trevelyan Miller et al., eds.,* The Photographic History of the Civil War in Ten Volumes *(New York: Review of Reviews Co., 1912), 10:199.*

Banks until Taylor was ready to meet him. The time it took Lee to move his men out of column and into attack formation, deal with the Texans, and then re-form into column bought Taylor time. When the Confederates melted away into the forests, Lee believed he had whipped them soundly and that the Rebels were not up to professional military standards; in fact, they were disciplined and completed their task as assigned. Wilson's Farm would not be the only incident of this type.

Lee picked his way another three miles beyond Wilson's Farm and decided to halt for the evening. He had marched six miles, fought a small battle, and he felt his men deserved a rest. Franklin sent word forward to Lee to keep moving so his infantry would have room to come forward the next morning without waiting for the cavalry train. Lee was ordered to move his cavalry unit as far forward as possible with his train and artillery.[182] This may have been a slight aimed at Lee by Franklin for questioning him earlier in the day. It may also have been retribution for Clark's bypassing Franklin when he sought help from Banks. Lee returned his men to their saddles and began riding up the narrow road again. The pine trees rarely gave way to open pasture and there was very little water. Lee was disgruntled. The cavalry slowly rode another four miles to Carroll's Mill. As Lee's cavalry neared the mill, Green's Texans again made a demonstration, which forced them to come into battle order. After a brief skirmish in the twilight, the Rebels melted into the woods. Lee posted pickets and halted for the night.[183]

Early in the morning of April 8, Franklin went to Banks and told him of the day's plans for the column. He thought his infantry had marched splendidly and deserved a rest. Franklin told Banks he intended for the column to shorten its length by the head of the column having a short day and the rear a much longer one.

At sunrise, Lee moved his cavalry out with Lucas's Brigade in the lead.[184] Almost immediately they encountered Green's Texans. Lee had to abandon the idea of his cavalry's probing their way on horseback. He ordered Lucas to dismount one of his cavalry regiments and deploy them as skirmishers, with two regiments of Landram's infantry as reinforcements.[185] Green slowed them every foot of the way, trying to buy time for Taylor and determine what reaction the men in blue would have to his slow withdrawal. This constant skirmishing tired the Federal troops, particularly the infantry.

Ransom began the march at 5:30 A.M. at Pleasant Hill and five hours later reached what he thought was Bayou San Patricio but was actually Ten Mile Bayou. He stopped as per his orders after covering ten miles. Ransom's men were going into camp when Lee asked for relief for his exhausted infantry. Franklin ordered Ransom personally to go forward with Vance's Brigade to see what was happening and to make sure that Emerson's men came back to the main column. Franklin still did not want a large body of infantry operating with the cavalry.[186]

With constant skirmishing, a frustrated Lee pushed the Confederate cavalry screen back six miles on the morning of April 8. Sometime between noon and 1 P.M. Lee and his men emerged from a thick woods and found themselves at an intersection of the road on which they were traveling and one that was used to take cotton to landings on the Red River. The intersection was called Sabine Cross Roads. The Confederate cavalry that had been a constant menace for the last day seemed to disappear. Lee, at the head of his column, rode another three-quarters of a mile to the edge of a huge clearing, 800 yards deep and 1,200 yards across, at the slope of a ridge called Honeycutt Hill.[187] Confederate skirmishers were there in force, and, as Lee and Landram marched forward, they gave way. The cavalry and infantry units moved to occupy the ridge. As Lee rode to the crest, he saw most of the Confederate army west of the Mississippi drawn up in line of battle across his front on both sides of the road and extending down and past his right flank.[188]

The decision to split the Union land and naval forces at Grand Ecore effectively severed the arms from cooperating until they were to rejoin below Shreveport. Faulty intelligence, poor maps, and an inappropriately constituted column all hindered Banks as he marched his men west then north. The frequent encounters since noon the previous day between the head of the column and Rebel cavalry made no impression upon him. His decision not to lead from the front ensured he would not understand the changing situation as the Confederates massed forces and prepared to fight. Banks's failure to seek and respond to information from his officers, particularly his cavalry commander, created tension within the ranks, led to conflicting or inadequate orders, and helped assure that the Union forces would have few advantages if attacked. Finally, Banks's belief that the Confederates were unwilling or unable to fight allowed him to send his men into a trap as the Confederates had found their place to make a stand.

After the campaign, the Joint Committee on the Conduct of the War received extensive testimony on the composition of the supply train, the order of march, and Banks's actions and inactions. The committee was particularly interested in Banks's delegation of authority and the elections he held. Members writing the majority report blamed Banks for leaving the fleet and marching inland. They derided him for holding elections and for not leading from the front of the column. Banks deflected some of the blame to Franklin, who simply stated he was following orders. Banks caused most of the problems. His march orders created hardships on his troops, illustrated a near total lack of military professionalism, and created the scenario for disaster.

# Chapter 5

## The Battles of Mansfield and Pleasant Hill

Banks's army faced the Confederates three miles southeast of the town of Mansfield in DeSoto Parish, Louisiana. The order of march precluded reinforcements from sweeping forward to assist the lead elements of the column. Both Banks and Franklin believed that the Rebels would not make a stand south of Shreveport, and this faulty belief influenced their actions on April 8 and 9. When Union cavalry commander Albert Lee saw Taylor's army for the first time, he confirmed that Banks's arrogance could spell doom for the Union forces. He saw before him the majority of the Confederate forces west of the Mississippi River arrayed for battle.

The Union army was endowed with seasoned military commanders, Lee among them. Yet they deferred to Banks, the political general. Banks had exhibited a reserved detachment, which was perceived by the troops as a lack of leadership. Initial pleas for reinforcements went unanswered. The order of march hampered the army's ability to send infantry forward when they were most needed. At this point in the campaign the difference in attitudes between the northern and southern forces was remarkable.

Richard Taylor believed he could retreat no farther north. His forces were gathered, rested, and armed, and he had instilled in them a high level of emotion against the invaders. The Louisiana troops believed they were protecting their sacred soil. The Texas troops desperately wanted to make a stand in Louisiana to protect their home state. Historical evidence suggests that Taylor was frustrated after waiting six hours for Banks to make his first move. No one is certain as to whether Taylor ordered the attack or whether his orders were misunderstood. The battle scene was set and the activities were about to begin.

Taylor was ready for the Union column, thanks to the time bought for him by the Texas cavalry. After a frustrating meeting with Kirby Smith on April 6, Taylor seized the initiative to prepare for the coming battle. He was furious with the commanding general for not specifically allowing him to fight the battle at the time and place of his choosing and with all the forces available.[1] Taylor wrote his commander concerning the need to do *something*, "Action, prompt, vigorous action, is required. While we are deliberating the enemy is marching. King James lost three kingdoms for a mass. We

*Heavily altered photograph of Lt. Gen. Richard Taylor. C.S.A.. Courtesy Mansfield State Historic Site, Mansfield, Louisiana.*

may lose three States without a battle."[2] Fortunately, Kirby Smith was so vague that Taylor had time and room to prepare for Banks.[3]

On April 7 Taylor rode south from Mansfield on the road to Pleasant Hill and found Green and his cavalrymen annoying the Federal column. After making sure that the Union column had halted at Carroll's Mill, Taylor rode the seventeen miles back to Mansfield. He told the Texan to harass the Union forces as much as possible until he met the main body of troops who would be waiting for him.[4] He chose his ground on the great field at Honeycutt Hill. This was an ideal site because any place north of this position would offer the enemy a choice of three roads to Shreveport.[5] Taylor had no other clear choice for his stand.

After arriving in Mansfield on the evening of the seventh, Taylor began issuing orders to his commanders. He sent a courier to Keachi to summon Major General Sterling Price's Arkansas and Missouri troops to Mansfield. The 4,400 troops had to force-march twenty miles beginning at dawn on the eighth. Walker and Mouton were ordered to break camp near Mansfield and concentrate their forces at the field.[6] To cover himself, Taylor's last official act on the evening of April 7 was to send another courier to Kirby Smith in Shreveport at 9 P.M. Taylor wrote, "I respectfully ask to know if it accords with the views of the lieutenant-general commanding that I should

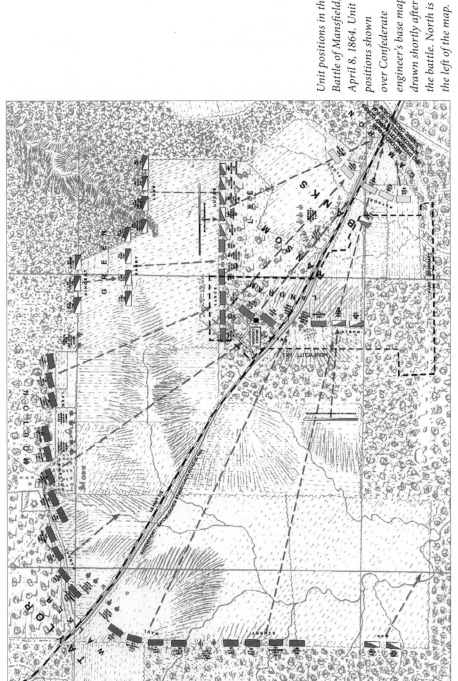

Unit positions in the Battle of Mansfield, April 8, 1864. Unit positions shown over Confederate engineer's base map drawn shortly after the battle. North is to the left of the map.

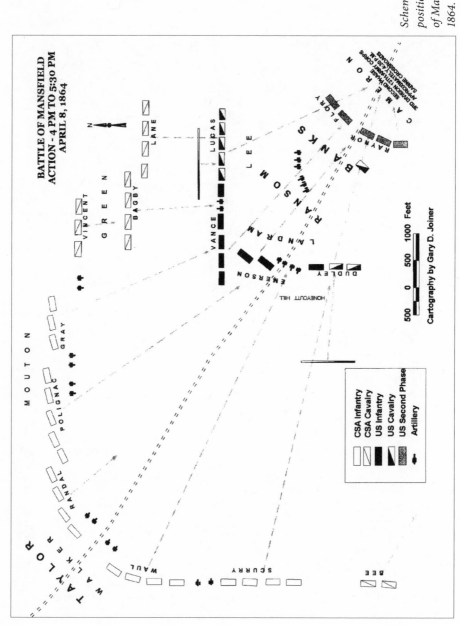

*Schematic of unit positions in the Battle of Mansfield, April 8, 1864.*

hazard a general engagement at this point, and request an immediate answer, that I may receive it before daylight to-morrow morning."[7] Taylor did not expect an answer and, anticipating the battle would be fought the next day, told his friend the Prince de Polignac, "I will fight Banks if he has a million men."[8]

At 9:40 the next morning, Taylor sent another message to Shreveport declaring, "I consider this as favorable a point to engage the enemy as any other."[9] The clearing formed a giant "L" lying on its side with the long axis facing east and the short axis facing south.[10] The Shreveport-Natchitoches stagecoach road entered the clearing at the vertex and ran to the southeast. Forests bordered the clearing on the west and north along ridgelines. Taylor's battle line extended more than three miles.

Taylor wanted his men with the forest to their backs. He did not want Banks to see how many men he had. He positioned his artillery to focus on the point on the road at which the Union forces would exit the woods and enter the field. He also needed the three-mile front to position his regiments. There is no doubt that Taylor expected Banks to act rashly and to charge his center position, at which time his two broad wings would collapse on the Union center like a closing door hinge.

On Taylor's far right, separated from the main body by several hundred feet, were two regiments of Green's cavalry. To their left were two brigades of Texas infantry from General Walker's Division. Between them was an artillery battery. Another battery occupied both sides of the stagecoach road. Here the "L" turned east with one-third

*The Prince de Polignac. Carte de visite in the collection of Gary D. Joiner.*

of Walker's brigades. Next in line were the Texas and Louisiana troops under General Mouton. These were the brigades under General Polignac, and to his left was the brigade under Colonel Gray. An artillery battery was positioned in front of Mouton's troops. Separated by several hundred feet and to the left of Gray was most of Green's cavalry, positioned in three tiers. They were the last to arrive and were placed to hold the most endangered flank.[11]

Green and his cavalrymen had performed their tasks admirably. They had slowed Banks's column until Taylor was ready to receive it. They were also able to tell Taylor what units were located within the column and where they were, to the location of the main supply train several miles from the head of the column. Taylor believed that he was fighting the 19th Corps and that A. J. Smith's ten thousand men were guarding Porter and the fleet.[12] This lack of knowledge would have serious implications the following day. Taylor promised Mouton and Gray they would draw first blood in honor of protecting their home state.[13] Their units were composed of battle-hardened veterans of the 18th Consolidated Infantry, the 28th Infantry, and the Consolidated Crescent regiments. These troops would take the brunt of the initial fighting.

Price's forces were still moving south, and Taylor did not know when they would arrive or in what shape they would be. With Green's arrival, Taylor's available force was complete. He now had approximately 5,300 infantry, 500 artillerymen, and 3,000 cavalry on the field.[14] Almost all the cavalry was to fight dismounted as infantry. With the line now in its final position, the Confederate troops saw the first Union troops come out from the woods shortly after noon.

Colonel William Landram's small Fourth Division of the 13th Corps had fought Green's cavalry for a day. The men were tired and wary of the Texans. They were frustrated at having to constantly change from marching in column to deploying for battle, only to have a short exchange and then watch the Rebels retreat. Lee and Landram saw the Confederates form skirmish lines in the open field on the southeastern slope of Honeycutt Hill. Landram had only one brigade and did not believe he had enough men to take a hill that size. He wanted reinforcements and ordered his second brigade forward.[15] The Confederate cavalry broke from their skirmish line and disappeared over the hilltop. Annoyed at this continued tactic, Lee and Landram followed with their regiments arrayed behind them. As they reached the hilltop, they viewed massed Confederate regiments drawn up in line of battle across their front and to their right.

The almost constant starting and stopping of the column annoyed Banks, who rode forward to see what Lee and his amateur equestrians were doing. As he left Franklin, Banks told his army commander that he would return if there were no heavy fighting. Franklin answered, "There will be no fighting."[16] Banks and his staff passed the wagon train, artillery batteries in limber, and then the infantry units that arrived at the base of the hill about 1 P.M. He found his forward infantry and cavalry units skirmishing with Confederates. Banks sent for Lee and asked him to describe the situation to their front. Lee later testified before Congress that he told Banks, "We must fall back immediately, or we must be heavily reinforced. I said the enemy must have 15,000 or 20,000 men there; four or five times as many as I had."[17] Lee described how he had his men deployed and Banks approved.[18] Banks told Lee that he would order the infantry to move forward.

Banks sent his assistant adjutant general, George Drake, back down the column to Franklin. Drake delivered a note from Banks to Franklin stating that "the commanding general desires me to say that the enemy are apparently prepared to make a strong stand at this point, and that you had better make arrangements to bring up your infantry, and to pass everything on the road. The general will send again when to move. He thinks you had better send back and push up the trains, as manifestly we shall be able to rest here."[19] Another message followed almost immediately, this one telling Franklin to begin moving his men forward as quickly as possible.

The first message is astounding. Either Lee did not communicate the seriousness of the threat poised in front of them or Banks did not take the threat seriously. Banks told Lee that infantry support was being called forward, yet he told Franklin to "make arrangements" to bring them up and that he would tell him when to move. Perhaps the answer lies in the last line in which Banks told Franklin to push up his trains, as "manifestly we shall be able to rest here."[20] Banks still did not believe the Confederates would fight him.

Landram's second brigade arrived on the hill about 3:30 P.M. Lee then had 4,800 infantry and dismounted cavalry in place.[21] He placed his men in a smaller replica of the Confederate line shaped in an "L" configuration. As the units came into place, the cavalry's wagon train pulled up to the crossroads about one-half mile behind the front line. The train, their teamsters, and guards from the Corps d'Afrique halted. Once again, the three hundred wagons blocked the road.[22]

About 4 P.M. Lee rode back to the crest of the hill after conferring with Banks. Thinking the infantry he requested would soon arrive, Lee was given an order by one of Banks's staff aides to move immediately on Mansfield. Lee was incredulous and said there must be a mistake in the order. He immediately rode over to Banks, who confirmed the order was correct. Lee later explained, "I told him we could not advance ten minutes without a general engagement, in which we should be most gloriously flogged, I did not want to do it."[23] Banks agreed to delay the advance and sent a courier to Franklin ordering the infantry up. This was the second message Franklin received. Banks's apparent confusion illustrates that he did not have a clear grasp of the situation. He exhibited a total lack of military expertise. Banks later blamed Lee for all the problems with unit positions.

Taylor watched the sun sink lower into the western sky, knowing that he had only about three hours of daylight left. He had counted on Banks being impetuous and acting rashly, but this was not happening. As his men watched, more Union regiments arrived, and their line was getting stronger by the hour. The Confederates had to act or they would lose the initiative. There is some question as to whether Taylor ordered Mouton to attack or told him they would soon attack. The reason for the confusion is the order in which the Confederate units began their charge. Rather than having the entire line moving in unison, Mouton advanced his regiments in echelon, staggering their lines. This resulted in high casualty rates from the Union troops focusing on specific regiments as they came close to their positions. This was not a tactic that

Taylor usually employed. Mouton's men had been waiting for their chance for most of the day, and their charge was magnificent, as recorded by both sides.[24] The division's officers rode their horses in order for their men to more easily see them, and this act of bravado led to catastrophic results.

On Honeycutt Hill Thomas E. G. Ransom joined Lee and Landram. When Mouton's men moved forward, Ransom ordered his five infantry regiments facing the Louisianians to leave the fence and engage them in the field. The two sides met at close range and fired volleys.[25] Losses were heavy and Mouton's attack faltered. The Union infantry began picking off the mounted officers, with Mouton one of the first casualties. Shortly after he fell, the commanders of the 18th Louisiana Infantry, 28th Louisiana Infantry, and the Consolidated Crescent regiments were also killed. One-third of Mouton's men were killed or wounded in the attack.[26] Mouton led the charge and was killed after his men passed the crest of Honeycutt Hill. Mouton's men then fell on the blue regimental line with a vengeance. The Confederate line stalled, and the accurate Union fire pushed the Confederates back to about two hundred yards from Ransom's right flank.[27] Within minutes of the beginning of the assault, Tom Green was the senior Confederate officer on Taylor's left wing.[28]

To Mouton's left, the Texas cavalry made their entry on foot. This placed the five Union regiments in danger of being flanked. The five regiments of Lucas's Union cavalry, also fighting on foot, were in danger of being turned. If these units folded, the entire Union line could be enveloped. Randal's Texas Brigade, holding the center of the Confederate line, anchored Mouton's right. As this brigade marched out in echelon, it found that it was squeezed between Polignac's charge and the road. Randal's men were forced to march more slowly.

With one leg draped across his saddle, Taylor smoked a cigar as he watched the Texans and Louisianans engage the enemy.[29] As soon as he saw the Union forces occupied with the first wave, he ordered Walker to unleash his Texas troops on the Federal left. The Texans, who had been listening but unable to see the action on the other side of the field, were anxious to attack and did so in rapidly advancing solid lines, not echelon formations.[30]

R. B. Scott of the 67th Indiana Infantry Regiment was at the vertex of Lee's "L." His regiment was to the right of Captain Ormand Nims's 2nd Massachusetts Battery on the stagecoach road. Scott saw the Texans coming at his position and wrote that they ran toward the Union line "like a cyclone. Yelling like infuriated demons."[31] The Texans ripped through the 3rd Massachusetts Cavalry Regiment and began to push the Union line in upon itself. Nims's battery kept a deadly fire, until three of its guns were captured, turned around, and used on the former friends.[32] The 23rd Wisconsin and 67th Indiana regiments were crushed. Ransom ordered the 83rd Ohio, the last infantry regiment on his right flank, to move in support of the left.[33] Green's Texans were already flanking them. When they shifted to their new position, they found that the left flank did not exist.[34] Ransom then ordered them back to support the Chicago Mercantile Battery.[35]

Ransom ordered his adjutant, Captain Dickey, to instruct Landram to retreat on the same line as the 83rd Ohio. Dickey left and almost immediately was shot in the head. The order was not carried out and most of the right-wing regiments were forced to surrender when surrounded. Two regiments, the 48th Ohio and the 130th Illinois, simply ceased to exist. There were not enough survivors to rally or formally surrender.[36] Ransom described his 13th Corps as being caught in a nutcracker. Shortly after Dickey's death, the entire Union line collapsed.[37] Ransom was mounted on his horse so his men could see him in the swirling fight. As he ordered the remnants of his 13th Corps into new positions, he fell from his horse when he was hit in the knee by shrapnel.[38] Some of his men lifted Ransom on their shoulders and took him to the rear. Cameron's small Third Division finally made its way around the cavalry train and set up between the battery and a copse of trees standing in front of the crossroads.[39] The head of the wagon train was at the crossroads. In thirty minutes of fighting, the Union advance had been crushed. Ransom was wounded, and both of Landram's Brigade commanders, Emerson and Vance, were wounded and captured.[40]

Franklin came to the front with Cameron. As they formed their line at the base of the hill behind Nims's battery, the remnants of the cavalry tried to rally to the new line. Lieutenant Colonel Lorenzo Thomas of the 3rd Massachusetts Cavalry yelled to his men to rally on the new line and to "try to think that you are dead and buried, and you will have no fear."[41] Franklin made an accurate assessment of the situation to his front and ordered Brigadier General William Emory to form his First Division of the 19th Corps in line of battle behind him on the first good position he could find.[42]

As Cameron's men solidified their line, they were met with a crashing charge, not from the Confederates but from the Union survivors of the opening phase of the battle. John Russell Young, a northern reporter described the scene. "We found ourselves swallowed up, as it were, in a hissing, seething, bubbling whirlpool of agitated men."[43] The rout was endangering both the men running and the men of Cameron's Division. Soldiers were shedding rifled muskets, knapsacks, and any gear that slowed them down.[44] The Confederates behind them were still giving the "Rebel Yell" and the cacophony at the crossroads was maddening.[45] Franklin, unhorsed by the mob, fell, and broke his left arm.[46] Banks tried to rally his men, but he was ineffectual. No one doubted his personal courage as he shouted to the soldiers, "Form a line here. I know you will not desert me."[47] But they did desert him.

The wagons could not be turned around, so the teamsters cut the lines to ride the horses and mules away from the disaster. With no opportunity to protect the wagons, their guards, the Corps d'Afrique, added their number to the tide of men in retreat. The wagons acted as a barrier to any organized retreat. No artillery limbers could pass the train, so they were captured piece by piece. Franklin was taken away to safety as Cameron tried to hold the line, but after only about twenty minutes his position collapsed as well.[48] Banks had only five regiments on this line and they were flanked on both left and right. Cameron's men also joined the exodus of blue trying to reach safety somewhere behind them. It was now about 5:30, and the sun was low in the western sky.

Emory and his men were coming forward from Ten Mile Bayou when they encountered trickles then masses of men, Union soldiers, running or riding toward and then past them.[49] This slowed his division's progress. The influx of men became a steady stream and then a flood. This chaos almost halted Emory's advance, as one soldier wrote, "On came a negro, bareheaded, and running for as if for life. Soon came more, and then by hundreds, on foot and mounted; nor knew they scarcely why they ran, only that the rebels were coming. There came cavalry, infantry, artillery, and wagons, crowding the road and each side, making advance almost an impossibility."[50] Another soldier described the rout, writing, "The road was blocked up with wagons, caissons, mules and run-away horses, while negro teamsters and cavalrymen were driving directly through the ranks."[51] Emory stopped at a house on a ridge overlooking the small creek called Chapman's Bayou. Next to the house was an orchard and, although there are no local records to state why, Emory called it Pleasant Grove.[52] Emory ordered his men to fix bayonets to push through the mob impeding his progress.[53] He positioned his men in front of the creek, correctly assuming that this was the only water for miles around and certainly the only water between him and Ten Mile Bayou, seven miles behind him, which was little more than a creek.[54] His fresh troops stood their ground better than did their predecessors.

The Confederates had lost unit cohesion in the wild assaults culminating in the third Union position of the day, and the final attack was made as a mad rush. Rebel troops hit Emory's line in a massive assault, but they were exhausted from continuous fighting. As darkness fell, the Confederates managed to push the Union troops behind the creek and claimed the water for themselves.[55] Emory redeployed his men on the low ridge above the bayou. The Rebels made a last push up the ridge in the waning light but failed to dislodge the Union infantry. Fighting ended with the darkness. As the combat was winding down, Taylor received the reply to his letter to Kirby Smith from the previous night. Smith told Taylor to avoid a general engagement. Taylor sent the courier back to Shreveport with a message for the commanding general: "Too late, sir, the battle is won."[56]

The losses that day were high for both sides. Landram's Fourth Division of the 13th Corps, the first line of Union infantry in the battle, lost almost half of its 2,400 men, with 25 killed, 95 wounded, and 1,018 reported missing. Many of these missing were killed in the opening minutes of the battle, and hundreds were captured within the first half hour of fighting.[57] Cameron's Third Division lost 317 of its 1,200-man roster. Lee's cavalry division lost 39 killed, 250 wounded, and 144 missing. Emory's Division lost 347 killed of his 5,000 men. The total Union losses were 113 killed, 581 wounded, and 1,541 missing, or 2,235 official casualties of a force of 12,000 participating in all three phases.[58] Taylor reported taking 2,500 prisoners.[59] The numbers of dead were certainly higher than Union estimates. They left their dead and wounded on the field to be cared for by Confederate doctors. Some Union doctors remained to help with the medical care.[60] An examination of individual regimental records increases the total casualties. The regimental casualty figures reveal 240 killed, 671 missing, and 1,508 missing, or 2,419 casualties in all.[61] Obviously the two casualties of 2,236 and 2,419 disagree. The latter is closer to the truth. The first figure was derived from division totals and apparently did not include attached personnel. Taylor's figure appears to have been rounded, and in the confusion after the battle some prisoners may have been counted twice.

Confederate losses were listed as approximately 1,000 killed and wounded of 8,800 combat soldiers. Although a few Confederates were taken prisoner, the number was insignificant. Two-thirds of these were from Mouton's Division and were captured due to the echelon attack. This is easily proven when comparing Walker's casualties.[62]

Taylor lost many of his favorite commanders that day, but he had stopped the Union advance on Shreveport. He never considered simply holding the ground he had won that day. He was confident that early the next morning he would crush Banks's 19th Corps. At 1:30 A.M. on April 9, Taylor penned a letter to Walker telling him what they would do the next day. This plan was simple. At dawn his force, led by Missouri and Arkansas troops, would sweep over the ridge to give the Texans and Louisianans a much-needed rest. Taylor ordered Green to take his cavalry to the Blair's Landing road to cut off the Union retreat and to try to keep reinforcements from joining Banks. In the plan, General Parsons's Division of Missouri infantry was to form the left wing and General Churchill's Division of Arkansas infantry was to form the right wing. Because the road was narrow, Churchill's men were to wheel around in the woods and attack the Union on their left flank.

Taylor told Walker that the only troops they faced were the 19th Corps consisting of about seven thousand men, many of whom were raw recruits "who will make no fight. Yankees whom we have always whipped."[63] Taylor also thought that Banks might pull back during the night. In that event, the Confederates would pursue them and push them behind Pleasant Hill, forcing them to return to Natchitoches. Once there the Rebels might force them to surrender. Taylor also mentioned that it was impossible for reinforcements to reach Banks before late in the day and cautioned that they must fight him quickly. Taylor's intelligence sources reported troop transports coming up the river.[64] This was Admiral Porter's force of six warships and twenty troop and supply transports coming to meet Banks at Springfield Landing. With the letter completed, Taylor slept a few hours on the battlefield. He would be ready for Banks in the morning.

Taylor's cavalry had not observed Banks's column to its fullest extent prior to the battle. The scouts had not seen the banners of the 16th and 17th Corps, composed of Sherman's veterans. Taylor believed with absolute certainty that the troops he faced were entirely easterners and that Sherman's men guarded the fleet. He had fought the easterners in Virginia and in Louisiana and he had little regard for their ability and discipline. This belief blinded him to another possibility. Why not hold his position and make Banks attack him? He held the only water for seven miles. He had most of Banks's supply train and the promised reinforcements were at his disposal. With the Rebels blocking the only road to Shreveport, Banks must either fight or retreat. Taylor wanted to exact vengeance for what the Union army had done to his state and believed that he could either capture or destroy the 19th Corps and perhaps the fleet.

Through the night the Confederates could hear the clanking and rustling sounds of troops being repositioned. What they did not know, but Taylor suspected, was that Banks was withdrawing to Pleasant Hill. Taylor did not know that A. J. Smith's 7,500 men forming the rear of the Union column had encamped at Pleasant Hill that night. Taylor's battle plan for the next day was set, but the location was to be fourteen miles down the road rather than over the ridge to his front.

The Battle of Mansfield proved the folly of Banks's organizational plans, from the order in which he placed units in the column to the positioning of the supply wagons between the cavalry and infantry. His forward commanders exhibited extraordinary bravery in a rapidly deteriorating position and their efforts saved many of their men. When the Union's first position collapsed and the second position was in danger of folding, Banks attempted to rally his troops but was not taken seriously. The battle was effectively decided before the Union position folded upon itself in the hinge-closing that Taylor anticipated.

Taylor picked the best location for his attack. He had adequate time to array his troops and was patient for most of April 8. However, when he launched his attack, he made a grave error in ordering, or allowing, an attack in echelon. He also permitted his Louisiana officers to ride their horses in the attack, causing huge losses among them. The second charge, a frontal assault by Texas soldiers against a collapsing wing of the Union line, resulted in comparatively few Rebel casualties. The momentum from this charge collapsed two Union attempts to rally their troops. Only darkness and the exhaustion of the Rebel forces halted the battle.

The fighting ended in a solid Confederate victory with the Rebels holding both the battlefield and the only available water source. Taylor had an opportunity to hold his position and force Banks either to fight him the next day or retreat. Because he wanted to punish Banks, he never considered this option. It was a very costly mistake.

That fall the Joint Committee on the Conduct of the War particularly wanted to hear testimony about Banks's role just before and during the battle. What emerged was the confusion typically found in a major battlefield defeat in which each witness knows only a piece of the puzzle. Uniform, however, was the chorus of voices describing Banks's detachment, confusion, and inability to grasp the situation. Banks placed partial blame on Franklin, but Franklin showered additional accusations on Banks. No witness wanted to take any share of the responsibility.

Taylor, in his letter to General Walker in the early hours of April 9, reminded his Texan commander that the Confederate army must defeat Banks at all costs, adding that "the safety of our whole country depends upon it."[65] He trusted his intelligence sources and his forces' will to fight. Before daybreak Taylor embarked on a fourteen-mile chase to catch Banks and punish him, using the battle plan he described in the letter. Even though different terrain confronted him, Taylor failed to change the tactical plan.

Union regiments at the rear of the retreating column were in constant contact with Rebel troops, but their commanders did not believe there would be another battle. Banks's attitude seemed to be lackadaisical and his staff seemed bored as they rested in Pleasant Hill. General Franklin did not deploy his forces to meet a Confederate threat. Ransom was wounded and offered no guidance. A. J. Smith and his veterans were encamped on the south and east sides of the village. They received no orders to prepare for battle, although they were the most able troops in Banks's army. Banks vacillated about the wisdom of another attempt against Taylor, versus rendezvousing with the fleet. As his senior officers began to question his abilities, he undoubtedly weighed the effects that the previous day's fighting and retreat might have on his political career. Banks was very pleased with Emory's stand as night fell on April 8. He considered the ridge above Chapman's Bayou an excellent defensive position and sent an aide back to Pleasant Hill to order A. J. Smith to bring his 16th Corps forward.[66]

Franklin, nursing his broken arm, pointed out that Smith would have just arrived at Pleasant Hill and he doubted Smith's ability to reach the ridge before the next morning. If they did arrive, would they be in any condition to fight after covering twenty-two miles in one day followed by an immediate march of an additional fourteen overnight? Franklin then pointed out the lack of water. Banks asked the opinion of his confidant Brigadier General William Dwight, a brigade commander in Emory's Division. Dwight advised Banks to retreat to safer ground and to do so promptly.[67] Banks agreed and at 10:00 P.M. the army began its retreat. Private Julius L. Knapp, of Company I, 116th New York Volunteer Infantry, wrote in his journal that night that Banks received information that Taylor had received fifteen thousand reinforcements under Major General Sterling Price. According to Knapp, this led to the decision to retreat.[68]

Banks allowed the 13th Corps to lead, followed by the cavalry, then the 19th Corps. Dwight's Brigade brought up the rear, guarding against Rebel attacks. The column moved slowly, picking its way through stragglers and hampered by the infantry's trains. The head of the column reached Pleasant Hill at 8:30 on the morning of April 9.[69] The village of Pleasant Hill was situated on the east side of large cleared fields that ran along the stagecoach road.[70] To the west of the village was a dense stand of pine trees, and beyond this was a very large open field.

After daylight some Confederate cavalry began harassing the rear of the column, mostly worrying stragglers and disrupting the 153rd New York Infantry.[71] A. J. Smith heard rumors that the 13th Corps had been cut to pieces early that morning. As clots of weary men walked, mounted riders trotted, and teamsters bullied their teams into the village, Smith knew the rumors were true.[72] He ordered the Second Brigade, Third Division, of his 16th Corps, commanded by Colonel William Shaw, to take up a position on the road west of the village. They were hampered by the retreating column, which was now streaming into the village. Shaw's men were forced to abandon the road and made their way through the dense woods.[73] Shaw reported to General Emory, who told him to relieve Brigadier General James McMillan's Brigade, located in a good location south of the road and perpendicular to it.

Shaw relieved the brigade and set up in line of battle three regiments of Iowans on the south side and one regiment of Missourians north of the road.[74] He also moved a four-gun battery north of the road. This position was detached from the closest friendly troops by a quarter mile. The latter were three regiments of New Yorkers and the 30th Maine led by Colonel Lewis Benedict. Dwight's Brigade was positioned parallel to Benedict and on the north side of the road, with his units facing north. This left both of Shaw's flanks exposed and Dwight with his left wing facing ninety degrees to the expected angle of attack. Benedict was positioned astride the Logansport road.[75] Most of A. J. Smith's men were located in and around the village of about fifteen buildings on the highest of some gently rolling ridges. Banks set up his headquarters on the east side of the village in the largest residence, the Childers House.[76] The house stood near the intersection of the road that led to Blair's Landing. Shaw's Brigade was in line of battle more than a mile to the west from most of the 16th Corps.

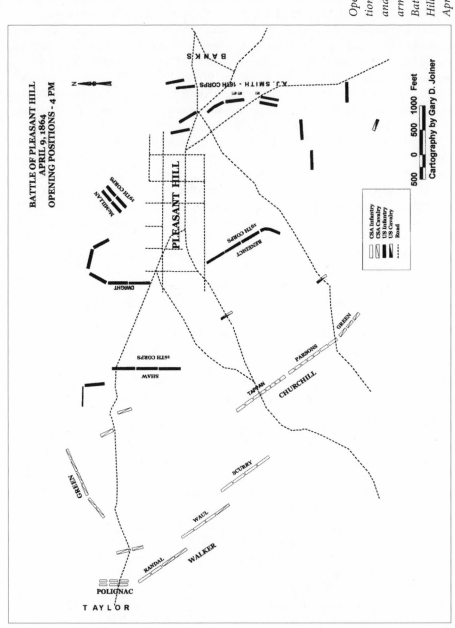

*Opening positions of the Union and Confederate armies at the Battle of Pleasant Hill, 4:00 P.M., April 9, 1864.*

Before dawn Taylor ordered his men to probe the ridge that was the scene of the end of the previous day's fighting, and they soon found that Banks had pulled out. In his message to Walker earlier that morning, Taylor told the Texan, "Arkansas and Missouri will lead the fight this morning. They must do what Texas and Louisiana did today [yesterday]."[77] During the remainder of the day, the plan he created the night before was followed.

Taylor and Green led the Texas cavalry down the road with orders for the infantry to follow. Six miles northwest of Pleasant Hill they found a large number of prisoners being herded back to the Confederate lines by Texas cavalrymen. About 9:00 A.M. Green's cavalry came into contact with McMillan's and Shaw's troops just as the former were to be relieved by Shaw. Taylor thought they were a rearguard protecting the trains. He ordered the cavalry to reconnoiter the Union position.[78]

About 1:00 P.M. Churchill's men arrived two miles west of Pleasant Hill.[79] Taylor talked to Churchill and found that the Arkansans had marched forty-five miles in the last thirty-six hours and were exhausted. Taylor told them to rest for a short time and that they would lead the attack.[80] Taylor then decided that all of his infantry units required a rest to perform at optimum ability. He delayed his attack for three hours with orders for all the units to rest for two hours.[81] Taylor knew he was wasting valuable daylight, but he also knew his men were tired. His cavalry scouts reported the basic layout of the Union forces but not the reserves' positions, including the 16th Corps.

*Brig. Gen. Thomas J. Churchill, C.S.A. Courtesy Arkansas History Commission and the Old State House Museum, Little Rock, Arkansas.*

Taylor used the concept for battle he had made the night before, making a slight variation. Churchill would sweep to the Confederate right over a mile into the woods.[82] On his right were three regiments of cavalry to cut off the Union retreat. Churchill would then extend past the Union left and hit them from behind, striking from the Shreveport-Natchitoches stagecoach road. Walker would form in line of battle south of the road and begin his advance when he heard Churchill's guns and link his right flank with Churchill's left. When it appeared the Union forces were drawn south of the road from the combined infantry attack, cavalry under Bee and Buchel were to charge down the road and through the village. Two more cavalry units were to block the Blair's Landing road. Mouton's Division, now under the command of the Prince de Polignac, was held in reserve. Taylor told his men to rely on the bayonet, "as we had neither time nor ammunition to waste."[83]

In the village, Banks and his commanders were bored and did not think there would be action that day.[84] They knew of little activity other than skirmishing down the road. Banks sent Admiral Porter a message telling him about Mansfield and that he intended to resume the advance to Shreveport that evening.[85]

At 3:00 P.M. Churchill and his men headed down the road for two miles and then began their trek though the dense woods. They formed up in line of battle with General Parsons's Division on the right and Churchill's own division on the left. The forest immediately posed problems to the two divisions, interfering with lines of approach and sight. As they swept to their right, Parsons's left flank came in contact with Federal units, so the entire force moved even farther to the right. With all

*Brigadier General Andrew Jackson Smith. From Francis Trevelyan Miller et al., eds.,* The Photographic History of the Civil War in Ten Volumes *(New York: Review of Reviews Co., 1912), 4:137.*

of these movements, forward progress became more difficult and the two divisions became disoriented.[86]

After the Missouri and Arkansas troops disappeared into the woods, Taylor began a countdown to initiate the battle. He gave Churchill an hour and a half to get into position. At 4:30 P.M. a Confederate twelve-gun battery began firing on the Union four-gun battery with Shaw's men to the north of road at a distance of about eight hundred yards. Within thirty minutes the counter battery fire had become so intense that the Union battery withdrew for its own safety.[87] As the Union battery withdrew, Churchill's men were heard yelling, signaling the beginning of their attack. Walker's Texans recognized this as the signal for their advance and at 5:00 P.M. they charged.[88] This was thirty minutes premature, but the Texans thought the Arkansans were in position.

Tom Green saw the Union battery limbering up. Believing that the forward Union units were collapsing under the weight of the Confederate artillery barrage, he ordered Bee to charge.[89] This decision was also made in error. Bee charged his men across an old track and was met with a furious volley from Shaw's Brigade. One-third of Debray's regiment died in the assault. Buchel forced the then-advancing Union infantry back to their original line and then fell, mortally wounded. Debray's horse was hit and fell on him. He survived by losing his boot and slightly injuring his ankle. He limped back to his line using his sword as a cane.[90]

Walker's men marched against Shaw's Brigade, exchanging volleys as they approached. Shaw's men were thinly protected in a band of trees and behind a rail fence. This position was exposed and had no flank support. Walker's men drove toward the 32nd Iowa Infantry just as the Texas cavalry, fighting dismounted, attacked the Union brigade's right flank.[91]

Positioned due east of the 32nd Iowa, and astride the westernmost dirt street of the village, was General Dwight's Brigade. It was composed of three New York regiments and another from Maine. The brigade had been rounding up stragglers since dawn and was then placed in this second line of battle.[92] The Easterners took the brunt of Walker's charge and held their ground while withstanding intense firing.

The most unusual Union soldier on the field at Pleasant Hill was a private named Lyons Wakeman of the 153rd New York Infantry, one of the regiments in this brigade.[93] The private's true name was Sarah Rosetta Wakeman, and she had fooled everyone into thinking she was a reclusive young man. Private Wakeman and her unit were under fire for the full battle.[94] She wrote her family, "I was under fire about four hours and laid on the field of battle all night. There was three wounded in my Co. and one killed."[95] She went on to say that one of the wounded received a head wound, the second soldier was wounded in the hip, and the third had one of his fingers shot off.[96]

Private Wakeman was not the only woman fighting as a man in the campaign, Private Albert D. J. Cashier of Company G, 95th Illinois Infantry, was actually Jennie Hodgers, an Irish immigrant. Her unit was part of the 17th Corps accompanying Porter on the river.[97] Cashier was well known for bravery in actions at Vicksburg the previous year where she participated in the May 22 assault on the Confederate works.[98]

A Union soldier penned a letter to his wife while his unit was pinned down during this phase of the battle. He apologized for his penmanship, for he was forced to write it on the top of his kepi while lying on his stomach to avoid being shot. He told her that the Union forces were outnumbered, that the fighting was desperate, and that this may be his last letter. Even in this dire situation, his humor was displayed as he wrote, "I don't know why this place is called Pleasant Hill—Seems to darned unpleasant to me right now. The Rebs are fighting like dogs but we will whip them, you can bet on that."[99]

Churchill's divisions, still in deeply wooded terrain, believed they were abreast of the Union line. They could hear the cannonade to their left rear. They saw a Union line ahead of them in a field, in the center of which lay a tree-filled dry streambed. This was Benedict's Brigade. Most of the enemy soldiers were in the thicket and Churchill charged them. The Confederates had no further use for their rifled muskets in the thick undergrowth, so they used their weapons as clubs. The Union regiments collapsed as a line and were routed. The three New York regiments broke first and the Maine soldiers retreated only after they were almost enveloped. Benedict was killed shortly after he told the Maine troops to pull back.[100] Flushed with this victory, Churchill's men captured the left section of Battery L, 1st U.S. Artillery Battery, and aimed for the village.[101] In their rush they did not notice A. J. Smith's men ahead and to their right. Churchill had wheeled too soon and had come into the Union lines almost in front of the Union left flank. It was a terrible mistake.[102]

In the center of the action, General Walker, wounded, was carried to the rear. Taylor called in Polignac's weary reserves. These were the men who had born the brunt of the fighting the previous day. They aimed for Shaw's Brigade. When Benedict's Brigade collapsed, there was no support on either side or to the immediate rear for Shaw. The 32nd Iowa, holding the center of the line, stubbornly refused to leave and bent itself into a semicircle, preparing to make a final stand. Adding to the pressure on Shaw were Green's dismounted cavalrymen who swept toward the Iowa regiment's right. Shaw urged Dwight to help, but Dwight refused to move, saying he had no orders to do so.[103] A. J. Smith ordered Shaw's Brigade to withdraw, and three regiments did so. The steadfast 32nd Iowa was surrounded and cut off.[104] Dwight decided that if he did not act, orders or not, he would suffer the same fate as Shaw. He ordered two of his regiments to cross the road and set up on the south side. General Emory then ordered McMillan's Brigade to fill the void created by Dwight. McMillan's troops had been relieved by Shaw and were held in reserve. They marched into a hailstorm of shells from both sides.[105] A soldier of the 30th Maine wrote that the "air seemed all alive with the sounds of various projectiles."[106]

At that point in the battle, both sides thought the Confederates were winning. The Union right and center had all but collapsed. The left seemed to have evaporated. The only large contingent of the command thus far not engaged was the 16th Corps except for Shaw's Brigade and they were waiting for their chance. The 58th Illinois, which had been concealed in a copse of trees, began pouring accurate fire into Churchill's men just after they passed their position. Other regiments of Lucas's Brigade joined in and A. J. Smith then ordered his entire line to charge the Confederates. Churchill's

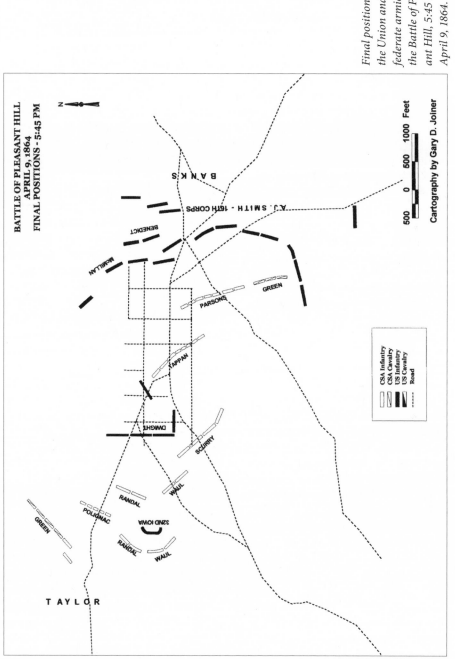

*Final positions of the Union and Confederate armies at the Battle of Pleasant Hill, 5:45 P.M., April 9, 1864.*

men still had forward momentum and reached the eastern side of the village.[107] They were then forced to fall back to the stream bottom where they overwhelmed Benedict's Brigade. The fighting was especially brutal here, and just as before muskets were used as clubs because of the dense undergrowth.[108]

Sergeant John H. Cook of Company A, 119th Illinois Infantry, was leading a company of skirmishers at the forefront of his regiment. His regiment had advanced into the stream bottom when Churchill's men charged. He later wrote that it seemed that the battle was lost. His position was facing north and near the far left flank of the Union forces. Cook saw the 13th and 19th Corps units being crushed. He also saw the Confederate forces sweep past him. Leading the skirmishers, he saw an old friend fall from a mortal head wound. The sight infuriated him and, realizing his breechloader rifle was empty, Cook waved his gun and cap and called out, "Come on boys!" His regiment followed him. This charge halted the Confederate advance. For his gallantry, Cook was awarded the Medal of Honor.[109]

As Parsons was driven back, Tappan, commanding Churchill's Division, was forced to retreat or his flank would be exposed and Smith's "gorillas" would drive a wedge between the two divisions. As they withdrew, they ran into Scurry's Brigade of Walker's Division of Texans and all three units were thrown into a tight position. Taylor had to send two brigades to Scurry's aid before he was enveloped.[110] Although the Union forces repelled Confederate attacks, the armies mutually separated at the end of the battle, and as darkness again fell on a battlefield for the second straight day, the fighting ended in a tactical draw.

During the battle the Confederates had forced the Union lines to bend back on the left and then had blown through their center, only to have their own right wing enveloped at great loss. Darkness finally separated the armies. Taylor's plan worked as it was designed to, except for the unknown quantity of the Union 16th Corps. Banks rode up to A. J. Smith and shook his hand, thankfully saying, "God bless you general. You have saved the army."[111] A. J. Smith had little to say to Banks and went back to his troops to see to their welfare and to make them ready in the event of another Confederate attack. He did not attend a conference of Union commanders who met with Banks to decide their next course of action. The dead of both armies lay on the battlefield that night, and the wounded of both armies were heard pleading for help and water. They were in no-man's-land. Neither side could afford to offer assistance.[112] It was in the midst of this chorus of misery that Banks decided on his next course of action.

Banks wanted to try again to take Shreveport and had told A. J. Smith of his intention.[113] In preparation, the commanding general ordered Lee to bring what was left of his trains back to Pleasant Hill.[114] Banks met with Franklin, Dwight, and Emory to seek their counsel. Franklin later told Congress that he held no hope for success in another battle. Franklin was so disgusted with Banks's leadership that he was "certain that an operation depending on plenty of troops, rather than upon skill in handling them, was the only one which would have a probability of success in his [Banks's] hands."[115] Both Franklin and Emory suggested that the most prudent option was to take the road to Blair's Landing and link with Porter and the fleet. The supply transports held all the equipment and rations the army needed. Dwight suggested that the army retrograde to Grand Ecore, telling Banks that no one had heard from Porter and that they did not know if Taylor's forces had captured or destroyed the fleet.[116] Banks listened to his friend over the objections of the two more seasoned generals. He decided to follow the same route by which they had come and delay any further actions until they reached Grand Ecore.

The night was filled with the sound of the army packing and preparing to leave for the small river port. Lee was ordered to turn his train around again. The dead and wounded were to be left on the field where they lay for the second time in two days.[117] Private Julius Knapp of the 116th New York Volunteer Infantry regiment noted in his diary that the "dead and wounded lay upon the field two days before they were taken care of [,] the rebels thinking we had possession of the ground and we thinking the Same of them."[118]

A. J. "Whisky" Smith was furious when he learned of Banks's plan after midnight. He stormed up to Banks to protest the action, telling him the reasons for not retreating. First, he was upset at the thought of not burying his dead and leaving his wounded for the Confederates to tend to if they could or would do so. Second, it would leave his 2,500 men under Brigadier General T. Kilby Smith, aboard the transports traveling with Porter, at risk without the benefit of support. Banks refused to alter his plans. Smith then pleaded with Banks to let him stay behind with his men to tend to the dead and dying. Banks refused this as well, saying that there was no water for the troops and they must return to Grand Ecore. The lack of water was certainly true, but Banks was to use this as the primary excuse for the upcoming retreat too often.[119]

A. J. Smith left Banks and visited Franklin. Smith was still seething at Banks's evident incompetence on the battlefield. He did not want to leave the dead and wounded as Banks had ordered. Smith asked Franklin to place Banks under arrest and take over the command of the army. He assured Franklin that he would have the support of the 13th, 16th, and 17th Corps. Franklin, still disgusted with Banks, considered this and then replied, "Smith, don't you know this is mutiny?" Since mutiny was an offense that was punishable by hanging upon conviction of the crime, the generals dropped the conversation.[120]

Union losses by regimental tally were 289 killed, 773 wounded, and 543 missing, for a total of 1,605.[121] Richard Taylor reported Confederate losses at Pleasant Hill as 1,200 killed and wounded and another 426 taken prisoner.[122] The twin battles fought over two consecutive days left dead and wounded soldiers over a twenty-mile corridor, with the majority of them on the two battlefields. Homes, schools, and all other available buildings were used as hospitals. Confederates and Federal soldiers were treated side by side for several days after.[123] The Union trains provided much-needed supplies, but the Confederate physicians were quickly overwhelmed by the number of wounded. Food was unavailable for three days.[124]

The fighting at Pleasant Hill was the most intense of the campaign. A careful analysis of unit positions at the beginning of the battle illustrates that A. J. Smith's decision to move Shaw's Brigade forward saved the Union from another catastrophic defeat. Shaw's stubborn resistance slowed the Confederate charge enough to allow units behind them to reposition. Without this the 16th Corps may have had less of an impact on the fighting. Many soldiers wrote of the sudden violence and the duration of the fighting, the uneven wooded terrain, the fading light of late afternoon and evening, and confusion between attacking and defending positions. Both sides were confused about who was winning. The deciding factor in this battle was Smith's veterans, who were both well positioned and ready for battle. Their position cannot be attributed to Banks's leadership. He kept the Westerners, whom he despised, near the back of his column. Smith's request to Franklin to arrest Banks speaks volumes about the soldiers' attitude toward their commander following the battle.

Richard Taylor was so focused on destroying the Union 19th Corps that he considered no alternatives to a direct confrontation. His military intelligence sources lacked knowledge of the location of A. J. Smith's men, and Taylor's assumption that they were guarding the fleet excluded them from his planning. When Banks evacuated the ridgeline he held the previous night, Taylor did not change his battle plan. Taylor's attitude toward the Union troops was not so much arrogance as it was practical knowledge. His faults generally lay in not adequately preparing for known contingencies. The wooded terrain through which his Arkansas and Missouri troops marched was uneven, and maneuvering in line of battle was difficult. Also, he did not assess the possibility that Smith's troops could be on the battlefield. He respected Smith's men, but not the Easterners. He blamed himself for Pleasant Hill. In his memoirs he stated that he should have personally led the right flank rather than leaving the task to Churchill, who was tired and unfamiliar with the terrain. He then added, "Herein lies the vast difference between genius and commonplace: one anticipates errors, the other discovers them too late."[125]

Nathaniel Banks seems to have retreated into numbness after the Battle of Pleasant Hill. His confidence was shaken by the Rebels' stand. He asked little advice from his senior commanders, and he could not decide whether to advance or retreat. His failure to deploy his men to face the Rebels was more turpitude than neglect.

Later that fall, the Joint Committee on the Conduct of the War heard testimony on Banks's lack of preparedness before the Battle of Pleasant Hill. A. J. Smith was particularly harsh, but Porter and several other commanders agreed with him. Banks could not divert blame on Franklin, and his excuse for retreating after the battle rang hollow. Lack of water was a lame excuse when the force could have marched due east to Blair's Landing. The retreat doomed any further incursion into Rebel-held territory. It destroyed Banks's presidential hopes, although Banks did not seem to realize this at the time. The retreat undoubtedly turned the tactical draw into a strategic defeat.

# CHAPTER 6

## The Campaign in Arkansas

Banks's plan had a northern column. A force was to descend upon Shreveport from Little Rock. This was intended to draw potential opponents away from the Union column advancing up the Red River and, if possible, to capture the Louisiana capital. This portion of the Red River Campaign, the Camden Expedition, acted as a counterbalance to the Louisiana incursion. The Confederates were forced to defend their territory on two fronts simultaneously. The methods chosen to successfully defend their territory placed great hardships on commanders and troops alike. The battles of Mansfield and Pleasant Hill, fought on April 8 and 9, sealed the fate of Nathaniel P. Banks's expedition into northwestern Louisiana, but there was no rapid method to inform the Arkansas Union forces contingent of events to the south. The northern prong was under way, but deep in the wilderness of pine barrens and river bottoms of another howling wilderness. The timing and planning of the campaign allowed the Union commander in Arkansas, Major General Frederick Steele, to select his route and, to a great degree, the extent of his participation in the campaign. This wide leeway created immediate concerns. Was Steele to capture Shreveport or simply support Banks? Was there to be a siege or an assault on the town? What was he to do if he faced most of Confederate forces that could be brought against him?

Steele was an unwilling participant, ordered by U. S. Grant to cooperate fully. He thought he knew more about campaigning in Arkansas than Grant did. He was reluctant to participate in any venture with Banks and he told Grant how he felt. Central Arkansas had many of the same characteristics as north Louisiana.[1] It was alternately hilly and barren, then low and swampy, all with little population and few opportunities to forage. In the spring, rains turned the few roads into bottomless muddy troughs. Steele had to contend with regular Confederate troops to the south and west, hostile Indians in the west, guerrilla units called "partisan rangers" operating freely in the countryside, and Jayhawkers, ostensibly pro-Union but mercenary enough to work for the highest bidder.[2]

Further complicating the campaign season was the mandate from President Lincoln to hold elections so that Arkansas and Louisiana would elect members to Congress, a governor, and state officials. Steele protested that the elections must

*Major General Frederick Steele as colo-nel of the Eighth Infantry. From Francis Trevelyan Miller et al., eds., The Photo-graphic History of the Civil War in Ten Volumes (New York: Review of Reviews Co., 1912), 10:175.*

take priority. He wrote to Grant that "the President is very anxious it [the election of Arkansas state officers] should be a success. Without the assistance of the troops to distribute the poll-books, with the oath of allegiance, and to protect the voters at the polls, it cannot succeed."[3] His remonstrations were ineffective.

Grant forced him to cooperate and Steele obeyed.[4] His orders were to take a force down to Shreveport and work in concert with Banks and the fleet under Admiral Porter. How this would be accomplished was left up to Steele and his staff. The Arkansas commander at first planned to move southwest from Little Rock and approach the Ouachita River somewhere between Hot Springs and El Dorado. From there he would descend to Monroe, Louisiana, located on the Ouachita River. This route offered several advantages. It was a straightforward line of travel that was devoid of major Confederate units until he reached Louisiana. If he did not cross the Ouachita River earlier, he would do so at Monroe and follow the uncompleted bed of the Southern Pacific Railroad west to the Red River. This alternative afforded Steele the support role he requested without requiring a large troop commitment. Although the route would take the Union force almost due south then west to the Red River, it was the safest route.

For some reason, perhaps to solve potential political problems, Steele changed his mind. He decided to veer to the southwest, to Arkadelphia and then to Washington, the capital of Confederate Arkansas, about seventy miles north of Shreveport.[5] This might drive the Arkansas government to Shreveport and he might overwhelm two state governments. He decided to gather forces from two locations and meet at Arkadelphia

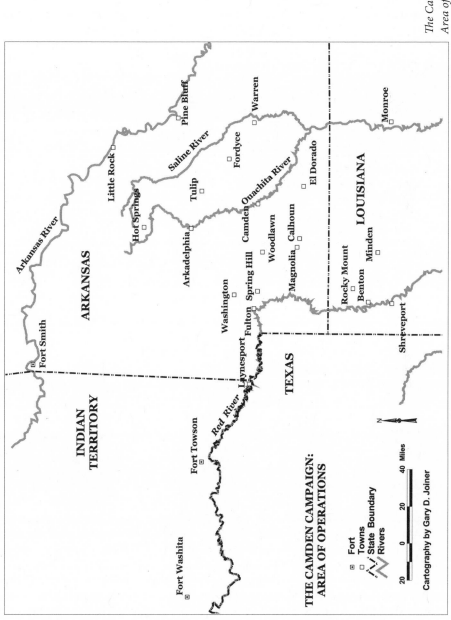

*The Camden Campaign
Area of Operations.*

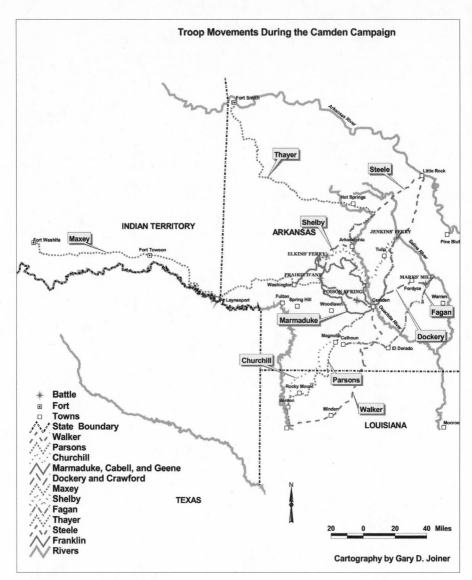

*Steele's campaign in Arkansas.*

and then march southwest to Shreveport. It was a variant of Banks's plan for the Union forces in Louisiana to meet at Alexandria after the 19th Corp under General Franklin marched west then north and General A. J. Smith and Admiral Porter came up the Red River on naval and transport vessels. Once Steele began the march, his faith in the timetable Banks had set was the only guidance he had. There would be little or no communication with Banks or Porter. Steele created a communications problem for himself by orchestrating a similar scenario in Arkansas.

On March 17 Steele ordered Brigadier General John Thayer, the commander at Fort Smith, to march his troops in the Frontier Division to Arkadelphia, where he would rendezvous with Steele's column coming from Little Rock. Steele gave Thayer until April 1 to march the 170 miles.[6] He then ordered the commander of the small garrison at Pine Bluff to send patrols to watch for any movement by Confederate forces to the south. Steele took the Third Division, 7th Corps, and two brigades of cavalry from Little Rock on March 23. Steele's force consisted of 6,800 men and Thayer added another 3,600, making a force of 10,400.[7] Each man was weighted down with full equipment for a campaign and forty rounds of ammunition.[8]

Steele's men, since September 1863, had not been campaigning but performing garrison duty. To ease them into the march, he set a leisurely pace. The column left Little Rock to the cadence of "Yankee Doodle."[9] The first day they traveled nine miles.[10] Early the next morning, according to A. F. Sperry, a soldier in the 33rd Iowa Infantry and perhaps the best chronicler of the campaign, noted that the predawn darkness was broken as "bugles rang as we had never heard them before. If an enemy had been in hearing distance, he must have thought we were at least a hundred thousand strong."[11] The column formed up before the sun rose and marched the entire day. That night Steele ordered half rations for his men, except coffee, for the duration of the march.[12] This was an odd order to be given so early in the expedition and the result was obvious. As the men, still unaccustomed to long marches, moved to the southwest, their hunger grew and the land was inhospitable for foraging.

The next day, March 26, the column reached the Ouachita River at the hamlet of Rockport, which they found deserted.[13] They easily crossed the shallow river, although they stopped to throw up a bridge in case rains made the stream rise. This activity slowed them, and for the next three days the column marched at a leisurely pace to a point a few miles outside Arkadelphia. The advance elements reached the town on March 29.[14]

The main body entered the town and many of the men began foraging. Most paid for the items they took. Sperry reported that one of the women in town told the Federal soldiers that "yur men treat us better than our own men do."[15] Steele expected to find Thayer's column from Fort Smith either waiting for him or arriving shortly thereafter. Neither happened. Arkadelphia was a small town and the forage opportunities for a force of 6,800 men were limited. Steele opened his commissary wagons to the men and waited for Thayer. Many of the troops, hungry from the trek on half rations, ate ravenously from the limited local fare and their own supplies.[16] Steele knew that this was not wise, but he had little choice. If there was scant forage left in the town for both men and animals, the surrounding region was even less hospitable. The Union commander had a limited number of options. He could stay in Arkadelphia and consume its supplies. He could retrace his route to Little Rock or veer east to Pine Bluff. The final option was to move the column toward Washington, the capital of Confederate Arkansas. That might afford the possibility of capturing Rebel supplies. Steele chose the latter.[17] The Confederates seemed to be ignoring them.

Confederate forces in Arkansas were scattered but highly mobile, consisting primarily of seasoned cavalry units. Their division and brigade commanders were excellent field officers. However, the Rebels had a disadvantage in the district commander,

Major General Sterling Price, who was only marginally competent. Kirby Smith was Price's immediate superior and close friend. The two had an unusual relationship. Smith at times took Price's advice almost as if he were listening to a sage. Price was a former governor of Missouri and had a forceful personality. Smith sometimes appeared to question Price's ideas but usually acquiesced to the Arkansas District commander's wishes. Later that year Price's plan to free Missouri would bear bitter fruit.

Prior to the Battle of Mansfield, Smith and Richard Taylor met to discuss plans. Taylor offered to take most of his forces and march to Arkansas, eliminate the threat posed by Steele, and return to Louisiana to stop Banks. Smith refused and gave Taylor a vague response.[18] Taylor defeated Banks and his Union column at Mansfield on April 8 and fought the Federals to a bloody standoff the next day at Pleasant Hill. Smith was not on the scene and withheld two divisions from action in an attempt to save the day if Taylor ran into trouble at Mansfield. These two divisions, previously called down from Arkansas, fought at Pleasant Hill on April 9.

Sterling Price saw his territory shrink drastically after the Union forces took Little Rock. Although his numbers were small, five brigades of cavalry, they were concentrated in the southwest portion of the state and were mostly tough veterans.[19] His brigades were scattered when Steele began his expedition. Two were east of the Saline River, one near Monticello, and the other near Mount Elba—halfway between Pine Bluff and Camden. Brigadier General John Marmaduke led the other three. Two of the three were with Marmaduke at Camden—one of these under Brigadier General Joseph Shelby; the other under Colonel Colton Greene. The third brigade, led by Brigadier General William "Old Tig" Cabell, was operating west of the Confederate capital of Washington on the Red River.[20] Marmaduke's brigades totaled 3,600 men. Price's forces were adequate to thwart a Union drive but not to destroy Federal columns sent against them in mass.

Marmaduke's intelligence gathering was suffering from a time lag. On March 25 the brigades were dispatched to specific points, only to discover that Steele's column was already approaching Arkadelphia. Marmaduke had intended to harass the Federal column from both front and rear and then attack the supply trains with a third brigade from the flank. When the cavalry reached their objective at Tate's Bluff, they found only hoof prints and wagon tracks. Marmaduke then decided to make a dash for the Little Missouri River and contest the crossing with three brigades.[21] This initial disposition of forces by the Confederates was the first in a long series of moves by both sides that highlighted the problems of campaigning in southern Arkansas. The Federals found both northern Louisiana and southern Arkansas to be a howling wilderness with few roads and lines of travel and communication that were difficult at best. The land was equally inhospitable to both sides. As the Confederate and Union columns marched and countermarched, this hostile environment left them with more questions than answers.

Steele arrived at Arkadelphia for his expected linkup with Thayer, but Thayer was missing. Steele waited for three days. As his men rested and ate voraciously from the commissary wagons and local fare, Steele became anxious and finally felt he could wait no longer. On April 1 Steele moved the column toward Washington.[22] Confederate General Cabell's Brigade of Fagan's Division began skirmishing with the Union Column almost immediately. That night Marmaduke ordered Colonel Greene's Brigade to take up a position on the Washington Road near the Little Missouri River.[23] The next morning Cabell was ordered to join Greene. Marmaduke's plan to hold at the Little Missouri crossing seemed to be working. As the two brigades prepared to hold their crossing, word came that the Union column had turned toward Elkin's Ferry, bypassing them.[24] There is no evidence that Steele knew of the trap prepared for him.

The Union troops seized and then began fortifying the ferry landing, mounting artillery on all the approach roads. General Shelby's Brigade attacked the rearguard with spirited cavalry charges but failed to dislodge the Federals.[25] On April 3 and 4 Steele's column crossed the Little Missouri while Shelby continued to attack. Marmaduke then assaulted the column while it was most vulnerable, crossing the river. He charged with 1,200 men and drove several regiments back. The Union soldiers stopped running when they joined the main concentration of Federal troops, in part because they could run no farther. The strengthened column then seized the initiative. Shortly thereafter Marmaduke was forced to withdraw.[26] The withdrawal allowed the Federal troops time to consolidate their position at the crossing. Shelby ceased attacks on the rearguard when it became apparent that the crossing was fortified and he had inadequate forces to contest the position. He then joined the other two brigades that night and the Confederates withdrew to Prairie d'Ane, where they hastily built earthworks. Marmaduke received reinforcements from the Indian Territory on April 6 in the form of Brigadier General Richard Gano's Brigade. These hard-riding

*Brigadier General John M. Thayer. From Francis Trevelyan Miller et al., eds., The Photographic History of the Civil War in Ten Volumes (New York: Review of Reviews Co., 1912), 10:221.*

Texans traveled from Fort Washita and Fort Towson and then from Laynesport in the southeastern corner of the Indian Territory. They had been posted there to prevent Steele or Thayer from raiding and harassing the Confederates living in and around Jefferson and Marshall, Texas.[27]

Steele finally received news from Thayer's column. They were trying to find him as they marched from Hot Springs. Steele halted his column to give Thayer time to catch up, still uncertain of the distance between the two groups. A spring rainstorm deluged the camp area, destroyed the corduroy roads, and threatened to float the pontoon bridges away.[28] Steele's men repaired the damage on April 8 and 9 while the twin battles of Mansfield and Pleasant Hill raged. Steele, of course, knew nothing about Banks's fortunes or Admiral Porter's problems with falling river levels, harassment by Confederate artillery, cavalry, and infantry sharpshooters north of Grand Ecore.[29] Thayer finally arrived and Steele's men were unimpressed by their reinforcements.[30] The second column seemed to consist of every type of soldier possible, pro-Union Indians and two regiments of blacks; Thayer's column had a variety of bulky wagons and other transportation that had been scavenged along the route.[31] Although they had many conveyances, they had no supplies. Thayer had expected Steele to resupply him, but Steele issued no orders to that effect. Steele's men, mules, and horses had been consuming rations and forage at a fast pace while waiting for Thayer, and Thayer's commissary stores were almost depleted. Steele was forced to request supplies from Little Rock, dispatching a train of empty wagons. His quartermasters were told to

*Brigadier General John Marmaduke. From Francis Trevelyan Miller et al., eds.,* The Photographic History of the Civil War in Ten Volumes *(New York: Review of Reviews Co., 1912), 10:279.*

resupply the column with thirty days of half rations for fifteen thousand men.[32] This order would reduce the number of wagons needed in this resupply effort and hopefully reduce the waiting time. Most of Steele's actions henceforth would be cast in the light of this severe lack of rations for his men and forage for his horses and mules.

On April 10 Steele moved across Prairie d'Ane, pushing two of Marmaduke's brigades before him. Shelby's and Brigadier General Thomas P. Dockery's brigades joined and stiffened their positions by late afternoon and the fight escalated. Both sides called up artillery. The lines were so close that Union troops reported seeing the Confederates' matches as they lit the cannon fuses (which is odd since friction primers were common at that time; perhaps they saw the Rebels smoking).[33] There was little fighting the next day, and that afternoon Steele tried to force the Confederates out of their lines by making a major demonstration. The Confederates would not accept the challenge to fight, and Steele returned to his camp of the previous night.[34] Under cover of darkness, Price, who had arrived at the battlefield, withdrew his men about eight miles toward Washington, abandoning the earthworks his men had thrown up without a fight.[35]

Price made a number of incomprehensible decisions during the campaign. The abandonment of earthworks that obviously annoyed Steele ranks in this category. Steele was not afraid to give battle, but he was wary of earthworks, perhaps remembering his failed attacks on Vicksburg on May 22, 1863. These works blocked the only road used on the Union column's approach. Due to the difficult terrain, there was little opportunity to implement a flanking movement. Price's gift bewildered the Federals.

Price had made a blunder, but he was surprised by Steele's next move. Steele's men occupied the earthworks on the morning of April 12. Shortly afterward, the column reversed its direction and marched for Camden.[36] Price had no way of knowing how short of supplies Steele was. The country was inordinately inhospitable. The primary problem Steele faced was not rations for his men but forage for his animals. The general wrote to chief of staff Henry Halleck that Camden was the most convenient place to set up a supply base, and until supplies arrived the combined Union column could not move toward Shreveport. He reasoned that "our supplies were nearly exhausted and so was the country. We were obliged to forage from 5 to 15 miles on either side of the road to keep our stock alive."[37] Many Union soldiers ignored orders against unauthorized foraging for themselves as they sought feed for their animals.[38] Sperry indicates that this was due to soldiers being on half rations for almost three weeks.[39] Many of the Union soldiers had not shared in the feast of the commissary wagons in Arkadelphia.

Steele's men marched toward Camden on April 12 and 13. On the thirteenth, the rearguard was repeatedly attacked by reinforcements that Price had received. These men were the remainder of the division of troops from the Indian Territory, Colonel Tandy Walker's Second Indian Choctaw Brigade.[40] The pro-Confederate Indians had a decided distaste for blue-coated soldiers who had enforced the reservation policies of the U.S. government. The Confederates made a combined attack on Thayer's rearguard. The Rebels were repulsed after most of the Union column turned back to help the beleaguered Frontier Division. The Rebels broke off the engagement and the march resumed. The spring rains once again beat, slowing the column.

Marmaduke marched his entire division sixty miles from near Washington, bypassing Steele's column, and took position across the road fourteen miles west of Camden. Steele had sufficient manpower to push the Confederates aside. His intent was not to deal a deathblow but to get past the Confederates and enter Camden where he could fortify until his supplies arrived.[41] This may seem an odd action for the Union commander. He could not put enough soldiers forward to destroy Marmaduke's force, but he could disperse them. He also had the supply problem at the forefront of his thoughts. On the other side, Marmaduke's men had just completed an extraordinary sixty-mile ride and were immediately thrown into battle formation. The action of both sides was a case of asking too much from the common soldier with too little time and preparation for a battle.

In Shreveport four days earlier, Kirby Smith decided to go after Steele. There were adequate cavalry units in Arkansas to curb the Union foragers capability, disrupt lines of communication, and block access to northern Louisiana, but there were not sufficient numbers to eliminate the threat to his Louisiana headquarters. Smith decided to play a safe hand of poker and perhaps grab some of the glory that heretofore had been Richard Taylor's alone after Banks was thwarted at the battles of Mansfield and Pleasant Hill. Smith's plans did not include Taylor, who was kept out of Arkansas.[42]

Smith prepared to support Price with three divisions and Taylor found this disconcerting. The divisions that Smith intended for use in Arkansas were the Texas, Missouri, and Arkansas units, leaving the Louisiana Division under Taylor's command. This small division had been badly mauled at Mansfield. All four were desperately needed if Taylor had an opportunity to trap Banks.

Taylor offered to lead his infantry against Steele until that Union column was either destroyed or forced to retreat to Little Rock. He would then return to Louisiana to fight Banks with both his and Price's forces.[43] Smith agreed to this arrangement, and on April 14 Taylor sent three divisions to Shreveport. These were General Walker's Texas Division, General Churchill's Division of Arkansas, and General Parsons's Missouri Division. The Prince de Polignac's small and hard-fought Louisiana Division was sent south down Red River to track Banks and make him think that Taylor was in pursuit.

Taylor rode to Shreveport the next day to lead his three divisions north and found an unpleasant surprise. He learned that Steele had turned his column toward Camden, about 110 miles from Shreveport. Smith told Taylor that he, not Taylor, would pursue Steele.[44] Smith then dismissed Taylor from the Arkansas expedition, telling him he could either remain in Shreveport or harass Banks at Grand Ecore.[45] Taylor, livid, returned to his troops. In their discussion, Smith had promised Taylor that he would return the infantry divisions through Minden to Campti when Steele no longer posed a threat.[46]

Kirby Smith was normally a cautious man, almost to the point of distraction. He enjoyed working out the details of campaigns, allocating sufficient numbers of troops for a mission, and planning routes of travel. He relied on his staff to handle the details. In his newfound desire for quick action to destroy Steele's force, Smith missed a crucial detail. His army would need pontoon's borne by wagons to cross rivers in the event they were swollen due to spring rains. Steele included adequate pontoons and engineering troops as part of his train. Smith brought only a few, although they were available. The 4th Confederate Engineer Battalion, Company H, was based in Shreveport. It was commanded by Kirby Smith's first cousin, Captain Smith Kirby. This company was responsible for the Army of Western Louisiana's pontoons. They were left in Shreveport, and rather than following the army into Arkansas, they operated on the Red River between Shreveport and Natchitoches from April 29 to May 25.[47] This lack of bridging equipment cost the Confederates dearly.

Smith marched his men out of Shreveport on April 15 and 16.[48] A soldier stationed in Shreveport, Private William Henry King, soon to be a member of the 4th Engineers, observed the divisions passing through the capital. In his diary he penned:

> April 15th, Friday.
> Gen'l Walker's brigade [*sic*] passed through here to-day, proceeding up the river. It is supposed they are to reinforce Gen'l Price.[49]

> April 16th, Saturday.
> Gen'ls Tappan, Parsons & Churchill passed through here to-day, proceeding up the River with their commands.[50]

The three divisions used three different roads to facilitate faster travel and greater ease of forage. Walker was sent to Minden, thirty miles to the east, and then north on the Fort Towson Road to guard against the possibility of Steele joining Banks. Walker's Division then encamped north of Minden until it was determined that Banks was not going to cross the Red River at Grand Ecore and move to Harrisonburg on the Ouachita or attempt a march up the Red or Ouachita rivers to reach Steele. Walker marched his men northeasterly toward Camden.[51] Parsons took the center road, crossing the Red River at Shreveport, then traveling north to Benton, then northeasterly to Rocky Mount and Shongaloo before heading north to Camden. Churchill took the western road, which followed the Benton Road north to Plain Dealling, at which point it paralleled Parsons's route and converged with it at Magnolia. Smith's force then marched north to Calhoun, only a few miles from Price's position.

Kirby Smith planned to block any chance of Steele combining with Banks or Porter and he planned to destroy the northern column. This would leave Little Rock and even eastern Arkansas devoid of Union presence.[52] He could then march into Little Rock as the conquering hero. The ultimate goal was to reach St. Louis and free both Arkansas and Missouri from Union influence and restore the 1862 border of the Confederacy west of the Mississippi River. This would outshine Taylor's exploits at Mansfield. Steele reached Camden the same day Smith left Shreveport.

The Federals were forced to lay corduroy road before the wagons and artillery could pass through the rain-soaked bottomlands.[53] On April 14, after an exhausting march through the stream valleys through which the Camden road passed, the Union commander received word from scouts that a large Confederate force was assembling between him and his future supply base.[54]

Steele was desperate for supplies. Camden was well fortified, but if he could not feed 11,000 men, the earthworks were useless to him.[55] He sent 198 wagons to forage for corn and food. He sent two cannon, 500 men of the 1st Kansas Volunteer Infantry (Colored), and 200 white cavalry.[56] The train moved west about eighteen miles and then scattered on various roads to forage. Most were successful in retrieving corn. On the morning of April 18 the train reassembled for the return to Camden. They had moved about four miles when they were met by reinforcements, including 375 infantry and 90 cavalry with two mountain howitzers.[57] A guard force of 1,000 men and four cannon were now with the train.

Marmaduke decided to attack the supply column and set out with 2,000 men. His plan was to hit the Union wagon train simultaneously from the front and the right flank. He received word of the reinforcements and halted, asking Price for permission to bring his entire force to interdict the supply train. Permission was granted and, after another flanking march, he set up a trap at Poison Spring. Price sent reinforcements and before the supply train arrived Marmaduke had 3,100 men waiting for the Federal column under Brigadier General Samuel B. Maxey, including Tandy Walker's Choctaw Brigade.[58]

When the supply column came in contact with Confederate troops, Colonel James Williams of the 1st Kansas (Colored) Infantry ordered the wagons as close together as possible to protect them. He then moved his regiment to the front and along the flanks of the train facing outward and the remaining men to the rear, also facing outward.[59]

The Confederates attacked the right flank first and the Union troops were so spread out protecting the 198 wagons that reinforcements could not reposition to counter new threats. Marmaduke then hit the train from the front, and the white Kansas cavalrymen broke and ran into the woods. The Confederates gave chase and cut them down.[60]

Williams believed Steele's men in Camden, only ten miles distant, would hear the commotion and rush to their assistance. This did not happen and the Confederates captured the train as the Union infantry and the remnants of the cavalry routed. The Confederate Choctaws chased the survivors through the woods.[61]

The Rebels captured 170 wagons and burned 28 others. They also captured the four cannon with ammunition and powder plus 100 prisoners.[62] Marmaduke suffered 115 killed, wounded, and missing. Union losses were 301 killed, wounded, and missing, with 182 of them from the 1st Kansas Colored Infantry.[63] The Confederates relished killing the black troops, at least on a scale that equaled or exceeded what had occurred at Fort Pillow six days before.[64] The survivors straggled back into Camden without any wagons or field pieces and with 300 fewer men. The loss of forage was devastating.

Steele hunkered down in Camden waiting for supplies from Pine Bluff. He could do little else. On April 18 a messenger arrived with word that Banks wanted Steele to join him. In the message Banks said he had won at Mansfield and Pleasant Hill but had withdrawn to Grand Ecore for supplies.[65] On April 22 Steele wrote General Sherman that he could not defeat everything that Kirby Smith could send against him if Banks were defeated.[66] Steele then sent a courier to Banks saying that he probably could not

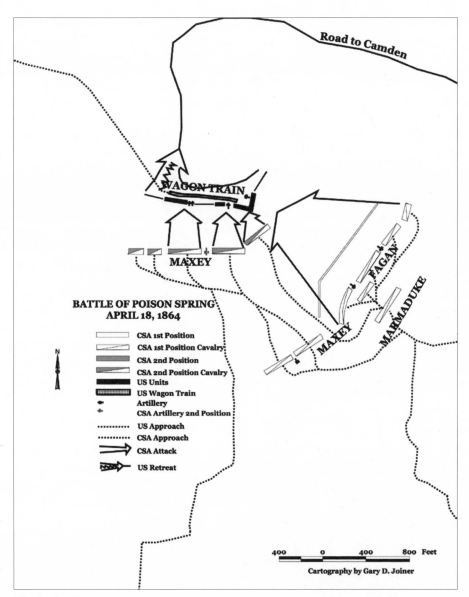

The Battle of Poison Spring.

link up with the southern column because he had received word that eight thousand Confederate infantry had just reinforced Price. Steele's letter rambled about possible lines of approach, each of which he dismissed.[67] In fact, Steele had no idea what he should or could do. The Confederates would decide for him.

Kirby Smith arrived at Calhoun, near Magnolia, with the three divisions of infantry on April 17 and immediately took command of field operations.[68] From Calhoun,

Smith had telegraph access to Shreveport.[69] He ordered Fagan's Division, with Shelby's Brigade attached, to place themselves between Steele and Little Rock, and while doing so, to attack Steele's supply bases on his main line of retreat.[70] Although this was logical, it created a problem later. Fagan was forced to range far to the east and cover a line from El Dorado on the Ouachita River to Mount Elba on the Saline River. He proceeded east to El Dorado. Communications between Fagan and the remainder of the Confederate forces were all but severed.

Smith then ordered Parsons and Churchill to converge on Camden. By the next day (April 20) they had moved to Magnolia, about half the distance to Little Rock from Shreveport. The movements of Parsons and Churchill were designed to make Steele believe that the main attack was on his fortified position at Camden.[71] Four days later Fagan arrived at El Dorado on the Ouachita and learned that Steele's supply train, having arrived from Pine Bluff, had been unloaded and was returning to Pine Bluff by way of the Moro Bottoms. Fagan then headed northwest to intercept it. Forty-five miles of fast riding placed Fagan crossing the Warren Road eight miles southeast of Marks' Mills. He allowed his exhausted men to bivouac at midnight. At dawn the next morning, Fagan moved to Marks' Mills, located on a road intersection on the Camden to Pine Bluff road, eight miles from Mt. Elba. Finding no trace of the supply train at the intersection, he prepared to attack.[72]

*Brigadier General James F. Fagan. From Francis Trevelyan Miller et al., eds., The* Photographic History of the Civil War in Ten Volumes *(New York: Review of Reviews Co., 1912), 10:257.*

Steele's supply train, commanded by Lieutenant Colonel Francis Drake, headed northeast en route back to Pine Bluff. At the core were 240 wagons. Guarding this train were three regiments of Union infantry, a total of 1,200 men and 240 cavalry troopers.[73] Oddly, for a column heading potentially in harm's way, there were large numbers of hangers-on, including local citizens, cotton speculators, and 300 blacks, who were referred to as contrabands.[74] The column encamped near Marks' Mill on the evening of April 24 without knowing that Fagan was just down the road.[75] Drake did not feel the need to post pickets.

At dawn Fagan hit the supply column with one brigade of Cabell's cavalry before it could reach the Saline River.[76] Dockery's brigade had lagged and struck the column. Cabell's Brigade, attacking the left flank, chased Steele's men from the train and into the woods on the opposite side. Cabell then realized that Union infantry were massing to attack one of his flanking regiments. At this point he ordered an about-face and fell upon the Union troops, thus avoiding a trap. Cabell's troops fought hand-to-hand for an hour and a half until Dockery's reinforcements arrived to crush the Union line. As the Union troops were pushed back to fighting among the wagons, Shelby's Brigade arrived after an eight-mile ride from the Mt. Elba crossing. At this point two Union regiments (the 43rd Indiana and 36th Iowa) surrendered when Drake was wounded.[77] The Confederates then directed attention to the third regiment, the 77th Ohio, that was still holding out and soon defeated them. Due to the way the column approached on one road, and the disposition of their forces, the Confederates were allowed to attack the Federals piecemeal, one or two units at a time, thereby granting the Southerners superiority in numbers at each surge of fighting. The Confederates then attacked the cavalry that had been conducting rearguard duty several miles behind the train. The Union cavalry were driven off and Fagan owned the day and the supply train.[78] The battle had lasted five hours, in which the Union suffered more than 1,300 military casualties. This did not include civilians, particularly blacks who had been killed.[79] Confederate casualty lists were incomplete. The numbers of killed, wounded, and missing were apparently about 500.[80] The battle at Marks' Mill was similar to that of Poison Spring in tactics and results.

Steele heard about the battle at Marks' Mills and its disastrous results and was immediately forced to halt his waiting game. The supply problem was critical and there was no chance to replenish his force. He had ten thousand men and nine thousand horses and mules in a land of pine barrens and swampy river bottoms—a country side that was devoid of forage. His generals disagreed on a course of action, but Steele had made up his mind regarding the only course open to save his command. The next day he evacuated Camden and began a retreat to Little Rock.[81]

At this point the Confederates achieved a strategic victory. The enemy was forced to retreat to his home base. The Union column was in an untenable position. They might fight their way to Shreveport and hope to secure supplies, but their animals, and perhaps their men, might starve. At the least the animals would be too weak to haul the wagons and gear. Napoleon's maxim that an army marches on its stomach rang true. If the Confederates did nothing, victory was theirs. Kirby Smith wanted more, to secure Little Rock and perhaps the entire state of Arkansas and perhaps

Missouri. Glory was his if he could only stop the fleeing Union column and force a battle leading to the annihilation of the enemy. This desire was his undoing.

The Union retreat took on the look of a rout, though more organized. Steele ordered that everything that could not be taken by the troops should be destroyed. This strangely included a large amount of hardtack and bacon that could not be distributed.[82] The column set out after dark on April 26 after decoying the Confederates into believing they were bedding down for the night. By midnight, the column had crossed the Ouachita, where they pulled up their pontoon bridge and slept along the road where they stopped.[83]

Smith had no idea that Steele had left. At 9:00 A.M. on April 27 the Confederates entered the abandoned works at Camden. The three infantry divisions that Smith brought with him from Louisiana all arrived late that afternoon. They could not quickly pursue due to the lack of a pontoon bridge. Smith then sent Maxey's Division back to the Indian Territory because he believed they would not be needed.[84] Smith's reasoning was flawed. Maxey's Division would have provided extra man- and firepower to either slow down or flank the retreating Union column. Tactically and strategically, the order made very little sense. Marmaduke's cavalry crossed the Ouachita by swimming, but not until darkness fell. The next morning, Smith ordered his troops to begin bridging the river.[85]

Steele pushed his men as hard as he could along the road to Jenkins' Ferry rather than the Pine Bluff road. This allowed him to avoid the swamps of the Moro Bottoms.[86] Men threw away gear they previously thought was important in order to lighten their loads. Rumors were rampant that the Confederates had overtaken them and were waiting somewhere ahead.[87] The Confederates, however, were having trouble of their own.

Fagan could not find a place to cross the Saline River. The water had risen because of constant rains, and he was forced to cross farther north. He finally gave up and led his men to Arkadelphia on April 29 to find supplies.[88] Southern Arkansas was inhospitable to both sides. With Fagan now in Arkadelphia and Maxey ordered to retire to the Indian Territory, Kirby Smith was short two veteran divisions. To Fagan's south, Marmaduke pressed closer to Steele's column.

Steele reached Jenkins' Ferry that afternoon and found the Saline River flood swollen as it had been for Fagan. He brought up the pontoons, loaded on wagons, and bridged the torrent after 4:00 P.M.[89] Steele then began moving the wagons and artillery across the bridge, leaving tactical command to Brigadier General Frederick Salomon. The infantry and cavalry would cross last. As the train moved over the pontoon bridge, Marmaduke closed on the Federal column.

Marmaduke began to skirmish with the Union rearguard the next morning— April 30—trying to pin them down until reinforcements arrived. He was unable to identify which units or their type that remained on the south side of the river. This lack of intelligence proved crucial. The Rebels incorrectly believed they were facing Steele's rearguard and that pursuit would begin the next morning after they bridged the Saline. Churchill's Division, the first to arrive, caught the Federal infantry on the west side of the Saline River.[90] The road leading to the ferry descended from a line of

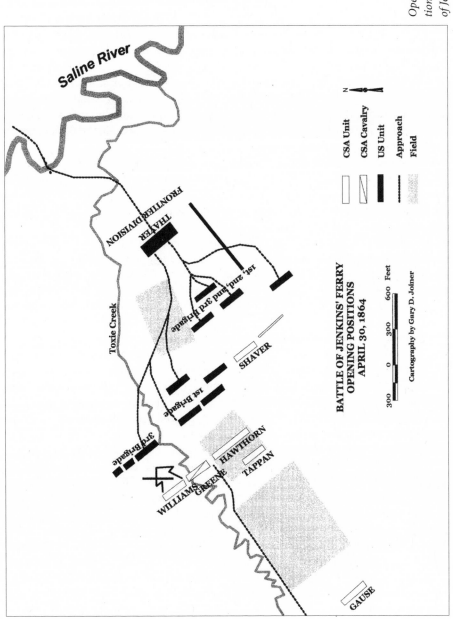

Saline River

Toxie Creek

FRONTIER DIVISION

THAYER

1st, 2nd, and 3rd Brigade

SHAVER

1st Brigade

3rd Brigade

WILLIAMS

GREENE

HAWTHORN

TAPPAN

GAUSE

**BATTLE OF JENKINS' FERRY
OPENING POSITIONS
APRIL 30, 1864**

300    0    300    600 Feet

Cartography by Gary D. Joiner

N

CSA Unit

CSA Cavalry

US Unit

Approach

Field

bluffs into a narrow valley bordered on the north by a line of bluffs, a small bayou, and a canebrake. To the south were fields separated by and ringed with timber. There was little area for either side to maneuver. In the fields close to the river, the Union infantry felled trees, creating an abatis with the trunks facing the defenders and the leafy growth facing the enemy. They also formed some of the trees into hastily contrived breastworks. The fields of fire were less than a quarter mile deep and wide.[91] The fields were flooded with almost two feet of water. Across this swamp and into the abatis and breastworks was the only Confederate approach. The Rebel line of attack and the Union defensive positions eerily resembled the battlefield at Gettysburg on July 3, 1863, but once off the bluffs and into the bottoms, it was as level as a billiard table. Pickett's charge would be replayed in the Saline bottoms of Arkansas with one major exception. There would be no grand push with all units marching forward. With Steele in retreat and such an inhospitable avenue of approach, the Rebels should have dug in and waited. They did not.

Price ordered first Marmaduke and then Churchill to attack. This was done piecemeal, committing individual regiments because of limited space.[92] Smith again made a major error using unsound military practice. There was no thought to smashing a single point in the Union line by a massive surge of men. The small bayou Toxie Creek (today known as Cox Creek) proved a problem for the advancing Confederates. Some of Steele's regiments, sent as skirmishers across the stream, poured enfilade fire on the advancing Rebels.[93] Smith decided there were not enough forces engaged, so he added all of Churchill's Division and then Parsons's Division, but incrementally. Marmaduke's inability to identify the number and nature of the enemy units to his front became critical. The Confederates did not realize that Steele had been unable to cross his infantry en masse over the Saline and that they were fighting the main force, not the rearguard. Both divisions were forced to retreat in the withering fire coming from their front and their left flank.[94] Visibility was limited because of a fog and the smoke from muskets and artillery. Both Price and Smith told the two divisions to pull back. About the same time, Walker's Division arrived and Smith committed them to attack on the Union left. Smith wanted all three of Walker's brigades to advance and overpower the Federal position. He finally realized that he must pour men into the area near the ferry landing, but by this time the Union line reconfigured for the onslaught. This was a senseless attack, and the brigade commanders suffered wounds, with Randal and Scurry mortally wounded.[95] Smith's orders caused senseless carnage. As the Confederates fell back, Steele crossed the remainder of his forces over the river in three hours. The Union troops then pulled the bridge to their side, dismantled it, but before they reached the bluffs, destroyed it.[96] Steele had no choice. His men were not physically able to fight a battle in a running pursuit. The river was the ally of the Union. The Federals had no way to know that the Rebels had inadequate bridging equipment. They still believed a major force was to their front, waiting to pounce. Their memories of Poison Spring and Marks' Mills were vivid.

The track behind Steele's retreat was littered with wagons that broke down and with horses and mules that were freed because they were too weak to pull wagons

*Brigadier General Mosby M. Parsons. From Francis Trevelyan Miller et al., eds.,* The Photographic History of the Civil War in Ten Volumes *(New York: Review of Reviews Co., 1912), 10:279.*

or artillery limbers. Military equipment previously thought to be essential was discarded when it became a burden. Water backed up from the Saline River had flowed into low areas, making some stretches of the road chest-deep in water.[97] As units at the front of the column discarded their equipment, those following were forced to move through these obstacles throughout May 1. They did not stop that night and marched until 4 A.M. without a break. Their meager food supplies gave out, and the column was finally given a short break before dawn.[98] After an all-too-brief respite, Steele began the march again, and by the afternoon the men reached Benton, where a supply train from Little Rock met them. Steele halted for the remainder of the day and evening.[99] The next morning—May 3—the lead elements of the column moved into Little Rock.[100] The hard march brought the Union troops to safety. They believed that the Confederates were trying to engage them in another battle, but this was not the case. Smith's lack of available pontoons halted the pursuit. The campaign ended with the Federals in Little Rock and the Confederates still south of the Saline River.

Smith and Price each showed poor judgment in their tactics at Jenkins' Ferry. Smith's lack of tactical skills and strategic vision caused the deaths of many brave men. Price fared no better. In hindsight, Marmaduke was by far the most capable leader for the Southerners. Confederate casualties at Jenkins' Ferry were listed as 800 to 1,000 killed, wounded, or missing out of 6,000 committed.[101] Union casualties were approximately 700 killed, wounded, and missing.[102]

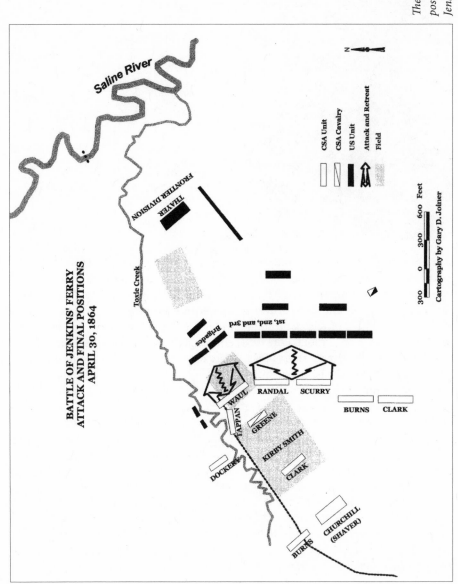

*The attack and final positions in the Battle of Jenkins' Ferry.*

In all the campaign in Arkansas, the Confederate losses were reported as 2,300 to the Union's 2,750.[103] Steele suffered huge losses in materiel, including 635 wagons, 2,500 mules, and 9 artillery pieces.[104] The Confederates, who did not travel with large trains, lost 35 wagons and 3 field pieces.[105]

Smith turned his army back to the little village of Tulip, located near the battlefield. On the night of April 30 both Scurry and Randal died of their wounds and were buried in the village graveyard.[106] For the next three days the army encamped while Smith pondered what to do. On May 3 he ordered his three divisions to return to Taylor.[107] They would not reach their Louisiana and Texas comrades in time to assist them in pursuit of Banks.

The Camden Expedition duplicated the failure of Banks's efforts in Louisiana. Banks's planning of broad aspects of the entire campaign left too many details for consideration. Steele did not want to participate in the expedition, but he had been compelled by Grant to do so. He faced unclear objectives. From the outset, Union commanders caused most of the difficulties encountered by their columns. The route planning for the columns was cumbersome and obtuse. Inadequate numbers of infantry were available and the cavalry failed to perform their primary mission of forward reconnaissance and foraging. The Federal columns were encumbered by large numbers of supply wagons and the men were allowed to consume rations too quickly. Steele allowed blacks to attach themselves to his column, placing their lives in danger, particularly if separated from it or captured during battle. Steele and his field commanders often placed their troops in exposed positions.

The Confederates exhibited a remarkable ability to march long distances quickly to counter the Union threat. Their field commanders, particularly Marmaduke and Fagan, displayed superb skills as tacticians. Marmaduke's and Walker's forces displayed extraordinary discipline, marching as much as sixty miles in quick order with little respite. However, the rapid marching took a toll on the men, and they were exhausted when ordered to attack. Price and Kirby Smith both displayed their meager talents as field commanders, resulting in useless retreats or, worse, the wholesale slaughter of their troops.

Smith brought three divisions to Arkansas, and the department commander largely destroyed each in a failed attempt to achieve glory. The three divisions were in a much better position to operate with Richard Taylor in Louisiana rather than chase an already fleeing enemy in Arkansas. If left in Louisiana the three divisions would have been in a position to trap the Union army on the Isle de Breville, or Cane River Island, south of Natchitoches. Adequate Confederate forces blocking the Union retreat at Monett's Ferry and larger numbers of cavalry pushing them south from Natchitoches may well have resulted in the loss of Banks's column and the destruction of Porter's fleet.

Ultimately, the Arkansas portion of the Union campaign ended with results similar to its counterpart in northwestern Louisiana—the primary objective was not taken, nor was it closely approached. Federal forces retreated in humiliation against determined foes that held the territory more firmly than they had prior to the Camden Expedition.

# CHAPTER 7

# Union Retreat in Louisiana

The battles of Mansfield and Pleasant Hill sealed the fate of the Union effort in Louisiana. Lack of communication continued to plague the Union forces. There was no feasible method for the Union column and the navy to check on the progress of the other. As the army found itself, under Banks's misguidance, in an almost inescapable trap, the navy also faced near destruction.

After Banks moved inland, Porter divided his fleet yet again. Only the shallow-draft gunboats could navigate the narrow river upstream from Grand Ecore, and these were used to protect the army's transport vessels. Porter found that his maps were better than those used by the army, but locations of streams and landings were not reliable. The admiral, learning that Banks had been defeated, began the difficult task of retrograding his fleet back to the relative safety of Grand Ecore. Both Porter and Banks discovered the problems of retreating from positions deep within hostile territory while at the same time contending with a determined opponent.

Confederate forces, now reduced in size by battle and the removal of three divisions to Arkansas, attempted to trap both the Union fleet and the army. Taylor found his forces were hard-pressed to accomplish both tasks. Local conditions on the Red River, thanks to the removal of most of the water into Bayou Pierre, slowed the progress of the fleet and gave the Confederate cavalry and artillery units opportunities to harass the fleet. Banks made another in a string of bad tactical decisions that allowed the Confederates both to chase and to flank his column. This offered perhaps the best opportunity during the campaign for the Confederates to capture the Union column.

Porter left Grand Ecore on the morning of April 7 with a much smaller but still powerful fleet. The slowly dropping river level forced him to leave the *Eastport* behind. His maps showed the river ahead to be narrow and winding, and the *Eastport*'s length and draft made the great ironclad a liability. Sandbars were emerging from the river's water, making shallow-draft vessels his only viable option. He chose his vessels for the final sprint to Shreveport for their firepower and their ability to navigate the tight meanders of the unpredictable river.[1]

Porter selected one ironclad and two monitors to lead this portion of the mission. The monitors were the *Osage* and *Neosho*. Each was equipped with two eleven-inch

*The* Osage. *Library of Congress LC 816-3126.*

naval smooth-bore guns in a single turret mounted at the bow. The monitors were sister boats, built by the great naval architect James Buchanan Eads of St. Louis. They were the only stern wheel monitors built during the war. In spite of their great weight, they needed only four and a half feet of water beneath their decks to float. With huge turrets in the bow and massive armored engine houses in the stern, the vessels tended to be unwieldy and difficult to steer in tight places. The ironclad was the *Chillicothe*. Two side-wheels and two screw propellers propelled this hybrid, which required almost seven feet of water below the waterline to get under way.[2]

The *Lexington,* constructed in 1860, was one of the oldest warships in the inland fleet. As a timberclad side-wheeler, *Lexington* used thick layers of wood to protect it from enemy guns and required six feet of water to stay afloat.[3]

Porter also selected two tinclads, vessels with thinner armor, usually one-half to three-quarters of an inch thick. These were the *Fort Hindman* and the *Cricket*. The *Fort Hindman* required only two feet four inches of water to float.[4] The *Cricket* was a stern-wheeler and had a draft of four feet.[5] Porter picked the *Cricket* as his flagship.

The remainder of the U.S. Navy's contingent consisted of the tugs *Dahlia* and *William H. Brown* and the supply transport *Benefit*. Of the three, the *William H. Brown* was the only one armed. It was large for a tug and was often used as a dispatch boat.[6]

These vessels guarded and herded the army's transports, at least twenty vessels. The quartermaster's boats held supplies for the main column and 1,600 of A. J. Smith's men of the 17th Corps under Brigadier General Thomas Kilby Smith. Kilby Smith had armed most, if not all, of these boats with army cannon mounted on the decks. He had also placed bales of cotton and sacks of oats on the decks from which his men could fire in relative safety.[7] Among the transports was Banks's headquarters boat, *Black Hawk*, which Porter detested as an insult to his own favorite command vessel by the same name.[8]

The fleet headed north and reached Campti at 5 P.M.[9] The next morning as the force got under way, the transport *Iberville* ran aground almost immediately and was wedged so tightly against a sand bar that it took several hours to get it afloat. The water level dropped at a steady rate. As Porter passed north of the Grand Ecore hill complex and the mouth of Bayou Pierre, he had no way of knowing that the river was starved for water because of the Confederate destruction of the Tones Bayou dam.

The *Iberville* was pulled off the bar, and the fleet slowly ascended the river as the crews called out the locations of snags in the channel bottom. Travel was slowed to just above steerage in the now gentle current. The fleet reached the town of Coushatta and the mouth of Bayou Coushatta or Coushatta Chute at 6 P.M. Kilby Smith sent a brigade ashore to guard the fleet from attack and they took two prisoners.[10]

At 9 A.M. on April 8 the fleet headed north again, moving in column due to the narrow, winding river. Porter saw the river road that Banks could have used. He also saw the fields of corn and herds of cattle upon which the army could have subsisted.[11] Other than the small band of Confederates seen at Coushatta, there was no opposition. The day passed uneventfully, as did the next. At 2 p.m. on April 10 the fleet reached the mouth of Loggy Bayou—or what Porter believed to be Loggy Bayou.[12] This body of water was not the same stream shown on his map.[13]

Lake Bistineau, lying to the east of the river, was one of several lakes created by the Great Raft. The lake had three outflows connecting to the Red River, the southernmost

*The* Fort Hindman. *Naval Historical Center Photo No. NH61569.*

*The* Cricket. *Naval Historical Center Photo NH 55524.*

being Coushatta Chute. The other two were channels of Loggy Bayou. The Union maps were not correct in the positions or names of these streams. In fact, Porter did not know specifically where he was. In his *Naval History of the Civil War* Porter said that he reached Springfield Landing, his rendezvous point, within an hour of his appointed time.[14] Springfield Landing is four miles west of the Red River. In his official report, he said he reached Loggy Bayou.[15] In his post-war *Incidents and Anecdotes,* Porter stated that he reached the mouth of the Shreveport River, a stream that does not exist.[16] We may never know just how far north he came. If the water level was sufficiently deep for his convoy to stay afloat, he must have traveled another four river miles and anchored opposite a small stream one mile south of the foot of Scopini's cutoff. It is possible that the admiral was as close as two miles south from Tones Bayou or as much as four to five miles below the bayou.[17]

While anchored opposite the stream, Kilby Smith sent a landing party to scatter some Confederates who were watching them. Then, after traveling another mile, Porter and Smith saw a sight that halted any further progress. Porter described it in a letter to General Sherman:

FLAG-SHIP CRICKET, OFF ALEXANDRIA, LA.,
April 16, 1864.
Maj. Gen. W. T. SHERMAN,
Comdg. Mil. Div. of the Miss., Nashville, Tenn.:

When I arrived at Springfield Landing I found a sight that made me laugh; it was the smartest thing I ever knew the rebels to do. They had gotten that huge steamer, New Falls City, across Red River, 1 mile above Leggy [*sic*] Bayou, 15 feet

of her on shore on each side, the boat broken down in the middle, and a sandbar making below her. An invitation in large letters to attend a ball in Shreveport was kindly left stuck up by the rebels, which invitation we were never able
to accept. . . .

DAVID D. PORTER,
Rear-Admiral.[18]


Porter began working on the problem of moving the *New Falls City* and Kilby
Smith landed troops to secure the position. Shortly after this, Captain William
Andres of the 14th New York Cavalry rode up with fifty of his troopers and told them
of Banks's defeat on the eighth. He carried with him several dispatches and specific
verbal orders for Kilby Smith to return to Grand Ecore.[19] No mention was made of
Porter's fleet.

Smith and Porter decided that they must return to Grand Ecore before the Confederates could bring their artillery to the banks of the river and effectively blockade
them. That could easily lead to either the capture or the destruction of the fleet. Porter
and Smith ordered additional artillery placed on the upper decks of the transports,
and barricades of any materials available were made for firing positions for the infan-
trymen.[20] Now the fleet began the arduous downstream passage from the deepest
penetration into the Red River Valley by Federal forces.

The fleet was in a difficult position. From the time they entered the Narrows the
vessels had to contend with the winding river and shallow channel bottoms. They
were wedged bow to stern with the *New Falls City* blocking them. The channel was
so narrow that they could not turn around. This forced the largest vessels to back

The New Falls City. *Howard Tilton Memorial Library, Tulane University, New Orleans.*

*The* Black Hawk, *Admiral Porter's flagship. Library of Congress LC 816-3140.*

down the river stern-first for several miles.[21] The physical strains of this type of move-ment over an extended course caused severe problems with steerage assemblies and major mechanical malfunctions. Snags in the channel and along the shore made the backward passage even more difficult. To make matters worse, the Confederates had hastily sent men and as much artillery as they could muster to high points along the banks north of Grand Ecore to harass the fleet.

Almost immediately the *Chillicothe* impaled itself on a submerged tree, which pierced the hull. This halted the fleet for more than two hours. The *Chillicothe* was unable to move until the *Black Hawk,* using the *Chillicothe's* hawser, freed it.[22] Other vessels suffered damage as rudders became unshipped and paddles splintered, a com-mon occurrence. As these boats were dealing with their own problems, the *Emerald* ran hard aground.[23] The Confederates began to fire at the fleet, and the sound of minié balls careening off hulls, casemates, and superstructure of the *Benefit, Black Hawk,* and *Osage* was ear shattering.[24] These vessels responded to the ineffective long arm fire with the *Osage's* eleven-inch naval guns, which "must have been like hunting par-tridges with a howitzer."[25] When the fleet reached Coushatta Chute on the morning of April 12, the *Lexington* collided with the transport *Rob Roy,* spearing the latter's wheelhouse and launch and damaging its chimneys.[26]

Later on the twelfth, the fleet approached Blair's Landing, which was due west of Pleasant Hill and approximately forty-five miles north of Grand Ecore. Tom Green's cavalry had moved there to harass and, if possible, halt the progress of the fleet. Porter's fleet, transports, and armed vessels alike passed the landing under cannon and small arms fire.[27] Some naval personnel were wounded and the vessels received damage from the Confederate artillery, which was well placed and concealed. Bringing up the rear of the flotilla were the timberclad *Lexington* and the monitor *Osage.* Strapped to the *Osage* was the transport *Black Hawk.* In making the tight turn above the landing, the *Osage* slewed and ran aground. Green and his 2,500 men were near the bank at this time. They dismounted, tied their horses, formed into three ranks, and began pouring fire into the three boats. Banks's *Black Hawk* took such devastating fire that forty soldiers on the decks had to be evacuated into the safe confines of the cramped metal hull of the *Osage*. All hands aboard followed. Later Porter stated upon examination of the *Black Hawk* "that there was not a place six inches square not perforated by a bullet."[28]

Porter was fortunate that the unprotected wooden transports had passed the landing earlier. If Green and his 2,500 men had had more artillery, the scene would have been much worse. Thomas O. Selfridge Jr., commanding the *Osage,* wrote to Admiral Porter some sixteen years later, recounting it as "one of the most curious fights of the war, 2,500 infantry against a gunboat aground."[29]

The *Osage* and the *Black Hawk* strapped together were still aground with the wooden surfaces of the *Black Hawk* riddled like Swiss cheese from musket and artillery fire. The vessels were forced to work the monitor off the bar and allow the *Lexington* to carry on the fight. After an intense engagement of more than an hour with no hint of the Confederates lessening the strength of their attack, the *Lexington* finally silenced Green's four-gun battery with eight-inch guns.[30] Shortly before this duel, the *Osage* managed to move from the bar on which it was grounded. It cut the lines to the *Black Hawk,* and Selfridge let the current move the boat close to the Confederates without the engines running. Selfridge brought one of his eleven-inch guns to bear on the troops and, at a distance of only twenty yards, fired a load of grape shot and canister, decapitating General Green. Selfridge aimed the big naval gun with mirrors rigged to function as a periscope, its first use in warfare.[31] The Confederates broke ranks and moved away from the riverbank.[32] There had been very few casualties, but Green's loss was catastrophic for Taylor. Although Union estimates of Confederate casualties estimated two hundred to five hundred killed and wounded, Confederate losses were quite low, perhaps less than ten. Union losses were also negligible.[33]

Porter kept the vessels moving past sunset and into the night. With only torches and perhaps moonlight to light the way, this was a very perilous journey. Normally the admiral did not take such risks, but the prospect of rejoining the vessels at Grand Ecore and of the support of the army to keep the Confederate army at bay were powerful incentives. The flotilla finally anchored at 1 A.M. on the morning of the thirteenth. Several transports had run aground during the night. After dawn the next morning, the quartermaster's boat *John Warner* went aground and delayed the progress of the fleet. Porter made several attempts to extricate the *John Warner* throughout the day. The Confederates, who had placed cannon on a high bank, began to fire at the vessels before *Osage* drove them off. The *Rob Roy* then lost its rudder and had to be placed undertow by the transport *Clara Bell.*[34]

The *John Warner* resisted all attempts to remove it from the sandy river bottom to which it was firmly affixed. Fearing that the Confederates were preparing a trap, Kilby Smith at daylight on the fourteenth ordered his transports and their protecting gunboats ahead to Campti. He left the tinclad *Fort Hindman* to stay with the *John Warner* for protection. The next day the *Fort Hindman* managed to pull the vessel off the bar and they rejoined the fleet at Grand Ecore on the fifteenth, where the

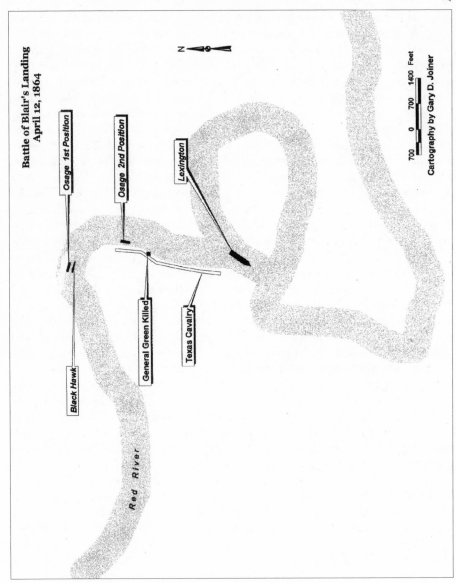

**Battle of Blair's Landing**
**April 12, 1864**

Osage 1st Position

Osage 2nd Position

Lexington

Black Hawk

General Green Killed

Texas Cavalry

Red River

N

700  0  700  1400  Feet

Cartography by Gary D. Joiner

*Battle of Blair's Landing.*

naval forces were safely under the army's guns.[35] The navy was now finally back in contact with the army, largely due to the skills and composure of Porter and T. Kilby Smith.[36]

Upon arriving at Grand Ecore, Porter visited Banks in his headquarters tent. The admiral found Banks's accommodations well appointed, even opulent for field conditions. Banks was dressed in a fine dressing gown, velvet cap, and comfortable slippers. He was reading *Scott's Tactics,* his nightly ritual.[37]

Banks made it plain that he considered he had won the Battle of Mansfield and that the subsequent Battle of Pleasant Hill was simply a withdrawing action. Banks gave Porter the same excuse he had used with A. J. Smith, that he only withdrew for lack of water. The admiral informed him that, if that were the case, he was only six miles from water at Mansfield. He left the general "under the delusion that he had won the battle of Mansfield, or Sabine Cross Roads, or whatever name that unfortunate affair was known by."[38] Disgusted with Banks and his excuses for retreat, the admiral later wrote "that he should have read it [*Scott's Tactics*] before he went to Sabine Cross Roads."[39] Porter told Banks that under no circumstance would the navy go back upstream.[40]

With the river falling rapidly at Grand Ecore, the fleet and the army were forced to withdraw from this region that had held so much promise for them. The army began marching along the river road to Alexandria. On April 16, with some navigation problems and further mechanical failures, the fleet proceeded downstream three miles, with *Eastport* in the lead. The Confederates in mid-March, knowing that the fleet could only return on the same route it took north, had placed six torpedoes (or mines) below the ferry at Grand Ecore.[41] The *Eastport* struck one of these Confederate torpedoes, but only a few people aboard felt the shock. The vessel took on water rapidly and came to rest on the bottom. Fortunately, the bottom was only a few feet at most below the keel and it settled into the soft sand.[42]

The *Eastport* became a potential obstacle as threatening as the *New Falls City,* but perhaps more deadly. It was wedged at the forefront of the flotilla and blocked its passage. The pump boat *Champion No. 5* was used to bilge out the water. The guns were removed and placed on flat rafts towed by the *Cricket.* The captain, Lieutenant Commander Seth Ledyard Phelps, and his crew worked day and night to save the vessel.[43] It was finally refloated on April 21, and with some groundings due to its still taking on water it proceeded downstream another forty miles. Near the town of Montgomery it ran into submerged snags and became firmly stuck on the twenty-sixth. The *Champion No. 3* and the *Fort Hindman* joined the pump boat *Champion No. 5* in attempts to wrest the vessel free. As the boats tried to move the behemoth back and forth, the efforts to save it only worsened the situation. The captain of the *Fort Hindman,* Acting Volunteer Lieutenant John Pearce and Phelps of the *Eastport* made several attempts to rock the *Eastport* free, but they were doomed to failure. Porter received news that the water level downstream was falling. Knowing that the fleet was in danger of being bottled up behind the great ironclad, Porter ordered a ton of powder placed throughout the vessel. Combustible materials available at the time were packed into the boat and at 1:45 P.M. on April 26 it was destroyed.[44]

The vessels that had been aiding and guarding the *Eastport*—the *Fort Hindman, Cricket, Juliet, Champion No. 3,* and *Champion No. 5* made their way downstream and approached the mouth of the Cane River. The Confederates had assembled four artillery pieces of Captain Florian O. Cornay's 1st (Louisiana) Battery, along with two hundred riflemen from Polignac's Division.[45] They heaped fire on the vessels, and the *Champion No. 3* was sunk. Below decks, more than one hundred slaves being carried to freedom were scalded to death. The *Champion No. 5* was heavily damaged, grounded and abandoned by the crew. The *Fort Hindman,* now commanded by Phelps, the *Cricket,* and the *Juliet* were severely damaged but passed through the gauntlet.[46] A tribute to the ferocity of this attack is that in five minutes the *Cricket* was hit thirty-eight times, and suffered twenty-five dead and wounded. This constituted fully half of the crew. The *Juliet* also lost half of its crew, suffering fifteen killed and wounded. The *Fort Hindman* suffered three killed and four or five wounded.[47]

Porter, aboard the *Cricket,* displayed great personal bravery in keeping the tinclad in the fight. A shell hit the aft gun and killed the gun crew. Another eliminated the forward gun and its crew. Cornay's Confederates were pouring accurate fire on the gunboats. A third shell hit the fire room, where the stokers kept steam pressure up in the boilers. All were killed but one man. Porter gathered some refugee slaves that the *Cricket* had taken aboard, showed them how to fire a gun, and turned them into a gun crew to try to keep the Confederates' heads down long enough for the vessel to escape. He then went to the engine room and, finding the chief engineer dead, put the assistant engineer in charge and told him to get the steam pressure up. Porter then went to the pilothouse and discovered that another shell had wounded one of the pilots and that the remaining crew on the bridge were hiding. With his customary aplomb, Porter took charge of the *Cricket* and moved it past the battery that had nearly sent it to the bottom.[48]

Porter's fleet limped into the northern approaches to Alexandria with the Red River falling rapidly. He had lost the most powerful ironclad in the fleet. Two of his tugs/pump boats had also been sunk, and three of his tinclads had been severely damaged. Most of the army transport vessels had received either mechanical or battle damage. To make matters worse, the river had fallen a full six feet and most of his fleet was now trapped above the Falls.[49]

With Porter's move upriver from Grand Ecore, the fleet was reduced in both firepower and effectiveness. The admiral left his largest ironclads at his forward base due to water conditions. The reduced fleet was still potent, but not the larger ironclad hunting squadron assembled for the expedition. Forced to retreat, Porter discovered this reduced flotilla was inadequate for the river environment. Determined attacks by the Confederates cost the navy boats and lives. Porter's most egregious loss was that of the *Eastport.*

The Confederates proved that with limited resources they could disrupt Union plans. This was particularly true of the Union navy when it was not protected by substantial numbers of soldiers. The Rebels used the engineering diversion at Tones Bayou to divert approximately 75 percent of the water from the Red River. They nearly stranded the fleet above Alexandria and, if not for the seamanship of Selfridge, may have captured the *Osage* for use against the fleet. Tom Green's death was a severe blow to Taylor's plans, but also put an end to serious attempts at capturing Porter's boats.

The army was also having its share of problems. After the retreat from Pleasant Hill, Banks made a series of very poor decisions. He tried to deflect the criticism he knew would come from his superiors. He fired veteran commanders who would offer opposing views, he marched his army onto an elongated island that led to potential entrapment, he chose a route on that island that kept the army away from the naval guns, and he barely escaped a Confederate trap.

Banks's column was full of griping, angry men who believed that they were betrayed by incompetent commanders. The words of improvised songs floated up and down the line. One ditty sung by Massachusetts troops to the tune of "When Johnny Comes Marching Home," had a chorus of "We all skedaddled to Grand Ecore." The troops sometimes ended the bitter song with a yell of "Napoleon P. Banks."[50] The soldiers began referring to the commanding general as "Mister Banks," referring to his lack of military training and his accession to the lofty rank of major general without ever wearing so much as a private's stripes.[51]

The column covered the distance from Pleasant Hill to Grand Ecore in three days. Banks ordered the men to expand the outer perimeter of the Confederates' former defenses with the army's thirty thousand men packed into a fortification of about six square miles.[52] He believed Taylor had twenty-five thousand men to contest him.[53] Banks, apparently panicked, ordered the remaining division at Alexandria under Brigadier General Cuvier Grover to come to Grand Ecore immediately.[54] He then sent a message to Pass Cavallo, Texas, instructing Major General John McClernand to strip his command of all but two thousand soldiers and bring most of his force to Grand Ecore. McClernand was to take over command of the 13th Corps, replacing the wounded Ransom.[55]

Banks then reported to Grant the details of the campaign thus far. His major points were the following: (1) Shreveport was the prime focus of the Confederates defenses; (2) the Confederates were on the defensive; (3) the Rebels had been planning an invasion of Missouri; (4) Steele's advance on the line he was using rendered Banks no assistance at all; and (5) gunboats were useless to the army, considering the shallow depth of the river. He concluded saying that he intended to advance on Shreveport using a different route.[56] Just as this missive was complete, word came from Sherman demanding the return of A. J. Smith and his men.[57] Banks countermanded Sherman's order since he was senior to Smith's commander.[58]

Banks made an effort to shift blame and bolster his own support, lagging among the troops and within his staff, and fired his chief of staff, Brigadier General Charles P. Stone.[59] He relieved Albert Lee from command of the cavalry division and sent him to New Orleans.[60] With Lee was "Gold Lace" Dudley, who was also relieved of command. Scathing letters were attached to the men's files.[61] Banks replaced Stone with his protégé William Dwight.[62]

While the navy bumped and scraped its way along the sandy, rock-scattered river bottom, Banks led his men south toward Alexandria. The high bluffs of Grand Ecore did not directly connect to the river road. Four miles south of Grand Ecore lay

Natchitoches. From there the road, which ran along Red River, crossed Cane River. The channel of Cane River had once been the main course of Red River. These two channels ran roughly parallel for thirty miles before joining at Monett's Ferry. He chose the Cane River Road; however, it afforded him little assistance from the fleet until he reached the ferry. It followed a channel that was located west of the river and was not open to the naval vessels.[63]

The river road followed the twisting channel of the Cane River, adding another fifteen miles to cross the island formed by the two streams. Had Banks taken an alternative route, traveling west and then turning south, he would have left the safety of the fleet and reentered the "howling wilderness."

Banks placed A. J. Smith's Division in Natchitoches as a safeguard between Richard Taylor and his own army. Smith's men would be the last to leave, and on April 21 at 5 P.M. the column began to move.[64] The men torched the few buildings in Grand Ecore.[65] Three brigades of cavalry, now allowed to perform their duties properly, screened the column. As twilight led to darkness, the cavalrymen burned homesteads and barns to light the way for the infantry and to exact some revenge. Following the cavalry was the infantry led by Grover's Division, just arrived from Alexandria. Banks positioned the combined trains behind these fresh troops. Next came the remainder of the 19th Corps, then the 13th Corps. After the column passed through Natchitoches, A. J. Smith's 16th Corps and one brigade of cavalry brought up the rear.[66]

Banks received messages that Taylor was moving his forces south to cut the Union forces off at Monett's Ferry.[67] If the Confederates made a strong position at the ferry,

*The defenses at Grand Ecore. Photograph taken by a U.S. Army photographer during the campaign. LSUS Archives, Noel Memorial Library, Louisiana State University, Baton Rouge.*

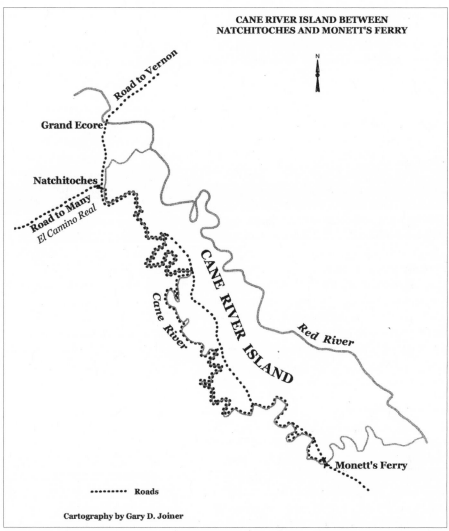

Map of Cane River Island.

the column would be cut off on this island and, possibly, forced to surrender. Banks now drove his men to reach the ferry before the Confederates could arrive. Rebel advance troops cut trees to block the road ahead of Banks, slowing the column and raising tensions. There were no large streams on the island from which the men could fill their canteens. The banks of the Cane River were steep and not easily traversed. The men were pushed to the limit of their endurance with some staggering, some sleeping while marching, and officers often asleep in their saddles.[68]

Taylor sent Green's cavalry, now under the command of Major General John Wharton, to harass the rearguard. The Confederate cavalry was adept at hit-and-run tactics and this added to the charged atmosphere of the column. Wharton's timely arrival saved Natchitoches from being torched by A. J. Smith's men.[69]

News of events at both the front and rear of the column moved quickly from unit to unit. The Union march took on the aura of a nervous herd of cattle ready to stampede. The angry troops devastated the countryside, leaving nothing of value behind. A. J. Smith's "gorillas" destroyed everything in sight.[70] Taylor later wrote that local residents told him that eastern troops under Banks tried to stop the westerners but were unable to do so.[71] The pattern of devastation continued to the end of the campaign.

The column pressed on through the night of April 21 and finally halted at 2:30 A.M. to allow the rear units to catch up. The lead elements had covered twenty miles in a little more than nine hours. At 11 A.M. on April 22, the cavalry and infantry units took up the march again, just as the rearguard units were closing on the column. As the men began to bed down, Banks received word from scouts that the Confederates were on his side of the ferry.[72] At midnight he ordered Emory to take the army except the rearguard and secure the ferry landing. Banks then ordered A. J. Smith to send a brigade to assist Emory. Smith refused, stating that he could not spare any men.[73] Emory pressed forward and by 4:30 A.M. drove the Confederate pickets across the river. As dawn broke, Emory and his men could finally see what awaited them. Across the river on a high and wooded bluff, the Confederates had mounted numerous cannons. The position overlooked any line of approach the Federal troops might mount on that narrow tip of the island.[74]

Taylor's troops, consisting of eight batteries of artillery and 1,600 cavalry were sent to seal off the ferry.[75] They commanded the best ground for miles around. General Bee was ordered by both Taylor and Wharton to hold the ferry crossing and not let Banks escape. What Emory and his men did not know was that Confederate infantry under Polignac had secured the ford opposite Cloutierville and that other infantry under Brigadier General St. John R. Liddell was in position at Colfax on the other side of Red River.[76] Wharton's cavalry was pressing A. J. Smith so hard it was possible that he might be unable to hold the Confederates at bay.[77] If the column was to retreat to Grand Ecore, it would be forced to fight every inch of the way. All avenues of escape for the Army of the Gulf had been blocked. Emory sent his cavalry forward only to be driven out of range by the Rebel artillery. He then formed a line with his infantry to watch the Confederates and sent the cavalry to find another exit.[78] None was found. Taylor had achieved his goal.

Some of the Union troopers approached a black man and asked him if there was a place to cross the river other than the ferry and were told of a point two miles behind them. The man led them to a ford that was not covered by the Confederates.[79] Grover's Division led by Brigadier General Henry Birge, Benedict's Brigade now led by Colonel Francis Fessenden, and the remnants of the 13th Corps were selected to make the flank attack.[80]

The Union troops led by Birge made a long loop around both Cane River and the Confederates blocking the ferry position. They approached in line of battle with skirmishers deployed to their front. This was a difficult maneuver because the terrain was wooded and interspersed marshy lands. They emerged unseen onto a broad cotton

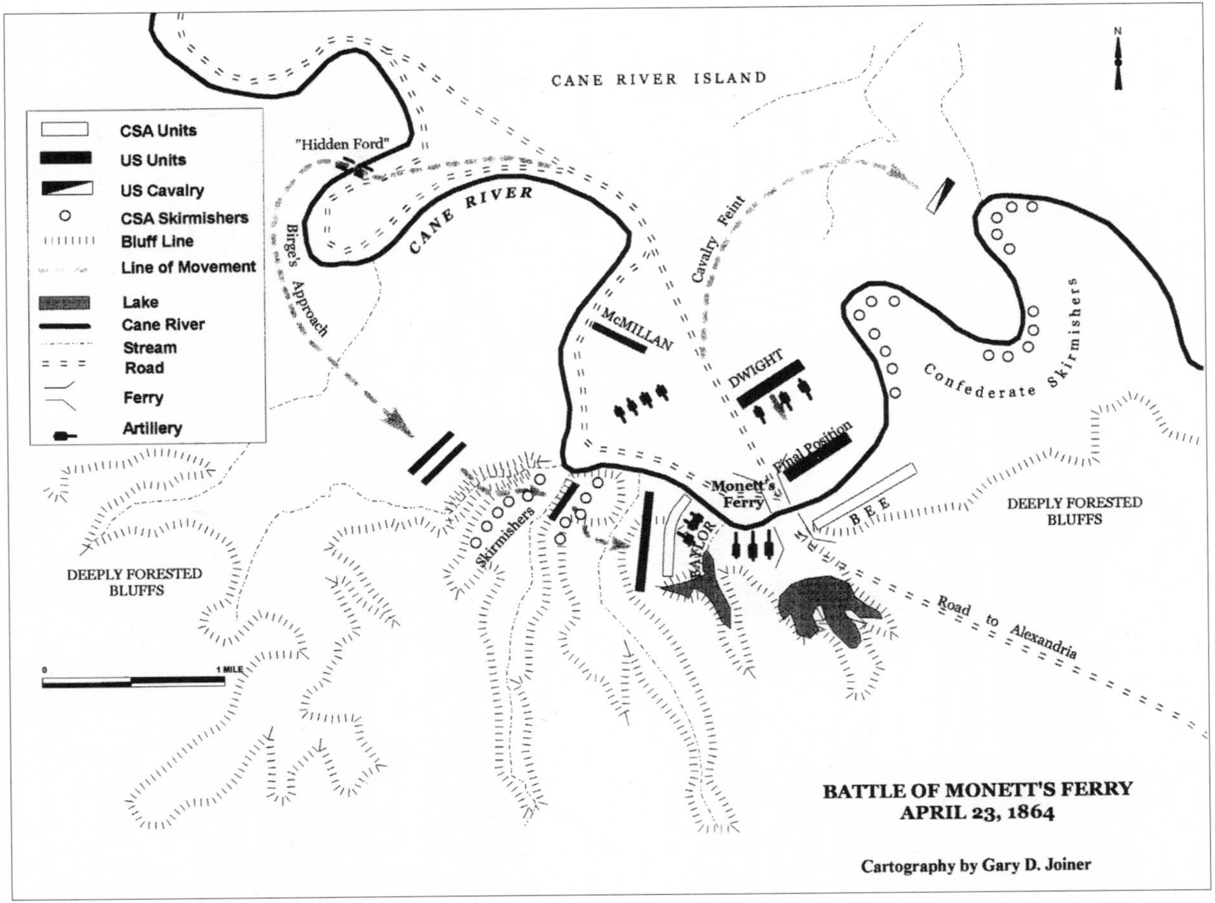

The Battle of
Monett's Ferry.

BATTLE OF MONETT'S FERRY
APRIL 23, 1864

Cartography by Gary D. Joiner

CANE RIVER ISLAND

CANE RIVER

"Hidden Ford"

Birge's Approach

Cavalry Feint

McMILLAN

DWIGHT

Final Position

Monett's Ferry

BEE

TAYLOR

Confederate

Skirmishers

Skirmishers

DEEPLY FORESTED
BLUFFS

DEEPLY FORESTED
BLUFFS

Road to Alexandria

N

CSA Units
US Units
US Cavalry
CSA Skirmishers
Bluff Line
Line of Movement
Lake
Cane River
Stream
Road
Ferry
Artillery

1 MILE
0

field. After crossing the field, the troops climbed a wooded ridge, where their skirmishers encountered Bee's pickets. From this ridge, Birge and his men could see the main Confederate position a quarter of a mile ahead and across an open field. They could also look down at some of their own troops on the opposite side of Cane River.[81]

Birge allowed Fessenden to prepare the attack. Benedict's old brigade held the right of the line and Birge's men held the left. Cameron's Division was in reserve. Fessenden ordered the men to fix bayonets and to wait to fire in volley in order to increase effectiveness of the fire. The Union line moved forward and Fessenden was one of the first casualties, suffering a wound to his right leg, later amputated. The line wavered as it descended the ridge and crossed a slough. The field they now crossed was in the shape of a trapezoid and this forced the troops to crowd closer together. As the Union line reached the foot of the ridge where the Confederates were lodged, they charged.[82]

The Confederates were Colonel George Baylor and the 2nd Arizona Cavalry. Seeing the size of the force to their front, the Rebels fell back to a line behind an overgrown fence. Here Colonel Isham Chisum's 2nd Texas Partisan Rangers Cavalry Regiment joined them. Baylor asked Bee for two regiments to plug a hole in his flank, but none were sent.[83]

Birge halted his men and dressed their line. He then rode with some of his staff to examine what lay ahead of them. As the men went into a gully they were hit by murderous artillery and small arms fire, the location of which they could not determine. At this moment Birge and his party rode back through the line to save themselves, creating confusion. The Union regiments simply hit the ground or broke and ran. Two regiments crossed into a ravine for cover.[84]

Emory watched from across Cane River and directed an artillery battery to provide fire support. He ordered his troops to make a feint as if forcing the ferry crossing to distract the Confederates. The ruse worked and the Rebels split their artillery fire between Birge and Emory. Bee then received word, incorrectly, that his right flank was being attacked.[85] There were no Federal forces there, but Bee concluded that Banks had out maneuvered him and that the battle was lost. Bee ordered Baylor, who was expecting fire support, to retreat.[86]

Taylor was south of Cloutierville doing his best to pin down A. J. Smith. The Confederates here were making progress and Taylor believed his trap was working.[87] Bee retreated and left the ferry landing open. Emory crossed and ordered the cavalry division to chase Bee. Emory's troops took a wrong road and missed the fleeing Confederates.[88] The road to Alexandria lay open for the Union column. A. J. Smith's men were the last to cross the river at two in the afternoon the next day. Wharton had driven them to the ferry just as Polignac joined up his forces with Taylor.[89] The Confederates were now at the narrow end of the island and the Union forces were gone. In the running battles of April 22 and 23, Union losses were three hundred killed, wounded, and missing. Confederate losses were less than half that. Bee had suffered only fifty casualties.[90]

Taylor censured Bee and later fired him.[91] Kirby Smith and Bee's peers defended him, but his premature actions in retreat placed the tactical blame squarely on him for the battle's loss.[92] Ultimately, perhaps the loss is equally the fault of Kirby Smith, who removed three divisions of infantry to chase Steele in Arkansas and thus left Taylor with inadequate resources to trap Banks. Taylor did not have enough men to keep the Union forces from creating a bridgehead at the ferry. Emory could have forced it by the next day, especially with Birge cooperating in a flanking maneuver.

The Union column force-marched into Alexandria with the lead elements entering the town on the afternoon of April 25.[93] At the rear of the column, A. J. Smith's men scorched the earth around them and arrived the next day.[94] As they marched in, hordes of runaway slaves entered with them, freed from the torched plantations along the river. Franklin issued orders against looting, pillaging, and burning, but the evidence of destruction was seen in the charred ruins of the plantations and homesteads north of Alexandria.[95]

Banks only vaguely realized the political firestorm in which he was involved. The campaign had begun five weeks before his return to the central Louisiana town. In that short time, Grant had become general in chief, Halleck was chief of staff, and Sherman was making final preparations for his thrust into Georgia. Banks's carefully worded messages to his superiors, to Lincoln, and to others concerning tactical situations had been mixed with exuberant exaggerations and expectations. He was not privy to conversations and letters exchanged among the people with whom he was communicating. He was also unaware of newspaper reports and letters from within his own command condemning his actions.[96]

Grant sent Banks orders on March 31 that were plainly stated. First, if Banks captured Shreveport, he was to hand over the city to Steele and let the navy handle the defense of the river. Second, with the sole exception of the Rio Grande River, Banks was to withdraw from every point he occupied on the Texas coast. Third, he was to reduce garrison posts and troop concentrations to compose a force of twenty-five thousand troops to take Mobile.[97] Banks received the orders on April 18 while the army was at Grand Ecore.[98] While Grant's orders were being delivered to Banks, Banks's message of April 2 was being forwarded to Grant. This letter told Grant of Banks's intention of chasing Kirby Smith into Texas.[99]

The letter infuriated Grant. It meant that that his timetable in the East would be delayed. He had planned for Mobile to be taken or at least attacked by May 1. Mobile was critical to the upcoming campaigns because it would tie down Confederate forces under Lieutenant General Leonidas Polk in Mississippi and Alabama and would keep them away from Sherman's path through Georgia. Failure to take Mobile would create another problem for Sherman. Once deep in Georgia, Sherman's anticipated rapid movement would strain his extended supply lines. Polk's army could be in a position southwest of Sherman, thereby creating the possibility of entrapment. With Mobile under no pressure of attack, Polk was free to operate as he saw fit.

On April 17 Grant sent Major General David Hunter to Banks with a copy of his orders. He was to make it very plain to Banks that Mobile was more important than Shreveport. If he found Banks had taken Shreveport and was in east Texas, he was to order Banks to retrace his steps and prepare for the attack on Mobile.[100] Hunter arrived in Alexandria on April 27.

On April 18 other correspondence was generated between Secretary of War Stanton and the naval base at Cairo, Illinois, Porter's headquarters. Stanton was told that navy dispatches had been received from Porter explaining that Banks had been defeated at Mansfield, retreated to Pleasant Hill, and had fought another battle there, which he had won.[101] At that point no mention was made of the retreat to Grand Ecore. Stanton also received the first newspaper reports about the battles. Stanton immediately sent the naval dispatches and newspaper reports to Grant.[102] Shortly after this, Stanton received word from Cairo that Sherman's aide, Brigadier General John M. Corse, had arrived there with word from A. J. Smith that Banks had lost four thousand men, sixteen guns, two hundred wagons, and had retreated to Grand Ecore with his force in very poor condition.[103] These were forwarded to Grant as well.

Grant was furious. He telegraphed Halleck that he wanted Banks removed from command and replaced by Major General Joseph J. Reynolds, then in command of New Orleans.[104] Halleck took Grant's telegram to President Lincoln, who told the chief of staff to delay action on Banks's removal. Lincoln needed New England in the upcoming November elections, so firing Banks was politically out of the question.[105]

On April 25 Grant issued an order countermanding his demand that A. J. Smith and his men be sent to Sherman.[106] This was done to protect the fleet and was based on reports from Porter to Secretary of the Navy Gideon Welles.[107] On the same day, Grant received an anonymous letter from (apparently) an officer in the 13th Corps railing against Banks's deplorable mismanagement.[108] This was too much. On April 27 Halleck ordered Banks to turn over command to the next ranking officer and return to New Orleans and carry out previous instructions, the attack on Mobile.[109] The order was not delivered since it was apparently aboard the *City Belle,* a transport packet, when it was attacked on May 4.[110] Grant abandoned the attack on Mobile, realizing that troops from west of the Mississippi could not feasibly be moved in time to coordinate attacks.[111] He then suggested that the Gulf region be reorganized. Grant even suggested to Halleck that he take over command of the Army of the Gulf. Halleck declined.[112] Grant and Halleck then informed Banks that no troops were to be withdrawn from the region at that time.[113]

Lincoln was silent on Banks's removal, certainly adding to the delay in action on reallocating forces for the spring campaigns. Although no formal written communication exists, Lincoln must have agreed to the wishes of Halleck and Grant.[114] On May 7 Major General Edward R. S. Canby was given command of the newly reorganized Military Division of West Mississippi, including the Departments of the Gulf and Arkansas.[115] A delicate balance was struck in this promotion. Canby was given broad discretionary powers in his command. Banks was to command the Department of the Gulf, but as a subordinate officer to Canby. Banks's position still carried the trappings of power, but it was only an illusion.[116] Banks, of course, knew nothing of this. He was in Alexandria with his army and the fleet was trapped above the Falls with Taylor and his Confederates at his heels.

Banks, faced with a disgruntled and potentially mutinous army, fired commanders not loyal to him. He shifted blame away from himself to save his career in any manner possible. His attempt to take a shortcut through Cane River Island, ostensibly to remain near the fleet, almost cost him the army. Only the lack of sufficient Confederate opposition and a faltering will by the Confederate general on the scene saved the Union army from ruin. Banks's loss of command discipline, particularly among western troops, led to the torching of the countryside between Natchitoches and Alexandria.

Banks's decision to move his army onto Cane River Island offered Taylor his best opportunity to trap the Union force. The Confederate stand at Monett's Ferry should have worked. Taylor's inability to provide Bee with reinforcements combined with Bee's lack of aggressive leadership allowed the Federal troops to escape to Alexandria.

Following the campaign, the Joint Committee on the Conduct of the War heard testimony from every officer that Banks fired. It gave each witness ample time and room to explain their actions and those of their commander. The views of the veteran officers were uniform in denouncing Banks's credibility as a soldier.

As the army struggled southeast, the navy was fighting for survival. The navy straggled into Alexandria following close fighting because Porter had lost vessels to enemy action and the vagaries of the river. Several of the army's transports required repair from pierced hulls and damage above the waterline from enemy fire and collisions. The admiral saw the water levels falling at an alarming pace and realized his fleet was trapped above the Falls. Normally confident, Porter's resolve was shaken as he considered the destruction of his fleet to keep it from falling into enemy hands. There seemed no way out of the dilemma. Near the time that a decision had to be made to destroy or abandon the fleet, Lieutenant Colonel Joseph Bailey suggested a solution that was to make him famous during the war and give him the highest awards his country bestowed.

The Confederates were placed in the unenviable situation of having their foe bottled up in a relatively small area and unable to do much about it. Taylor observed his enemy trapped within a defensive ring surrounding Alexandria. The river in places appeared to be a string of ponds connected by rivulets. The fleet barely floated in the shallows, stranded upstream from the falls, the lowest water that the boats would have to cross before reaching safety in the deep water beyond. The Confederates had adequate artillery and cavalry to keep the enemy in sight and occupied but inadequate infantry to lay siege to the town. Taylor dispatched units to harass naval units below Alexandria, but he could not control the river and totally stop naval traffic. When it appeared that the fleet might be his, Taylor and his men witnessed an engineering miracle that changed the course of the campaign.

Taylor was in a peculiar position. He had surrounded an army of thirty-one thousand men with eighty cannon and a huge fleet of warships, with only six thousand men.[117] Banks had pulled everyone he could into Alexandria and had begun fortifying the town. This left the interior of Louisiana devoid of Union forces. Taylor had cavalry patrols operating at Fort DeRussy and on Bayou Teche.[118] He positioned artillery batteries at various points on the river below Alexandria, including Dunn's Bayou and the very important crossing at David's Ferry.[119] Union forces were bottled up at

Plaquemine in Iberville Parish, Baton Rouge, New Orleans, Brashear City, and of course, Alexandria. Taylor waited for the divisions that had been diverted to Arkansas to return, but they never arrived.

Captain John A. West's Grosse Tete (Louisiana) Flying Artillery, under Lieutenant W. H. Lyne, was sent to David's Ferry, located on the Red River about thirty miles below Alexandria. They almost immediately engaged and burned the transport *Emma* on May 1.[120] On May 4 they attacked and captured the *City Belle* on its way to Alexandria with reinforcements. On board were seven hundred men of the 120th Ohio Infantry. About half of these men were captured and the remainder were killed or wounded.[121] Subsequent reports stated that the *City Belle* was destroyed in the attack but later salvaged by the Rebels.[122]

The same day, the *John Warner* and the *Covington* left Alexandria. They were joined by the *Signal*. The *John Warner* carried the men of the 56th Ohio Infantry who were leaving on veterans' furloughs.[123] The vessels had received small arms fire throughout the day. At night the small convoy tied up on the riverbank about twenty miles south of Alexandria. Confederates fired at them as they ate their evening meal.[124] The next morning the gunboats got under way and at 4:45 A.M., as they reached Dunn's Bayou, the *Warner* was fired upon by artillery and musketry. The *Covington* and *Signal* fired back on the attackers. The Confederate artillery disabled the *Warner's* rudders and it drifted to the south bank below the attack. The Rebel artillery continued to fire at the vessel and was joined by Confederate cavalry. It was pounded into a floating pile of debris.[125] The 56th Ohio, still aboard, was torn to shreds. The *Covington* tried to torch the boat to sink it rather than allow it to be captured after the captain of the *Warner* raised the white flag. The colonel of the 56th Ohio pleaded with the party from the *Covington* not to burn the ship because it still held 125 of his men who lay dead or dying on the decks.[126]

The artillery from Dunn's Bayou then arrived to pour more fire on the gunboats. The *Covington* and *Signal* tried to retire upstream, but the *Signal* lost its steering assembly and port engine. The *Covington* used a towline to pull the *Signal* against the current. An artillery shell then hit one of the *Signal's* steam pipes and the crew believed the boilers were going to explode. The *Covington* cut *Signal* loose and tried to escape, but its rudder had been hit as well. The captain tied the vessel to the south bank and his crew returned fire for a short time, until they ran out of ammunition. The captain ordered the guns spiked and set fire to the tinclad. The *Signal* was forced to surrender under the combined battery fire after the *Covington* began to burn. The Confederates reported that they drove off another gunboat that tried to offer assistance.[127] The navy suffered more losses in vessels and men than it had on April 22 below Grand Ecore.[128] But they were not alone in their adversity. Inside the defensive perimeter at Alexandria, Porter was dealing with other problems.

The navy was in desperate straits. The water level had fallen until the sand and rocks of the falls were bared. The river level at the chute or navigable channel was only three feet four inches deep.[129] The *Louisville* and the other Pook turtles needed more than six and one-half feet to float. The transports and gunboats that had been left behind as the remainder of the fleet ascended the river had been ordered below the falls as the river began to fall. The transports that accompanied Porter upstream were ordered to pass the Falls as well. But the potential disaster lay ahead in the fact that the majority of the most powerful vessels were trapped above the rocks. These included the *Lexington, Osage, Neosho, Mound City, Louisville, Pittsburg, Carondelet, Chillicothe, Ozark,* and *Fort Hindman.*[130] If the navy retreated, these vessels would have to be destroyed. It was unthinkable to lose these very expensive, powerful boats, and their loss would seriously harm or destroy Porter's career. Porter's report to Gideon Welles resulted in Grant's decision to keep A. J. Smith's men with Porter to protect the fleet, and this was fortunate for the navy.

The number of possible actions was limited if the fleet was to be saved. A huge number of men would be tied down at Alexandria waiting for the autumn rains to raise the river level and that appealed to no one, particularly with Richard Taylor and his army nearby. The only other possibility was to force the water level to rise at Alexandria. Colonel Bailey of Wisconsin, one of Franklin's engineers, advanced this option.

Bailey had worked in the logging industry in Wisconsin and was familiar with the practice of building temporary dams to increase water levels to float logs downstream to sawmills in dry weather. He had used the technique in Thompson Creek near Port Hudson to salvage two steamers the previous year. Bailey had watched the water levels drop for three weeks, and he suggested dams might be needed to float the fleet.[131] He told Franklin about his idea, and although Franklin was favorably impressed he became distracted by command issues and nothing was done. After the *Eastport* sank, Franklin gave Bailey a letter of introduction to Porter, who gave little credence to an idea from an army officer offering a means to save his fleet.[132]

Franklin was also an engineer and appreciated Bailey's approach. Once again Franklin attempted to convince Porter, now at Alexandria.[133] By this time Porter's options were even more limited and the water level was lowering with each passing hour. On April 29, Bailey attended a meeting with Banks and Hunter, who had been in Alexandria for two days. Banks was interested because Hunter's message from Grant made it imperative that the army should withdraw from central Louisiana as quickly as possible. Banks also could not afford to leave Porter with Hunter there watching him. Sherman's belief that Banks would leave the fleet stranded if the army was forced to leave might have become a reality had Hunter not been sent with the message from Grant. Hunter, though skeptical, agreed to Bailey's proposal since Franklin promoted it.[134] The same day, construction began. Franklin sought a leave of absence due to his wound and left Alexandria for convalescence.[135] Emory was elevated to the command of the 19th Corps and McMillan replaced Emory as division commander.[136]

Bailey's task of dam building was more difficult than he expected. First, he had trouble securing work gangs. Some regimental commanders thought it was a waste of time.[137] Second, the site he chose for the main dam was 758 feet wide. The water level varied from four to six feet, and as the dam was formed the level rose and the current increased to ten miles per hour.[138] Third, building materials for the dam were not uniform. He began to disassemble buildings in Alexandria and across the river in Pineville. Bricks, stones, wall segments, even pieces of furniture were used. Ironically,

*Lieutenant Colonel Joseph Bailey. From Francis Trevelyan Miller et al., eds., The Pho-tographic History of the Civil War in Ten Volumes (New York: Review of Reviews Co., 1912), 1:77.*

some of the dam's structure included portions of Sherman's beloved Louisiana Semi-nary for Learning and Military Institute from across the river in Pineville.[139] Soldiers from Maine, most of whom had been lumbermen, felled trees and chopped them to appropriate lengths. Bricks and stones were gathered into barges to make cribs to meet the tree dam.[140] The structure was formed from both sides of the river, meeting in the center. Construction of the dam became quite a spectacle attracting the interest of bored soldiers. Primarily, the Maine soldiers and U.S. Colored Troops of the Corps d'Afrique built the dam.[141]

After a week of work the tree dam extended three hundred feet from the western bank. Four coal barges loaded with brick and stone were lashed together and sunk to extend it farther. From the other side, the crib dam was extended to meet the barges on May 8.[142] The lightest draft vessels, the *Osage, Neosho,* and *Fort Hindman* floated to the area above the dam. The others did not follow, although the water was deep enough for them to do so. The ironclads were still filled with cotton. Removing the cotton would have lightened them sufficiently to pass through the dam on May 8, but they were not willing to lose the white gold. The water level was rising significantly and exerting pressure on the cribs and barges. Finally, at 5 A.M. on May 9 the river pushed the center barges aside. Porter ordered the *Lexington* through the gap before the water level fell and it managed to pull through with a full head of steam. The *Osage, Neosho,* and *Fort Hindman* followed, with only the *Neosho* suffering minor hull damage from the rocks.[143]

*Bailey's dam under construction at Alexandria. From Francis Trevelyan Miller et al., eds., The* Photographic History of the Civil War in Ten Volumes *(New York: Review of Reviews Co., 1912), 1:78–79.*

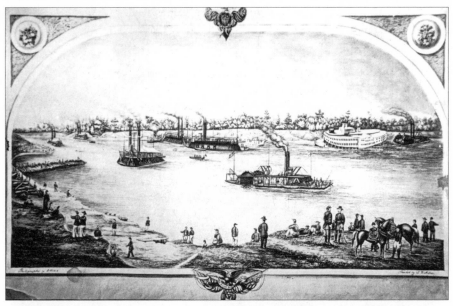

*Mississippi Squadron vessels trapped above the Falls. Photograph from an engraving. Image 48750102, John Langdon Ward Magic Lantern Slide Papers, Louisiana and Lower Mississippi Valley Collection, LSU Libraries, Louisiana State University, Baton Rouge.*

The other vessels had not been moved into the pool above the dam, so when the water level decreased they were unable to get through.[144] Bailey immediately began repairs on the dam and decided that other structures called wing dams must be built to channel the water above the main dam. This delay affected Banks's plan for evacuation. By May 9 McClernand had arrived from Texas and Banks now had more troops to deal with.[145] Although Banks had anticipated evacuating Alexandria on May 9, he did not do so. By May 11 Banks sent word to Porter that the navy must be ready to move its boats as soon as the wing dams were built.[146]

Porter believed that Banks was ready to bolt and leave the fleet. Banks wrote Grant that forage supplies were running very low for the animals upon which the train and artillery depended.[147] He then expressed his concern to Porter that it would be perilous to remain in Alexandria more than one more day.[148] Whether there was actual cause for Porter's suspicions is uncertain, but the admiral attempted to halt any plans of abandoning the navy.[149] A. J. Smith assured the admiral that he and his men would remain with Porter regardless of Banks's actions.[150] Porter promised Banks that once the river rose another foot, the boats could move and Banks would be free to leave. Porter was very condescending to Banks and treated him as he would a small child, even going so far as to say, "Now general, I really see nothing that should make us despond. You have a fine army, and I shall have a strong fleet of gunboats to drive away an inferior force in our front."[151] Banks replied that he never intended to abandon the fleet, but that he had received complaints that the army was doing all the work on the dams and that the navy was doing nothing to rescue its own boats.[152]

The Forest Rose *at Bailey's dam. Library of Congress 419078LC.*

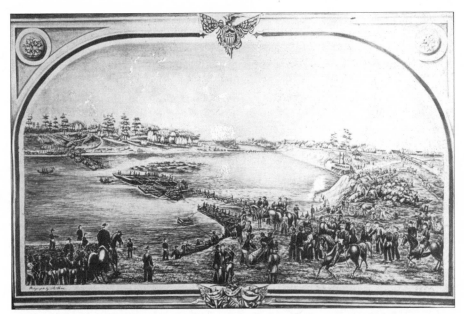

*Union forces building Bailey's dam. Photograph from an engraving. Image 48750103, John Langdon Ward Magic Lantern Slide Papers, Louisiana and Lower Mississippi Valley Collection, LSU Libraries, Louisiana State University, Baton Rouge.*

Porter began removing guns and iron plating from the ironclads to lighten their weight and decrease their draft. The guns, ammunition, and needed supplies were placed on wagons and carried below the falls. Iron plating was removed from some of the ironclads and dumped in the river. Tar was then smeared on the exposed wood to fool anyone who saw the vessels without their armor.[153] Porter chose not to carry eleven 32-pounder smoothbore cannon and had them spiked and dumped into the river.[154] By May 11 the wing dams were complete, but water was not rising sufficiently to float the vessels over the dam. A bracket dam was hastily built. Two days later the water was high enough for the ironclads to shoot through the gap.[155]

Bailey's complex series of dams were designed to utilize every aspect of the Red River near Alexandria. The river made a gentle curve just above the town, and at both ends of the arc were the boulders that formed the Falls. The wing dams were located at the northern end, supported by the bracket dams. The tree dam, supported by the cribs, was placed downstream near the wharves on the town's riverfront.[156]

Bailey had a limited amount of time to construct the dams; thus his design was crude but effective. Hampered by a shortage of willing manpower and construction materials, he used his wing and bracket dams to trap and pool river water. Rather than construct a lock-and-dam structure with a sluice gate and channel to regulate the level of water below the tree dam, he chose a faster but riskier method. The vessels would build up steam, then the cribs were to be moved, allowing the vessels to rapidly shoot through the gap just created. Two photographs show the main dam under construction and the roiling water as the gap was closed.[157] Another image, in the form of a watercolor, portrayed the *Osage* and *Neosho* plunging through the torrent.[158] Other engravings depict efforts to build the dam and the difficulties associated with the project. The dam system was a daring, innovative undertaking.[159] For his efforts and ingenuity, Joseph Bailey was awarded the Medal of Honor and the "Thanks of Congress." By May 15 Porter pushed his fleet out of the Red River and into the wide waters of the Mississippi. He wrote to his mother, "I am clear of my troubles and my fleet is safe out in the broad Mississippi. I have had a hard and anxious time of it."[160]

After sending only positive reports to Washington, Banks entered Alexandria. The true picture, leaked from sources within his command, was different. Naval officers also filed negative reports. He had little if any idea of the true feeling of his superiors toward him. Grant and Halleck wanted to remove him from command, but the president countermanded the sanction against his fellow Republican. Although Banks was unaware of it at the time, his ability to make command decisions was diminished by the creation of a new level of military bureaucracy, the Military Division of West Mississippi. This new organization combined the Departments of the Gulf and Arkansas under a single umbrella, a step needed before the campaign. Although the president concurred that Banks should be fired, he had political reasons for leaving Banks in his command, so he ensured instead that Banks's position as commander of

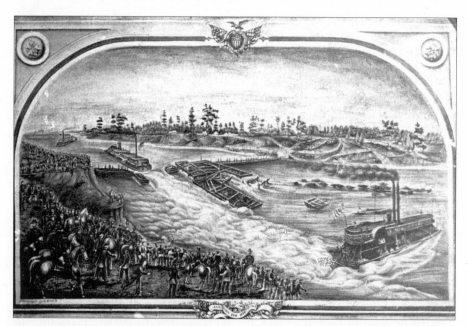

*Mississippi Squadron vessels passing the dam. Photograph from an engraving. Image 48750104, John Langdon Ward Magic Lantern Slide Papers, Louisiana and Lower Mississippi Valley Collection, LSU Libraries, Louisiana State University, Baton Rouge.*

the Department of the Gulf would now be subordinate to the division commander, E. R. S. Canby. Banks in fact had lost all command authority. He was unaware of the change while he was in Alexandria.

Before the dams were constructed, Porter's gunboats were separated above and below the low water of the Falls. The admiral erred by failing to send more of his gunboats through the shallows when sufficient depth remained. Among the boats Porter retained above the falls were the city class ironclads and the monitors. It appears his concern over Confederate naval forces to his rear led to this decision. Ultimately, he was compelled to contemplate the destruction of his most prized vessels. At the same time, Porter was anxious because he believed that Banks was considering abandoning the fleet. Porter urged the general to remain in the town, despite the prospect of a Confederate army of undetermined size lurking outside his defensive perimeter.

Colonel Bailey undoubtedly saved the fleet from destruction. He offered hope to Porter and Banks, who were both skeptical about his plan. Maine lumbermen and the African American troops of the Corps d'Afrique provided most of the labor building the dams. The Maine troops had previously built such structures and, ironically, the African American troops whom Banks detested readily offered their labor when most infantry units scoffed at the idea.

Taylor's opportunity to capture or destroy the fleet vanished with the construction of the dams. He had insufficient infantry to capture the army or destroy the fleet. He felt capturing or destroying a number of Banks's army units was a suitable objective, but a capture of the fleet would have been a great prize. The elimination of the fleet would have freed the western waters for the Confederates' usage for several months before the vessels could be replaced. Although highly speculative and almost impossible to achieve if some vessels had been captured with their guns intact, Taylor might have seriously endangered the Union hold on Baton Rouge, New Orleans, and Vicksburg for a brief time. The recapture of any of the three cities could have done harm to the Union's plans and morale with a general election in early November, six months in the future.

Porter's command on the lower Red River was not solid. He lost more large vessels and men south of Alexandria than were destroyed above the town. The loss of *Covington, Signal,* and *John Warner* intensified the anxiety of the Union commanders and their troops while trapped in Alexandria.

For the army, any hope Banks held for continuing the campaign was extinguished in Alexandria. The expedition that began five weeks before with overwhelming numbers of men, warships, and firepower had gone badly. The fleet had faced what seemed certain destruction and the army was demoralized. During the building of the dams, Banks, at least in Porter's mind, considered abandoning the fleet and any army units that would not follow him to safety. Porter's treatment of Banks is evidence of this. As the navy finally departed Alexandria following their ordeal, Banks faced the prospect of a final retreat and an uncertain future. His political aspirations were damaged, if not ruined.

Banks wanted to leave Alexandria as quickly and quietly as possible. Tired and disgruntled, he had no intention of offering battle to Taylor. Grant, chief of staff Halleck, and the president had castigated him for his failures, and his presidential plans were in ruins. An ambitious but honest man, he observed the events crushing his career with detached bemusement. He never seemed to understand how the promising campaign turned into a major embarrassment. Remaining was the task of extricating his army from the valley. He continued to overestimate the number of Confederate troops that operated against him.

The demoralized army was a source of problems. Banks did not trust A. J. Smith's men or officers, and he believed they would wreak havoc on the local citizens and their property, and this was counterproductive to the president's plans for reconstruction. Smith's men had burned buildings between Natchitoches and Alexandria. Banks believed that if Alexandria were put to the torch, Taylor might contest his passage all the way to Simmesport. He made preparations against the incendiary proclivities of the Westerners, but he could not be sure that his favored eastern troops would decline to participate in such activities.

Taylor was still hoping for his three divisions to return from Arkansas. He watched helplessly as the Union fleet left. His only hope of defeating or capturing the Union force was to hold them inside Alexandria or to block their retreat at some point to the south. He had inadequate resources to lay siege to the town, but he could observe his opponents' movements. He prepared to meet Banks's column when they retreated, again at a place of his choosing. He watched anxiously, praying for his reinforcements to arrive.

After the dam broke on May 9, Banks had time to prepare for his departure in more detail. He was evidently worried that A. J. Smith's "gorillas" might cause problems and make Taylor aware of the army's impending departure. He ordered Brigadier General Richard Arnold, his new chief of cavalry, to place five hundred cavalrymen under "reliable" officers inside the town during the departure to prevent a conflagration.[161] Smith's men were not pleased, and Brigadier General Oliver Gooding was overheard to say, "This is just like old Banks."[162]

The first troops left Alexandria at 7 A.M. on May 13. A little over an hour later, with most of the column still in town, buildings began to burn. Some Union soldiers, and possibly pro-Union residents of the town, had buckets with a mixture of turpentine and camphene (a precursor to napalm) and mops. These men smeared the volatile mixture on buildings and one was reported as saying they were "preparing the place for Hell!"[163] The town turned into an inferno. One man reported that the cavalry officers who were assigned to protect the town were actually directing the burning.[164] Even stout pro-Unionists, who had been under the protection of the army until then, saw their homes torched. People whose sons had just enlisted in the Union army were burned out, and they asked for refuge on the boats, knowing that their neighbors would seek retribution.[165] Several members of Banks's staff and the provost guards tried to stop the flames. Explosives were used to try to extinguish the fire, but the sources were too numerous and a wind fanned the conflagration. In three hours the entire center of town had ceased to exist.[166] Banks had not ordered the torching, but he certainly failed to halt it. His ultimate purpose for not burning the town had not been accomplished. The flames could be seen for miles, and Taylor certainly knew the Union forces were on the march.

Banks set his usual order of march, although he allowed the cavalry to screen forward and to the flanks. Next came the 19th Corps, the combined supply train, the 13th Corps, and then Smith's 16th and 17th Corps units.[167] The men torched buildings all along the road, and nothing was left usable for the people of the region.[168] Taylor was doing his best with the forces at his disposal. His cavalry was harassing the column from both front and rear. His men blocked the roads beginning twelve miles southeast of Alexandria, trying to buy time for reinforcements that never came.

The next day Banks's pioneers cleared the road and spanned Bayou Choctaw with a pontoon bridge. That evening they bivouacked beside the wrecks of the *John Warner,* the *Signal,* and the *Covington* and saw their mail strewn over the ground.[169] On May 15 the column slowly traversed the Bayou Choctaw Swamp and ascended to the tablelands of the Avoyelles Prairie. The lead elements were attacked several times by Wharton's cavalry. The 19th Corps finally brought enough troops to the open country to push the Rebels back. The Confederates retreated to set up again farther down the road, and the head of the column continued until at nightfall they entered Marksville.[170]

On the morning of May 16 Banks found that Taylor had drawn all of his available forces to meet him six miles ahead at the village of Mansura. Taylor used the buildings of the village as his center and placed eight cavalry regiments on his right with nineteen cannon. Polignac and his infantry were on the left with thirteen guns.[171] Also on the left were two regiments of cavalry. About half of the field guns aimed at the Federal troops had been taken from them at Mansfield. The Union troops formed a line of battle and an artillery duel ensued. Taylor later said that it was a beautiful sight with the lines of battle being three miles long on prairie land as "smooth as a billiard table."[172]

Both sides recorded the beauty of the scene as regiments marched into order. Cavalry skirted about seeking a place to charge, and myriad silken flags fluttered in the late spring breezes. The air was filled with glittering accoutrements of war and many diaries and reports reflected the grandeur of the spectacle.[173] The 19th Corps moved forward but Taylor's former Union guns kept them at bay. A sporadic artillery duel lasted nearly four hours until A. J. Smith's men were brought up from the rear and the entire line moved forward at the pace set by the Westerners. Taylor, confronted by eighteen thousand men against his six thousand, retreated.[174] There were few casualties, which added to the vivid memories of the diarists.[175]

Banks pushed on to Bayou de Glaise. From there the road led to Moreauville, Yellow Bayou, Simmesport, Old River, and the Atchafalaya. The army was close to safety even though Confederate cavalry vigorously skirmished with the rearguard and slowed them down. The Confederates also tried to attack the wagon train, but with little success. When the lead elements arrived at Simmesport, or the charred ruins of where it had been located, they believed the campaign was over. The army drew up in and around the former town.[176]

A. J. Smith was tired of Confederate cavalry harassing him while he guarded the tail of the column. He sent Joe Mower back to Yellow Bayou with three brigades

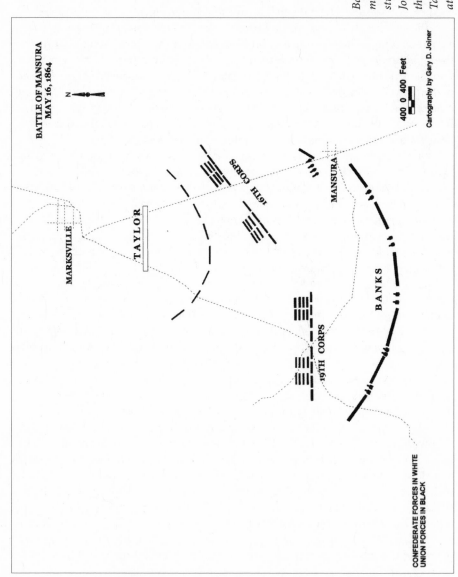

*Battle of Mansura. This map is based on a field study by Union Colonel John Clark and represents the line of Battle after Taylor's original position at Mansura.*

to push the Rebels back. Mower crossed the Yellow Bayou on May 18 and pushed on another two miles where he found Wharton's cavalry and Polignac's infantry drawn up in line of battle.[177]

Polignac fired his artillery and then advanced his infantry. Mower's men pushed them back and then withdrew. He was worried that he might be advancing into a trap. Polignac advanced again but was repulsed. The fighting moved into a thicket of dry trees and brush which caught fire. The Confederate artillery prevented Mower from giving chase. Polignac had about 5,000 men on the field to Mower's 4,500. Polignac lost 608 men killed, wounded, and missing. Mower lost 350.[178] Taylor simply did not have enough men to trap Banks, and the battle at Yellow Bayou proved it. Mower's men could pridefully boast that they were the first in and last out in the campaign and had certainly seen more than their share of the fighting.

As the men of Banks's column came to the landing to leave the Red River country, they encountered high water, something they had missed during the entire campaign. Pontoon bridges were not useful in the fast-flowing current. The army again faced the possibility of being trapped. It seemed as if the earth itself was on the side of the Confederates. Bailey, undoubtedly one of the most resourceful engineering officers in the Union army, made a floating bridge by anchoring the steamboats to each shore and lashing them together side by side. Using the boats as a roadbed, he put a plank road across them for the supply trains and artillery to cross the deep-channeled Atchafalaya River.[179] The infantry was ferried over in transports making bank-to-bank journeys. The entire force was able to cross on May 19 and 20. After the last man crossed, the transports were unlashed, the anchors were hoisted, and there was no way for Taylor to pursue any farther.[180] An Iowa soldier wrote, "General Banks looked dejected and worn, and is hooted at by his men."[181]

General E. R. S. Canby arrived at Simmesport on May 18 and was waiting for Banks. He informed Banks of the reorganization ordered by Washington. Banks returned to New Orleans and became primarily a political officer, writing reports and doing nothing that Canby did not approve.[182] That fall he secured a leave of absence to go to Washington and tried to salvage his career.[183] By that time the presidential elections were over and Lincoln had no reason to help him. He was picked to lead the Reconstruction government in Louisiana for the president and that put him in disfavor with the Radical Republicans in Congress.[184]

In December 1864 Congress reconvened the Joint Committee on the Conduct of the War to investigate the Red River Expedition, chaired by Senator Ben Wade.[185] Testimony was given from December 14, 1864, through April 21, 1865. Banks was the first in a long list of witnesses. The Radicals were out for blood and Banks was a easy target. Banks appears to have tried to answer everything with honesty and integrity. No one could make a case that he had personally gained from the campaign. The Wade Committee published its findings and walked away in disgust. When the committee finished, no direct action was taken against any of the officers. Lincoln sent Banks back to Louisiana to reorganize the government, but before Banks had reached New Orleans the president was assassinated and Andrew Johnson became president. In June 1865 Banks resigned from the army and returned to Massachusetts.[186]

*Battle of Yellow Bayou.*

*Colonel Bailey's bridge of boats across the Atchafalaya River. Photograph from an engraving. Image 48750101, John Langdon Ward Magic Lantern Slide Papers, Louisiana and Lower Mississippi Valley Collection, LSU Libraries, Louisiana State University, Baton Rouge.*

In Shreveport, Kirby Smith had returned from Arkansas believing that he had saved his department. Taylor could not stand the sight of the commanding general. On June 5 he wrote a letter that blamed Smith for Taylor's inability to capture the fleet and Banks's army. He asked to be relieved of command.[187] Smith put Taylor under arrest five days later and sent a message to President Davis regarding his actions.[188] The same day, June 10, the Confederate Congress passed a joint resolution praising Taylor.[189] Troops loyal to Taylor almost came to blows with troops loyal to Smith. Soon after, Taylor was promoted to lieutenant general and given command of the Department of Alabama, Mississippi, and East Louisiana. He surrendered that department to General Canby at Citronelle, Alabama, on May 4, 1865.

Shreveport, in 1865, was the last Confederate capital to fall. Kirby Smith had tried to reach Mexico to continue the rebellion there. He was captured at Galveston, Texas, on June 2. Kirby Smith approved the convention entered into by Lieutenant General Buckner on his behalf on May 26 with a representative of E. R. S. Canby for surrender of Confederate forces in the Trans-Mississippi. Union troops entered Shreveport on June 6, just short of two months after Robert E. Lee surrendered at Appomattox courthouse.

The campaign that began with such promise ended with nothing substantive to show for the great effort by the Union army and navy. The Confederates felt cheated as well. Richard Taylor wrote, "I feel bitterly about this [the removal of the three divisions to Arkansas], because my army has been robbed of the just measure of its glory and the country of the most brilliant and complete success of the war."[190]

Union attitudes were almost uniform in their disgust. A reporter for the St. Louis *Daily Missouri Republican* summarized the campaign as "a fit sequel to a scheme, conceived in politics and brought forth in iniquity."[191] President Lincoln, citing the "disaster at Red River" among other reasons, declared a day of "fasting, humiliation, and prayer."[192] General Sherman perhaps offered the best summary from the Union side. When asked his opinion of the campaign, the great general replied, "One damned blunder from beginning to end."[193]

Wasted opportunities, too much bloodshed, and incredible blunders by Union and Confederate commanders all served to bury the campaign in the dustbin of history. Evidence of this is seen in the volume of literature regarding other campaigns in 1864 compared to only a few scholarly publications studying the Red River Campaign that occurred in that long-forgotten spring in the interior of Louisiana.

# CHAPTER 8

## Congressional Investigation

The disaster that was the Red River Campaign provided Congress with an opportunity to examine witnesses, place blame, and direct its ire at the president's plans and policies. The stunning Confederate victory at Mansfield, the near loss of most of the Mississippi Squadron's vessels, the delays in the campaign in order to hold elections and gather cotton, and the headlong, at times panic-stricken, retreat back to Union-held territory led to a major Congressional investigation. The Radical Republicans controlling both the House of Representatives and the Senate did not trust Lincoln's so-called easy Reconstruction policies. They also viewed Banks as the president's puppet. The debacle of the campaign offered them a very public venue to vilify Lincoln and Banks's actions.

Several of the senior field commanders believed that the hearings would place blame where it was deserved. T. E. G. Ransom wrote to William B. Franklin "our Red River campaign will be ventilated."[1] He also delighted in the fact that Banks's political enemies were going to use hearings to ruin any chance for a presidential bid.[2]

The hearings began after the presidential elections. The delay was caused by several factors. Parliamentary rules forced a late call to convene the proceedings. Lincoln won the Republican nomination in June negating the desire among most committee members to hamper the president's bid. Finally, Banks had been removed from field command so there was no sense of urgency to begin testimony.[3]

The Joint Committee on the Conduct of the War heard the testimony. Historians have typically disagreed with its actions and motivations.[4] It was at times meddlesome and self-righteous, admittedly radical, and almost always critical of military failures and what it perceived as ineptitude. The committee was created in late 1861 and was composed of three senators and four congressmen. By 1864 all but one member, a congressman, were Republicans. Senator Benjamin Wade of Ohio served as chair. Vice President Hannibal Hamlin appointed the other senators, Zachariah Chandler of Michigan and Benjamin Harding of Oregon. The House members, appointed by Speaker of the House of Representatives Galusha Grow, consisted of George Julian of Indiana, Daniel Gooch of Massachusetts, Benjamin Loan of Missouri, and Moses Odell of New York, the sole Democrat.

The committee as a whole was vehemently opposed to Lincoln's "10-percent rule" of holding elections when 10 percent of the prewar electorate of a state swore an oath of allegiance to the United States and formed a new government, thus sending representatives and senators to Washington. The committee members agreed with their radical Republican colleagues, believing this policy was much too easy on the rebellious states and that they should be harshly punished. They also believed the influx of loyal-but-Southern senators would tip the balance against the radicals, thus leading to a soft reconstruction of the entire South. The Red River Campaign offered the venue for the committee to stake the legal ground for its own brand of reconstruction of the South.

Although the committee ultimately divided over the allocation of blame, it entered the hearings in unanimity with preconceived conclusions. Each member knew the expedition was a failure and that blame must be assessed. The committee had a history of meddling in military affairs to the detriment of the president and the command staff. They viewed themselves as an important tool in the system of checks and balances—that is, the cornerstone of American government. As a whole they were displeased with Lincoln's ideas concerning an easy reconstruction of the rebellious Southern states. The difference between the majority view, led by Wade, and the minority view, held by Gooch alone, was the degree of Banks's blame.

The two most significant members, for their outspoken participation and influence, were Wade and Gooch. Wade served as chairman and exhibited the most forceful personality. Gooch asked the most insightful questions and often delved deeper into issues than either the committee or witnesses desired. Gooch was a loyal Republican and staunch defender of the committee; however, he differed with his colleagues on two occasions. He wrote forceful minority reports against the majority in praising John C. Frémont's leadership as commander of the Department of the West and, more important for the purposes here, an impassioned defense of Nathaniel Banks after the Red River Campaign.

In December of 1864 Congress reconvened this Joint Committee on the Conduct of the War to examine what went wrong with the Red River Campaign. The testimony of these hearings fills the majority of a volume of published reports and findings.[5] It was apparent from the start of the hearings that Lincoln's policies and Banks's implementation of them were primary targets. The committee focused on the elections that Banks organized in New Orleans, Baton Rouge, Alexandria, and Grand Ecore. They sought to determine if those elections were constitutionally legal and whether or not they delayed the campaign. They also closely examined the methods by which the Union advance was conducted and the leaders responsible for these actions.

The congressional committee heard testimony from every surviving senior Union commander who participated in the campaign, several midlevel army and navy officers, the Union army chief of staff, and several civilians, including Banks's riverboat pilot. Military planners and senior commanders were placed in the unenviable position of defending a campaign based on economic and political goals and not urgent military needs. The committee delved into routine military matters such as how many wagons were in the supply trains, the order of march, and internal communication within the columns. Officers close to Banks and those who distrusted him all had their say, and almost all abandoned him.

The committee released two reports, the majority report and the minority report. The sole dissenter, Daniel Gooch, authored the minority report. In both reports, the results were presented in a narrative style rather than in point-by-point findings as in a legal brief. The majority report consisted of fourteen pages, and the minority report was twice its length. Together, they comprised the first forty-nine pages of the document. The committee processed hundreds of pages of transcribed testimony and agreed on the bulk of findings. The primary difference of opinion came in apportioning the degree of blame for the failure of the expedition.

The bulk of both reports recounted facts and included copies of orders and testimony. Differing interpretation of these led to the dissention by Gooch. In both reports, the legislators were hampered because they had not visited the sites to understand why some events happened. A visit by the committee was not possible because the area traversed in the campaign was still in Rebel hands. The committee met in Washington and had no desire to travel to Louisiana or Arkansas. They were particularly kind to the navy. They did not criticize the types of vessels Admiral Porter took up the river, nor did they chastise naval staff for confiscating cotton under the Naval Prize Law.

The majority report found that there were both military and political pressures to conduct the campaign. The first mention was in a letter from General Halleck to General Banks in November 1862. Banks had been given command of the Department of Gulf, and Halleck made clear what he wanted: "It is also suggested that having Red river in our possession, it would form the best base for operations in Texas."[6] This letter was sent seven months prior to the siege of Vicksburg, and the flow of supplies from west to east was still vigorous. Just after the fall of Vicksburg, Halleck wrote to Banks, "There are important reasons why our flag should be hoisted in some point of Texas with the least possible delay. Do this by land, at Galveston, at Indianola [Matagorda Bay], or at any other point you may deem preferable."[7] The president, his cabinet, and Halleck were worried the French and their puppet emperor Maximilian might attempt to reunite Texas with Mexico. Banks's first two attempts to invade Texas by sea ended in failure, with the exception of planting the flag and garrisoning troops on one of the barrier islands near Brownsville, Texas. It failed to adequately address the president's need for a strong presence on the Gulf Coast or inland in Texas.

The committee also acknowledged that Halleck's correspondence was always in the form of suggestions and not direct orders. Banks, always anxious to please both Lincoln and Halleck, enthusiastically tried to divine their wishes. Lacking firm orders, he had trouble making decisions, and this was not surprising given his lack of military leadership training. The result of his interpretations was continued failure to invade Texas. The committee used Banks's willingness and indecisiveness against him.

The majority report described the force composition and the timetable established by Banks and noted that March 17, 1864, was the date fixed for the rendezvous at Alexandria. It briefly described the actions on the lower Red River by Admiral

Porter and A. J. Smith, including their arrival on schedule in the central Louisiana town. The report then recounted Banks's testimony that "he was detained in New Orleans, by order of the President, to arrange for a civil organization of the State."[8] Banks's land contingent did not arrive in Alexandria until March 26. The report later determined that this delay, together with others caused by electioneering, interfered with the campaign and that political issues seemed more important than military necessities.[9] Banks was under great pressure from Washington to reconstruct Louisiana as a model and he had a short time to return Sherman's troops back east. The committee believed his potential run for the presidency to be a distraction. In short, it appeared that Banks's political nature won the contest over his military duties. He saw the need to run the New Orleans political machine as more pressing than personally leading his forces into the interior of Louisiana.

Banks laid blame for the tardiness of his troops squarely on General Franklin, who was not only the 19th Corps commander but also was given the responsibility of day-to-day command by Banks. The committee duly noted Banks's position and added that Franklin's testimony proved that Banks's orders were impossible to carry out. Franklin testified that he was not told until March 10 about the rendezvous at Alexandria. At that time he had only three thousand troops to form his column. He had to gather the men, beginning the trek on March 13 or 14. The 175-mile march was accomplished by March 26. The committee then noted that the delay did not retard the progress of the expedition due to low river levels. The committee majority believed Franklin and did not chastise him for being nine days late to the rendezvous, choosing to lay blame on Banks for not giving Franklin his orders earlier. There is no doubt that this position is correct. Banks was preoccupied with elections and political processes and was not interested in his army at that point. Franklin's march schedule was fairly rigorous between Brashear City and Alexandria. The column could have made better time by moving along multiple roads. The infantry commanders complained about moving through muddy terrain churned up by the cavalry and the wagons. Torrential rains offered a good excuse for the delay, but better utilization of resources may have reduced the problems. The march between Brashear City and Alexandria is comparable to Grant's march from Milliken's Bend to Hard Times Plantation in eastern Louisiana during the Vicksburg Campaign the previous year. The use of a single road created havoc for the infantry who were following supply trains.[10]

The majority report described the army's march to Grand Ecore and the move inland to Pleasant Hill and Mansfield. The order of march was detailed, as were the movements of the navy. The report ignored Banks's decision to move inland and Porter's plea to perform a reconnaissance upriver. The committee, as Banks did before it, believed the testimony of the river pilot Withenbury as if it were gospel. It is astounding that a body so critical of the commanding general of a failed campaign did not pursue his reasons for leaving the safety of the navy's big guns to traverse inhospitable ground.

The committee examined the order of march between Grand Ecore and Mansfield.[11] It heaped criticism on the poor planning, the fact that the cavalry's wagons hampered reinforcing infantry from coming to the front, and the position of the senior commanders several miles behind the lead elements. The body also focused on the use of a single narrow road with the column extended to between twenty and thirty miles, thus making it impossible for the most able supporting units to rush forward from the rear of the column. This criticism is well founded. The order in which the column was assembled was the second greatest error by the Union commanders, surpassed only by the decision to move inland away from the protection of the navy. The infantry regiments, particularly Sherman's veterans, should never have been relegated to the rear of the column. Banks's petty snobbery over the Westerners is directly to blame for this.

The majority report described the battles of Mansfield and Pleasant Hill as told by the survivors. It criticized Banks for deciding to make a stand on Honeycutt Hill when he might have pulled back to the ridge above Chapman's Bayou, also called Pleasant Grove by Union officers. In this assumption, the report deferred to General Albert Lee, the cavalry commander. Lee was disgusted with Banks, who had subsequently fired him. The report followed accounts common to both Union and Confederate participants until the third phase. Then it described the Confederates as "repulsed with heavy loss, and forced to retire."[12] The heaviest losses suffered by the Rebels came during the first twenty minutes of fighting. Exhaustion of the pursuing Confederate soldiers and the fall of darkness ended the fighting. The committee also commented that in the fighting at Pleasant Hill "the enemy attacked with great vigor, but were completely repulsed, and retired some distance from the field of battle."[13] To be completely repulsed, the Confederates would have made a headlong retreat to the safety of their interior lines. In fact the two sides performed something of a wheel clockwise. After four hours of vicious fighting, the two sides drew apart and neither retreated for several hours. Both stood their ground, but at a respectful distance from the other. The battle ended in a tactical tie.

Senator Wade and his fellow legislators writing the majority report determined that the campaign was abandoned on the night of April 9 following the Battle of Pleasant Hill. At that time Banks gave orders to retreat to Grand Ecore. The committee also mentioned that the retreat was conducted in such haste that the dead and wounded were left on the field of battle as they had been on the previous day. It surmised that Banks had abandoned the initiative of the campaign before the battle when he ordered what was left of his cavalry division to take the remaining wagons back to Grand Ecore. This may be correct, but Banks obviously saw his presidential hopes slipping away and believed he could still resurrect them. At Grand Ecore he tried to convince Porter to make another run at Shreveport, this time upriver, but Porter refused.

The naval officers who testified were unanimous in their belief that Banks would have abandoned the navy "in his desire to return with his army to New Orleans, after it was determined to abandon the expedition."[14] Admiral Porter, who was adamant about the point in his testimony, may have fostered this uniform opinion. The majority report followed this statement by adding that Banks and his men did all that they could to protect the fleet. According to Porter, Banks had to be treated almost as a child to keep him from bolting, leaving the flotilla stranded above the rapids at Alexandria.

The majority report commended the actions of Colonel Bailey in creating the dams that saved the vessels. It added that the army built the dams and that the only losses to the navy were "one or two gunboats and some transports."[15] In fact, both the army and naval commanders were wary of Bailey's project, and he had to lobby for labor. Black troops of the 97th and 99th engineering regiments and volunteers from some of the Maine infantry units worked on the dam until they were officially ordered to undertake the task. The "one or two gunboats and some transports" were lost in heavy action just below Alexandria and included two powerful tinclads, the *Signal* and the *Covington,* and the large transport *John Warner.*

Senator Wade and his coauthors discussed the need for the campaign, stating that no witness felt or indicated that a beneficial result could be expected. They placed the blame on Banks for wanting the campaign and more or less excused Halleck for urging Banks to undertake the venture. The report made a very important accusation: "They (witnesses) state that had the town of Shreveport been reached there would have been nothing to be done but to return by the very route they had travelled in going there."[16] This ignores the notion of invading Texas for both political and strategic reasons, however critical the actual military need. The committee then wrote: "General Banks states most positively that he never considered a movement upon that line [Red River] practicable. Why, then, he should have commenced it, with the discretion allowed him, or have continued it beyond Alexandria after he had ascertained that the river was so very low at so late a season, your committee cannot understand. It certainly could not have been from any very great deference to the opinion of the then general-in-chief, for he undertook movements against which General Halleck expressed opinions so strong that they almost partook of the nature of commands."[17] Senator Wade and his coauthors used this rhetorical paragraph to justify their primary indictment of Banks's blame. In their view the primary reasons for failure lay in two areas: cotton and presidential policy.

The committee pointed to cotton procurement as the major reason for failure. The majority committee members used one-third of their document quoting from witnesses, finally summarizing the issue of cotton procurement.[18] They attempted to discover whether some cotton speculators had presidential passes to purchase cotton wherever they found it. They tried to link Banks directly to these men and illustrated that these men traveled under the protection of the army. There is no doubt that several cotton speculators accompanied Banks to Alexandria on the transport *Black Hawk.* It is also evident that at least two men carried passes signed by the president from the previous year. Banks was willing to help them since his power base was New England, the eventual destination of the bales. However, Banks was not particularly interested in enriching himself, even at the exorbitant prices of 1864. Although the committee was silent on the subject, confiscation of cotton was a vehicle for Banks. It would have allowed him to continue the support of his benefactors in his presidential bid. It would also please Lincoln by appeasing New England, although it was a powerful lure. Confiscation of cotton was not the primary reason for the campaign.

The majority report focused on the abuse of presidential reconstruction practices, with which it was diametrically opposed. The report stated that the holding of elections in the army's camps at both Alexandria and Grand Ecore was "clearly a usurpation on the part of the military authorities, the execution of which was as weak and inefficient as the attempt was improper and illegal."[19] The report ended with this statement.

Representative Gooch of Massachusetts was the sole dissenting voice in the Joint Committee on the Conduct of the War. His minority report exhaustively quotes sources, some identical to the majority report. He poses two questions: Upon whom does the responsibility of the expedition rest? What were the objectives expected to be accomplished from it?[20]

Gooch exhaustively detailed the correspondence between Halleck and Banks.[21] He then concluded that the responsibility for the expedition lay in Washington and primarily with Halleck. He described Halleck's particular talent of making strong suggestions that could be read as orders. Halleck was adamant that the Red River approach offered the best corridor into Texas. Gooch reminded the committee that Halleck's suggestions could be read as orders if the expedition failed, incriminating the recipient of the "order." Gooch wrote: "And when he [Banks] had found it impossible to comply with views expressed 'as suggestions only, and not instructions,' he was told, by way of censure, 'In regard to your Sabine and Rio Grande expeditions, no notices of your intentions to make them were received here until they were actually undertaken.'"[22] The congressman asserted that his superior bullied Banks into leading the expedition. Banks was following the lead of several masters. Gooch points to Halleck as the sole source, but this is not so. Halleck was working at the behest of the president, who wanted the flag placed in Texas for several reasons. Members of the cabinet, principally Secretary Seward, were pushing for it. Major General George McClellan had suggested it as well. Seen from the aspect of Grand Strategy, the campaign was a useful part of the Anaconda Plan, which had been discarded but resurrected in 1864. Finally, Banks was serving his own desire to be a hero and become president. This, perhaps more than any other reason, was the driving force behind the campaign.

Gooch asserted that Banks did not have enough troops, contending that he was actually outnumbered.[23] He stated that pressing needs forced Banks to leave troops at various points, and, in one case (the Mississippi Marine Brigade) some were sent away. Indirectly, although not in the manner of his argument, Gooch was correct. The committee overestimated the number of Confederates available on the field of battle at any one time. It did not realize that Kirby Smith withheld several thousand men in multiple divisions. Banks did not have full use of his cavalry division, keeping one brigade as flankers and a division of infantry to garrison Alexandria, meaning that the column was shorter by that exact number of men. The cavalry would have been of more use if it were allowed to remain with the division at the head of the column. Lee would have had more men to hold Honeycutt Hill for a time, but the result would have yielded the same results. Richard Taylor had ample forces in place for the attack and prosecuted his plan with vigor. Due to the length of the column and the disposition of the troops within it, additional troops could not have moved up in support in any great numbers until the wagons were moved out of the way. There was simply no time to do this, and there was no strong leadership from Banks to make the decision to do so. The leaders who could act on it (Lee, Ransom, and Cameron) were too involved to supervise the operation.

Gooch blamed Franklin for the organization and disposition of the column and for remaining several miles behind the lead elements at Mansfield. The congressman portrayed Banks as doing all that he could to make the best of an admittedly bad situation. He portrays Franklin as being overconfident, lazy, and perhaps even feebleminded for the orders he gave, as well as the orders he did not give. The latter would include removing the wagons as obstacles, bringing up sufficient infantry and artillery support, and digging entrenchments on the Pleasant Grove ridge. Gooch's portrayal of Banks is too kind. Banks should not have been in Grand Ecore holding an election. He should have been at the head of the column, or at least near enough to make command decisions during the entire movement from Grand Ecore. Banks relied too heavily on Franklin. For his part, Franklin should also have been closer to the front to determine the needs of his elements engaging the Confederates. He was so confident that there would be no battle and that Lee was a meek commander at best that he disregarded information from the front.

Gooch's grasp of the battles and the predicament of the navy are shallow. He parrots the information of the majority report. He briefly recounts the loss of the *Eastport* and effort to save the fleet at Alexandria, making the points of little importance to his thesis. This illustrates that either he did not care or had difficulty understanding what was happening to Porter and his fleet. The strategic implication of the loss of almost all combatant vessels in the Mississippi River was tremendous. Vicksburg was left unguarded during the campaign. With no vessels to control the Mississippi River, the Confederates might have forced Sherman to divert from the Georgia campaign. No other forces were available between Banks and Sherman for a relief operation.

Gooch blames the failure of the campaign on a series of factors.[24] First, it was the understanding that the campaign must be a combined operation between the army and navy and that it could only be successfully accomplished when the river was full. The river did not cooperate, thanks to the Confederate engineers at Tones Bayou. Second, Banks had no control over the removal of troops he deemed vital to the operation. Third, Gooch blamed Steele for not linking up with Banks south of Shreveport when Banks requested assistance.

The congressman's contention about the river is perfectly sound. Porter's choice of vessels required river levels to be high to float his largest hulls. The second assessment, concerning the removal of troops, is somewhat irrelevant due to the order of march and the improper positioning of the best fighting men at the rear. The third contention is fanciful at best. Steele was requested to meet Banks south of Shreveport, although too late. The Arkansas commander's plan of operation had always been to approach Shreveport from the north or east. Banks had no way of knowing Steele's predicament in Arkansas. The request for Steele to join the main body of troops south of Shreveport was simply Banks grasping at straws. Gooch discussed the option of obtaining support from Steele because he either believed it (which is difficult if he looked at a map) or he wished to provide the committee with another possibility for the campaign's failure other than Banks's errors. The latter is most probable.

Gooch also dismissed the cotton speculation and electioneering as a smoke screen by his fellow members on the committee. Cotton gathering was very important to the operation, and Banks acknowledged this; however, to dismiss it as unimportant is more partisan politics than logic, considering the circumstances. Gooch contended that the elections caused no appreciable delay in the operations. This point may be debated. Banks wasted valuable time overseeing elections at both Alexandria and Grand Ecore, leaving Franklin to handle the daily routine of the army. Perhaps the most important aspect of the elections is that Banks had very little idea about Franklin's activities and seemed not to care what he did.

Although the committee did not delve into naval matters to a great degree, they should have indicated that Porter's choice of vessels was inappropriate for the river conditions. The admiral relied on the word of General Sherman about water conditions in previous years and failed to conduct reconnaissance missions. Fearing a fleet of ironclads, and perhaps submarines, at Shreveport, Porter chose to believe scanty intelligence sources and made no attempt to confirm the rumors. His choice of vessels almost proved the fleet's undoing. Massive firepower was useless since the guns could not be brought to bear on the enemy in an effective manner.

The force was composed of both appropriate and inappropriate vessels. Fears of a large Confederate fleet upstream on the narrow, twisting river colored Porter's thinking. River monitors and tinclads were best suited as gun platforms for a mission up the Red River. Forward reconnaissance and search-and-destroy raids were their forte. Instead, they were used primarily as escorts for the army transports or cotton hauling. The four City Class ironclads were powerful weapons in moderate depth waters of seven to nine feet. These vessels could seize a strong point on the river and hold it until infantry units arrived. They were mishandled and their effectiveness was nullified. The largest of the ironclads, *Eastport, Choctaw, Lafayette, Benton,* and *Essex* were not suited for the shallow river. The small role played by the rubberclads, heavily armed vessels that were coated in India rubber for armor, and the older ironclads proved this point. Porter's insistence on leading with the *Eastport* caused many delays and created the scenario for the potential loss of the fleet in the journey downriver.

The majority report points the blame squarely at Banks. Banks was indeed the culprit of most of the problems before and during the campaign, but not all. The hearings allowed many officers and civilians to express views otherwise ignored or buried in official reports. The majority correctly directed witnesses' testimony toward many weak points of the expedition. Cotton gathering, holding elections, force composition, and horribly simplistic orders of march were all factors in the failure. It is evident, however, that the committee's questions had two underlying themes. First, Lincoln's reconstruction policy of early elections to increase loyalty to the Union hampered if not disrupted the campaign. Second, Banks served as the president's lackey and that he was so involved with the reconstruction issue that he neglected his military duties. The majority certainly had favorite witnesses. Admiral Porter was received graciously and held in high esteem by the members. Their questions were soft and Porter was allowed to shift blame almost exclusively to Banks. No naval officers received harsh treatment. John Clark, Banks's topographical engineer, was given free rein to discuss both Banks's and Franklin's obstinacy in refusing the cavalry's pleas for assistance.

Wade and his allies were stern with witnesses they believed were at fault and let others have an easier time. Banks and Franklin both testified on several occasions and were grilled each time. Cotton brokers also received close scrutiny. The only witness who shared blame for altering the campaign and was not harshly interrogated was Wellington W. Withenbury, the riverboat pilot. Withenbury played perhaps the most important role in the outcome of the campaign for convincing Banks to turn inland at Grand Ecore. The majority only wanted to know about river conditions, elections, and cotton speculators. They did not ask a single pointed question and the pilot was vague whenever possible.

Although the majority tried from the outset to discredit both the president and Banks, they were proficient in identifying the issues surrounding the campaign. Banks was not a great military leader and was out of his element on the field of battle. Franklin was thrust in the role of his superior, handling the day-to-day operations of the army on the march. At the same time, he was subservient to Banks's wishes, attempting to stay in the commander's favor. This balancing act made Franklin a somewhat ineffective political flunky and a martinet. The committee fully exploited this relationship, allowing Banks to blame Franklin for the order of march and Franklin to rail against Banks's ineptitude. The majority's zeal for exposing cotton procurement and operational delays caused by electioneering were both appropriate.

Gooch agreed with the committee on most points, but his staunch defense of Banks is the basis for his minority view. Gooch was so vigorous defending Banks that he moved the majority to increase the proportion of blame to Franklin. Gooch might have also spread part of the blame on Porter and Withenbury, among others, but failed to do so.

With the exception of Gooch's opinion of Banks's role, the majority and minority opinions concurred. In spite of the committee issuing two reports, both the majority and minority opinions are correct in most of their findings. Both reports recognize the need to assess blame. Both reports showed disdain for political and economic meddling in a military operation. The oversights of the two reports were more significant than their more obvious problems: a total lack of attention to Confederate operations, inappropriate Union naval force composition, and a discussion of why the campaign was fought. The committee was not interested in the combat effectiveness of the Confederates or their prowess on the battlefield. In its opinion it was Banks's campaign to lose. The committee members all but ignored naval issues and the portion of blame shared by Porter for the selection of vessels and the disposition of his forces. The committee also granted very little time to the military necessity of the campaign, focusing instead on how poorly it was managed.

The majority also focused heavily on Reconstruction policy. The committee as a whole did not agree with President Lincoln's methods of reconstructing the rebellious states. They were particularly interested in Banks's role as a tool of presidential policy. Banks's divergent roles as politician and military leader were placed in separate areas of questioning, but the political agenda was the most scrutinized. This thread of questioning was directed at witnesses of all levels of authority, from Halleck down to civilians. Wade and other members ordered witnesses to testify as to whether Banks was in their presence at specific times, particularly in the early days of the campaign, at Alexandria, and at Grand Ecore before the army moved inland. The intent of this line of questioning was to ascertain whether Banks was doing his job as military commander or whether he was otherwise engaged in political activities. If Banks was not present, witnesses were asked their knowledge of the commander's whereabouts. If Banks was in their presence, the committee delved into his actions. The majority attempted to prove that Banks was absent from his command for at least eight days at the beginning of the campaign and arrived only after the gubernatorial inauguration was accomplished in Baton Rouge. A second line of questioning in this vein was the obsession with cotton and ministering to cotton brokers accompanying the general. A third line of questioning involved elections held in Alexandria and Grand Ecore and whether these events delayed the campaign in any way. The committee's lines of questions on matters directly related to military activities were tied to Banks's support of the president's Reconstruction policy of increasing the number of loyal voters to 10 percent of the population to bring the rebellious state into the Union fold.

The committee also covered Banks's military abilities. Questions focused on his activities, attitudes, demeanor, and focus. Officers with knowledge of orders given by Banks and Franklin were asked their opinions of military necessity and whether the witness considered the instructions to be proper for the situation in which they were given. Even those officers loyal to Banks through most of the campaign turned against him in a chorus, describing ineptitude, moodiness, aloofness, and gross incompetence. Cavalry commanders, particularly Albert Lee, indicated they were mystified by the orders, actions, and attitudes of both Banks and Franklin. Western commanders were particularly harsh toward Banks's actions. Porter's testimony reads like a description of misdeeds performed by a wayward child. In every case the witnesses tried to use the best light on their actions, making Banks the center of all that went wrong.

# CONCLUSION

The Red River Campaign was the largest gathering of combined arms west of the Mississippi River in the Civil War. It was the last foray by the U.S. Navy deep into Rebel-held territory. Following the expedition, the Union navy only patrolled inland waters and the U.S. Army did not venture far from its bases west of the river. The Confederates securely held more territory after the campaign than before it began. The last Rebel capital to fall was Shreveport, which was occupied one day shy of two months after Robert E. Lee capitulated in Virginia.

Shreveport served as both capital of Confederate Louisiana and as headquarters of the Army of the Trans-Mississippi. It was the nexus of the Rebel military-industrial complex west of the Mississippi River. The town was also the major cotton exporting port north of New Orleans. The combination of the undefeated Rebel army operating deep in the Union rear, the existence of the war-making potential, and tens of thousands of bales of cotton were a strong lure to the Union planners. All of these points made Shreveport a viable prime target for the invasion.

The Union commanders undertook the campaign with a tremendous air of arrogance. Why did they have an almost total disregard for their opponents? They discovered that overwhelming Union superiority in manpower and naval firepower was not enough to compensate for bad decisions by politicians and military planners. Both Banks and Porter believed that enough men and equipment would carry the day, regardless of the Confederate threat. Banks had been defeated by Richard Taylor in earlier battles but did not learn any lessons from these experiences. Porter trusted his friend William T. Sherman's information about river conditions rather than performing his own reconnaissance missions. His armada was far superior to any vessels the Rebels could send against him, but he relied too heavily on brute strength.

Perceived economic gain and politics overshadowed military necessity in planning the operation. Did political interference doom the expedition before it began? Actually, these factors were intertwined. The political needs, as perceived by Abraham Lincoln, of placating the New England industrial and banking interests overshadowed military necessity after the fall of Vicksburg. The economic lure of tens of thousands of bales of cotton attracted Banks and his potential run for the presidency. This combination of factors led to an overly complex plan, which was almost unworkable given the assets applied to the mission, the distance between the cooperating forces, and the personalities involved.

The army and navy were obsessed by the prospect of valuable cotton vulnerable and ripe for military "grabbing" at certain points during the campaign. Did this affect the planning and ultimately contribute to the defeat of their forces? Political and economic exigencies superceded military necessities in the reasoning behind the campaign. It seems clear that presidential politics had more impact on rationale than did military need. The campaign was conducted in the spring of 1864 with the knowledge that, if successful, it could play a large role in the presidential elections that fall. President Lincoln desperately wanted to return both Louisiana and Texas to the Union. This would solve two problems that occupied him early in 1864. First, it would increase the number of moderates in Congress and promote the Reconstruction process he envisioned for the South. Second, through the capture of the vast amounts of cotton grown in the Red River Valley and in eastern Texas it would supply the raw material needed for textile mills in New England, returning tens of thousands of unemployed workers to their jobs. The New England Radical Republicans would be placated before the fall elections.

Following the campaign, Congress placed most of the blame for the expedition's failure on Nathaniel Banks. Was this deserved or was Banks a scapegoat for an ill-conceived, as some historians have contended, cotton raid? Lincoln's choice to command the expedition, a political general from Massachusetts with no military experience prior to the war, was arguably the most popular favorite-son politician from New England. Banks had presidential aspirations, hoping to run against Lincoln in the fall Republican primaries. Oddly, Lincoln trusted Banks to carry out his wishes on Reconstruction and bring Louisiana and Texas into the Union camp. Banks energetically attempted to do both, and, although his political background (as a former Speaker of the U.S. House of Representatives and three-term governor of Massachusetts) allowed him to work through the political intricacies of Reconstruction, his lack of military knowledge made him an abysmal choice as commander.

Communication among the army's three prongs was all but impossible. Could the plan have been simplified to create less confusion? The plan lacked a clear military purpose as well as detailed goals and objectives. Banks was given total control of force composition of army units. His plan utilized elements from five army corps and three separate commands, over forty thousand men, moving on Shreveport from three starting points as far as four hundred miles apart. The naval force was to support one of the prongs of the advance. The goal was the capture of Shreveport, the capital of Confederate Louisiana, followed by the invasion of Texas. Unbelievably, there was no indication of what should be done or where the force was to go after crossing into Texas.

With some notable exceptions, army and navy commanders did not trust each other. Regional rivalries existed among the Union troops. Did this discord seriously hamper the operation? Issues between the armed services were evident. Interservice rivalries between the army and navy had been longstanding and cooperation was difficult to achieve, yielding an air of mistrust. Interservice cooperation had been a marriage of convenience until the Vicksburg Campaign. That operation brought together the three most dynamic Union leaders of the Civil War in the western theater—Major General Ulysses S. Grant, Major General William T. Sherman, and Rear Admiral David D. Porter. After an awkward beginning, the three men came to trust each other implicitly, each relying on the others under the most difficult conditions. This bond unintentionally created a problem in the Red River Campaign.

The navy entered the campaign with reckless abandon, bringing many vessels unsuitable for the river in which they were to operate. What was the proper mix of boats, and could the naval plan have been altered to achieve success? Both the army and navy entered the mission with a lack of intelligence capability that made them almost blind to local geographic conditions. The navy signed on for the mission with great enthusiasm when Porter was told that Sherman would lead the operation. He committed the vast bulk of the inland navy to the mission without regard to river conditions on the shallow Red River, confident that Sherman would assist the fleet if it ran into trouble. Banks, instead of Sherman, was named to command the expedition, but at that point Porter felt he could not withdraw or reduce the force he had committed. Porter made no attempt to perform reconnaissance upstream to determine potential threats. Instead, he relied on scanty, uncorroborated intelligence to choose which vessels would ascend the river. Porter was skeptical of Banks's abilities, and the loan of ten thousand veterans by Sherman, ostensibly to protect the fleet from abandonment by Banks, reinforced his belief.

Porter made some poor choices as he prepared for the operation. He committed almost his entire command to the expedition, leaving barely enough vessels to patrol the Mississippi and its major tributaries. This mix of vessels was inappropriate for the conditions of the river and the admiral gave little thought to the geographic environment it was about to enter. He had received some information from intelligence sources, mostly incorrect or exaggerated, and he chose not confirm the hearsay. His ultimate belief in naval firepower to reduce threats was only partially correct. The near loss of the fleet was sobering to the admiral, and he made no attempt to repeat the venture.

Both army and navy commanders had a total disregard for Confederate leadership west of the Mississippi River and its ability to defend the territory under its control. Banks had faced the Confederate field commander, Major General Richard Taylor, and had been bested by the Rebel more than once. However, Banks believed using huge numbers of troops would be a sufficient counterweight to any opposition the Rebels could offer. That may have been the case, but he lacked a plan to deploy them in an effective manner. Porter had received intelligence information that the Confederates were building an ironclad fleet and possibly submarines. His answer to this potential threat was huge ironclads fitted with large bore guns. On the eve of the campaign, neither Union military leader appeared concerned about the opposition.

Perhaps the most neglected question concerning the campaign is "To what extent did Confederate forces and policy contribute to the Union failure?" Northern sources almost uniformly ignored Confederate preparations for an attack. They were ignorant of the depth and quality of the defensive positions since the Union forces did not

Conclusion
179

see most fortifications. Lacking knowledge of Confederate plans for troop allocation, most Union reports greatly exaggerated the number of Rebel troops present on the battlefields.

The Confederates had worked feverishly for a year preparing for such an invasion. The Confederates prepared war-related industries, defensive positions, and laid elaborate traps for the navy. The Rebel army in Louisiana had been repositioned in preparation for an attack up the Red River. Although political turmoil within the Confederate leadership hindered their plans, the Rebel army was prepared to meet the Union force on the battlefield.

The Rebels responded to rapidly changing Union plans with speed and efficiency, but occasionally with confusion. Was this reaction enough to disrupt Union plans or did the Union commanders basically bring the debacle upon themselves? As the Union forces penetrated deeper into north Louisiana, logistical and deployment problems became apparent. The campaign unfolded, and promised schedules failed to materialize. Cockiness among the Union commanders, particularly Banks, William B. Franklin (Banks's second in command), and Porter, created trouble. Banks chose to take the bulk of his army inland at the village of Grand Ecore in Natchitoches Parish, away from the massive fire support offered by the navy. The most remote of the Union columns was in Arkansas, descending upon Shreveport from Little Rock. This column was completely cut off from communications with the Louisiana portion and suffered accordingly. Porter was forced to parse his squadron into segments on the narrow, twisting, often shallow Red River and to leave deeper draft vessels at safe points along the way.

Edmund Kirby Smith was ill-suited as commander of the Department of the Trans-Mississippi in Shreveport. He was a soldier of the old school, believing strongly in strings of fortifications with garrisons to protect surrounding areas. The department was simply too large and its geography too complex for a system like this to be maintained, particularly with limited manpower. Smith should have realized that the fall of well-established bastions as Fort Pulaski on the Savannah River in Georgia and Fort Pickens in Florida, and, more locally, Fort Jackson and Fort St. Philip below New Orleans, proved the folly of relying solely upon static fortifications. A headstrong man, he rarely listened to opposing views. Conversely, his manner was subservient to those he respected, even those who were his subordinates. This created a pattern of inconsistency in his orders and prompted contempt within his staff.

Smith was both erratic and ineffective in his treatment of the district commanders. He refused to order John Magruder, the Texas district commander, to send troops to Louisiana when the campaign began. He did not want to confront Magruder on most matters. This left the Texas district as an almost autonomous authority. Smith also seemed to follow any suggestion his Arkansas district commander made. Sterling Price, a political general roughly equivalent to Nathaniel Banks in aptitude, was authoritative, decisive, and, quite often, wrong in his decisions. Smith believed Price to be very capable, and this caused great problems for the department during the Camden Campaign. Richard Taylor, the commander of the Western District of Louisiana, had a contentious relationship with Smith, resulting in constant tensions within the Louisiana command.

Smith and Taylor, key commanders in the Trans-Mississippi, came from different backgrounds and had different philosophies regarding tactics and strategies. Smith, a native of Florida and a veteran of the Mexican War, taught mathematics at West Point from 1849 to 1852. He held a deep appreciation for fortifications and believed in protecting an area with strings of fortified positions garrisoned by large numbers of troops. Taylor was a member of the Southern aristocracy, the son of President Zachary Taylor and brother-in-law to President Jefferson Davis. He possessed a sharp intellect, was very well educated, and developed a well-honed aptitude for military matters. He was competent and fiercely aggressive. Stonewall Jackson instilled in him that rapid movement and decisive action by a smaller, highly motivated army could overcome a much larger force, especially when weak commanders led the opposition. Taylor disdained fortifications, believing they were places to trap an army, rather than a strong point to defend an area. Considering their differences, it is surprising that the Confederate forces achieved the success they did in the Red River Campaign. Had the two commanders been more congenial in their personal relationship and more alike in their professional philosophies, the Confederates could likely have enjoyed even greater success.

The differences in the command philosophies of Smith and Taylor created problems. Smith created an extensive series of fortifications that lacked sufficient heavy artillery. Taylor wanted all major components of the Army of the Trans-Mississippi to be available to stop a threat from any direction and be available for rapid deployment wherever they were needed. Garrison duty interfered with this concept, so he refused to assign units to specific forts. The most important result of this dichotomy of command style was an impressive array of defenses with no firm plan of action. The two men carried on a war of words over almost every detail of allocation of guns and men. Animosity between the two generals reached new levels just before and during the campaign.

Once the campaign began, Taylor found himself without a reconnaissance force and this left him at a distinct disadvantage. Magruder did not release large numbers of cavalry, and the only Louisiana cavalry units were captured. Taylor was placed in the unenviable situation of using Fabian tactics of retreat before Banks's force because he had no way of knowing how large the size or direction of movement of opposing troops. He did not offer serious opposition until he was near Mansfield, abandoning both Alexandria and Natchitoches without a fight. Taylor had ample cavalry when Magruder released Tom Green's force for use in Louisiana. Their arrival, combined with the repositioning of other Texas and Louisiana units, gave Taylor the force he needed to halt the Union thrust. The strategic withdrawal had two consequences. First, it afforded Taylor a shorter supply line and the ability to assemble his forces with greater ease. Second, it left Banks with a false sense of security, believing that the Rebels lacked both the ability and the heart to fight his superior force. This may have lulled Banks and Franklin into their actions with the composition of the Federal column.

Taylor's belief that he was only fighting Banks's 13th and 19th Corps led to incorrect assumptions. The Confederate general's plan to fight Banks the next morning was not changed after the Union column retreated, and this was the greatest tactical mistake by Taylor during the campaign. The Battle of Pleasant Hill was fought with Arkansas and Missouri troops who arrived late and were exhausted from the force-march at Keachi. The unaltered battle plan from the previous night called for them to make a wide sweep to the right through dense forest. They became disoriented and wheeled too soon, placing them in front of Sherman's seasoned veterans. The result was a bloody stalemate, a tactical tie that ended in a strategic victory for the Confederates thanks to Banks's retreat.

One of Taylor's primary goals in the campaign was to capture as many Union warships as possible and use them against the U.S. Navy. He developed a theory the previous year that naval vessels could be attacked and captured by using overwhelming force by infantry or cavalry—if the vessels were close to a riverbank. Taylor's bold attempt to capture part of Porter's fleet at Blair's Landing was launched too late, but it achieved a limited success. Although the loss of Tom Green was grievous, the battle proved that ironclads and monitors were not all-powerful in confined areas. Taylor's theory may have worked had more men been used in the attack and had the troops arrived earlier.

After the Battle of Pleasant Hill, Smith pulled the Arkansas, Missouri, and Texas divisions from Taylor's command to chase Steele in Arkansas. This infuriated Taylor, who believed he had an excellent opportunity to trap both the Union army and fleet. Smith was still trying to retrieve his lost glory in a move that was unneeded, ill timed, and resulted in the near destruction of the three veteran divisions.

The three missing divisions would have played a major part in harassing the fleet and bottling Banks's force on Cane River Island. The Rebel force was too small to stop the Union column. The three additional divisions would have supplied ample troops to cover all potential exits, provide firepower from the adjacent ridges onto the flat tablelands of the island, and halt the exodus, thereby trapping the 13th, 16th, and 19th Corps units. With no infantry support other than the small 17th Corps contingent, Porter would have faced surrender or destruction of the fleet.

The missing divisions could have enhanced the Confederate victory. Taylor lacked troops to prevent the construction of Bailey's dams, pooling water to save the fleet. He was unable stop the burning of farms near Alexandria or the torching of the town. His small Louisiana Division had been greatly reduced in the opening charge at Mansfield. It could only offer limited resistance to Banks's column as it snaked southward toward Simmesport. In short, Taylor had too few men to offer any real measure of resistance or to prevent Union troops from crossing the Atchafalaya to safety.

Confederate actions in the field were boldly executed. When sufficient numbers of men were on the field, success was on the side of the Rebels. However, the rivalry between Smith and Taylor led to lost opportunities to capture or destroy the fleet at several points and Banks's army on Cane River Island. Smith's attempt to capture glory in Arkansas closely paralleled Banks's attempt to gain fame on the battlefield in Louisiana. Kirby Smith should be blamed for Confederate inconsistencies and the inability to achieve complete victory by capturing the fleet and possibly the army.

Following the campaign, the Union army was not eager to try a second attempt as well. For the remainder of the war, the army was content to hold New Orleans, Baton

Rouge, and the swampy land surrounding the two cities. It also allowed the navy to carry the flag on the rivers, with the sole exception of the Red and its tributaries. Almost all of the fighting force was removed to the Shenandoah Valley in Virginia. These troops were pivotal in the defense of Washington, arriving to thwart Jubal Early's raid on the city in July 1864. They were also the backbone of Sheridan's operation that devastated the Shenandoah Valley shortly thereafter. This operation deprived the Army of Northern Virginia of supplies, particularly foodstuffs, and helped end the war sooner.

The unanswered (and unanswerable) questions from the Confederate point of view are tantalizing. What might the Rebels have done with an intact Mississippi Squadron with free reign of the Mississippi River for several months? With the Mississippi and its tributaries compromised, could the Union have held New Orleans, Memphis, and Chattanooga? Would the Union Army of the Tennessee have supplied itself without material pouring across the Ohio River at Cincinnati and other ports? With Sherman marching on Atlanta and its supply lines cut, how would the army have reacted? Finally, with Banks's army destroyed or captured, army induction riots occurring in New York, and a resurgent George B. McClellan running on a Democratic Party peace platform, how would the presidential election of 1864 have played?

What were the most significant military and political consequences of the campaign? Combined operations with army and naval forces entered into a new phase with the Red River Campaign. Although major combined operations were conducted before and after the expedition, the Red River Campaign offered a showcase of what could be done and what should not be attempted.

The numbers of naval units participating in the campaign were larger than any riverine force heretofore. Following the campaign, the navy relegated itself to support of coastal and tidal river operations and to patrol the Mississippi River and its tributaries, excluding the Red River. Large-scale combined operations have since become a staple of American military strategy. The navy learned not to take inappropriately large vessels into tight quarters, regardless of their firepower potential. In fact, the campaign was the last mission of its type in the Civil War.

The army was taught a lesson in command and control issues by its failure to give clear authority to a single on-the-scene commanding officer. The importance of firm goals and objectives as a vital part of strategic planning was reinforced. Following the campaign the Union army dispersed the units to fight in Tennessee and in the Shenandoah Valley of Virginia. No attempt was made to strike at the Confederate Army of the Trans-Mississippi, although Banks's successor, E. R. S. Canby, proposed such an operation.

Innovations in the use of technology and in combat engineering were elevated to new heights in the campaign. Bailey's dam was a brilliant adaptation of logging industry techniques for military use. Lieutenant Colonel Joseph Bailey was promoted to the rank of brigadier general, given the thanks of Congress, and awarded the Medal of Honor. Another innovation, not recognized for its significance at the time, was the first use of a periscope to direct a weapon at an enemy.

The Red River Campaign was a pivotal operation for both the Union army and navy during the course of the war and afterward. It was the last great incursion deep into enemy-held territory by combined forces in the Civil War. Following the campaign, military planners in both services redirected cooperative ventures to areas better suited for their various strengths. The operation provided valuable hindsight for later plans.

The failure to take Shreveport and invade Texas was correctly perceived as a personal failure by Nathaniel Banks. This altered the political landscape in the fall presidential elections in 1864 and destroyed Banks's political career. In three short months Banks fell from the position of the favorite son of New England and strongest Republican contender against President Lincoln to the position of a high-ranking departmental staff officer with no power and few political friends.

The campaign forced ten thousand veteran troops originally assigned to operate in Georgia during the pivotal Atlanta Campaign to be redirected, thus delaying the end of the war by weeks or months. The troops of the 16th and 17th Corps were some of Sherman's best fighters. An additional ten thousand veterans on the Atlanta Campaign might have made the advance on Atlanta and March to the Sea progress at a faster pace. Grant's plan for Sherman to swing north from South Carolina and place Robert E. Lee's Army of Northern Virginia between the two great armies might have forced the surrender of Confederate forces earlier in 1865. The campaign also delayed the capture of Mobile by drawing off needed men and equipment from a much more important mission. The Red River Campaign allowed Confederate forces under Lieutenant General Leonidas Polk to move west of Atlanta rather than protect Mobile, thus slowing Sherman's forces.

The campaign had a tremendous effect on the navy. The inland fleet, or "brown water navy," never operated large vessels deep into Rebel-held territory again. Joint or combined operations continued, but in a different manner. From the end of the campaign to the close of the war, the navy participated in several operations, but only in coastal waters or tidal rivers.

The expedition was very important to naval strategy through the end of the war and beyond. No further naval expeditions were made up small rivers and streams. From the end of the campaign to the final spasm of fighting, the Mississippi Squadron patrolled the Mississippi River and its tributaries, but not the Red River. One could argue that there were no targets of opportunity left by this time, but the Red River still stood as an unconquered stream, and Shreveport was still in Rebel hands, fully functional, with an intact army ready to protect it.

Following the campaign, Union forces simply left the Trans-Mississippi to its own devices. Even on the Atlantic seaboard and the coast of the Gulf of Mexico, subsequent naval expeditions were made into bays and sounds, not into the feeder tributaries.

The last great naval attack on the Gulf coast was a major operation in August 1864, in which Admiral Farragut brought his West Gulf Blockading Squadron into Mobile Bay. In so doing, he closed the South's last major port. From that point forward the two Gulf of Mexico blockading squadrons performed sentinel duties and little else.

The chronology of combined operations during the Civil War clearly illustrates that the Red River Campaign was the apex in the scale of cooperation between the

Union army and navy in narrowly focused operations. Prior to the operation the two armed services learned each other's strengths and weaknesses. Following the campaign, the navy was more reserved in applying its power against deep penetration targets of the Confederacy. Although the expedition was one of several combined operations, its place as a turning point on the path to tactical doctrine makes it worthy of study.

Congressional oversight of military operations was affirmed. This is, perhaps, the most enduring legacy of the campaign for the U.S. military. Economic gains and political posturing towering over military objectives were never again so blatantly put to the forefront in military operations during the Civil War. This point can be argued during later conflicts, but not until the end of the war.

On the Southern side, Shreveport was spared the destruction experienced by other Southern towns. It did not have to rebuild, as did Atlanta. Shreveport became the economic capital for the Ark-La-Tex region, a position the city retains. The former Confederate capital of Louisiana continued to be the second largest city in the state until the last quarter of the twentieth century.

The campaign that the Union initiated with such promise ended with nothing to show for its efforts. Wasted opportunities, too much bloodshed, and incredible blunders by both sides all served to bury the campaign in the dustbin of history. Perhaps this is why so little historical attention has been given to this campaign as compared to others that occurred in 1864.

# APPENDIX 1

## Mississippi Squadron Vessels Deployed in the Red River Campaign, March–May 1864

Following are the Union vessels that participated in the Red River Campaign. The list includes U.S. naval vessels, U.S. Army Quartermaster Corps vessels (QMC), and vessels of the Mississippi Marine Brigade.

| Vessel Name | Type |
| --- | --- |
| Benton | Converted ironclad |
| Choctaw | Converted ironclad |
| Eastport*[1] | Converted ironclad |
| Essex | Converted ironclad |
| Lafayette | Converted ironclad |
| Carondelet | Ironclad |
| Louisville | Ironclad |
| Mound City | Ironclad |
| Pittsburg | Ironclad |
| Chillicothe | Ironclad |
| Neosho | River monitor |
| Osage | River monitor |
| Ozark | River monitor |
| Black Hawk | Large tinclad |
| Ouachita | Large tinclad |
| Lexington | Timberclad |
| Argosy | Tinclad/stern-wheeler |
| Avenger | Tinclad/side-wheeler |
| Covington*[2] | Tinclad/side-wheeler |
| Fort Hindman | Tinclad/side-wheeler |
| Gazelle | Tinclad/side-wheeler |
| Cricket | Tinclad/stern-wheeler |
| Forest Rose | Tinclad/stern-wheeler |
| Juliet | Tinclad/stern-wheeler |

| | |
|---|---|
| *General Bragg* | Tinclad-side-wheeler |
| *Naiad* | Tinclad-stern-wheeler |
| *Nymph* | Tinclad-stern-wheeler |
| *Signal*\*3 | Tinclad/stern-wheeler |
| *Saint Clair* | Tinclad/stern-wheeler |
| *Tallahatchie* | Tinclad/stern-wheeler |
| *General Sterling Price* | Ram/armed supply vessel |
| *New National* | Mail/supply/receiving vessel |
| *General Lyon* | Ordnance/stores, dispatch vessel |
| *Benefit* | River service vessel side-wheeler |
| *William H. Brown* | River service vessel side-wheeler |
| *Champion No. 3*\*4 | Tug/pump boat/side-wheeler |
| *Champion No. 5*\*5 | Tug/pump boat/side-wheeler |
| *Dahlia* | Tug |
| *Fern* | Tug |
| *Thistle* | Tug |
| *Judge Torrence* | Ordnance boat |
| *Samson* | Floating machine shop |
| *Alf Cutting* | Mississippi Marine Brigade/tug |
| *Autocrat* | Mississippi Marine Brigade |
| *Baltic* | Mississippi Marine Brigade |
| *Cleveland* | Mississippi Marine Brigade/tug |
| *Diana* | Mississippi Marine Brigade |
| *John Raine* | Mississippi Marine Brigade |
| *Lioness* | Mississippi Marine Brigade |
| *Little Rebel* | Mississippi Marine Brigade/gunboat |
| *T. D. Horner* | Mississippi Marine Brigade |
| *Woodford*\*6 | Mississippi Marine Brigade |
| *Bell Darlington* | Mississippi Marine Brigade/tug |
| *Adriatic* | U.S. Army QMC transport vessel |
| *Alice Vivian* | U.S. Army QMC transport vessel |
| *Any One* | U.S. Army QMC transport vessel |
| *Arizona* | U.S. Army QMC transport vessel |
| *Bella Donna* | U.S. Army QMC transport vessel |
| *Belle Creole* | U.S. Army QMC transport vessel |
| *Black Hawk* | U.S. Army QMC transport vessel |
| *City Belle*\*7 | U.S. Army QMC transport vessel |
| *Clarabelle* | U.S. Army QMC transport vessel |
| *Colonel Cowles* | U.S. Army QMC transport vessel |
| *Des Moines* | U.S. Army QMC transport vessel |
| *Diadem* | U.S. Army QMC transport vessel |
| *Emerald* | U.S. Army QMC transport vessel |
| *Emma*\*8 | U.S. Army QMC transport vessel |

| | |
|---|---|
| Gillum | U.S. Army QMC transport vessel |
| Hamilton | U.S. Army QMC transport vessel |
| Hastings*⁹ | U.S. Army QMC transport vessel |
| Henry Chouteau | U.S. Army QMC transport vessel |
| Iberville | U.S. Army QMC transport vessel |
| Ike Davis | U.S. Army QMC transport vessel |
| Illinois | U.S. Army QMC transport vessel |
| J.C. Lacy | U.S. Army QMC transport vessel |
| James Battle | U.S. Army QMC transport vessel |
| Jennie Rogers | U.S. Army QMC transport vessel |
| John H. Groesbeck | U.S. Army QMC transport vessel |
| John Warner*¹⁰ | U.S. Army QMC transport vessel |
| Kate Dale | U.S. Army QMC transport vessel |
| La Crosse*¹¹ | U.S. Army QMC transport vessel |
| Laurel Hill | U.S. Army QMC transport vessel |
| Liberty | U.S. Army QMC transport vessel |
| Louisiana Belle | U.S. Army QMC transport vessel |
| Luminary | U.S. Army QMC transport vessel |
| Madison | U.S. Army QMC transport vessel |
| Mars | U.S. Army QMC transport vessel |
| Meteor | U.S. Army QMC transport vessel |
| Mittie Stephens | U.S. Army QMC transport vessel |
| Pauline | U.S. Army QMC transport vessel |
| Polar Star | U.S. Army QMC transport vessel |
| Red Chief No. 2 | U.S. Army QMC transport vessel |
| Rob Roy | U.S. Army QMC transport vessel |
| Sallie Robinson | U.S. Army QMC transport vessel |
| Shreveport | U.S. Army QMC transport vessel |
| Silver Wave | U.S. Army QMC transport vessel |
| Sioux City | U.S. Army QMC transport vessel |
| South Wester | U.S. Army QMC transport vessel |
| Starlight | U.S. Army QMC transport vessel |
| Superior | U.S. Army QMC transport vessel |
| Texas | U.S. Army QMC transport vessel |
| Thomas E. Tutt | U.S. Army QMC transport vessel |
| Universe | U.S. Army QMC transport vessel |
| W. L. Ewing | U.S. Army QMC transport vessel |

**Total Vessels: 104**

U.S. Navy: 42
Mississippi Marine Brigade: 11
U.S. Army QMC: 51

\* Vessel lost during the expedition
 1. Sunk April 16, 1864, by Confederate torpedo.
 2. Destroyed by Confederate artillery at Dunn's Bayou, twenty miles below Alexandria on May 5, 1864.
 3. Destroyed by Confederate artillery at Dunn's Bayou, twenty miles below Alexandria on May 5, 1864.
 4. Destroyed by Confederate artillery and infantry at mouth of Cane River on April 26, 1864.
 5. Destroyed by Confederate artillery and infantry at mouth of Cane River on April 26, 1864.
 6. Ran aground and burned at Alexandria prior to March 27, 1864.
 7. Captured by Confederate artillery at David's Ferry (Snaggy Point), thirty miles below Alexandria on May 5, 1864.
 8. Destroyed by Confederate artillery at David's Ferry on May 1, 1864.
 9. Snagged and lost at Alexandria April 23, 1864.
10. Destroyed by Confederate artillery at Dunn's Bayou, twenty miles below Alexandria on May 4, 1864.
11. Destroyed by Confederate artillery at Egg Bend April 12, 1864.

# Appendix 2

## Orders of Battle for the Red River Campaign

### *Operations in Louisiana, March–May 1864*

#### Confederate Forces

General Edmund Kirby Smith commanding the Army of the Trans-Mississippi
Maj. Gen. Richard Taylor commanding the District of Western Louisiana
    Headquarters Escort Company (Louisiana Cavalry)—Capt. Joseph Benjamin
Unattached—2nd Battalion Louisiana Reserves

#### First Infantry Division

Maj. Gen. John G. Walker

First Brigade—Brig. Gen. Thomas N. Waul
        12th Texas Infantry—Col. Overton C. Young
        18th Texas Infantry—Col. Wilburn H. King
        22nd Texas Infantry—Col. Richard B. Hubbard
        13th Texas Cavalry, Dismounted—Col. Anderson F. Crawford
        Haldeman's Texas Battery—Capt. Horace Haldeman

Second Brigade—Col. Horace Randal (promoted brigadier general April 13)
        11th Texas Infantry—Col. Oran M. Roberts
        14th Texas Infantry—Col. Edward Clark
        28th Texas Cavalry, Dismounted—Lt. Col. Eli H. Baxter Jr.
        6th (Gould's) Texas Cavalry Battalion—Lt. Col. Robert S. Gould
        Daniel's Texas Battery—Capt. James M. Daniel

Third Brigade—Brig. Gen. William R. Scurry
        3rd Texas Infantry—Col. Phillip N. Luckett (attached about April 15)
        16th Texas Infantry—Col. George Flournoy
        17th Texas Infantry—Col. Robert T. P. Allen
        19th Texas Infantry—Col. Richard Waterhouse Jr.

16th Texas Cavalry, Dismounted—Col. William Fitzhugh
Edgar's Texas Battery—Capt. William Edgar

First Division Artillery
Haldeman's Texas Battery—Capt. Horace Haldeman
Gibson's Battery
Daniel's Texas Battery—Capt. James M. Daniel
Edgar's Texas Battery—Capt. William Edgar

## Second Infantry Division

Brig. Gen. Jean Jacque Alexandre Alfred Mouton (killed April 8), Brig. Gen. Camille Armand Jules Marie, Prince de Polignac

First Brigade—Col. Henry Gray
18th Louisiana Consolidated Infantry—Col. Leopold L. Armant (killed April 8), Lt. Col. Joseph Collins (promoted colonel)
28th Louisiana Infantry—Lt. Col. William Walker (killed April 8), Maj. Thomas W. Pool (promoted colonel)
Consolidated Crescent Regiment—(Louisiana) Regiment—Col. James Beard (killed April 8), Col. Abel W. Bosworth, Capt. William C. C. Claiborne, Jr.

Second Brigade—Brig. Gen. Camille J. Polignac, Col. James R. Taylor (killed April 8), Lt. Col. Robert D. Stone (killed April 8), Co. James E. Harrison
15th Texas Infantry—Lt. Col. James E. Harrison (promoted colonel April 15), Maj. John W. Daniel (promoted lieutenant colonel April 15)
17th Texas Consolidated Cavalry, Dismounted—Col. James R. Taylor, Maj. Thomas F. Tucker
22nd Texas Cavalry, Dismounted—Lt. Col. Robert D. Stone, Maj. George W. Merrick
31st Texas Cavalry, Dismounted—Maj. Frederick J. Malone
34th Texas Cavalry, Dismounted—Lt. Col. John H. Caudle
Artillery—Maj. Thomas A. Faeries
Confederate Regular Battery, Capt. John T. M. Barnes
Bell (La.) Battery—Capt. Thomas O. Benton
Boone's Louisiana Battery (siege guns)—Lt. Maunsel Bennett
St. Mary (La.) Cannoneers—Capt. Florian O. Cornay (killed April 26), Lt. John B. Tarleton.

Second Division Artillery—Maj. Joseph L. Brent (promoted lieutenant colonel)
Reserve Battalion—Maj. Charles W. Squires
West's Arkansas Battery—Capt. Henry C. West
Pelican (La.) Battery—Capt. B. Felix Winchester

## Detachment, District of Arkansas

Brig. Gen. Thomas James Churchill

## First Division

Brig. Gen. James C. Tappan

Tappan's Brigade—Col. H. L. Grinstead
  19th (Dawson's) and 24th Arkansas Infantry—Lt. Col. William R. Hardy
  27th and 38th Arkansas Infantry—Col. R G. Shaver
  33rd Arkansas Infantry—Col. Hiram L. Grinstead
  Etter's Arkansas Battery—Capt. Chambers B. Etter

Gause's Brigade—Col. Lucien C. Gause
  26th Arkansas Infantry—Lt. Col. Iverson L. Brooks
  32nd Arkansas Infantry—Lt. Col. William Hicks
  36th Arkansas Infantry—Col. James M. Davie
  [? 39th Arkansas Infantry—Col. James W. Rogan?]
  Marshall's Arkansas Battery—Capt. John G. Marshall

## Second Division

Brig. Gen. Mosby M. Parsons

First Brigade—Brig. Gen. John B. Clark Jr.
  8th Missouri Infantry—Col. Charles S. Mitchell
  9th Missouri Infantry—Col. Richard H. Musser
  Ruffner's Missouri Battery—Capt. Samuel T. Ruffner

2nd Brigade—Col. Simon P. Burns
  10th Missouri Infantry—Col. William M. Moore
  11th Missouri Infantry—Lt. Col. Thomas H. Murray
  12th Missouri Infantry—Col. Willis M. Ponder
  16th Missouri Infantry—Lt. Col. Pleasant W. H. Cumming
  9th Missouri Battalion Sharpshooters—Maj. Lebbeus A. Pindall
  Lesueur's Missouri Battery—Capt. Alex A. Lesueur

## Cavalry Corps

Brig. Gen. Thomas Jefferson Green (killed April 12), Brig. Gen. Hamilton P. Bee,
Maj. Gen. John A. Wharton

## First Division

Brig. Gen. Hamilton P. Bee (relieved May 14), Brig. Gen. Arthur P. Bagby

  Debray's Brigade—Col. Xavier B. Debray (promoted brigadier general)
    23rd Texas Cavalry—Col. Nicholas C. Gould (arrived April 9–10)
    26th Texas Cavalry—Lt. Col. John J. Meyers
    36th Texas Cavalry—Col. Peter C. Woods (arrived April 9–10)

Buchel's Brigade—Col. Augustus C. Buchel (mortally wounded April 9), Col. Arthur P.
Bagby (promoted brigadier general April 13), Col. Alexander W. Terrell

1st Texas Cavalry—Lt. Col. William O. Yager
35th (Likens') Texas Cavalry—Col. James B. Likens, Lt. Col. James R. Burns
(arrived April 9–10, detached to Sub-District of North Louisiana)
Terrell's Texas Cavalry—Col. Alexander W. Terrell

## First Division

Brig. Gen. James P. Major

Lane's Brigade—Col. Walter P. Lane (wounded April 8), Col. George W. Baylor
1st Texas Partisan Rangers—Lt. Col. R. P. Crump, Maj. W. P. Saufley
2nd Texas Partisan Rangers—Col. Isham Chisum, Lt. Col. Crill Miller
2nd Regt., Arizona Brigade—Col. George W. Baylor, Lt. Col. John W. Mullen
3rd Regt., Arizona Brigade—Lt. Col. George T. Madison

Bagby's Brigade—Col. Arthur P. Bagby, Col. William P. Hardeman, Lt. Col. George J.
Hampton, Lt. Col. Edward Waller Jr.
4th Texas Cavalry—Col. William P. Hardeman, Lt. Col. George J. Hampton,
Maj. Charles Lesueur
5th Texas Cavalry—Maj. Hugh A. McPhaill
7th Texas Cavalry—Lt. Col. Philemon T. Herbert Jr. (promoted colonel;
mortally wounded April 8), Lt. Col. Gustave Hoffman
13th Texas Cavalry Battalion—Lt. Col. Edward Waller Jr., Capt. W. A.
McDade

Vincent's Brigade—Col. William G. Vincent (operated independently)
2nd Louisiana Cavalry—Col. William G. Vincent, Maj. Winter O. Breazeale
4th (7th) Louisiana Cavalry—Col. Louis Bush

Horse Artillery—Maj. Oliver J. Semmes
Grosse Tete (La.) Flying Artillery Battery—Capt. John A. A. West
Gibson's Texas Battery—Capt. William E. Gibson (arrived about May 10)
McMahan's Texas Artillery Battery—Capt. Martin Van Buren McMahan
Moseley's Texas Artillery Battery—Capt. William G. Moseley
Valverde (Tex.) Artillery Battery—Capt. Thomas D. Nettles

Louisiana State Guard
1st Louisiana Battalion Cavalry—Lt. Col. Benjamin W. Clark, Maj.
Thomas J. Caldwell
2nd Louisiana Battalion Cavalry—Lt. Col. Henry M. Favrot

Miscellaneous
Harrison's Louisiana Cavalry Battalion—Lt. Col. William Harrison
Red River Scouts (La.) Cavalry Battalion (two companies)—Capt. Willis A.
Stewart
1st Trans-Mississippi Cavalry Battalion—Maj. Thomason J. Bird
King's Louisiana Battery (siege guns)—Capt. Edward T. King
Crescent Artillery (Company A)—Capt. T. H. Hutton

## Sub-District of North Louisiana - Operating East of Red River

Brig. Gen. St. John R. Liddell (relieved May 10), Col. Isaac F. Harrison

Harrison's Brigade—Col. Isaac F. Harrison
    3rd Louisiana Cavalry—Lt. Col. Francis W. Moore
    4th Louisiana Cavalry—Col. A. J. McNeill
    5th Louisiana Cavalry—Col. Richard L. Capers
    8th Missouri Cavalry (detachment)—Lt. Col. Samuel J. Ward
    35th (Likens') Texas Cavalry—Col. James B. Likens, Lt. Col. James R. Burns

Artillery—Capt. T. Kinlock Fauntleroy
    2nd Louisiana Heavy Artillery Battalion (siege guns)—Lt. Col. George W. Logan, Capt. Daniel Scully
    Cameron's Louisiana Battery (one section)—Lt. T. Jefferson Key
    Battery H, 1st Mississippi Light Artillery Regiment (one section)—Lt. J. Wood Coleman

# Union Forces

Major General Nathaniel Prentiss Banks, Commander Department of the Gulf

## 13th Army Corps (Detachment)

Brig. Gen. Thomas E. G. Ransom

## Third Division

Brig. Gen. Robert A. Cameron

First Brigade—Lt. Col. Aaron M. Flory
    46th Indiana Infantry—Capt. William M. DeHart
    29th Wisconsin Infantry—Maj. Bradford Hancock

Second Brigade—Col. William H. Raynor
    24th Iowa Infantry—Maj. Edward Wright
    28th Iowa Infantry—Col. John Connell
    56th Ohio Infantry—Capt. Maschil Manring Artillery
    1st Missouri Light Artillery, Battery A—Lt. Col. Elisha Cole
    Ohio Light Artillery, 2nd Battery—Lt. William H. Harper

## 4th Division

Col. William J. Landram

First Brigade—Col. Frank Emerson
    77th Illinois Infantry—Lt. Col. Lysander R. Webb
    67th Indiana Infantry—Maj. Francis A. Sears

19th Kentucky Infantry—Lt. Col. John Cowan
23rd Wisconsin Infantry—Maj. Joseph E. Greene

Second Brigade—Col. Joseph W. Vance.
    130th Illinois Infantry—Maj. John B. Reid
    48th Ohio Infantry—Lt. Col. Joseph W. Lindsey
    83rd Ohio Infantry—Lt. Col. William H. Baldwin
    96th Ohio Infantry—Lt. Col. Albert H. Brown Artillery
    Indiana Light Artillery, 1st Battery—Capt. Martin Klauss
    Chicago Mercantile Battery—Lt. Pinkney S. Cone

## 19TH ARMY CORPS

Maj. Gen. William B. Franklin

## FIRST DIVISION

Brig. Gen. William H. Emory

First Brigade
Brig. Gen. William Dwight
    29th Maine Infantry—Col. George L. Beal
    114th New York Infantry—Lt. Col. Henry B. Morse
    116th New York Infantry—Col. George M. Love
    153rd New York Infantry—Col. Edwin P. Davis
    161st New York Infantry—Lt. Col. William B. Kinsey

Second Brigade—Brig. Gen. James W. McMillan
    15th Maine Infantry—Col. Isaac Dyer
    160th New York Infantry—Lt. Col. John B. Van Petten
    47th Pennsylvania Infantry—Col. Tilghman H. Good
    13th Maine Infantry—Col. Henry Rust Jr.

Third Brigade—Col. Lewis Benedict
    30th Maine Infantry—Col. Francis Fessenden
    162nd New York Infantry—Lt. Col. Justus W. Blanchard
    173rd New York Infantry—Col. Lewis M. Peck
    165th New York Infantry—Lt. Col. Gouverneur Carr Artillery
    1st Delaware Battery—Capt. Benjamin Nields
    Battery L, 1st U.S. Artillery—Lt. Franck E. Taylor
    1st Vermont Battery—Capt. George T. Hebard

## CAVALRY DIVISION

Brig. Gen. Albert L. Lee

First Brigade—Col. Thomas J. Lucas
    14th New York Cavalry—Maj. Abraham Bassford
    16th Indiana Mounted Infantry—Lt. Col. James H. Redfield
    2nd Louisiana Mounted Infantry—Maj. Alfred Hodsdon

Third Brigade—Col. Harai Robinson
    1st Louisiana Cavalry (U.S.)—Maj. Algernon S. Badger
    87th Illinois Mounted Infantry—Lt. Col. John M. Crebs

Fourth Brigade—Col. Nathan A. M. "Goldlace" Dudley
    2nd Illinois Cavalry—Maj. Benjamin F. Marsh Jr.
    3rd Massachusetts Cavalry (31st Massachusetts Mounted Infantry)—
        Lt. Col. Lorenzo D. Sargent
    2nd New Hampshire Cavalry (8th New Hampshire Mounted Infantry)—
        Lt. Col. George A. Flanders

Fifth Brigade—Col. Oliver R Gooding
    18th New York Cavalry, Companies K and D—Capt. William Davis
    3rd Rhode Island Cavalry (detachment)—Maj. George R Davis
    2nd New York Veteran Cavalry (?)—Col. Morgan H. Chrysler

Artillery
    Rawles's Battery (Battery G, 5th U.S. Light Artillery)—Lt. Jacob B. Rawles
    6th Missouri Cavalry, Howitzer Battery—Capt. H. H. Rottakan
    2nd Battery (B) Massachusetts Light Artillery—Capt. Ormand F. Nims

## 16TH ARMY CORPS, ARMY OF THE TENNESSEE

Brig. Gen. Andrew J. Smith

Also under Smith's command was the Provisional Division of the 17th Corps and the Mississippi Marine Brigade.

## FIRST DIVISION

Second Brigade—Col. Lucius F. Hubbard
    47th Illinois Infantry—Col. John D. McClure
    5th Minnesota Infantry—Maj. John C. Becht
    8th Wisconsin Infantry—Lt. Col. John W. Jefferson

Third Brigade—Col. Sylvester G. Hill
    35th Iowa (nonveterans 8th and 12th Iowa attached)—Lt. Col. William B.
        Keeler
    33rd Missouri (nonveterans, 11th Missouri attached)—Col. William H. Heath

## Third Division

Brig. Gen. Joseph A. Mower

First Brigade—Col. William F. Lynch
    58th Illinois Infantry—Maj. Thomas Newlan
    119th Illinois Infantry—Col. Thomas J. Kinney
    89th Indiana (nonveterans, 52nd Indiana attached)—Col. C. D. Murray

Second Brigade—Col. William T. Shaw
    14th Iowa Infantry—Lt. Col. Newbold
    27th Iowa Infantry—Col. James J. Gilbert
    32nd Iowa Infantry—Col. John Scott
    24th Missouri (nonveterans, 21st Missouri attached)—Maj. Robert W. Fyan

Third Brigade—Col. Risdon M. Moore
    49th Illinois Infantry—Thomas W. Morgan
    117th Illinois Infantry—Lt. Col. Jonathan Merriam
    178th New York—Col. Edward Wehler

Artillery
    3rd Indiana Battery—Capt. James M. Cockefair
    9th Indiana Battery—Capt. George R. Brown

## 17th Corps

Detached to Brig. Gen. A. J. Smith (16th Corps)

## Second (Provisional) Division

Brig. Gen. Thomas Kilby Smith

First Brigade—Col. Jonathan B. Moore
    41st Illinois Infantry—Col. John M. Nale
    3rd Iowa Infantry—Lt. Col. James Tullis
    3rd Wisconsin Infantry—Maj. Horatio H. Virgin

Second Brigade—Col. Lyman M. Ward
    81st Illinois Infantry—Lt. Col. Andrew W. Rogers
    95th Illinois Infantry—Col. Thomas W. Humphrey
    14th Wisconsin Infantry—Capt. Carlos M. G. Mansfield

Artillery
    1st Missouri Light Artillery, Battery M—Lt. John M. Tiemeyer

## Mississippi Marine Brigade

Brig. Gen. A. W. Ellet

Infantry Regiment—Col. Charles R. Ellet
Cavalry Battalion—Maj. James M. Hubbard

## Corps d'Afrique—U.S. Colored Troops

### First Division

First Brigade—Col. William Dickey
    73rd Regiment USCT—Col. Chauncey J. Bassett, Maj. Hiram E. Perkins
    75th Regiment USCT—Col. Henry W. Fuller
    84th Regiment USCT—Col. James H. Corrin
    92nd Regiment USCT—Col. Henry N. Frisbie, Lt. Col. John C. Chadwick

Engineer Brigade—Col. George D. Robinson
    97th Regiment USCT—Lt. Col. George A. Harmount
    99th Regiment USCT—Lt. Col. Uri B. Pearsall

Garrison Troops holding Alexandria that did not actively participate in the campaign farther north but were sent to Grand Ecore as reserves after the battles of Mansfield and Pleasant Hill:

### 19th Army Corps

Maj. Gen. William B. Franklin

### Second Division

Brig. Gen. Cuvier Grover

Second Brigade—Col. Edward L. Molineaux
    13th Connecticut Infantry—Col. Charles D. Blinn
    1st Louisiana Infantry—Col. William O. Fiske
    90th New York Infantry (three companies)—Maj. John C. Smart
    159th New York Infantry—Lt. Col. Edward L. Gaul

Third Brigade—Col. Jacob Sharpe
    38th Massachusetts Infantry—Lt. Col. James P. Richardson
    128th New York Infantry—Col. James Smith
    156th New York Infantry—Capt. James J. Hoyt
    175th New York Infantry—(three companies) Capt. Charles McCarthey

Artillery
    7th Massachusetts Battery—Capt. Newman W. Storer
    26th New York Battery—Capt. George W. Fox
    Battery F, 1st U.S. Artillery—Lt. Hardman P. Norris
    Battery C, 2nd U.S. Artillery—Lt. John I. Rodgers

Cavalry
    3rd Maryland Cavalry—Col. C. Carroll Tevis

Reinforcements ordered to Alexandria from Texas following the battles of Mansfield and Pleasant Hill. They did not actively participate in the campaign farther north and did not participate in the battles of Mansura and Yellow Bayou.

## 13TH ARMY CORPS

Maj. Gen. John A. McClernand

### FIRST DIVISION

Second Brigade—Brig. Gen. Michael K. Lawler
  49th Indiana— Lt. Col. James Keigwin
  69th Indiana—Lt. Col. Oran Perry
  34th Iowa—Col. George W. Clark
  22nd Kentucky—Col. George W. Monroe
  16th Ohio—Lt. Col. Philip Kershner

# Operations in Arkansas, April–May 1864

## Confederate Forces

Lt. Gen. (later Gen.) Edmund Kirby Smith, Department Commander and Commander of the Army of Arkansas

District of Arkansas—Maj. Gen. Sterling Price

Escort—14th Missouri Cavalry Battalion—Maj. Robert C. Woods

### FAGAN'S CAVALRY DIVISION

Brig. Gen. James F. Fagan

Cabell's Brigade—Brig. Gen. William L. Cabell
  1st Arkansas Cavalry—Col. James C. Monroe
  2nd Arkansas Cavalry—Col. T. J. Morgan
  4th Arkansas Cavalry—Col. A. Gordon
  7th Arkansas Cavalry—Col. John F. Hill
  Trader's Regiment of Arkansas State Troops—Col. W. H. Trader
  Gunter's Arkansas Cavalry Battalion—Lt. Col. T. M. Gunter
  Blocher's Arkansas Battery

Crawford's Brigade—Col. William A. Crawford
  2nd Arkansas Cavalry—Capt. O. B. Tebbs
  Crawford's Arkansas Cavalry Regiment—Col. William A. Crawford
  Wright's Arkansas Cavalry Regiment—Col. J. C. Wright
  Poe's Arkansas Cavalry Battalion—Maj. J. T. Poe
  McMurtrey's Arkansas Cavalry Battalion—Maj. E. L. McMurtrey

Dockery's Brigade—Brig. Gen. Thomas P. Dockery
  18th Arkansas Mounted Infantry
  19th Arkansas (Dockery's) Mounted Infantry—Lt. Col. H.G.P. Williams

20th Arkansas Mounted Infantry
12th Arkansas Mounted Infantry Battalion (Sharpshooters)

Artillery
Hughey's Arkansas Battery—Capt. W. M. Hughey

## Marmaduke's Cavalry Division

Brig. Gen. John S. Marmaduke

Greene's Brigade—Col. Colton Greene
3rd Missouri Cavalry—Lt. Col. L. A. Campbell
4th Missouri Cavalry—Lt. Col. William J. Preston
8th Missouri Cavalry—Col. William L. Jeffers
10th Missouri Cavalry—Col. Robert R. Lawther
Harris's Missouri Battery—Capt. S. S. Harris

Shelby's Brigade—Brig. Gen. Joseph O. Shelby
1st Missouri Battalion Cavalry—Maj. Benjamin Elliot
5th Missouri Cavalry—Col. B. Frank Gordon
11th Missouri Cavalry—Col. M. W (or V). Smith
12th Missouri Cavalry—Col. David Shanks
Hunter's Missouri Regiment—Col. DeWitt C. Hunter
Collins's Missouri Battery—Capt. Richard A. Collins

## Maxey's Cavalry Division

Brig. Gen. Samuel B. Maxey

Gano's Brigade—Col. Charles DeMorse
29th Texas Cavalry—Maj. J. A. Carroll
30th Texas Cavalry—Lt. Col. N. W. Battle
31st Texas Cavalry—Maj. Michael Looscan
Welch's Texas Company—Lt. Frank M. Gano
Krumbhaar's Texas Battery—Capt. W. Butler Krumbhaar

Second Indian Brigade—Col. Tandy Walker
1st Choctaw Regiment—Lt. Col. James Riley
2nd Choctaw Regiment—Col. Simpson W. Folsom

## First Infantry Division—Department of Arkansas

Brig. Gen. Thomas James C. Tappan

Tappan's Brigade—Col. Hiram L. Grinstead
19th (Dawson's) and 24th Arkansas Infantry—Lt. Col. William R.
Hardy
27th and 38th Arkansas Infantry—Col. R. G. Shaver

33rd Arkansas Infantry—Col. Hiram L. Grinstead
Etter's Arkansas Battery—Capt. Chambers B. Etter

Gause's Brigade—Col. Lucien C. Gause
    26th Arkansas Infantry—Lt. Col. Iverson L. Brooks
    32nd Arkansas Infantry—Lt. Col. William Hicks
    36th Arkansas Infantry—Col. James M. Davie
    [? 39th Arkansas Infantry—Col. James W. Rogan?]
    Marshall's Arkansas Battery—Capt. John G. Marshall

## SECOND DIVISION

Brig. Gen. Mosby M. Parsons

First Brigade—Brig. Gen. John B. Clark Jr.
    8th Missouri Infantry—Col. Charles S. Mitchell
    9th Missouri Infantry—Col. Richard H. Musser
    Ruffner's Missouri Battery—Capt. Samuel T. Ruffner

Second Brigade—Col. Simon P. Burns
    10th Missouri Infantry—Col. William M. Moore
    11th Missouri Infantry—Lt. Col. Thomas H. Murray
    12th Missouri Infantry—Col. Willis M. Ponder
    16th Missouri Infantry—Lt. Col. Pleasant W. H. Cumming
    9th Missouri Battalion Sharpshooters—Maj. Lebbeus A. Pindall
    Lesueur's Missouri Battery—Capt. Alex A. Lesueur

## WALKER'S TEXAS DIVISION

Maj. Gen. John G. Walker

First Brigade—Brig. Gen. Thomas N. Waul
    12th Texas Infantry—Col. Overton C. Young
    18th Texas Infantry—Col. Wilburn H. King
    22nd Texas Infantry—Col. Richard B. Hubbard
    13th Texas Cavalry, Dismounted—Col. Anderson F. Crawford
    Haldeman's Texas Battery—Capt. Horace Haldeman

Second Brigade—Brig. Gen. Horace Randal
    11th Texas Infantry—Col. Oran M. Roberts
    14th Texas Infantry—Col. Edward Clark
    28th Texas Cavalry, Dismounted—Lt. Col. Eli H. Baxter Jr.
    6th (Gould's) Texas Cavalry Battalion—Lt. Col. Robert S. Gould
    Daniel's Texas Battery—Capt. James M. Daniel

Third Brigade—Brig. Gen. William R Scurry
    3rd Texas Infantry—Col. Phillip N. Luckett
    16th Texas Infantry—Col. George Flournoy

17th Texas Infantry—Col. Robert T. P. Allen
19th Texas Infantry—Col. Richard Waterhouse Jr.
16th Texas Cavalry, Dismounted—Col. William Fitzhugh
Edgar's Texas Battery—Capt. William Edgar

# Union Forces

Maj. Gen. Frederick Steele, Commander, Department of Arkansas and the Army of Arkansas

Headquarters Escort
Co. D., 3rd Illinois Cavalry—Lt. Solomon M. Tabor
Co. H., 15th Illinois Cavalry—Capt. Thomas J. Beebe

## THIRD DIVISION

Brig. Gen. Frederick Salomon

First Brigade—Brig. Gen. Samuel A. Rice
50th Illinois Infantry—Lt. Col. Thomas H. Benton Jr.
29th Iowa Infantry—Col. Thomas H. Benton Jr.
33rd Iowa Infantry—Maj. Hiram D. Gibson
9th Wisconsin Infantry—Col. C. E. Salomon

Second Brigade—Col. William E. McLean
43rd Indiana Infantry—Maj. Wesley M. Norris
36th Iowa Infantry—Col. Charles W. Kittredge
77th Ohio Infantry—Col. William B. Mason

Third Brigade—Col. Adolph Engelmann
43rd Illinois Infantry—Lt. Col. Adolph Dengler
40th Iowa Infantry—Col. John A. Garrett
27th Wisconsin Infantry—Col. Conrad Krez

Artillery—Capt. Gustave Strange
Battery E, 2nd Missouri Light Artillery—Lt. Charles Peetz
Springfield Illinois Light Artillery (Vaughn's Illinois Battery)—
Lt. Charles W. Thomas
Company F, 9th Wisconsin Infantry (Voegele's Wisconsin Battery)—
Capt. Martin Voegele

## FRONTIER DIVISION

Brig. Gen. John M. Thayer

First Brigade—Col. John M. Edwards
1st Arkansas Infantry—Lt. Col. Elhanon H. Searle

2nd Arkansas Infantry (eight companies)—Maj. Marshall J. Stephenson
18th Iowa Infantry—Capt. William M. Duncan
2nd Battery, Indiana Light Artillery—Lt. Hugh Espey

Second Brigade—Col. Charles W. Adams
1st Kansas Colored Infantry—Col. James M. Williams
2nd Kansas Colored Infantry—Col. Samuel J. Crawford
12th Kansas Infantry—Lt. Col. Josiah E. Hayes
1st Battery, Arkansas Light Artillery—Capt. Denton D. Stark

Third (Cavalry) Brigade—Lt. Col. Owen A. Bassett
2nd Kansas Cavalry—Maj. Julius G. Fisk
6th Kansas Cavalry—Lt. Col. William T. Campbell
14th Kansas Cavalry—Lt. Col. John G. Brown

## CAVALRY DIVISION

Brig. Gen. Eugene A. Carr
Co. B., 13th Illinois Cavalry—Capt. Adolph Bechand
3rd Iowa Cavalry (detachment)—Lt. Franz W. Arnim
1st Missouri Cavalry (eight companies)—Capt. Miles Kehoe
2nd Missouri Cavalry—Capt. William H. Higdon

3rd Brigade—Col. Daniel Anderson
10th Illinois Cavalry—Lt. Col. James Stuart
1st Iowa Cavalry—Lt. Col. Joseph W. Caldwell
3rd Missouri Cavalry—Maj. John A. Lennon

## GARRISON TROOPS AT PINE BLUFF

Col. Powell Clayton
18th Illinois Infantry—Lt. Col. Samuel B. Marks
1st Indiana Cavalry (eight companies)—Maj. Julian D. Owens
5th Kansas Cavalry (ten companies)—Lt. Col. Wilton A. Jenkins
7th Missouri Infantry—Maj. Henry P. Spellman
28th Wisconsin Infantry—Lt. Col. Edmund B. Gray

# APPENDIX 3

## David Dixon Porter Letter

MISSISSIPPI SQUADRON
FLAGSHIP BLACK HAWK
Off Alexandria LA
March 24, 1864.

Sir,

I have the honor to report for adjudication and condemnation, Two-Thousand, one hundred & twenty nine bales of cotton; - 28 barrels of molasses, and Eighteen bales of wool, captured from Rebels, and belonging to Confederate Government. This cotton, wool & molasses was captured in presence of the following vessels, which are all entitled to share in the prize.

would respectfully request that the cotton may be sold as soon as possible, as it is badly baled, and it may accidentally burnt and lost to the navy.

I also request that previous to being sold, it may be advertised in the Cairo papers.

Vessels entitled to share—
"Black Hawk"
"Eastport"
"Lafayette"
"Neosho"
"Ozark"
"Choctaw"
"Osage"
"Chillicothe"
"Louisville"
"Carandelet"
"Benton"
"Pittsburg"
"Mound City"
"Essex"

"Lexington"
"Ouichita"
"Fort Hindman"
"Cricket"
"Gazelle"
"General Price"

Very Respectfully
Your Obt. Servant
David D Porter
Rear Admiral

Hon. JH Treat
U.S. Dist. Judge
   Springfield
   Illinois

# Appendix 4

## Richard Taylor Letter

1:30 AM

April 9, 1864

HQ for D.W. La

Mansfield, La

General [Walker]:

Churchill and Parsons are starting on the right of the road. Churchill has been moved to take position on the right of the road. Parsons will march by his left, and take position on the left of the road. They will lead the attack at *early Dawn*. Time is every thing to us. Dispatches just received from the river show that the enemy has troops on the east side, and is again trying to get transports covered with troops up the river. This shows the enemy has divided his forces. We must take advantage of this error. Your men and Polignac's will have some relief as Arkansas and Missouri lead the fight in the morning. They must do what Texas and Louisiana did today. Show this to Gen'l Green and tell him we must push our left vigorously to occupy the road from Pleasant Hill to Blair's landing as this road is the shortest for the enemy to reinforce upon, and it is important to push him behind Pleasant Hill, which forces him to return to Natchitoches to reunite with his column on the river. Gl [General] Major should push some cavalry on the Blair's landing road as soon as possible even a squadron, as it would materially delay the enemy should he attempt to cross Bayou Pierre at Jordans Ferry. Given the nature of the position any resistance at Jordan's Ferry would be fatal to an attempt to cross. The enemy cannot receive anything from the river before late in the day tomorrow, so it is all important to punish him vigorously. [There is] nothing in our front but the troops we beat to day and the 19th Corps all Yankees whom we have always whipped. The corps is about seven thousand strong—many recruits who will make no fight. Should the enemy have disappeared in the morning, which is probable, the cavalry must make an active pursuit, at least to Dupont's Bridge and further if possible. One or two reg'ts [regiments] of cavalry will be in from Logansport early in the day. I will be in the field at early dawn, but if we detained a little later, the attack must be pressed at early light. The safety of our whole country depends upon it. Marmaduke badly managed the enemy on the Little Missouri, taking many wagons in his rear.

Your Obdt. Servant

R. Taylor
Major Gen'l

# APPENDIX 5

## Chronology of Combined Operations

April 12, 1861     Fort Sumter in Charleston, South Carolina, fired upon by South Carolina batteries and hostilities began.

April 22, 1861     Union troops coming by water land at Annapolis and save Washington from threat of occupation by Confederate forces.

May 16, 1861     Commander John Rodgers ordered to form a Union naval force on the western rivers. The three ships purchased and outfitted by Rodgers, the *Conestoga, Lexington,* and *Tyler,* formed for the nucleus of brown water navy. Rodgers was ordered by the secretary of the navy to operate under the command of the army.

May 24, 1861     Commander S. C. Rowan of the USS *Pawnee* demanded the surrender of Alexandria, Virginia, across the Potomac River from Washington, D.C. An amphibious force from the Washington Navy Yard occupied the town.

August 29, 1861     Flag Officer S. H. Stringham and Maj. Gen. Benjamin F. Butler received the unconditional surrender of Confederate forts Hatteras and Clark, closing Pamilico Sound to commerce raiding and blockade running.

September 12, 1861     Rodgers was replaced by the head of the Brooklyn Navy Yard Flag Officer Andrew H. Foote and the command was called the Mississippi Flotilla. Foote arrived at Cairo on September 12, 1861. Quartermaster General Montgomery Meigs had contracted with James Buchanan Eads to build the City Class ironclads on August 7, 1861. Samuel Pook built them, thus they were called "Pook Turtles." The first one delivered was the *St. Louis* (*Baron de Kalb*), on October 12, 1861.The first four were built at

| | |
|---|---|
| | Carondelet, the last three at Mound City. They were soon followed by the *Benton* and the *Essex*. This gave the flotilla twelve powerful gunboats. |
| **February 6, 1862** | Naval forces under Flag Officer Andrew H. Foote captured Fort Henry on the Tennessee River after receiving extensive damage to the gunboats. |
| **February 7–8, 1862** | Joint amphibious expedition under Flag Officer L. M. Goldsborough and Brig. Gen. A. E. Burnside captured Roanoke Island, thus compromising Albemarle Sound for the Confederates. This cut Norfolk off from its primary supply line and doomed it as a major naval base for the Confederacy. |
| **February 14, 1862** | Gunboats under Flag Officer Foote attacked Fort Donelson on the Cum-berland River in conjunction with land forces under Brig. Gen. Ulysses S. Grant. The fort surrendered February 16. This led to the fall of Nashville, a major supply depot for the Rebels. |
| **April 7, 1862** | Island No. 10, the key to Rebel defenses on the upper Mississippi River, surrendered to the Union forces commanded by Maj. Gen. John Pope. This opened the river to near Memphis for the Union gunboats from Cairo, Illinois, and allowed the attack on Fort Pillow. |
| **April 6–7, 1862** | The Battle of Shiloh. The Union gunboats *Tyler* and *Lexington* arrived to provide fire support for Brig. Gen. Grant against Rebel artillery batteries. This allowed Grant to hold his position and renew fighting the next day when reinforcements arrived by transport. |
| **April 24, 1862** | Flag Officer David G. Farragut's fleet ran past Fort Jackson and Saint Phillip, destroyed the defending Confederate naval forces, and took New Orleans the next day. |
| **June 17, 1862** | White River expedition in Arkansas cleared the Confederate defense fleet seeking refuge there. The navy was accompanied by a single army regiment. |
| **July 16, 1862** | Farragut promoted to rear admiral, the first officer to hold that rank in U.S. naval history. |
| **October 15, 1862** | Porter made the second rear admiral and arrived at Cairo. Mississippi Flotilla became the Mississippi Squadron. |
| **October 1862–July 1863** | Vicksburg Campaign and water experiments and naval operations. |

| | |
|---|---|
| December 12, 1862 | *Cairo* sunk. |
| March 14, 1863 | Farragut passed the batteries at Fort Hudson with two of seven ships to blockade Red River. |
| July 4, 1863 | Vicksburg surrendered. |
| July 9, 1863 | Port Hudson surrendered. |
| March 12, 1864 | Porter moved up Red River. The campaign lasted until late May. |
| July 11, 1864 | Jubal Early's raid on Washington was thwarted by the Potomac flotilla and the army. |
| August 5, 1864 | Farragut steamed into Mobile Bay closing the South's last major Gulf Coast port. |
| December 24–25, 1864 | Porter and Butler unsuccessfully tried to take Fort Fisher. |
| January 13–15, 1865 | Amphibious assault by Porter and Maj. Gen. Alfred H. Terry took Fort Fisher, the key defensive position guarding Wilmington, N.C., the last open Atlantic port held by the Confederates. |
| February 17–18, 1865 | Charleston was evacuated when faced by Sherman on the land and a naval-army amphibious assault from Bull's Bay. |
| February 22, 1865 | Wilmington, North Carolina, evacuated as Porter steamed up the Cape Fear River and Gen. J. M. Schofield marched into the city. |

# APPENDIX 6

## David French Boyd Letter

GRAND ECORE
April 14th, 1864
General Taylor,
Com. of Confederate Forces.

General:

Two iron-clad gunboats were lying at the mouth of Red river on 7th inst: The Essex at Fort DeRussey on 7th. The Benton at Alexandria on 8th; and on 12th a brigade of infantry, and one of cavalry, and four (4) light batteries at Alexandria (last is the statement of a private (Zauker [?])), who left that place on 12th inst.

At Grand-Ecore four (4) heavy iron-clad *Three* (3) of *Nine* (9) guns, and *One* (1) monitor of *Two* (2) guns. [This was the USS *Osage*.] Some Four (4) transports also.

Mostly the whole of Banks' Army is here (Grand-Ecore). A pontoon bridge spans the River; and a large forage train is encamped on East Bank, half (1/2) mile below the town; and evidently some cavalry and infantry are encamped on that side.

The enemy is said to be fortifying in rear of Grand-Ecore. They are foraging a great deal on East Bank. Some twenty (20) transports are *above*—between Grand-Ecore & Coushatta; and from the best information I can receive, they are protected by three (3) heavily plated gunboats, one (1) monitor and another, a *Ram,* and six (6) Tin-Clads; and it is certain that a large body of infantry is aboard the transports—probably the whole of one (1) Division, belonging to 17th Army Corps, commanded by Kilby Smith. [He was correct.]

The River is falling slowly—about four (4) inches last night (13th inst.). Scant six (6) feet of water is on the Falls. *Move heaven and earth to close up Scopini's Cut-Off!* A fall of two (2) feet more in the River would ruin the enemy. If the Fleet is lost, General banks considers himself ruined. He has been heard to say so. He is certainly much disturbed.

If Plaisance could be seized, and your 24 pounders and 30 pounder Parott placed there, I think you w*d* [would] reap a rich harvest, th' your Battery was finally

lost. Such a movement—if Plaisance were tenaciously held—would completely para-
lyze General Banks.

I have just now heard from a reliable source that there are but three (3) regiments & a squadron of Cavalry (Whites), and some negro troops (number not
known) at Alexandria. To that number add about 500 Whites sent down on 13th.
Three (3) boat loads, about 1500 men, came up from Alexandria on 12th.

I *wd* [would] have put-down this information *neatly* in a letter; but as the returning surgeon will be most likely required to carry out no letters but those examined & approved by the Federal authorities, I have thought it best to resort to this
means -o- [unknown mark on letter by Boyd] of communicating with you.

I hope you will give our enemies another good thrashing. They acknowledge
themselves badly whipped.

We have now been on this Boat Ten (10) days, and many men are sick. I am well,
and in good spirits, but bitterly regretting that my ignominious capture x- [*his mark*]
has prevented my participating in your glorious victory.

Resp'y

D. F. Boyd[1]

1. Letter in the Archives of Jackson Barracks (Louisiana National Guard
   Archives), New Orleans, LA.

# APPENDIX 7

## Red River Campaign Time Line

| | |
|---|---|
| March 7 | Lead elements of the U.S. 13th and 19th Corps assemble in and near Brashear City (Morgan City). They are five days behind schedule. These troops are to meet the navy in Alexandria on March 17. |
| March 8 | The advance of the column, led by the Cavalry Division of the 19th Corps heads west from Brashear City toward Opelousas. |
| March 10 | U.S. Brig. Gen. A. J. Smith of William T. Sherman's command (13th, 16th, and 17th Corps) leaves Vicksburg aboard transports. |
| March 11 | Evening—Army transports and Mississippi Squadron under Rear Adm. David Dixon Porter rendezvous at mouth of the Red River. |
| March 12 | Combined fleet enters Red River. |
| | Simmesport secured as bridgehead. |
| March 13 | Advance units of Mississippi Squadron move upriver. |
| | A. J. Smith marches inland to Marksville after taking four unfinished Confederate forts at Yellow Bayou, two miles from Simmesport. |
| March 14 | Admiral Porter clears piling dam, and Smith's forces take Fort DeRussy with support from USS *Eastport*. |
| | CSA First (Texas) Division under Maj. Gen. John G. Walker withdraws to Bayou de Glaize. |
| March 15 | Admiral Porter orders USS *Osage* to demand surrender of Alexandria. The town surrenders without firing a shot. |
| March 15–16 | A. J. Smith's men attempt to destroy Fort DeRussy and USS *Benton* and USS *Essex* pound the fort and fail to destroy it. |

| March 16 | CSA Maj. Gen. Richard Taylor orders forces to gather west of Alexandria and for all Confederate vessels and army units to evacuate the town. |
|---|---|
| | Third Division of 16th Corps under Brig. Gen. Joseph Mower takes control of Alexandria. |
| | Admiral Porter arrives at Alexandria with the fleet minus the USS *Benton* and USS *Essex*. |
| March 16–24 | The fleet and A. J. Smith's men at Alexandria stealing more than three thousand bales of cotton from surrounding area. |
| | Porter monitors the river falling and does not understand its failure to rise after the spring rains. |
| March 17 | Arkansas—Union Maj. Gen. Frederick Steele orders Brig. Gen. John Thayer of the Frontier Division to lead a force from Fort Smith to Arkadelphia and link up with him for the drive on Shreveport. Steele, coming from Little Rock, is the senior Union commander in Arkansas. His two columns are to join and draw off Confederate forces against Banks. |
| March 18 | CSA Trans-Mississippi Department commander Lt. Gen. Edmund Kirby Smith orders a huge transport, *New Falls City*, to be removed from Cou-shatta Chute (Bayou Coushatta) and to be taken to the foot of Scopini's Cutoff (near the village of Robson in southern Caddo Parish) and to be wedged across the river to block it. |
| | A chain forged at a local plantation is being strung across the river upstream from the *New Falls City*. |
| | Smith also orders a dam (the Hotchkiss Dam) at Tones Bayou (about two miles south of Louisiana State University, Shreveport, on the Port of Shreveport–Bossier property) to be blown up and water diverted from Red River into Bayou Pierre, thus starving the river of water and hopefully trapping the Union fleet. |
| March 21 | CSA 2nd Louisiana Cavalry Regiment under Col. William Vincent captured at Henderson's Hill near Boyce. The Confederates have no reconnaissance arm. |
| | Union Maj. Gen. Nathaniel Prentiss Banks, the senior Union army commander, leaves Baton Rouge after installing the new governor in office. Rather than march with his men, he ascends the river aboard a U.S. Army quartermaster vessel, the *Black Hawk*. He has with him several cotton speculators. |

| | |
|---|---|
| March 23 | Arkansas—Steele leaves Little Rock with his column. |
| March 25 | Lead elements of the XIX Corps Cavalry Division encamp outside Alexandria, seven days late. The Union column extends behind the lead units for about twenty-five miles. |
| | Banks arrives at the wharf in Alexandria late in the day and is thwarted in cotton stealing by the navy. |
| | Arkansas—Confederate Brigadier General John Marmaduke sends out units to find the Union columns. Marmaduke is at Camden. |
| March 26 | The last regiments in Banks's column march into Alexandria. |
| | 2,500 African American troops of the Corps d'Afrique arrive by steamboat. |
| | Banks now has 32,500 combat troops in Alexandria. |
| | Banks orders the Cavalry Division to advance upstream to Grand Ecore, the port of Natchitoches. The column follows. |
| | Porter leaves about half the fleet at Alexandria due to low water. The remainder accompanies the army up the river. |
| | Banks receives a letter from Lt. Gen. U. S. Grant informing him that Sherman's ten thousand veterans must be returned no later than April 15 and that Banks is not to enter Texas. |
| | Arkansas—Steele reaches Arkadelphia. Thayer is not there. |
| March 28 | The last of the army's column leaves Alexandria that morning. |
| | Banks stays behind to organize elections. |
| March 30 | Cavalry division arrives at Natchitoches. No Confederates are there. |
| April 1 | Banks holds elections in Alexandria. |
| | First U.S. infantry units arrive at Natchitoches. |
| | Banks sends a letter to army Chief of Staff Henry Halleck stating that he would be at Shreveport by April 10 and would chase the Confederate army into Texas if needed, ignoring Grant. |
| | Porter anchors his fleet at Grand Ecore, four miles from Natchitoches. |
| | Richard Taylor orders the brigades from the Louisiana and Texas divisions to meet at Mansfield. He also requests |

that the Texas Cavalry Corps be released for action in Louisiana and that the Arkansas and Missouri divisions in southern Arkansas be marched to Shreveport and then Mansfield.

Arkansas—Steele leaves Arkadelphia for Washington, Arkansas, the Confederate provisional capital.

**April 2**    Banks leaves for Grand Ecore aboard an army transport vessel.

**April 3**    Banks arrives at Grand Ecore.

**April 4**    Porter sends a raiding party upstream to Campti, where two Confederates are captured.

Banks decides to hold an election in Grand Ecore.

Banks receives bad advice about roads and determines to march his army inland away from the protecting guns of the navy.

Porter and Banks have a conference in which they determine to meet at Springfield Landing (on Smithport Lake in northern DeSoto Parish) on April 10.

Porter pleads to wait until he can perform an armed reconnaissance along the river, but Banks refuses.

The Confederate commander of the District of Texas, Maj. Gen. John B. Magruder, releases the Texas Cavalry Corps under Brig. Gen. Thomas Green, for operations in Louisiana. The cavalrymen leave camp in Hemphill, Texas, and ride toward Logansport.

**April 5**    Banks holds elections at Grand Ecore.

**April 6**    The Union Cavalry Division takes the lead west out of Natchitoches along the old Spanish Royal Road (LA Hwy 6). They turn northwest at White's Store (Robeline) and continue north at Crump's Corner (Bellmont). They then head north on the Natchitoches-Shreveport Stagecoach Road (LA Hwy 175).

Green's Texas cavalry reach Keachi where they bivouac for the night.

The Union Cavalry Division beds down at Pleasant Hill (then in southern DeSoto Parish).

Arkansas—Marmaduke receives reinforcements from the Indian Territory (Oklahoma).

**April 7**    Porter selects six gunboats to escort twenty transports upriver for the final push on Shreveport. The river level is too low for his largest vessels.

Green meets Richard Taylor at Mansfield and is ordered to range forward to slow down the Union column.

Taylor picks a large field three miles south of Mansfield to lay his trap for the Federal column.

Green blocks the road at Wilson's Farm, about three miles northwest of Pleasant Hill. A short fight ensues, delaying the Union column.

Green harasses the Union cavalry for another seven miles until the Federals stop for the night at Carroll Jones's mill, about halfway between Pleasant Hill and Mansfield.

**April 8**

Green slows the Union column down for about four hours until they reach Honeycutt Hill, three miles south of Mansfield.

Taylor positions his two divisions of infantry across the road in a giant "L" shape and waits for Banks to attack him.

The Union cavalry Division supported by the small Union 13th Corps prepares a smaller "L" line to respond to the Confederates about noon.

Banks is seven miles behind the forward units. He begins to ride forward after reinforcements are requested.

A small division of infantry in the Union XIX Corps is brought up behind the forward line and sets up at Sabine Cross Roads (today at the intersection of DeSoto Parish Addison Road and LA Hwy 175).

Another division is brought forward to the ridge south of Chapman's Bayou.

Kirby Smith refuses to allow the Arkansas and Missouri divisions to come to the battlefield before the battle.

At 4 P.M. the Confederates attack.

The wagon train of the Cavalry Division blocks the road from Honeycutt Hill back more than three miles, keeping adequate reinforcements from coming forward and blocking the retreat of the Union forces.

Within an hour and a half the initial Union line is destroyed.

The second Union line collapses about 5:30.

The third Union line is pushed back across Chapman's Bayou and darkness ends the fighting about 7 P.M.

Confederate casualties are about 1,000 men including 11 field commanders.

Union casualties are approximately 2,500 including the commander of the 13th Corps and two of the brigade leaders.

Arkansas—Steele bridges the Little Missouri River during torrential spring rains.

Banks leaves the field during the night and withdraws his army to Pleasant Hill.

**April 9**   At 1:30 A.M. Taylor lays out his plans for the next day's battle.

At dawn Taylor gives chase and catches Banks army at Pleasant Hill.

The battle begins at 4 P.M. with the Confederates employing Taylor's plan of the night before.

The Arkansas and Missouri divisions attack through the woods on the Confederate right but wheel too soon and enter the battlefield in front of A. J. Smith's men. Taylor did not believe Smith's people were there, but on the river guarding the fleet. They had always been at the back of the column.

The Louisiana and Texas divisions attack down the road and the battle ends with darkness, as the day before, but this time in a tactical draw.

Arkansas—Steele and Thayer join. Thayer's column is low on supplies as is Steele's. Steele sends an empty supply train back for supplies to Little Rock.

**April 10**   Arkansas—Steele pushes the Confederates back at Prairie d'Ane.

Kirby Smith removes the Texas, Arkansas, and Missouri divisions from Taylor's command, sends them to Shreveport, and prepares for operations in Arkansas.

Admiral Porter, with six gunboats and twenty transports, reaches what he thinks is the mouth of Loggy Bayou. He is in fact four to five miles north of it, one mile south of Tones Bayou. His progress is stopped by the *New Falls City*.

A Union cavalry unit finds Porter and tells the army escort of the 17th Corps to return to Grand Ecore, that Banks has met with a reversal.

The fleet begins the retreat.

**April 11**   Arkansas—Confederates abandon Camden and gather at Old Washington.

| April 12 | Tom Green and 2,500 Texan cavalry attempt to trap the fleet at Blair's Landing (now in southern Red River Parish). Green fights a two-and-a-half-hour battle against the USS *Osage*, the USS *Lexington*, and a transport. There are very few casualties, except Green, who was decapitated by a canister round from the *Osage* in the first use of a periscope in battle. |
|---|---|
| | Banks's column arrives at Grand Ecore after a three-day retreat. Banks begins to fortify the bluffs. |
| April 12–13 | Arkansas—Steele's combined column enters Camden. |
| | Kirby Smith sends the Texas, Arkansas, and Missouri divisions to Arkansas via separate routes. The units are to rendezvous at Calhoun, Arkansas. |
| April 13 | Porter's fleet anchors at Grand Ecore at 1 A.M. |
| April 16 | The USS *Eastport* is sent downriver from Grand Ecore before the fleet. Two miles downstream it strikes a mine laid by the CSS *Missouri*, based in Shreveport, before the fleet reached Grand Ecore. Efforts to refloat the vessel take several days. |
| April 18 | Arkansas—Maxey destroys Steele's supply train at Poison Spring. |
| | Arkansas—Steele receives a message from Banks to join him at Grand Ecore. Steele does not comply, as he has no supplies and believes there is no way to get his force to the South. |
| April 19 | Arkansas—Kirby Smith arrives at Calhoun, Arkansas, with the Arkansas, Texas, and Missouri divisions. |
| April 21 | The *Eastport* is refloated and begins its run downstream. Efforts to raise the vessel from the shallow river are successful, but the gash in its hull proves a problem. The *Eastport* will almost trap the fleet behind it on several occasions as it makes its way downstream. The vessel will travel another forty miles and become wedged in a logjam near the village of Montgomery (in Grant Parish). All efforts to extricate the vessel are in vain. |
| | Banks moves the column away from Grand Ecore and the river at 5 P.M. A. J. Smith's men torch the buildings of Grand Ecore. |
| | Through the night the column covers twenty miles. They do not torch Natchitoches because Confederate cavalry, now under Brig. Gen. James P. Major, harasses the rear units. |

Banks makes another major tactical error. He marches the column onto Cane River Island, the land between the Cane and Red rivers. He hugs the western road away from the fleet and finds that there are no exits except far to the south at Monett's Ferry (Bluff).

Taylor dispatches cavalry under Brig. Gen. Hamilton Bee to block Monett's Ferry. The Louisiana Division, under the Prince de Polignac, is sent south to cover any possible crossing north of the ferry. Taylor pleads for the Texas, Arkansas, and Missouri divisions to be returned.

April 23    Bee fails to stop the Union column from exiting Cane River Island. An African American runaway slave leads the Union troops to a ford behind the Confederates and Bee is outflanked. This is the last great chance to capture Banks's column.

April 25    The lead elements of Banks's column enter Alexandria.

Arkansas—A second Union supply train is ambushed at Marks' Mill, ending hopes of reinforcements for Steele.

April 26    Arkansas—Steele abandons Camden heading for Little Rock.

Porter decides to destroy the *Eastport* by putting a ton of black powder aboard and detonating it. The fleet loses its most powerful warship.

April 27    Arkansas—Confederates enter the abandoned Camden.

Confederate cavalry and infantry attack the fleet near the mouth of Cane River. Porter loses *Champion No. 3* and *Champion No. 5*. The *Cricket* and *Juliet* are heavily damaged.

Porter's fleet limps into the area just above Alexandria in the evening. He finds the river so low that the rocks forming the falls are clearly visible. His fleet is now trapped in two groups, those above the falls and those below. His most heavily armed vessels are above the town.

April 28    Porter begins to remove the ironclads' guns from the armor plating to lighten the vessels.

April 29    Porter and Banks accept a plan by Lt. Col. Joseph Bailey to construct a dam to raise the water level in the Red River and allow the fleet to pass into the deeper water downstream. Construction begins using African American engineering troops of the Corps d'Afrique and Maine troops who were lumbermen.

Arkansas—Kirby Smith catches Steele's column trying to cross the Saline River at Jenkins' Ferry. Part of the Union column had crossed. Smith makes an ill-fated frontal attack reminiscent of Pickett's Charge at Gettysburg in 1863 and wastes a large portion of his three divisions. Two of the three Texas Division brigade commanders are mortally wounded.

Arkansas—Steele crosses the river and destroys his pontoon bridge. Kirby Smith has no pontoon bridges and cannot follow. Steele returns to Little Rock.

| | |
|---|---|
| May 1 | Confederate artillery sinks the transport *Emma* at David's Ferry (near Echo). |
| May 2–9 | Bailey's dam is constructed. On May 9 the large dam gives way due to excess water pressure. Bailey begins to reconstruct the dam and adds two wing dams a short distance upstream to ease the water pressure on the main dam. |
| May 3 | Arkansas—Smith releases the three divisions for operations with Richard Taylor, but they will return too late to have any effect on fighting in Louisiana. |
| May 4 | Confederate artillery sinks the transport *City Belle* at David's Ferry. |
| May 5 | Confederate artillery sinks the *John Warner, Signal,* and *Covington* at Dunn's Bayou. |
| May 10 | The *Lexington,* the monitors *Osage* and *Neosho,* and the ironclads *Mound City, Carondelet,* and *Pittsburg* cross the falls. |
| May 13 | The first troops of Banks's column leave Alexandria at 7 A.M.<br><br>The *Ozark, Louisville,* and *Chillicothe* cross the falls.<br><br>Union troops set fire to Alexandria and burn most of the business district and downtown residences. |
| May 15 | The *St. Clair* engages Confederate artillery at Eunice's Bluff below Alexandria. |
| May 16 | Richard Taylor attempts to block the Union column at Marksville. The two armies sidestep each other and the two forces fight an artillery duel at Mansura.<br><br>Backflow water from the Mississippi River extends up the Red River to near Alexandria and increases the depth to the extent that the Mississippi Squadron steams downstream and out into the great river without difficulty. |

| | |
|---|---|
| **May 18** | The Confederates make a final attempt to halt the retreat of the Union army at Yellow Bayou, four miles west of Simmesport. They fail to stop the Union column. |
| | Union Maj. Gen. E. R. S. Canby arrives at Simmesport and notifies Banks that he has been fired, the command has been reorganized, and that Banks now works for him in an administrative capacity. |
| **May 19–20** | High water almost traps the army, but Colonel Bailey again rescues the troops by building a bridge by lashing the army's steamboats together and building a plank road across them. After the last units cross the Atchafalaya River, the steamboats are separated and the Confederates cannot follow. This ends the campaign. |

# NOTES

## Introduction

1. J. Cutler Andrews, *The North Reports the Civil War* (Pittsburgh, 1955).

2. Charles Dufour, *The Night the War Was Lost* (Garden City, NY, 1960).

3. U.S. War Dept., *War of the Rebellion: The Official Records of the Union and Confederate Armies*, 128 vols. (Washington, DC, 1890–1901) (hereinafter cited as *OR* and followed by series, volume, part number, and page reference); U.S. War Dept., *Official Records of the Union and Confederate Navies in the War of the Rebellion*, 31 vols. (Washington, DC, 1895–1929) (hereinafter cited as *ORN* and followed by volume and page reference); U.S. Cong., *Report on the Joint Committee on the Conduct of the War, 1863–1866*, vol. 2, *Red River Expedition* (Millwood, NY, 1977) (hereinafter cited as *JCCW*).

4. Ludwell Johnson, *The Red River Campaign: Politics and Cotton in the Civil War* (Kent, OH, 1993).

5. William Riley Brooksher, *War along the Bayous: The 1864 Red River Campaign in Louisiana* (Washington, DC, 1998).

6. Gary D. Joiner, *One Damn Blunder from Beginning to End: The Red River Campaign of 1864* (Wilmington, DE, 2003).

## 1. The Campaign in Context

1. Adoption papers were never formalized.

2. Grady McWhiney, *Cracker Culture: Celtic Ways in the Old South* (Tuscaloosa, AL, 1988), 1–49.

3. U.S. Army Corps of Engineers, *Red River Index, ARK.-TEX. to Mississippi River, Index of 1990 Mosaics* (Vicksburg, MS: U.S. Army Engineer District, Vicksburg Corps of Engineers, 1990). River miles are given in post–Red River Navigation Project miles.

In 1864, the Red River was almost twice as long as it became after straightening and channeling works. In Louisiana, counties are called parishes.

4. Settlers of European descent.

5. Louisiana State site form 16CD246, Division of Archaeology, Baton Rouge, LA.

6. Map of the inner defenses of Shreveport entitled "Shreveport and Environs" by Confederate Major Richard Venable, 1864, in Jeremy Francis Gilmer papers, Southern Historical Collection, University of North Carolina, Chapel Hill, copy at Louisiana State University in Shreveport, Archives and Special Collections, Noel Memorial Library. Hereinafter cited as Venable Map. Fredricka Doll Gute and Katherine Brash Jeter, *Historical Profile of Shreveport: 1850* (Shreveport, LA, 1982), 3.

7. Gute and Jeter, *Historical Profile,* 1.

8. Albert Harris Leonard, "Memoirs," MS, Cammie G. Henry Research Center, Eugene P. Watson Memorial Library, Northwestern State University of Louisiana, Natchitoches, 35–70.

9. Gute and Jeter, *Historical Profile,* 4.

10. Evidence of Improvements, block 39, lot 16; block 51, lot 9; and block 42, lots 12 and 13, Caddo Parish Assessor's Office records, Shreveport, LA.

11. Venable Map.

12. James Arthur Lyon Fremantle, *The Fremantle Diary, Being the Journal of Lieutenant Colonel James Arthur Lyon Fremantle, Coldstream Guards, on His Three Months in the Southern States,* edited by Walter Lord (Boston, 1954), 66.

13. Leonard, "Memoirs," 39.

14. U.S. Dept. of Commerce, Seventh Decennial Census (1850), Caddo Parish and Bossier Parish, unpublished tabulations in the National Archives and Records Administration. Hereinafter cited as Seventh Decennial Census.

15. Ibid.

16. Conveyance Book 3, Records of Caddo Parish, LA, p. 626; "Early Shreveport Developer was Black," *Shreveport Times,* Jan. 28, 1979.

17. *Shreveport Times,* Jan. 28, 1979.

18. Seventh Decennial Census.

19. Ibid.

20. Ibid. Joyce Shannon Bridges, ed., *Biographical and Historical Memoirs of Northwest Louisiana* (Nashville, 1890), 107.

21. Jeffrey Rogers Hummel, *Emancipating Slaves, Enslaving Free Men: A History of the American Civil War* (Chicago, 1996), 38.

22. Seventh and Eighth Decennial Census. Eric J. Brock, "A Necropolis of Graves at Oakland Cemetery," MS, Archives and Special Collections, Noel Memorial Library, Louisiana State University, Shreveport.

23. Ibid. Eric Brock, "Slavery in 1860 Caddo-Bossier," *Journalpage,* in *Shreveport Times,* Nov. 22, 1999.

24. Personal communication with Clifton Cardin, official Bossier Parish historian, Nov. 5, 2001.

25. Ibid.

26. Maude Hearn O'Pry, *Chronicles of Shreveport and Caddo Parish* (Shreveport, LA, 1928), 167.

27. John D. Winters, *The Civil War in Louisiana* (Baton Rouge, 1963), 211. Francis Fearn, ed., *Diary of a Refugee* (New York, 1910), 29–34.

28. Fearn, *Diary of a Refugee,* 29–34.

29. Perry Snyder, "Shreveport, Louisiana: 1861–1865: From Secession to Surrender," *Louisiana Studies* 11, no. 1 (Spring 1972).

30. *OR,* series 1, vol. 6, pt. 1:677–68.

31. *JCCW,* 285.

32. Ibid.

33. Venable Map.

34. *OR,* series 1, vol. 32, pt. 2: 122.

35. "The Beginning of the End, A Greeting for the New Year," *Atlantic Monthly* 3 (1864): 112–22.

36. Alfred H. Guernsey and Henry M. Alden, eds., *Harper's Pictorial History of the Civil War* (1866), 2:531–76; Louis S. Moat, ed., *Frank Leslie's Illustrated History of the Civil War* (1865), 309–494.

37. Guernsey and Alden, *Harper's,* 429–82.

38. Ibid., 525–76.

39. Douglas Southall Freeman, *R. E. Lee: A Biography* (New York, 1934–35), 3:253; *OR,* series 1, vol. 33, pt. 1:462.

40. Joseph E. Johnston, *Narrative of Military Operations* (New York, 1874), 272–86.

41. Johnson, *Red River Campaign,* 80.

42. *New York Times,* Oct. 30, 1862.

43. Benjamin F. Butler, memorandum dated January 1862 in Edwin M. Stanton Papers, Division of Manuscripts, Library of Congress.

44. Ibid.

45. *De Bow's Review* 2, rev. ser. (1866): 419.

46. Frederick L. Olmsted, *A Journey through Texas* (New York, 1857), 140–41, 172–83, 358–60, 414–15, 428–41; Laura W. Roper, "Frederick Law Olmstead and the Western Texas Free-Soil Movement," *American Historical Review* 56 (1950–51): 58–64.

47. Butler memorandum dated January 19, 1862, Stanton Papers, Library of Congress.

48. George B. McClellan, *McClellan's Own Story* (New York, 1887), 103–4.

49. Robert U. Johnson and Clarence C. Buel, eds., *Battles and Leaders of the Civil War* (New York, 1887–88), 2:23–25; David Dixon Porter, *Incidents and Anecdotes of the Civil War* (New York, 1891), 63–66.

50. *OR*, ser. 1, vol. 6, pt. 1:677–8.

51. Benjamin F. Butler memorandum dated January 1862, Stanton Papers, Library of Congress.

52. Dufour, *The Night the War Was Lost.*

53. *OR*, series 1, vol. 15, pt. 1:426.

54. Winters, *The Civil War in Louisiana,* 132.

55. Johnson, *Red River Campaign,* 20.

56. Fred H. Harrington, *Fighting Politician.*

57. *OR*, ser. 1, vol. 15, pt. 1:590.

58. *OR*, ser. 3, vol. 3, pt. 1:522; U.S. Senate, Executive Documents, No. 2, 38th Cong., 2nd sess., no. 2, 459–60, 470.

59. Adam Badeau, *Military History of Ulysses S. Grant* (New York, 1868), 2:70.

60. *JCCW*, 5.

61. Ibid.; *OR*, ser. 1, vol. 26, pt. 1:673.

62. *OR*, ser. 1, vol. 26, pt. 1:287–88.

63. Ibid., 288–97.

64. Nathaniel Banks to his wife, dated September 22, 1863, Banks Papers, Essex Institute, Salem, MA. Microfilm copy at University of Texas, Austin. Hereinafter cited as Banks Papers.

65. *OR*, ser. 1, vol. 26, pt. 1:292. Richard Taylor, *Destruction and Reconstruction: Personal Experiences in the Civil War* (New York, 1890), 150.

66. *OR*, ser. 1, vol. 26, pt. 1:397.

67. Ibid., 20–21.

68. Harrington, *Fighting Politician,* 133.

69. *OR*, ser. 1, vol. 26, pt. 1:683, 807.

70. Ibid., 834–35.

71. Ibid., 683, 807; *OR,* ser. 1, vol. 34, pt. 2:267.

72. William T. Sherman, *Memoirs of Gen. W. T. Sherman* (New York, 1892), 1:172–93.

73. *OR*, ser. 1, vol. 34, pt. 2:46; *JCCW,* 227.

74. Abraham Lincoln, *The Collected Works of Abraham Lincoln,* edited by Roy P. Basler (New Brunswick, 1953), 7:90.

75. C. A. Dana, *Recollections of the Civil War* (New York, 1898), 103.

76. *OR,* ser. 1, vol. 26, pt. 1:888–90.

77. Lincoln, *Collected Works of Lincoln* 6:1–2, 7, 90, 364–65.

## 2. Confederate Preparations

1. *OR,* ser. 1, vol. 26, pt. 2:117, 293–94, 341–2; *OR,* ser. 1, vol. 34, pt. 2:819.

2. Taylor, *Destruction and Reconstruction,* 153.

3. Map of Shreveport and Environs by Major Richard Venable, Jeremy Francis Gilmer papers, Southern Historical Collection, University of North Carolina, Chapel Hill. Hereinafter cited as Venable Map.

4. Gary D. Joiner and Stephen R. James, "Phase I Cultural Resources Investigation: Harrah's Entertainment Project, City of Shreveport, Caddo Parish, Louisiana," Archives of the Division of Archaeology, State of Louisiana, Baton Rouge, 1997, 19. Hereinafter cited as "Harrah's."

5. Charles Pearson, "Historical Survey and Assessment of Waterborne Commerce and Transportation and an Inventory of Underwater Cultural Resources on the Red River," Archives of the Division of Archaeology, State of Louisiana, Baton Rouge, 1995, 6.

6. Conveyance Book 24, Records of Natchitoches Parish, Natchitoches, LA, 345.

7. Gary B. Mills, *Of Men and Rivers: The Story of the Vicksburg District* (Vicksburg, MS, 1978).

8. Joyce Shannon Bridges, ed., *Biographical and Historical Memoirs of Northwest Louisiana* (Nashville, 1890), 210.

9. Ibid., 210.

10. George W. Shannon Jr., "Cultural Resources Survey of the Port of Shreveport-Bossier, Caddo and Bossier Parishes, Louisiana, unpublished report for the Caddo/Bossier Port Commission," Archives of the Division of Archaeology, State of Louisiana, Baton Rouge, 1996, 20.

11. Scopini's Plantation after the war became known as Scopena Plantation, the name it goes by today. In the *Official Records of the War of the Rebellion* it was mistakenly transcribed as Scopern's.

12. Act 243 of the Louisiana Legislature, 1860; *Bossier Banner,* May 18–25, 1860.

13. Shannon, "Cultural Resources," 25.

14. Joiner and James, "Harrah's," 27.

15. *OR,* ser. 1, vol. 22, pt. 2:1137–39; Waldo Moore, "The Defense of Shreveport—The Confederacy's Last Redoubt," in *Military Analysis of the Civil War: An Anthology by the Editors of Military Affairs,* ed. T. Harry Williams (New York, 1977), 396.

16. Venable Map.

17. Caddo Parish Records, Conveyance Book N, folio 295.

18. Joiner and James, "Harrah's," 27.

19. William N. Still Jr., *Iron Afloat: The Story of the Confederate Armorclads* (Columbia, SC, 1988), 226.

20. For a thorough treatment of the *Missouri* and Lieutenant Carter, see Katherine Brash Jeter, ed., *A Man and His Boat: The Civil War Career and Correspondence of Lt. Jonathan H. Carter, CSN* (Lafayette, LA, 1996).

21. Carter to the directors of the Vicksburg, Shreveport and Texas Railroad, Feb. 28, 1863, in Jonathan H. Carter, "Carter Correspondence Book" (MS), National Archives and Records Administration.

22. Venable Map.

23. Report of the Vicksburg, Shreveport and Texas Railroad, January, 1861, 3. Hill Memorial Library, Louisiana State University, Baton Rouge.

24. Lawrence Estaville, *Confederate Neckties: Louisiana Railroads in the Civil War* (Ruston, LA, 1989), 62.

25. Ibid. *ORN* 26:438–39. Mark K. Ragan, *Union and Confederate Submarine Warfare in the Civil War* (Mason City, IA, 1999), 288 n.

26. *ORN* 22:103–4.

27. Special Orders No. 22, May 20, 1864, RG 109, National Archives and Records Administration.

28. Un-filed Papers and Slips Belonging in the Confederate Compiled Service Records, RG 109, Entry M347, Naval Receipts, vol. 22, 104. Ragan, *Union and Confederate,* 288 n.

29. *ORN* 26:438–39.

30. Certificate of Death of James O'Leary, RG 68, Feb. 14, 1864, Louisiana State Museum, New Orleans.

31. Carter to Mallory, Feb. 1, 1863, "Carter Correspondence Book"; Jeter, *A Man and His Boat,* x; Joiner, *One Damn Blunder,* 41.

32. Copy in the collection of Katherine Brash Jeter, Shreveport, LA.

33. Johnson, *Red River Campaign,* 80.

34. *OR,* ser. 1, vol. 22, pt. 2:781–82.

35. William R. Boggs, *Military Reminiscences of Gen. Wm. R. Boggs, C.S.A.,* edited by William K. Boyd (Durham, NC, 1913), 57.

36. Ibid.

37. Ibid., x.

38. Paul D. Casdorph, *Prince John Magruder* (New York, 1996), 24; D. H. Mahan, *Treatise on Field Fortification, Containing Instructions on the Methods of Laying Out,*

*Constructing, Defending and Attacking Intrenchments, with the General Outlines Also of the Arrangement, the Attack and Defense of Permanent Fortifications* (New York, 1863).

39. Boggs, *Military Reminiscences,* xiii.

40. Ibid., xix.

41. *OR,* ser. 1, vol. 26, pt. 2:216–18.

42. Ibid., 322.

43. *OR,* ser. 1, vol. 34, pt. 1:574–76; Taylor, *Destruction and Reconstruction,* 148–49.

44. Ibid.

45. Johnson, *Red River Campaign,* 91.

46. *OR,* ser. 1, vol. 26, pt. 2:216–18.

47. *OR,* ser. 1, vol. 15, pt. 1:1051.

48. Johnson and Buel, *Battles and Leaders* 4:362. This was Thomas O. Selfridge.

49. Taylor, *Destruction and Reconstruction,* 155.

50. Ibid.

51. Gary D. Joiner and Charles E. Vetter, "Union Naval Expedition on the Red River," *Civil War Regiments* 4, no. 2 (1994): 41.

52. Ibid.

53. Porter, *Naval History,* 496.

54. Journal of Mrs. Thomas Pope Fullilove, 1915. Annotated in 1982 by Mrs. Jane Fullilove from the original handwritten manuscript. Copy in the collection of the Mr. Bill Stephenson. Tom to his father, Dec. 21, 1863, 27. Hereinafter cited as Fullilove Diary.

55. Tom to Lizzie, Dec. 15, 1863, Fullilove Diary, 26.

56. Ibid., 28.

57. Ibid., Dec. 18, 1863, 27.

58. Ibid., Jan. 31, 1864, 29–30. Note the similarity to the official engineers' drawing in Map 196.

59. Ibid., 30.

60. Ibid., 31.

61. Grant, *Personal Memoirs,* 19.

62. *OR,* ser. 1, vol. 34, pt. 2:126.

63. *OR,* ser. 1, vol. 26, pt. 2:256–57.

64. Ibid.

65. Ibid.

66. *OR*, ser. 1, vol. 26, pt. 2:288.

67. Ibid., 891–92.

68. Some historians estimate that 80–90 percent of all Trans-Mississippi documents are missing, misplaced, or lost.

69. *OR*, ser. 1, vol. 26, pt. 2:322.

70. Ibid. 54–55.

71. Ibid.

72. Ibid., 323.

73. Bridges, *Biographical and Historical Memoirs,* 210.

74. Lavender U.S. Soil Survey map of 1906, archives, Louisiana State University, Shreveport.

75. Ibid.

76. Shannon, "Cultural Resources," 53.

77. W. W. Heartsill, *Fourteen Hundred and 91 Days in the Confederate Army: A Journal by Kept by W. W. Heartsill for Four Years, One Month and One Day or Camp Life; Day by Day, of the W. P. Lane Rangers from April 19th, 1861 to May 20th, 1865,* edited by Bill Irvin Wiley (Wilmington, NC, 1992), 211.

78. Ibid. Today the Red River has changed course and this fort sits on the east bank of the stream. The ravages of floods have almost completely destroyed it.

79. Clifton Cardin, *Bossier Parish History: The First 150 Years 1843–1993* (Shreveport, LA, 1993), 62.

80. Bridges, *Biographical and Historical Memoirs,* 210.

81. Heartsill, *Fourteen Hundred,* 211.

82. Frederick Way Jr., *Way's Packet Directory, 1848–1994,* rev. ed. (Athens, OH, 1983), 344.

83. *OR*, ser. 1, vol. 34, pt. 2:1056–57. The *OR* transcription incorrectly names the place as "Scopern's."

84. See Appendix 6 for the full text of the letter.

85. Lavender Map.

86. Unpublished family diary in the collection of James Marston, Shreveport, LA.

87. *OR*, ser. 1, vol. 34, pt. 2:161–62.

88. Venable Map

89. Eric J. Brock, "City Geared for Battle That Never Came," Presence of the Past column, *Shreveport Journal Page,* Nov. 25, 1995.

90. Mahan, *Treatise on Field Fortification,* Plate I.

91. For a full explanation of the locations of fortifications, see Brock, "City Geared for Battle"; Venable Map; and O'Pry, *Chronicles of Shreveport.*

92. Gary D. Joiner, "40 Archaeological Sites in the Red River Campaign," unpublished report to the Louisiana State Department of Culture, Recreation and Tourism, Division of Archaeology, 1997.

93. Edwin Bearss and Willie Tunnard, *A Southern Record: The Story of the 3rd Louisiana Infantry, C.S.A.* (Dayton, 1988), 326.

94. Venable Map.

95. *OR,* ser. 1, vol. 34, pt. 1:489.

96. Ibid., 494.

97. Ibid., 479, 494; pt. 2, 1027.

98. Ibid., 479.

99. Taylor, *Destruction and Reconstruction,* 154–55.

100. *Atlas to Accompany the Official Records of the Union and Confederate Armies* (Washington, DC, 1891–95), Plate LII (hereinafter cited as *OR Atlas*); *OR,* ser. 1, vol. 34, pt. 1:599.

101. Map of Fort DeRussy in the John Clark collection of the Cayuga County Museum in Auburn, NY.

102. Paul D. Casdorph, *Prince John Magruder: His Life and Campaigns* (New York, 1996).

103. Albert Castel, *General Sterling Price and the Civil War in the West* (Baton Rouge, LA, 1968).

# 3. Union Plans

1. James G. Hollandsworth Jr., *Pretense of Glory: The Life of General Nathaniel P. Banks* (Baton Rouge: Louisiana State Univ. Press, 1998), 1.

2. Ibid.

3. *Congressional Globe,* 33rd Cong., 1st sess., 1854, Appendix, 77–81. *Boston Post,* Mar. 7, 1849; Hollandsworth, *Pretense of Glory,* 3–32.

4. Harrington, *Fighting Politician,* 13.

5. Ibid., 21–22.

6. *Congressional Globe,* 34th Cong., 1st sess., 1855, 75.

7. Hollandsworth, *Pretense of Glory,* 28.

8. Ulrich Bonnell Phillips, ed., *The Correspondence of Robert Toombs, Alexander H. Stephens, and Howell Cobb* (1913; reprint, New York, 1970), 460.

9. William Eldon Baringer, *Lincoln's Rise to Power* (St. Clair Shores, MI, 1971), 218.

10. Hollandsworth, *Pretense of Glory,* 42.

11. William K. Ackerman, *Historical Sketch of the Illinois Central Railroad* (Chicago, 1890), 94.

12. Hollandsworth, *Pretense of Glory,* 45–52.

13. *New York Times,* June 6, 1862.

14. Richard C. Goodwin to his mother, Goodwin Papers, Massachusetts Historical Society, Boston.

15. Hollandsworth, *Pretense of Glory,* 66–68.

16. John M. Gould, *History of the First-Tenth-Twenty-ninth Maine Regiments* (Portland, ME, 1871), 174–76.

17. Robert K. Krick, *Stonewall Jackson at Cedar Mountain* (Chapel Hill, NC, 1990), 232–50.

18. *OR,* ser. 1, vol. 19, pt. 2, 202, 214.

19. *New York Herald,* Nov. 1, 1863. Harrington, *Fighting Politician,* 91–92.

20. Richard B. Irwin, *History of the Nineteenth Army Corps* (New York, 1892). 56.

21. Lawrence Lee Hewitt, *Port Hudson: Confederate Bastion on the Mississippi* (Baton Rouge, LA, 1987).

22. *OR,* ser. 1, vol. 26, pt. 1:664, 672–73; Johnson, *Red River Campaign,* 35.

23. Lincoln, *The Collected Works of Abraham Lincoln* 6:364.

24. *OR,* ser. 1, vol. 26, pt. 1:18–19, 285–312, 783.

25. Ibid., 341, 354, 779.

26. *OR,* ser. 1, vol. 34, pt. 2:133.

27. Ibid., 15, 42, 46, 145, 267. *JCCW,* 227.

28. Ibid.

29. Banks Papers, various correspondence from Aug. 20, 1863, through Feb. 1864.

30. *OR,* ser. 1, vol. 34, pt. 2:10.

31. Ibid., 224–25.

32. Ibid.

33. *ORN* 26:747–48.

34. Sherman, *Memoirs,* 1:425–26.

35. Ibid.

36. Ibid.

37. Ibid.

38. *OR,* ser. 1, vol. 32, pt. 3:289. This was in a letter dated Apr. 8, 1864.

39. M. A. DeWolfe Howe, ed., *Home Letters of General Sherman* (New York, 1909), 286–87.

40. Thomas H. S. Hamersly, comp. and ed., *Complete Army Register,* pt. 2:513; pt. 2:5, 16, 42, 97.

41. *OR,* ser. 1, vol. 34, pt. 1:68; pt. 2:545.

42. *OR,* ser. 1, vol. 34, pt. 2:481, 494, 496.

43. Stephen E. Ambrose, *Halleck: Lincoln's Chief of Staff* (Baton Rouge, 1962), 161.

44. Rowena Reed, *Combined Operations in the Civil War* (Lincoln: Univ. of Nebraska Press, 1978), 324.

45. *OR,* ser. 1, vol. 32, pt. 2:224–25.

46. John Scott, *Story of the Thirty Second Iowa Volunteers* (Nevada, IA, 1896), 136; Wickham Hoffman, *Camp, Court and Siege, A Narrative of Personal Adventure and Observation during Two Wars, 1861–1865, 1870–1871* (New York, 1877), 93. Harrington, *Fighting Politician,* 152–53.

47. Brooksher, *War along the Bayous,* 50.

48. Harrington, *Fighting Politician,* 152–3.

49. Ibid.

50. *OR,* ser. 1, vol. 34, pt. 1:179–80.

51. Sherman, *Memoirs,* 1, 425–26.

52. *OR,* ser. 1, vol. 34, pt. 2:576.

53. Ibid., 616.

54. Ibid., 179, 266.

55. *JCCW,* 19.

56. *OR,* ser. 1, vol. 34, pt. 2:293.

57. Ibid.

58. *ORN* 26 1:747–48.

59. Johnson and Buel, *Battles and Leaders* 4:366; Porter, *Naval History,* 494–533, 548–53. See Appendix 1 for a complete list of all vessels that participated in the campaign.

60. *OR,* ser. 1, vol. 34, pt. 1:68, 203; Johnson and Buel, *Battles and Leaders* 4:350–51.

61. Ibid.

62. See Appendix 1

63. Silverstone, *Warships of the Civil War,* 156.

64. *ORN* 26:36. Perhaps the most difficult problem in determining what information Porter had and when he obtained it is that some documentation is missing from the *OR* and *ORN.* This is evident from several matter-of-fact reports in which information about the *Missouri* is mentioned as common knowledge. Similarly, the submarine information appears in the same manner.

65. A contract for a second ironclad, identical to the *Missouri,* was let, but action on it was delayed until the *Missouri* was completed. The Confederate government proposed three additional ironclads. Carter to Mallory, Feb. 1, 1863, "Carter Correspondence Book"; Jeter, *A Man and His Boat,* x.

66. H. B. Sprague, *History of the 13th Infantry Regiment of Connecticut Volunteers* (Hartford, 1867), 186.

67. *OR*, ser. 1, vol. 34, pt. 1:167–68; Johnson and Buel, *Battles and Leaders* 4:366. Not all troops involved in the campaign were combat troops (effectives.) Effective strength is calculated at 93 percent for infantry units and 85 percent for cavalry regiments. These averages for effectives compared to support troops are standard for this period of the war. Johnson, *Red River Campaign,* 100 n. See Appendix 2 for a full list of all units that participated in the Red River Campaign, both in Louisiana and Arkansas. This list includes Union and Confederate units.

68. *OR*, ser. 1, vol. 34, pt. 3:601.

69. *JCCW,* 154–57.

70. Venable Map.

71. *OR*, ser. 1, vol. 34, pt. 2:638, 707.

72. Ibid., 704.

# 4. The Union Advance

1. *OR*, ser. 1, vol. 34, pt. 1:167. Included in this figure are the 2,500 U.S. Colored Troops of the Corps d'Afrique, which arrived separately by transport vessels within a few days of Banks's arrival at Alexandria.

2. See Appendix 1 for a list of vessels.

3. *OR*, ser. 1, vol. 34, pt. 1:168.

4. *JCCW,* 400.

5. Scott, *32nd Iowa,* 130; Edmund Newsome, *Experience in the War of the Rebellion* (Carbondale, IL, 1880), 111; Walter G. Smith, ed., *Life and Letters of T. Kilby Smith* (New York, 1898), 356.

6. *OR*, ser. 1, vol. 34, pt. 1:304.

7. Ibid.

8. *ORN* 25:787–88.

9. *OR*, ser. 1, vol. 34, pt. 1:312; Ezra Warner, *Generals in Blue: Lives of the Union Commanders* (Baton Rouge, 1992), 338–39.

10. Newsome, *Experience in the War,* 111–12.

11. *OR*, ser. 1, vol. 34, pt. 1:599; Johnson, *Red River Campaign,* 91.

12. *OR*, ser. 1, vol. 34, pt. 1:599.

13. Ibid.

14. Taylor, *Destruction and Reconstruction,* 155–56.

15. *OR*, ser. 1, vol. 34, pt. 1:305.

16. Scott, *32nd Iowa,* 132.

17. Ibid., *OR,* ser. 1, vol. 34, pt. 1:305, 338–39.

18. *ORN,* ser. 1, vol. 26, pt. 1:25.

19. Porter, *Naval History,* 397.

20. *OR,* ser. 1, vol. 34, pt. 1:305; Scott, *32nd Iowa,* 131.

21. *OR,* ser. 1, vol. 34, pt. 1:305, 338–39.

22. James P. Jones and Edward F. Keuchel, eds., *Civil War Marine: A Diary of The Red River Expedition, 1864* (Washington, 1975), 37.

23. Porter, *Naval History,* 496.

24. Ibid.

25. Porter, *Incidents and Anecdotes,* 214–15.

26. Ibid.

27. *OR,* ser. 1, vol. 34, pt. 1:306.

28. *ORN* 26:28, 30–31

29. Ibid., 32.

30. Johnson and Buel, *Battles and Leaders* 4:362.

31. Ibid.; Joiner and Vetter, "Union Naval Expedition on the Red River," 43.

32. Taylor, *Destruction and Reconstruction,* 181–83; *OR,* ser. 1, vol. 34, pt. 1:506, 561.

33. *OR,* ser. 1, vol. 34, pt. 1:506, 561.

34. *OR,* ser. 1, vol. 26, pt. 2, 54–55, 323; *Biographic and Historic Memoirs,* 210; Lavender Map.

35. Lavender Map.

36. See chap. 3.

37. *OR,* ser. 1, vol. 34, pt. 1:561.

38. Taylor, *Destruction and Reconstruction,* 156.

39. *OR,* ser. 1, vol. 34, pt. 1:496, 500, 578.

40. Ibid.

41. Ibid.

42. Gary B. Mills, *The Forgotten People: Cane River's Creoles of Color* (Baton Rouge, 1977), 215 n.

43. Johnson, *Red River Campaign,* 96; *OR Atlas,* Plate LII.

44. Taylor, *Destruction and Reconstruction,* 157.

45. Richard H. Zeitlin, *Old Abe the War Eagle: a True Story of the Civil War and Reconstruction* (Madison, 1986), 53.

46. Ibid.; *OR,* ser. 1, vol. 34, pt. 1:315–16, 334–35, 463–64, 501; Taylor, *Destruction and Reconstruction,* 157; Joseph P. Blessington, *The Campaigns of Walker's Texas Division*

(New York, 1875), 178; James K. Ewer, *The Third Massachusetts Cavalry in the War for the Union* (Maplewood, MA, 1903), 137–39.

47. Richard Lowe, *Walker's Texas Division, CSA: Greyhounds of the Trans-Mississippi* (Baton Rouge, 2004), 180.

48. *JCCW*, 28–29.

49. *ORN* 26:41.

50. B. F. Stevenson, *Letters from the Army 1862–1864* (Cincinnati, 1886), 307.

51. *OR*, ser. 1, vol. 34, pt. 2:513.

52. *JCCW*, 28.

53. Ibid.

54. Sprague, *13th Connecticut*, 186.

55. *OR Atlas*, Plate LII.

56. Scott Dearman, "Statistical Report of Union Troop Strength at the Battle of Mansfield, Louisiana April 8, 1864," unpublished report at Mansfield State Historic Site, Mansfield, LA.

57. *JCCW*, 28.

58. Ibid., 28–29.

59. T. H. Bringhurst and Frank Swigart, *History of the Forty-Sixth Regiment Indiana Volunteer Infantry* (Logansport, IN, 1888), 85–86.

60. *OR Atlas*, Plate LII.

61. *OR*, ser. 1, vol. 34, pt. 1:426–27.

62. Johnson, *Red River Campaign*, 99; Joiner and Vetter, "Union Naval Expedition," 47. There are discrepancies in the spelling of Banks's vessel. Some sources list it as *Blackhawk*, while others name it the *Black Hawk*. Even Admiral Porter used them interchangeably. I will use the two-word naming convention for both vessels.

63. Johnson and Buel, *Battles and Leaders* 4:366; Porter, *Naval History*, 494–533.

64. Ibid., 18, 71, 74, 224–25.

65. Thomas O. Selfridge, *What Finer Tradition: The Memoirs of Thomas O. Selfridge, Jr.* (New York, 1924), 96.

66. Ibid., 96.

67. Dispatch in the personal collection of Mr. Richard Self, Shreveport, LA. The full letter is reproduced in Appendix 3.

68. Photograph in the Lord-Eltinge Collection at Duke University, Raleigh, NC.

69. Winters, *Civil War in Louisiana*, 331.

70. *JCCW*, 285.

71. Ibid.

72. Porter, *Naval History*, 499.

73. Johnson, *Red River Expedition,* 118.

74. *OR,* ser. 1, vol. 34, pt. 1:426–27.

75. Porter, *Naval History,* 499–501.

76. Ibid., 501.

77. Scott, *32nd Iowa,* 136.

78. *JCCW,* 18, 71, 74, 224–25.

79. Ibid., 224–25, 284.

80. *OR,* ser. 1, vol. 34, pt. 3:18.

81. Ibid., 4.

82. *JCCW,* 281, 335.

83. *OR,* ser. 1, vol. 34, pt. 2:494, 610–11.

84. Ibid.

85. Ibid.

86. *JCCW,* 281–3.

87. Porter, *Naval History,* 500.

88. *JCCW,* 8–9; *ORN* 26:50.

89. *JCCW,* 8–9.

90. Ibid., 275; *ORN* 26:50.

91. *JCCW,* 282.

92. Ibid.

93. Ibid., 282–83.

94. Silverstone, *Warships of the Civil War Navies,* 156.

95. *OR,* ser. 1, vol. 34, pt. 2:1056–57.

96. Lavender Map.

97. *OR,* ser. 1, vol. 34 pt. 3:172.

98. *OR Atlas,* Plate LII.

99. *JCCW,* 282.

100. Ibid., 282–83.

101. Ibid.

102. Ibid.; *ORN* 26, 50.

103. *JCCW,* 282–83.

104. Ibid.

105. Ibid., 322.

106. Ibid., 7, 322.

107. *OR,* ser. 1, vol. 34, pt. 2:735; Crandall and Newell, *History of the Ram Fleet,* 378.

108. *JCCW,* 322; *OR,* ser. 1, vol. 34, pt. 2:746, 768.

109. Johnson and Buel, *Battles and Leaders* 4:350–51; *JCCW,* 322.

110. *OR,* ser. 1, vol. 34, pt. 1:167; pt. 2:769.

111. *JCCW,* 335.

112. Ibid., 280.

113. Jones and Keuchel, *Civil War Marine,* 41.

114. Scott, *32nd Iowa,* 135; Ewer, *3rd Massachusetts Cavalry,* 139; Irwin, *Nineteenth Corps,* 294.

115. *OR,* ser. 1, vol. 34, pt. 1:179–80.

116. Nicolay and Hay, *Abraham Lincoln: A History* (New York, 1909), 8:291.

117. Orton S. Clark, *The One Hundredth and Sixteenth Regiment of New York Volunteers* (Buffalo, NY, 1868), 149–55; Elias P. Pellet, *History of the 114th Regiment, New York State Volunteers* (Norwich, NY, 1866), 190–91.

118. William H. Stewart, Diary, Southern Historical Collection, University of North Carolina, Chapel Hill, 17; Thomas J. Williams, *An Historical Sketch of the 56th Ohio Volunteer Infantry* (Columbus, OH, 1899), 66.

119. *OR,* ser. 1, vol. 34, pt. 1:428, 445; Bringhurst and Swigart, *46th Indiana,* 86.

120. *OR Atlas,* Plate LII.

121. Lloyd Lewis, *Captain Sam Grant* (Boston, 1950), 114–30.

122. *JCCW,* 282, 286.

123. *OR Atlas,* Plate LII.

124. Ibid. See, for example, "Little River" rather than Cane River in its actual channel. The map also shows the location of the town of Red Bluff, which was never built. It was planned at the time the original source map was undergoing field research in the early 1840s.

125. *JCCW,* 286–87.

126. National Archives and Records Administration (NARA), RG 77, folio M72. All National Archives documents hereinafter cited as NARA. Hereinafter cited as LaTourette Map. John Clark's copy of the map is in the Cayuga County Museum, Auburn, NY.

127. The resulting base map, created during the campaign and edited on a daily basis, is the map found in the *OR Atlas,* Plate LII.

128. NARA, RG 77, folios M103-1 and M103-2.

129. Senate Documents, 62nd Cong., 3rd sess., no. 987, p. 256.

130. *JCCW,* 285.

131. Ibid.

132. Susan E. Dollar, "The Red River Campaign, Natchitoches Parish, Louisiana: A Case of Equal Opportunity Destruction," *Louisiana History* 52, no. 4 (Fall 2002): 411–32.

133. *OR Atlas,* Plate LII; LaTourette Map.

134. Fort Smith, Arkansas, was both a military fortification and a town of the same name. This thesis uses the "Fort Smith" naming convention for this location.

135. *JCCW,* 286–87.

136. Ibid.

137. Ibid.

138. *ORN* 26:60.

139. Banks Papers, Banks's letter to his wife, Apr. 4, 1864.

140. Ibid., 194.

141. Ibid., 281.

142. Ibid., 32, 58, 323.

143. Personal communication with Edwin C. Bearss, chief military historian emeritus of the U.S. National Park Service, June 7, 2001; Jean Edward Smith, *Grant* (New York, 2001), 298.

144. Ewer, *3rd Massachusetts,* 201, 276, 323.

145. *JCCW,* 201, 276, 323.

146. *OR Atlas,* Plate LII.

147. *OR,* ser. 1, vol. 34, pt. 1:284; *JCCW,* 323; *ORN* 26:51.

148. Johnson and Buel, *Battles and Leaders* 4:363.

149. *ORN* 26:51; *JCCW,* 201, 323; Newsome, *Experience in the War,* 124.

150. *JCCW,* 32.

151. *OR,* ser. 1, vol. 34, pt. 1:284, 322, 331, 428, 446; *JCCW,* 32, 58.

152. Ibid.

153. Irwin, *Nineteenth Army Corps,* 296.

154. Ewer, *3rd Massachusetts,* 142.

155. J. Cutler Andrews, *The North Reports the Civil War* (Pittsburgh, 1985), 506.

156. Andrews, *The North Reports the Civil War,* 506–7.

157. Scott, *32nd Iowa,* 135–36; Pellet, *114th New York,* 193.

158. Scott, *32nd Iowa,* 136; Harrington, *Fighting Politician,* 152–53; Hoffman, *Camp, Court and Siege,* 93.

159. Taylor, *Destruction and Reconstruction,* 178; Francis R. Lubbock, *Six Decades in Texas* (Austin, TX, 1900), 536.

160. Taylor, *Destruction and Reconstruction,* 158; *OR,* ser. 1, vol. 34, pt. 2:1029.

161. Taylor, *Destruction and Reconstruction,* 158; Lubbock, *Six Decades in Texas,* 536.

162. Johnson, *Red River Campaign,* 120.

163. Ibid., 121; Taylor, *Destruction and Reconstruction,* 153.

164. Ibid.

165. Ibid., 521–22.

166. Taylor, *Destruction and Reconstruction,* 159; *OR,* ser. 1, vol. 34, pt. 1:480, 485; Johnson and Buel, *Battles and Leaders* 4:371.

167. *OR,* ser. 1, vol. 34, pt. 1:528.

168. Ibid., 485; Boggs, *Military Reminiscences,* 75–76.

169. *OR Atlas,* Plate LII.

170. *OR,* ser. 1, vol. 34, pt. 1:520; Taylor, *Destruction and Reconstruction,* 158.

171. Ewer, *3rd Massachusetts,* 152; *OR,* ser. 1, vol. 34, pt. 1:257, 420, 454.

172. *JCCW,* 194.

173. *OR,* ser. 1, vol. 34, pt. 1:449; *JCCW,* 185.

174. *JCCW,* 185.

175. *OR,* ser. 1, vol. 34, pt. 1:450, 616–17; *JCCW,* 58.

176. *JCCW,* 194.

177. Ibid., 32, 59, 88, 194.

178. Ibid., 194.

179. Ibid.

180. *OR,* ser. 1, vol. 34, pt. 1:167, 290; pt. 3:72; *JCCW,* 29, 59–60, 194–95.

181. *JCCW,* 64.

182. Ibid., 58–59.

183. Ibid.

184. *OR,* ser. 1, vol. 34, pt. 1:290.

185. Irwin, *Nineteenth Corps,* 200.

186. *JCCW,* 32, 61–62, 68.

187. The hill was named for the family that farmed the ridge and had a homestead on the west side of the road. Personal communication with Scott Dearman, Mansfield State Historic Site, Dec. 1, 2001; John G. Belisle, *History of Sabine Parish Louisiana* (Many, LA, 1912), 159.

188. Irwin, *Nineteenth Corps,* 299; *OR,* ser. 1, vol. 34, pt. 1:291, 456; Taylor, *Destruction and Reconstruction,* 160–61; *JCCW,* 60–62.

## 5. The Battles of Mansfield and Pleasant Hill

1. *OR,* ser. 1, vol. 34, pt. 1:512–13, 517, 519.

2. Ibid., 522.

3. Ibid., 528.

4. Johnson, *Red River Campaign*, 129.

5. Taylor, *Destruction and Reconstruction*, 159.

6. *OR*, ser. 1, vol. 34, pt. 1:563; Taylor, *Destruction and Reconstruction*, 161; Blessington, *Walker's Division*, 181–83.

7. *OR*, ser. 1, vol. 34, pt. 1:526; Taylor, *Destruction and Reconstruction*, 161.

8. Mary L. B. Bankston, *Camp-Fire Stories of the Mississippi Valley Campaign* (New Orleans, 1914), 148.

9. *OR*, ser. 1, vol. 34, pt. 1:526.

10. Map of the Mansfield battlefield dated April 1864 by Major Richard Venable, Chief Topographic Engineer of the Department of the Trans-Mississippi, District of Western Louisiana and Arkansas, Jeremy Francis Gilmer Papers, Southern Historical Collection, Wilson Library, University of North Carolina, Chapel Hill.

11. *OR*, ser. 1, vol. 34, pt. 1:563–64; Taylor, *Destruction and Reconstruction*, 162; Blessington, *Walker's Division*, 185–86.

12. Richard Taylor letter to Maj. Gen. John Walker, Mansfield, 1:30 [A.M., Apr. 9, 1864], Walker Papers, Southern Historical Collection, Wilson Library, University of North Carolina, Chapel Hill.

13. Taylor, *Destruction and Reconstruction*, 162.

14. Ibid.

15. *OR*, ser. 1, vol. 34, pt. 1:464; *JCCW*, 61.

16. *JCCW*, 10.

17. Ibid., 60.

18. Ibid.

19. Ibid., 30.

20. Johnson, *Red River Campaign*, 129.

21. *OR*, ser. 1, vol. 34, pt. 1:167, 264, 266; Irwin, *Nineteenth Corps*, 303.

22. *OR*, ser. 1, vol. 34, pt. 1:464; *JCCW*, 61.

23. *JCCW*, 61.

24. *OR*, ser. 1, vol. 34, pt. 1:564.

25. Ibid., 266–67, 295–96, 300–301; Irwin, *Nineteenth Corps*, 304.

26. *OR*, ser. 1, vol. 34, pt. 1:564. Bankston, *Camp-Fire Stories*, 152–53. John Dimitry, "Louisiana," in *Confederate Military History* 10 (1899): 140–41; Napier Bartlett, "The Trans-Mississippi," *Military Record of Louisiana: Including Biographical and Historical Papers Relating to the Military Organization of the State* (New Orleans, 1875), 13, 42.

27. *OR*, ser. 1, vol. 34, pt. 1:266–67, 295–96, 300–301; Irwin, *Nineteenth Corps*, 304.

28. *OR*, ser. 1, vol. 34, pt. 1:564.

29. Bartlett, "The Trans-Mississippi," 13.

30. *OR*, ser. 1, vol. 34, pt. 1:564.

31. R. B. Scott, *The History of the 67th Regiment Indiana Infantry* (Bedford, IN, 1892), 71–72; *OR*, ser. 1, vol. 34, pt. 1:462; Frank M. Flinn, *Campaigning with Banks in Louisiana, '63 and '64, and Sheridan in the Shenandoah Valley in '64 and '65* (Lynn, MA, 1887), 108.

32. Scott, *67th Indiana*, 462; Flinn, *Campaigning with Banks*, 108.

33. *OR*, ser. 1, vol. 34, pt. 1:266–67, 300–301; T. B. Marshall, *History of the Eighty-Third Ohio Volunteer Infantry, The Greyhound Regiment* (Cincinnati, 1913), 134.

34. Marshall, *83rd Ohio*, 134.

35. Huffstodt, *Hard Dying Men*, 177.

36. John A. Bering and Thomas Montgomery, *History of the Forty-Eighth Ohio Veteran Volunteer Infantry* (Hillsboro, OH, 1880), 132; Belisle, *Sabine Parish*, 161.

37. Huffstodt, *Hard Dying Men*, 177.

38. Ibid., 179; *OR*, ser. 1, vol. 34, pt. 1:273–74, 292, 302; Irwin, *Nineteenth Corps*, 304.

39. *OR*, ser. 1, vol. 34, pt. 1:274–75.

40. Ibid., 274–75, 292, 301; Irwin, *Nineteenth Corps*, 304.

41. *OR*, ser. 1, vol. 34, pt. 1:; Ewer, *3rd Massachusetts Cavalry*, 156.

42. *OR*, ser. 1, vol. 34, pt. 1:257, 273–74.

43. Frank Moore, ed., *The Rebellion Record: A Diary of American Events* (New York, 1862–71), 8:548.

44. *OR*, ser. 1, vol. 34, pt. 1:273–74; Ewer, *3rd Massachusetts Cavalry*, 149; Scott, *67th Indiana*, 72; Hoffman, *Camp, Court and Siege*, 89; John M. Stanyan, *A History of the Eighth Regiment of New Hampshire Volunteers* (Concord, NH, 1892), 409.

45. *OR*, ser. 1, vol. 34, pt. 1:273–74; Ewer, *3rd Massachusetts Cavalry*, 149.

46. *OR*, ser. 1, vol. 34, pt. 1:273–74; medical certificate in the William B. Franklin Papers, Division of Manuscripts, Library of Congress.

47. Ewer, *3rd Massachusetts Cavalry*, 149; Scott, *67th Indiana*, 72; Henry M. Shorey, *The Story of the Maine Fifteenth Volunteer Infantry Regiment* (Brighton, ME, 1890), 83–84.

48. *OR*, ser. 1, vol. 34, pt. 1:257; Ewer, *3rd Massachusetts Cavalry*, 155; Flinn, *Campaigning with Banks*, 109.

49. *OR*, ser. 1, vol. 34, pt. 1:391–92; Harris H. Beecher, *Record of the 114th, New York N.Y.S.V. Where It Went, What It Saw, and What It Did* (Norwich, NY, 1866), 311.

50. Lydia M. Post, ed., *Soldier's Letters from Camp, Battlefield and Prison* (New York, 1865), 357–58.

51. Beecher, *114th New York*, 311.

52. Belisle, *Sabine Parish,* 163.

53. L. David Norris, James C. Millican, and Odie B. Faulk, *William H. Emory: Soldier Scientist* (Tucson, AZ, 1998), 229.

54. *OR Atlas,* Plate LII.

55. *OR,* ser. 1, vol. 34, pt. 1:392, 421–22, 429, 606–7, 616–17; Taylor, *Destruction and Reconstruction,* 164; Clark, *116th New York,* 155–57; Williams *56th Ohio,* 66.

56. Sarah H. Dorsey, *Recollections of Henry Watkins Allen* (New York, 1866), 263.

57. *OR,* ser. 1, vol. 34, pt. 1:167, 263–64, 273.

58. Ibid., 263, 421.

59. Taylor, *Destruction and Reconstruction,* 164.

60. Dr. Benjamin A. Fordyce, *Echoes: From the Letters of a Civil War Surgeon,* ed. Lydia P. Hecht (n.p., 1996), 248.

61. Unpublished casualty lists and reports at Mansfield State Historic Site, Mansfield, LA; interview with Steve Bounds, site manager at Mansfield State Historic Site, Mansfield, LA, Sept. 15, 2001 (hereinafter cited as Mansfield SHS).

62. *OR,* ser. 1, vol. 34, pt. 1:553; Bartlett, "The Trans-Mississippi," 13, 42.

63. Taylor, Walker letter.

64. Ibid.

65. Taylor, Walker letter.

66. *JCCW,* 77.

67. Ibid.

68. Diary of Julius L. Knapp in the collection of James Sandefur, Shreveport, LA. Entry for Apr. 8, 1864.

69. *OR,* ser. 1, vol. 34, pt. 1:392, 422.

70. Pellet, *114th New York,* 193–94; Beecher, *114th New York,* 308; S. F. Benson, "The Battle of Pleasant Hill, Louisiana," *Annals of Iowa* 7 (1906): 500; Henry H. Childers, "Reminiscences of the Battle of Pleasant Hill," *Annals of Iowa* 7: 514–15; *DeSoto Parish History: Sesquicentennial Edition, 1843–1993* (Mansfield, LA, 1995), 104.

71. Ibid.

72. Scott, *32nd Iowa,* 136–37.

73. Ibid., 136–46.

74. *OR,* ser. 1, vol. 34, pt. 1:354.

75. Ibid., 354, 423.

76. Map of the Battle of Pleasant Hill at Mansfield State Historic Site showing the locations of buildings and streets as well as unit dispositions. (hereinafter cited as Mansfield SHS Pleasant Hill Map); Map by Col. John Clark (No. 8) of the Red River Campaign, in the John Clark Collection, Cayuga County Museum, Auburn, NY; Map by CSA Maj.

Richard Venable of Pleasant Hill, Jeremy Francis Gilmer Papers, Southern Historical Collection, Wilson Library, University of North Carolina, Chapel Hill (hereinafter cited as Venable Pleasant Hill Map).

77. Taylor, Walker Letter.

78. Ibid., 565; Blessington, *Walker's Division,* 194; Hamilton P. Bee, "Battle of Pleasant Hill-An Error Corrected," *Southern Historical Society Papers* 8 (1880): 184–86; Blessington, *Walker's Division,* 193.

79. *OR,* ser. 1, vol. 34, pt. 1:566, 605.

80. Taylor, *Destruction and Reconstruction,* 166; *OR,* ser. 1, vol. 34, pt. 1:566, 605.

81. *OR,* ser. 1, vol. 34, pt. 1:566, 605.

82. Venable Pleasant Hill Map.

83. Taylor, *Destruction and Reconstruction,* 166; *OR,* ser. 1, vol. 34, pt. 1:566–71.

84. *Philadelphia Press,* Apr. 10, 1864; Moore, *Rebellion Record* 8:549–50.

85. *JCCW,* 176, 218; *OR,* ser. 1, vol. 34, pt. 1:308; pt 3, 99; *Philadelphia Press,* Apr. 10, 1864; Moore, *Rebellion Record* 8:549–50.

86. Taylor, *Destruction and Reconstruction,* 167; *OR,* ser. 1, vol. 34, pt. 1:602.

87. Taylor, *Destruction and Reconstruction,* 166–69; *OR,* ser. 1, vol. 34, pt. 1:567, 608, 617.

88. *OR,* ser. 1, vol. 34, pt. 1:567, 608, 617.

89. Taylor, *Destruction and Reconstruction,* 166–69.

90. X. B. Debray, "A Sketch of Debray's Twenty-Sixth Regiment of Texas Cavalry," *Southern Historical Society Papers* 8 (1885): 158–59.

91. Scott, *32nd Iowa,* 140, 180–83.

92. Mansfield SHS Pleasant Hill Map.

93. Lauren Cook Burgess, ed., *An Uncommon Soldier: The Civil War Letters of Sarah Rosetta Wakeman, Alias Pvt. Lyons Wakeman, 153rd Regiment, New York State Volunteers, 1862-1864* (New York, 1995). Burgess provided copies of the original letters to the author.

94. Ibid., 71.

95. Ibid.

96. Ibid.

97. Ibid., 5–6, 70.

98. Personal communication with Mr. Terrence Winschel, historian at Vicksburg National Military Park, Vicksburg, MS, Dec. 7, 2001.

99. Letter from a Union soldier named Thomas, last name unknown, in the collection of James Sandefur, Shreveport, LA. The soldier was a member of the Thirty-eighth Massachusetts Volunteer Infantry Regiment.

100. *OR*, ser. 1, vol. 34, pt. 1:430–31; Scott, *32nd Iowa*, 198.

101. Ibid., 410–11.

102. Ibid., 392; *JCCW*, 218.

103. *OR*, ser. 1, vol. 34, pt. 1:392.

104. Scott, *32nd Iowa*, 145–47; Taylor, *Destruction and Reconstruction*, 169; *OR*, ser. 1, vol. 34, pt. 1:355–56, 361, 363, 366, 369, 423–44.

105. *OR*, ser. 1, vol. 34, pt. 1:392–93, 417–18, 423–24.

106. Edwin B. Lufkin, *History of the Thirtieth Maine Regiment* (Brighton, ME, 1898), 85.

107. *OR*, ser. 1, vol. 34, pt. 1:341–42, 345–46, 350; Henry A. Shorey, *15th Maine*, 97.

108. Shorey, *15th Maine*; *OR*, ser. 1, vol. 34, pt. 1:317, 328, 350, 373.

109. Joseph B. Mitchell, *The Badge of Honor: Letters from Civil War Medal of Honor Winners* (Shippensburg, PA, 1997), 32–36.

110. Taylor, *Destruction and Reconstruction*, 168–69; *OR*, ser. 1, vol. 34, pt. 1:605.

111. *OR*, ser. 1, vol. 34, pt. 1:309.

112. Johnson, *Red River Campaign*, 163.

113. *JCCW*, 13, 62, 195–96.

114. Ibid.

115. Ibid., 35.

116. Ibid., 189.

117. Scott, *32nd Iowa*, 230–35; Hoffman, *Camp, Court and Siege*, 96–97; *OR*, ser. 1, vol. 34, pt. 1:309.

118. Knapp Diary entry for Apr. 9, 1864.

119. *OR*, ser. 1, vol. 34, pt. 1:309; Scott, *32nd Iowa*, 230–35. Hoffman, *Camp, Court and Siege*, 96–97; Johnson, *Red River Campaign*, 163–64.

120. Ibid.

121. Bounds, Mansfield SHS; Taylor, *Destruction and Reconstruction*, 167–71.

122. Taylor, *Destruction and Reconstruction*, 171.

123. Ben Van Dyke, "Ben Van Dyke's Escape from the Hospital at Pleasant Hill, Louisiana," revised by S. F. Benson, *Annals of Iowa* (1906): 524.

124. Shorey, *15th Maine*, 105.

125. Taylor, *Destruction and Reconstruction*, 171.

## 6. The Campaign in Arkansas

1. *OR*, ser. 1, vol. 34, pt. 1:576.

2. Ibid., 246, 519, 547, 576.

3. *OR*, ser. 1, vol. 34, pt. 2:448.

4. Ibid., 616.

5. Ibid.

6. *OR*, ser. 1, vol. 34, pt. 2:638, 707.

7. Ibid., 704; pt. 1, 657, 692.

8. A. F. Sperry, *History of the 33d Iowa Infantry Volunteer Regiment* (Des Moines, 1866), 61.

9. Ibid.

10. Ibid.

11. Ibid.

12. Ibid.

13. *OR*, ser. 1, vol. 34, pt. 1:673.

14. Sperry, *33rd Iowa*, 62–65.

15. Ibid.

16. Johnson, *Red River Campaign*, 173.

17. *OR*, ser. 1, vol. 34, pt. 1:673, 679; pt. 2:77–78; Sperry, *33rd Iowa*, 66; Johnson, *Red River Campaign*, 173.

18. *OR*, ser. 1, vol. 34, pt. 1:480, 485; Taylor, *Destruction and Reconstruction*, 159.

19. *OR*, ser. 1, vol. 34, pt. 1:821.

20. Ibid., 673, 679, 821; pt. 3:77–78; Sperry, *33rd Iowa*, 66.

21. *OR*, ser. 1, vol. 34, pt. 1:821.

22. Ibid. 673, 679; pt. 3, 77–78; Sperry, *33rd Iowa*, 66.

23. *OR*, ser. 1, vol. 34, pt. 1:821–22; Sperry, *33rd Iowa*, 66.

24. *OR*, ser. 1, vol. 34, pt. 1:821–22.

25. Ibid., 660, 693, 822; pt. 3, 77–78; Sperry, *33rd Iowa*, 67.

26. *OR*, ser. 1, vol. 34, pt. 1:660, 823; Sperry, *33rd Iowa*, 67.

27. Ibid., 552–61.

28. Ibid., 660, 675, 780, 824–25; pt. 3, 77–78.

29. Joiner, *One Damn Blunder*, 45–106, 137–75.

30. *OR*, ser. 1, vol. 34, pt. 3:77–79.

31. Sperry, *33rd Iowa*, 68.

32. *OR*, ser. 1, vol. 34, pt. 3:77–79.

33. Johnson, *Red River Campaign*, 178.

34. Sperry, *33rd Iowa*, 68–72; *OR*, ser. 1, vol. 34, pt. 1:675, 687, 780, 824–25.

35. Sperry, *33rd Iowa*, 72; *OR*, ser. 1, vol. 34, pt. 1:687, 780, 824–25.

36. *OR,* ser. 1, vol. 34, pt. 1:675.

37. Ibid., 661.

38. Sperry, *33rd Iowa,* 72–73.

39. Ibid.

40. *OR,* ser. 1, vol. 34, pt. 1:780.

41. Ibid.

42. Johnson, *Red River Campaign,* 180–82.

43. Ibid., 571–72.

44. Ibid.

45. Taylor, *Destruction and Reconstruction,* 180.

46. *OR,* ser. 1, vol. 34, pt. 1:481.

47. William Henry King, "A Journal Camp Life as Private Soldier," MS, Texas State Archives, Austin, Apr. 29–May 25, 1864.

48. Ibid., Apr. 15, 16, 1864.

49. Ibid., Apr. 15, 1864.

50. Ibid., Apr. 16, 1864.

51. Joseph P. Blessington, *The Campaigns of Walker's Texas Division* (New York, 1875), 243–44.

52. *OR,* ser. 1, vol. 34, pt. 1:486–87, 534; pt. 3:766.

53. Ibid., 675, 687.

54. Ibid., 675, 687–88, 695, 781, 825, 838–39.

55. Sperry, *33rd Iowa,* 78–79; *OR,* ser. 1, vol. 34, pt. 3:770.

56. Noah Andre Trudeau, *Like Men of War: Black Troops in the Civil War, 1862–1865* (Edison, NJ, 2001), 182–200.

57. *OR,* ser. 1, vol. 34, pt. 1:661, 668.

58. Ibid., 848–49.

59. Ibid., 744–45.

60. John M. Harrell, "Arkansas," in vol. 10 of *Confederate Military History* (Atlanta, 1899), 250.

61. *OR,* ser. 1, vol. 34, pt. 1:744–45, 791–92, 842, 848.

62. John N. Edwards, *Shelby and His Men: Or, The War in the West* (Cincinnati, 1867), 276.

63. Harrell, "Arkansas," 276.

64. *OR,* ser. 1, vol. 34, pt. 1:746.

65. Ibid., 661–62.

66. Ibid., 663.

67. *OR,* ser. 1, vol. 34, pt. 3:267–68.

68. *OR,* ser. 1, vol. 34, pt. 1:781; Edwin C. Bearss, *Steele's Retreat from Camden and the Battle of Jenkins' Ferry* (Little Rock, 1966), 49.

69. Bearss, *Steele's Retreat from Camden,* 49.

70. *OR,* ser. 1, vol. 34, pt. 1:481, 781.

71. Ibid., 781; pt. 3:267–68; Sperry, *33rd Iowa,* 83.

72. *OR,* ser. 1, vol. 34, pt. 1:788.

73. Ibid., 712–13.

74. Ibid.

75. Ibid., 788–89.

76. Ibid.

77. Ibid., 789, 794, 835–36.

78. Edwards, *Shelby and His Men,* 279; *OR,* ser. 1, vol. 34, pt. 1:668.

79. *OR,* ser. 1, vol. 34, pt. 1:692, 713–14; Edwards, *Shelby and His Men,* 279.

80. *OR,* ser. 1, vol. 34, pt. 1:787, 795; Johnson, *Red River Campaign,* 193.

81. *OR,* ser. 1, vol. 34, pt. 1:665, 668, 671, 681, 683.

82. Sperry, *33rd Iowa,* 85; *OR,* ser. 1, vol. 34, pt. 1:680.

83. Sperry, *33rd Iowa,* 86–87; *OR,* ser. 1, vol. 34, pt. 1:688.

84. *OR,* ser. 1, vol. 34, pt. 1:845–46; pt. 3:794–95, 797–98.

85. *OR,* ser. 1, vol. 34, pt. 1:782, 826–27, 829.

86. Ibid., 668–69.

87. Sperry, *33rd Iowa,* 87.

88. *OR,* ser. 1, vol. 34, pt. 1:669; Sperry, *33rd Iowa,* 87.

89. *OR,* ser. 1, vol. 34, pt. 1:677.

90. Ibid., 782, 799–800.

91. Blessington, *Walker's Division,* 249; Sperry, *33rd Iowa,* 90–91; *OR,* ser. 1, vol. 34, pt. 1:782, 800, 802, 809, 815, 817; Harrell, "Arkansas," 265.

92. *OR,* ser. 1, vol. 34, pt. 1:801–2, 829–30.

93. Ibid., 697, 725, 808.

94. Ibid., 556–57, 758, 800, 802–7, 812–13.

95. Ibid., 556–57, 677, 725–26, 817; Compte de Paris, *History of the Civil War in America* (Philadelphia, 1875–88), 4:557.

96. *OR,* ser. 1, vol. 34, pt. 1:668, 670, 677, 690.

97. Sperry, *33rd Iowa,* 94–95; *OR,* ser. 1, vol. 34, pt. 1:670, 678, 680–81.

98. Sperry, *33rd Iowa,* 97, Johnson, *Red River Expedition,* 201–2.

99. Sperry, *33rd Iowa,* 96–98; *OR,* ser. 1, vol. 34, pt. 1:393–94.

100. Ibid.

101. Edwards, *Shelby and His Men,* 297; *OR,* ser. 1, vol. 34, pt. 1:557, 787–88, 801, 812, 815.

102. *OR,* ser. 1, vol. 34, pt. 1:691, 758.

103. Ibid., 770–71, 779–80.

104. Ibid., 684.

105. Johnson, *Red River Campaign,* 203–4.

106. Blessington, *Walker's Division,* 254–60.

107. Ibid., 260; *OR,* ser. 1, vol. 34, pt. 1:482.

## 7. Union Retreat in Louisiana

1. Silverstone, *Warships of the Civil War Navies,* 149. *ORN* 26:xvi–xvii, 51, 59–60; *JCCW,* 275–76; Johnson and Buel, *Battles and Leaders* 4:366; H. Allen Gosnell, *Guns on the Western Waters,* 15; Francis T. Miller ed., *The Photographic History of the Civil War* (New York, 1911), 5:145.

2. Silverstone, *Civil War Navies,* 153.

3. Ibid., 158–59.

4. Ibid., 168.

5. Ibid., 170.

6. Ibid., 183.

7. *OR,* ser. 1, vol. 34, pt. 1:168, 179–80.

8. The similarity between the two names confused army and naval officers writing official reports, newspaper reporters covering the campaign, and historians chronicling the campaign. This led to many false reports of Admiral Porter's flagship engaged in actions where it never sailed. Even the Library of Congress and the National Archives have photographs and reports in which the two vessels were interchanged.

9. *OR,* ser. 1, vol. 34, pt. 1:168, 179–80.

10. Ibid., 380.

11. *ORN* 26:60.

12. *OR,* ser. 1, vol. 34, pt. 1: 380.

13. *OR Atlas,* Plate LII; La Tourette Map.

14. Porter, *Naval History,* 502.

15. *OR,* ser. 1, vol. 34, pt. 1:380.

16. Porter, *Incidents and Anecdotes,* 232.

17. Lavender Map.

18. *OR,* ser. 1, vol. 34, pt. 3:172.

19. *OR,* ser. 1, vol. 34, pt. 3:98–99; *ORN* 26, 51, 60, 789; *JCCW,* 203.

20. *OR,* ser. 1, vol. 34, pt. 1:168, 179–80.

21. Newsome, *Experience in the War,* 126.

22. Robert L. Kerby, *Kirby Smith's Confederacy,* 309; abstract log of USS *Chillicothe,* Mar. 7, 1864–June 8, 1864; *ORN* 26:777–78.

23. *OR,* ser. 1, vol. 34, pt. 1:381.

24. *ORN* 26:778, 781, 789; *OR,* ser. 1, vol. 34, pt. 1:633.

25. *ORN* 26:778, 781, 789; *OR,* ser. 1, vol. 34, pt. 1:633.

26. Abstract log of USS *Lexington,* Mar. 1, 1864–June 28, 1864, *ORN* 26:789.

27. Taylor, Walker Letter; *OR,* ser. 1, vol. 34, pt. 1:570–71; Anne J. Bailey, "Chasing Banks Out of Louisiana: Parsons' Texas Cavalry in the Red River Campaign," *Civil War Regiments* 2, no. 3 (1992): 219.

28. Porter, *Naval History,* 512.

29. Selfridge, *Memoirs,* 102; *ORN* 26:49.

30. Porter, *Naval History,* 512–13.

31. Selfridge, *What Finer Tradition,* 102.

32. Ibid.

33. *ORN* 26:49, 55; *OR,* ser. 1, vol. 34, pt. 1:172–204, 571, 633.

34. *OR,* ser. 1, vol. 34, pt. 1:382.

35. Ibid.

36. Pellet, *114th New York,* 222.

37. Porter, *Incidents and Anecdotes,* 235–36.

38. Ibid.

39. Ibid.; Porter, *Naval History,* 517.

40. *OR,* ser. 1, vol. 34, pt. 1:190.

41. Ibid., 505; *ORN* 26:62.

42. *ORN* 26:62.

43. Ibid., 78.

44. Ibid., 72–77.

45. Ibid., 74–75, 167, 169, 781–82, 786.

46. Ibid., 75, 81, 83.

47. Ibid., 26, 76; Taylor, *Destruction and Reconstruction,* 218.

48. Porter, *Naval History,* 523–24. Although prone to epic bouts of self-aggrandizement, Admiral Porter's actions were noted by fellow officers.

49. Ibid., 524.

50. John Homans, "The Red River Expedition," in *Papers of the Military Historical Society of Massachusetts* (Boston, 1895–1913), 8:85–86.

51. Hoffman, *Camp, Court and Siege*, 97; Sprague, *13th Connecticut*, 190; Lufkin, *13th Maine*, 87; George W. Powers, *The Story of the Thirty Eighth Regiment of Massachusetts Volunteers* (Cambridge, 1866), 133.

52. Map of Grand Ecore Defenses (Union), April 1864, archives of Jackson Barracks (Louisiana National Guard), New Orleans.

53. *OR*, ser. 1, vol. 34, pt. 1:186.

54. *OR*, ser. 1, vol. 34, pt. 3:128, 592.

55. Ibid.

56. *OR*, ser. 1, vol. 34, pt. 1:185, 187–88.

57. *OR*, ser. 1, vol. 34, pt. 3:24; *OR*, ser. 1, vol. 32, pt. 3:242.

58. *OR*, ser. 1, vol. 34, pt. 3:175, 265–66.

59. Irwin, *Nineteenth Corps*, 327; Scott, *32nd Iowa*, 230.

60. *OR*, ser. 1, vol. 34, pt. 3:211, 294, 259.

61. *JCCW*, 17.

62. Ibid., 193.

63. *OR Atlas*, Plate LII.

64. *OR*, ser. 1, vol. 34, pt. 1:310, 428; pt. 3:222, 244; Irwin, *Nineteenth Corps*, 328; Sprague, *13th Connecticut*, 192.

65. Powers, *38th Massachusetts*, 136–37; Sprague, *13th Connecticut*, 192; Lubbock, *Six Decades in Texas*, 539.

66. *OR*, ser. 1, vol. 34, pt. 1:310, 428; pt. 3, 222, 244. Irwin, *Nineteenth Corps*, 328; Sprague, *13th Connecticut*, 192.

67. *OR*, ser. 1, vol. 34, pt. 1:190.

68. Sprague, *13th Connecticut*, 193; D. H. Hanaburgh, *History of the One Hundred and Twenty-eighth Regiment, New York Volunteers* (Poughkeepsie, NY, 1894), 103; Thomas J. Williams, *56th Ohio Volunteer Infantry*, 87–88; Lufkin, *13th Maine*, 87–88.

69. Lubbock, *Six Decades in Texas*, 540; Pellet, *114th New York*, 229; *OR*, ser. 1, vol. 34, pt. 1:581.

70. Ibid.

71. Taylor, *Destruction and Reconstruction*, 193–94.

72. *OR*, ser. 1, vol. 34, pt. 1:262, 394–95, 460.

73. Ibid.; Ewer, *3rd Massachusetts Cavalry*, 164.

74. Ibid.

75. *OR*, ser. 1, vol. 34, pt. 1:580; Taylor, *Destruction and Reconstruction*, 180.

76. Ibid.

77. *JCCW*, 15, 34–35.

78. *OR*, ser. 1, vol. 34, pt. 1:262, 460.

79. Sprague, *13th Connecticut*, 195; Woods, *96th Ohio*, 74.

80. *OR*, ser. 1, vol. 34, pt. 1:262.

81. Sprague, *13th Connecticut*, 195–96.

82. Ibid., 196–97; *OR*, ser. 1, vol. 34, pt. 1:262, 275, 434, 613.

83. *OR*, ser. 1, vol. 34, pt. 1:619.

84. Ibid., 434; Sprague, *13th Connecticut*, 198–200.

85. *OR*, ser. 1, vol. 34, pt. 1:396, 407, 620.

86. Ibid., 611.

87. Lubbock, *Six Decades in Texas*, 539.

88. Clark, *116th New York*, 170; Ewer, *3rd Massachusetts Cavalry*, 166.

89. *OR*, ser. 1, vol. 34, pt. 1:63, 580; Ewer, *3rd Massachusetts Cavalry*, 166; Lubbock, *Six Decades in Texas*, 539; Sprague, *13th Connecticut*, 201.

90. *OR*, ser. 1, vol. 34, pt. 1:190, 432–35, 580, 611.

91. Taylor, *Destruction and Reconstruction*, 152.

92. *OR*, ser. 1, vol. 34, pt. 1:580, 611–15; Taylor, *Destruction and Reconstruction*, 152.

93. Sprague, *13th Connecticut*, 201.

94. Ibid.; Ewer, *3rd Massachusetts Cavalry*, 166.

95. *OR*, ser. 1, vol. 34, pt. 3:307.

96. *OR*, ser. 1, vol. 34, pt. 1:211, 220, 221, 235, 244; pt. 3:252–53; *OR*, ser. 1, vol. 32, pt. 3:407, 420, 422, 437.

97. *OR*, ser. 1, vol. 34, pt. 1:11.

98. Ibid., 206.

99. Ibid., 110–11.

100. *OR*, ser. 1, vol. 34, pt. 3:190–92.

101. Ibid., 211, 220–21, 235, 244.

102. Ibid.

103. Ibid.

104. Ibid., 252–53.

105. Ibid.

106. Ibid., 278–79.

107. *ORN* 26:50–54.

108. *OR*, ser. 1, vol. 34, pt. 1:181–85; pt. 3:278–79.

109. *OR*, ser. 1, vol. 34, pt. 3:279, 293–94, 306–7.

110. *OR*, ser. 1, vol. 34, pt. 1:474.

111. *OR*, ser. 1, vol. 35, pt. 3:331–32, 357.

112. Ibid.

113. Ibid., 357–58.

114. Ibid., 409–10.

115. Ibid., 491.

116. Ibid.

117. *OR*, ser. 1, vol. 34, pt. 1:168, 443; pt. 3:294, 296.

118. Taylor, *Destruction and Reconstruction*, 186; *ORN* 26:102; *OR*, ser. 1, vol. 34, pt. 1:585.

119. Taylor, *Destruction and Reconstruction*, 186.

120. Ibid.; *ORN* 26:102.

121. *OR*, ser. 1, vol. 34, pt. 1:475; Taylor, *Destruction and Reconstruction*, 186.

122. Charles Dana Gibson and E. Kay Gibson, *Dictionary of Transports and Combatant Vessels, Steam and Sail, Employed by the U.S. Army, 1861–1868* (Camden, ME, 1995), 60.

123. Williams, *56th Ohio*, 73.

124. Ibid.

125. *ORN* 26:113, 117–18; Williams, *56th Ohio*, 74–78.

126. Ibid.

127. Williams, *56th Ohio*, 74–78; *ORN* 26:114, 118–19, 134.

128. *ORN* 26:114, 119, 123, 134; Taylor, *Destruction and Reconstruction*, 185–86; *OR*, ser. 1, vol. 34, pt. 1:442, 475, 621, 623.

129. *ORN* 26:94; *OR*, ser. 1, vol. 34, pt. 3:316; Silverstone, *Warships of the Civil War Navies*, 151–53. The actual depth of the keel was six feet on *Cairo* or *River Cities* class ironclads.

130. *ORN* 26:94; *OR*, ser. 1, vol. 34, pt. 3:316.

131. Johnson and Buel, *Battles and Leaders* 4:358.

132. *JCCW*, 15; Johnson and Buel, *Battles and Leaders* 4:358; *OR*, ser. 1, vol. 34, pt. 1:402–3.

133. *JCCW*, 15.

134. *OR*, ser. 1, vol. 34, pt. 1:403; pt. 3:333, 391.

135. Surgeon's certificate and attached correspondence, Apr. 30, 1864, Franklin Papers.

136. *OR*, ser. 1, vol. 34, pt. 1:403; pt. 3:333, 391.

137. E. Cort Williams, "Recollections of the Red River Expedition," *Papers Read before the Ohio Commandery of the Military Order of the Loyal Legion* (Cincinnati, 1888), 2:84.

138. *OR*, ser. 1, vol. 34, pt. 1:403, Johnson and Buel, eds., *Battles and Leaders* 4:358.

139. *ORN* 26:130–31.

140. Ibid.

141. Ibid., 132; *OR*, ser. 1, vol. 34, pt. 1:405.

142. *OR*, ser. 1, vol. 34, pt. 1:209, 254; *ORN* 26:131.

143. Ibid.

144. Porter, *Naval History*, 526.

145. *OR,* ser. 1, vol. 34, pt. 1:68, 443; pt. 3:294, 296.

146. *ORN* 26:136;

147. Banks to Grant, May 4, 1864, Banks Papers; *ORN* 26:147.

148. *ORN* 26:136.

149. Johnson, *Red River Campaign,* 264–65.

150. Ibid., 140; Scott, *32nd Iowa,* 250–51.

151. *ORN* 26:140–41.

152. Ibid., 141.

153. Ibid., 132, 149; *OR,* ser. 1, vol. 34, pt. 1:255; *JCCW,* 84; Williams, "Recollections of the Red River Expedition," 115.

154. *ORN* 26:132, 149; *OR,* ser. 1, vol. 34, pt. 1:255; *JCCW,* 84; Williams, "Recollections of the Red River Expedition," 115.

155. *ORN* 26:132, 149; *OR,* ser. 1, vol. 34, pt. 1:255; Johnson and Buel, *Battles and Leaders* 4:373.

156. *OR Atlas,* Plate LIII.

157. Photographs in the Civil War Photographs collection of the Library of Congress, 419078 LC-B8171-3162 and 2119078 LC-B8184-3163.

158. Watercolor by James Alden, 1864, NH 91999-A KN, Commander George M. Bache Collection, Naval Historical Center, Washington, D.C.

159. For a thorough treatment of the dam, see Michael C. Robinson, *Gunboats, Low Water, and Yankee Ingenuity: A History of Bailey's Dam* (Baton Rouge, 1991).

160. David Dixon Porter to his mother, May 18, 1864, David D. Porter Papers, Division of Manuscripts, Library of Congress; *ORN* 26:130–35.

161. *OR,* ser. 1, vol. 34, pt. 3:521.

162. *Official Report to the Conduct of Federal Troops in Western Louisiana, during the Invasions of 1863 and 1864, Compiled from Sworn Testimony under Direction of Governor Henry Watkins Allen* (Shreveport, 1865), 72–73, 99.

163. G. P. Whittington, "Rapides Parish, Louisiana—A History," *Louisiana Historical Quarterly* 18 (1935): 26–28.

164. Ibid.

165. Ibid., 28–30.

166. *JCCW,* 335; Allen, *Report on the Conduct of Federal Troops,* 79; Whittington, "Rapides Parish," 26–28, 31–32, 37.

167. *OR,* ser. 1, vol. 34, pt. 3:517, 558–59, 568.

168. Ibid.; Bringhurst and Swigart, *46th Indiana,* 93.

169. Sprague, *13th Connecticut,* 207; Beecher, *114th New York,* 347–48.

170. *OR,* ser. 1, vol. 34, pt. 1:277, 592–93, 623; Sprague, *13th Connecticut,* 209–10.

171. *OR,* ser. 1, vol. 34, pt. 1:593.

172. Ibid.

173. Scott, *32nd Iowa,* 275; Sprague, *13th Connecticut,* 212; Ewer, *3rd Massachusetts Cavalry,* 181; Pellet, *114th New York,* 234; Bryner, *47th Illinois,* 114–15; Hanaburgh, *128th New York,* 114, Lufkin, *13th Maine,* 92; Clark, *116th New York,* 179–80; Shorey, *15th Maine,* 119; Powers, *38th Massachusetts,* 147–48; Beecher, *114th New York,* 349–51; *OR,* ser. 1, vol. 34, pt. 1:425.

174. *OR,* ser. 1, vol. 34, pt. 1:325, 593; pt. 3:616; Sprague, *13th Connecticut,* 212–13; Lubbock, *Six Decades in Texas,* 542–43.

175. Scott, *32nd Iowa,* 275.

176. *OR,* ser. 1, vol. 34, pt. 1:443–44; Scott, *32nd Iowa,* 276; Beecher, *114th New York,* 353–54.

177. Taylor, *Destruction and Reconstruction,* 191.

178. *OR,* ser. 1, vol. 34, pt. 1:304, 320, 329, 337, 347–48, 357, 364, 367, 370, 467, 594, 624, 631; Taylor, *Destruction and Reconstruction,* 191; Scott, *32nd Iowa,* 259, 277.

179. Johnson and Buel, *Battles and Leaders* 4:60.

180. *OR,* ser. 1, 34, pt. 3:644; Jones, *22nd Iowa,* 69.

181. Jones, *22nd Iowa,* 69.

182. Irwin, *19th Corps,* 347–48.

183. Harrington, *Fighting Politician,* 163–64.

184. Ibid., 164; Lincoln, *Collected Works of Lincoln* 8:121 n.

185. *JCCW,* iii.

186. Harrington, *Fighting Politician,* 167–69.

187. *OR,* ser. 1, vol. 34, pt. 1:546–48.

188. Ibid., 540–48.

189. Ibid., 597.

190. *OR,* ser. 1, vol. 34, pt. 1:594; Johnson and Buel, *Battles and Leaders* 4:360–61.

191. *St. Louis Daily Missouri Republican,* June 10, 1864.

192. Lincoln, *Collected Works of Abraham Lincoln* 8:348.

193. Lloyd Lewis, *Sherman: Fighting Prophet* (New York, 1932), 350.

# 8. Congressional Investigation and Reconstruction

1. T. E. G. Ransom to William B. Franklin, May 31, 1864, Franklin Papers.

2. Ibid.

3. Bruce Tap, *Over Lincoln's Shoulder: The Committee on the Conduct of the War* (Lawrence, KS, 1998), 215.

4. T. Harry Williams, *Lincoln and the Radicals* (Madison, WI, 1941); Hans Trefousse, *The Radical Republicans: Lincoln's Vanguard for Racial Justice* (New York, 1969); and Tap, *Over Lincoln's Shoulder*.

5. *JCCW*.

6. *JCCW*, iv.

7. Ibid.

8. Ibid., v.

9. Ibid., xiv.

10. Personal communication with Warren Grabeau, former chief of the U.S. Army Corps of Engineers Waterways Experiment Station, Vicksburg, MS, July 12, 2003; Warren E. Grabeau, *Ninety-Eight Days: A Geographer's View of the Vicksburg Campaign* (Knoxville, TN, 2000), 29–38.

11. *JCCW*, vii–viii.

12. Ibid., vii.

13. Ibid.

14. Ibid., viii.

15. Ibid.

16. Ibid., ix.

17. Ibid.

18. Ibid., x–xiv.

19. Ibid., xv.

20. Ibid., xvi.

21. Ibid., xvi–xxxii.

22. Ibid., xxxiii.

23. Ibid., xxxiv.

24. Ibid., xliii.

# SELECTED BIBLIOGRAPHY

## Primary Sources

### Manuscripts

Allen, N. S., Papers. Archives and Special Collections, Noel Memorial Library, Louisiana State Univ., Shreveport.

Banks, Nathaniel P., Papers. Essex Institute, Salem, MA. Microfilm copy at Univ. of Texas, Austin.

Barron, Amos J. "A History of Pleasant Hill." MS. Mansfield State Historic Site, Mansfield, LA.

Carter, Jonathan H. "Correspondence Book." MS. National Archives and Records Administration, RG45, Washington, DC.

Dearman, Scott. "Order of Battle of the Confederate Army at the Battle of Mansfield, Louisiana. Major General Richard Taylor, April 8, 1864." Compiled by Park Historian Scott Dearman, Mansfield State Historic Site, Mansfield, LA, n.d.

———. "Order of Battle of the Union Army at the Battle of Mansfield, Louisiana. Major General Nathaniel Prentiss Banks, April 8, 1864." Compiled by Park Historian Scott Dearman, Mansfield State Historic Site, Mansfield, LA, n.d.

Fowler, W. S. "Medical Register, 1863–1865." Univ. of Texas Archives, Austin.

Franklin, William B., Papers. Division of Manuscripts, Library of Congress.

Goodwin, Richard C., Papers. Massachusetts Historical Society, Boston.

Johnson, Andrew. Papers. Division of Manuscripts, Library of Congress.

Joiner, Gary D. "A Place Name Geography of Union Parish, Louisiana." MS. Louisiana Tech Univ., Ruston. Copy in the Union Parish Library, Farmerville, LA.

King, William Henry. Diary. Texas State Archives, Austin.

Lale, Max S. "New Light on Battle of Mansfield." TS. N. S. Allen Collection, Noel Memorial Library, Louisiana State Univ., Shreveport.

Leonard, Albert Harris. "Memoirs." MS. Archives of Eugene P. Watson Memorial Library, Northwestern State Univ., Natchitoches, LA.

Lord-Eltinge. Papers. Archives, Wilson Library, Duke Univ., Raleigh, NC.

McClung, R. L. "Three Years in the C.S. Army (P.A.C.S.)." TS. Mansfield State Historic Site, Mansfield, LA.

Porter, David Dixon. Papers. Division of Manuscripts, Library of Congress.

Shackelford, Ellen. Papers. Southern Historical Collection, Univ. of North Carolina, Chapel Hill.

Stanton, Edward F., Papers. Division of Manuscripts, Library of Congress.

Stewart, William H., Diary. Southern Historical Collection, Univ. of North Carolina, Chapel Hill.

# Diaries and Letters

Boyd, David French, to General Richard Taylor. Apr. 14, 1864. Original in the collection of Jackson Barracks Archives, New Orleans.

Brock, Eric. "A Necropolis of Graves at Oakland Cemetery." MS, Eric Brock Papers, Archives and Special Collections, Noel Memorial Library, Louisiana State Univ., Shreveport.

Fullilove, Mrs. [Elizabeth] Thomas Pope. Journal. 1915. Copy in the collection of Mr. Bill Stephenson, Shreveport, LA.

Fullilove, Tom. Confederate diary, 1862–65. In the collection of William Lane Stephenson, Shreveport, LA.

Knapp, Julius L., Diary, Jan.–Dec. 1864. Company I, 116th New York Volunteer Infantry Regiment. Original in the collection of Jim Sandefur, Shreveport, LA.

Knox, R. A., Letter. 2nd Texas Cavalry, 1864. Original in the collection of Jim Sandefur, Shreveport, LA.

Marston, James. Family diary. Collection of James Marston, Shreveport, LA.

Pearce, F. W., Letter. 2nd Maine Cavalry. Original in the collection of Jim Sandefur, Shreveport, LA.

Porter, David Dixon. Letter. Collection of Richard Self, Shreveport, LA.

Spyker, Leonidas Polk. Diary. Archives and Special Collections, Noel Memorial Library, Louisiana State Univ., Shreveport.

Taylor, Richard, to General John George Walker. Apr. 9, 1864. John George Walker Papers #910Z, Southern Historical Collection, Univ. of North Carolina, Chapel Hill.

Union letter. From "Tom," 38th Massachusetts Infantry Regiment, 1864. Original in the collection of Jim Sandefur, Shreveport, LA.

Union log book. From sailor "Eli," Alexandria to Shreveport, 1864. Original in the collection of Jim Sandefur, Shreveport, LA.

Wentworth, Thomas. Letters. 15th Maine Infantry Regiment 1864. Original in the collection of Jim Sandefur, Shreveport, LA.

# Government Documents

Caddo Parish (LA) Assessor's Office Records. Block 39, lot 16; block 51, lot 9; and block 42, lots 12 and 13.

———. Conveyance Book N, folio 295.

*Congressional Globe.* 34th Cong., 1st sess. (1855).

Illinois Military and Naval Dept. *Report of the Adjutant General of the State of Illinois.* Vols. 3, 5–8. Springfield, IL: Phillips, 1901.

Indiana Adjutant General's Office. *Report of the Indiana Adjutant General's Office for 1861–1865.* 8 vols. Indianapolis: Samuel M. Douglass, 1866.

Iowa Adjutant General's Office. *Roster and Records of Iowa Soldiers in the War of the Rebellion Together with Historical Sketches of Volunteer Organizations, 1861–1865.* Vols. 1, 3–5. Des Moines: E. H. English, 1908.

———. *35th Infantry Regiment First and Second Reunions of the Thirty-fifth Iowa Infantry Held at Muscatine, Iowa.* Muscatine, IA: Journal Printing Co., 1889–90.

Kansas Adjutant General's Office. *Official Military History of Kansas Regiments during the War for the Suppression of the Great Rebellion.* Leavenworth, KS: W. S. Burke, 1870.

———. *Report of the Kansas Adjutant General's Office for the Year 1864.* Leavenworth, KS: P. H. Hubbell, 1865.

Maine Adjutant General's Office. *Annual Report of Maine Adjutant General's Office for the Years 1864 and 1865.* Augusta, ME: Stevens and Sayward, 1866.

Maryland Commission on the Publication of the Histories of the Maryland Volunteers during the Civil War. *History and Roster of the Maryland Volunteers, War of 1861–5.* Vol. 1. Silver Spring, MD: Family Line Publications, 1987.

Massachusetts Adjutant General's Office. *Massachusetts Soldiers, Sailors and Marines in the Great Civil War.* Vols. 4–6. Norwood, MA: Norwood Press, 1931.

Minnesota Board of Commissioners on Publication of History of Minnesota in the Civil and Indian Wars. *Minnesota in the Civil and Indian Wars.* Vol. 1. St. Paul, MN: Pioneer Press, 1890.

"Mississippi Squadron Papers." Feb.–June 1864. National Archives and Records Administration, RG 45, microfilm, vols. 27–34.

Missouri Adjutant General's Office. *Annual Report of the Missouri Adjutant General's Office for 1864.* Jefferson City, MO: W. A. Curry, 1865.

———. *Annual Report of the Missouri Adjutant General's Office for 1865.* Jefferson City, MO: Emory S. Foster, 1866.

Natchitoches Parish (LA) Records. Conveyance Book 24.

New Hampshire Adjutant General's Office. *Revised Register of New Hampshire Soldiers and Sailors of the War of the Rebellion, 1861–1866.* Concord, NH: Ira C. Evans, 1895.

New York Adjutant General's Office. *Annual Report of the New York Adjutant General's Office for the Year 1894.* No. 4. Albany, NY: J. B. Lyon, 1895.

———. *Annual Report of the New York Adjutant General's Office for the Year 1897.* No. 15. Albany, NY: Wynkoop, Hallenbeck, Crawford, 1898.

———. *Annual Report of the New York Adjutant General's Office for the Year 1901*. No. 31. Albany, NY: J. B. Lyon, 1902.

———. *Annual Report of the New York Adjutant General's Office for the Year 1903*. No. 37. Albany, NY: Oliver Quayle, 1904.

———. *Annual Report of the New York Adjutant General's Office for the Year 1904*. No. 39. Albany, NY: Brandow, 1905.

———. *Annual Report of the New York Adjutant General's Office for the Year 1904*. No. 40. Albany, NY: Brandow, 1905.

Ohio Roster Commission. *Official Roster of the Soldiers of the State of Ohio in the War of the Rebellion*. Vols. 1, 4–7. Akron: Werner Printing & Manufacturing Co., 1887.

Rhode Island Adjutant General's Office. *Names of Officers, Soldiers and Seamen in Rhode Island Regiments . . . Who Lost Their Lives in the Defense of Their Country in the Suppression of the Late Rebellion*. Providence, RI: Providence Press, 1869.

———. *Official Register of Rhode Island Officers and Soldiers Who Served in the United States Army and Navy, from 1861 to 1866*. Providence, RI: General Assembly, 1866.

State of Louisiana (C.S.A.). *Official Report to the Conduct of Federal Troops in Western Louisiana, during the Invasions of 1863 and 1864, Compiled from Sworn Testimony under Direction of Governor Henry Watkins Allen*. Shreveport: Confederate State of Louisiana, 1865.

U.S. Congress. *Acts of the U.S. Congress, the Second Confiscation and Militia Act of 1862*, July 17, 1862, Section 15. Washington, DC: Government Printing Office.

———. *Report on the Joint Committee on the Conduct of the War, 1863–1866*. Vol. 2, *Red River Expedition*. Millwood, NY: Krauss Reprint, 1977.

U.S. Dept. of Commerce. 7th Decennial Census (1850), Caddo Parish and Bossier Parish. Unpublished tabulations in the National Archives and Records Administration, Washington, DC.

———. 8th Decennial Census (1860), Caddo Parish and Bossier Parish. Unpublished tabulations in the National Archives and Records Administration, Washington, DC.

"USS *Chillicothe* Abstract Log." Mar. 7–June 8, 1864. RG 45. National Archives and Records Administration. Microfilm.

"USS *Lexington* Abstract Log." Mar. 1–June 28, 1864. RG 45. National Archives and Records Administration. Microfilm.

U.S. War Dept. *Atlas to Accompany the Official Records of the Union and Confederate Armies*. Washington: U.S. Government Printing Office, 1891–95.

———. *Official Records of the Union and Confederate Navies in the War of the Rebellion*. 31 vols. Washington, D.C., 1895–1929.

———. *War of the Rebellion: The Official Records of the Union and Confederate Armies*. 128 vols. Washington, 1890–1901.

Vermont Adjutant and Inspector General's Office. *Revised Roster of Vermont Volunteers Who Served in the Army and Navy of the United States during the War of the Rebellion, 1861–1865*. Montpelier, VT: Watchman, 1892.

Wisconsin Adjutant General's Office. *Roster of Wisconsin Volunteers, War of the Rebellion, 1861–1865*. Vols. 1–2. Madison, WI: Democrat Printing, 1866.

———. *History of the Third Regiment of Wisconsin Veteran Volunteer Infantry, 1861–1865.* Madison, WI: Democrat Printing Co., 1891.

———. "Some Experiences of a Veteran in the Rear." In *Glimpses of the Nation's Struggle. Military Order of the Loyal Legion of the United States,* MN, 4:112–23. St. Paul, MN: Collins, 1898.

———. 23rd Infantry Regiment. *Roster of the Survivors of the Twenty-third Regiment, Wisconsin Volunteer Infantry.* Neehah, WI: Blair & Huie, 1889.

———. "William T. Sherman." In *War Papers. Military Order of the Loyal Legion of the United States,* WI, 2. Milwaukee: Burdick, Armitage & Allen, 1898.

## Maps

Hunter, Cammie. Collection. Watson Library Research Center, Northwestern State Univ., Natchitoches, LA.

Clark, John. Fort DeRussy. John Clark Collection, Cayuga County Museum, Auburn, NY.

———. Grand Ecore Defenses (Union). April 1864. Archives of Jackson Barracks, Louisiana National Guard, New Orleans.

———. Map No. 8 of the Red River Campaign. John Clark Collection, Cayuga County Museum, Auburn, NY.

LaTourette. LaTourette Map, ca. 1850. RG 77, folio M72. National Archives and Records Administration, Washington, DC.

Lavender Soil Map (1906). Archives and Special Collections, Noel Memorial Library, Louisiana State Univ., Shreveport.

Morse, George. Survey Map (1842). Louisiana Department of State Lands, Baton Rouge.

Pleasant Hill Battle Map. Mansfield State Historic Site, Mansfield, LA.

U.S. Army Corps of Engineers. *Red River Index, ARK.-TEX, to Mississippi River, Index of 1990 Mosaics.* Vicksburg, MS: U.S. Army Engineer District, 1990.

U.S. Army Topographic Engineers. Maps (1864), RG 77, folio M103-1, M103-2. National Archives and Records Administration, Washington, DC.

Venable, Maj. Richard. "Shreveport and Environs." 1864. Jerome Gilmer Papers, Southern Historical Collection, Univ. of North Carolina, Chapel Hill.

———. "Map of the Battlefield at Mansfield." 1864. Jerome Gilmer Papers, Southern Historical Collection, Univ. of North Carolina, Chapel Hill.

———. "Map of the Battlefield at Pleasant Hill." 1864. Jerome Gilmer Papers, Southern Historical Collection, Univ. of North Carolina, Chapel Hill.

## Newspapers and Periodicals

*Annals of Iowa,* ser. 3, vol. 1 (1893); ser. 3 (1895)

*Atlantic Monthly* 3 (1864)

*Bivouac* 3 (1885)

*Bossier (LA) Banner,* May 18–25, 1860

*Brooklyn Advance* 11 (1884)

*DeBow's Review* (rev. series) 2 (1866)

*Galaxy* 1–2 (1866); 10 (1870)

*Land We Love* 5 (Oct. 1868)

*Military Order of the Loyal Legion of the United States (MOLLUS)*, MN, vols. 2, 4; IA, vols. 1, 2; MA, vol. 1; ME, vols. 1, 4; OH, vols. 2, 5, 6; WI, vol. 2

*New York Herald,* Nov. 1, 1863

*New York Times,* June 6, Oct. 30, 1862

*Philadelphia Press,* Apr. 10, 1864

*Pennsylvania Folklife* 37, no. 3 (1988)

*Rhode Island History* 18 (Oct. 1959); 19 (Jan. 1960)

*Southern Historical Society Papers* 7 (1879); 8 (1880); 13 (1885)

*Western Life-Boat and Journal of Biography, History and Geography* 1, pt. 1–3 (1873–74); pt. 6 (1874)

## Other Printed Primary Sources

Allen, John Fisk. *Memorial of Pickering Dodge Allen, by His Father.* Boston: Henry W. Dutton and Son, 1867.

Allen, William P. "Three Frontier Battles." In *Glimpses of the Nation's Struggle. Military Order of the Loyal Legion of the United States,* MN, 4. St. Paul, MN: H. L. Collins, 1898.

"An Anthology of Experiences of Daniel Albaught, Co. C, 24th Regt., Iowa Infantry." N.p., n.d.

Arkansas Adjutant General's Office. *Report of the Adjutant General of Arkansas for the Period of the Late Rebellion, and to November 1, 1866.* Washington, DC: Government Printing Office, 1867.

"Army Life and Stray Shots." Memphis, TN: Argus, 1863.

Bacon, Edward. *Among the Cotton Thieves.* Detroit: Free Press Steam Book and Job Print, 1867. Reprint, Bossier City, LA: Everett Companies, 1989.

Baird, Henry C. *Washington und Jackson Huber die Neger Als Soldaten. General Banks Huber die Tapferkeit der Neger-Truppen, und das Zweite Louisiana Regiment, von G. H. Boker.* Philadelphia: Johnson, 1863.

Baird, Samuel. *With Merrill's Cavalry: The Civil War Experiences of Samuel Baird, 2nd Missouri Cavalry, U.S.A.* San Marcos, CA: Book Habit, 1981.

Barker, Harold R. *History of the Rhode Island Combat Units in the Civil War (1861–1865).* N.p., 1964.

Barrett, Joseph O. *History of "Old Abe," the Life War Eagle of the Eighth Wisconsin Volunteers.* Chicago: Dunlop, Sewell & Spalding, 1865.

———. *The Soldier Bird, "Old Abe": The Live War-Eagle of Wisconsin That Served a Three Years' Campaign in the Great Rebellion.* Madison, WI: Atwood and Culver, 1876.

Bartlett, Napier. *Military Record of Louisiana: Including Biographical and Historical Papers Relating to the Military Organization of the State.* New Orleans: L. Graham and Co., 1875.

Bartlett, Robert Franklin. *Roster of the Ninety-Sixth Regiment, Ohio Volunteer Infantry, 1862 to 1865.* Columbus, OH: Press of Hann and Adair, 1895.

Basler, Roy P., ed. *The Collected Works of Abraham Lincoln.* New Brunswick, NJ: Rutgers Univ. Press, 1953.

Bearss, Edwin C., ed. *A Louisiana Confederate: The Diary of Felix Pierre Poché.* Natchitoches: Louisiana Studies Institute, Northwestern State Univ., 1972.

Bearss, Edwin C., and Willy H. Tunnard. *A Southern Record: The Story of the 3rd Louisiana Infantry, C.S.A.* Dayton, OH: Morningside, 1988.

Bee, Hamilton P. "Battle of Pleasant Hill—An Error Corrected." *Southern Historical Society Papers* 8 (1880): 184–86.

Beecher, Harris H. *Record of the 114th New York N.Y.S.V. Where It Went, What It Saw, and What It Did.* Norwich, NY: J. F. Hubbard Jr., 1866.

Benedict, George C. *Vermont in the Civil War: A History of the Part Taken by Vermont Soldiers and Sailors in the War of the Union, 1861–1865.* Vol. 2. Burlington, VT: Free Press Association, 1888.

Benefiel, John K. *The Diary of John K. Benefiel for Year 1864, a Civil War Soldier, 46th Reg., Indiana Vol., Reflecting the Experiences of a Pulaski County, Indiana Soldier.* Lompoc, CA: Mrs. R. Q. McKinney, 1972.

Benson, S. F. "The Battle of Pleasant Hill." *Annals of Iowa.* Des Moines: Henry H. English, 1906.

Bentley, William H. *History of the 77th Illinois Volunteer Infantry.* Peoria, IL, 1883.

Bering, John A. *History of the Forty Eighth Ohio Veteran Volunteer Infantry Giving a Complete Account of the Regiment.* Hillsboro, OH, 1880.

———. "Reminiscences of a Federal Prisoner." In *Publications of the Arkansas Historical Association,* 2:372–78. Hillsboro, OH: N.p., [1908].

Berry, Daniel. *Letters Written by Dr. Daniel Berry to Marry Berry Crebs during the Civil War.* Carmi, IL: H. B. Vaught, 1976.

Blackburn, George M., ed. *"Dear Carrie—": The Civil War Letters of Thomas N. Stevens.* Mount Pleasant: Central Michigan Univ., 1984.

Blake, Ephraim. *A Succinct History of the 28th Iowa Volunteer Infantry.* Belle Plain, IA: N.p., 1896.

Blessington, J. P. *The Campaigns of Walker's Texas Division.* Austin: State House Press, 1994.

Boggs, William R. *Military Reminiscences of Gen. Wm. R. Boggs, C.S.A.* Durham, NC: Seeman Printery, 1913.

Bonner, T. R. "Sketches of the Campaign of 1864: Walker's Division—Retreat up Red River—Battle of Mansfield." *The Land We Love* 5 (Oct. 1868): 459–66.

Bowen, James L. *Massachusetts in the War, 1861–1865.* Springfield, MA: Clark W. Bryan, 1889.

Bowers, Stephen C. "The Civil War Diary of Chaplain Stephen C. Bowers." Edited by Glenna R. Schroeder. *Indiana Magazine of History* 79 (June 1983): 167–85.

Boyd, D. F. "General Richard Taylor, C.S.A." *Confederate Veteran* 36 (Dec. 1928): 412–13.

Bridges, Joyce Shannon, ed. *Biographical and Historical Memoirs of Northwest Louisiana.* Nashville: Southern Printing Co., 1890.

Bringhurst, T. H., and Frank Swigart. *History of the Forty-Sixth Regiment Indiana Volunteer Infantry.* Logansport, IN: Wilson Humphreys and Co. Press, 1888.

Britton, Wiley. *The Civil War on the Border: A Narrative of Operations in Missouri, Kansas, Arkansas and the Indian Territory during the Years 1861–62.* 2 vols. New York: Putnam's, 1890–99.

———. "Resume of Military Operations in Missouri and Arkansas, 1864–65." *Battles and Leaders of the Civil War.* Vol. 4. New York: Yoseloff, 1956.

———. "Union and Confederate Indians in the Civil War. *Battles and Leaders of the Civil War.* Vol. 1. New York: Yoseloff, 1956.

———. *The Union Indian Brigade in the Civil War.* Kansas City, MO: Franklin Hudson, 1922.

Brockway, Emmett Addiss. *Civil War Diary of Pvt. Emmett Addiss Brockway, Company B, 35th Iowa Vol. Infantry, 1861–1867.* West Des Moines, IA: J. H. Brockway, 1994.

Bryant, Edwin E. *History of the Third Regiment of Wisconsin Veteran Volunteer Infantry, 1861–1865.* Madison, WI: Democrat Printing Co., 1891.

Bryner, Byron Cloyd. *Bugle Echoes, The Story of the Illinois 47th.* Springfield, IL: Phillips Brothers, 1905.

Burdette, Robert Jones. *The Drums of the 47th.* Indianapolis, IN: Bobbs-Merrill Co., 1914.

Burgess, Lauren Cook, ed. *An Uncommon Soldier: The Civil War Letters of Sarah Rosetta Wakeman, Alias Private Lyons Wakeman, 153rd Regiment, New York State Volunteers, 1862–1864.* New York: Oxford Univ. Press, 1995.

Bush, James C. *A Short History of the Fifth Regiment, U.S. Artillery.* Governor's Island, NY: N.p., 1895.

Camp, Daniel W. *The Civil War Letters of Dan Camp, 24th Iowa Volunteers.* Fort Collins, CO: A. J. Morris, 1984.

Campbell, Randolph B., and Donald K. Pickens, eds. "'My Dear Husband': A Texas Slave's Love Letters, 1862." *Journal of Negro History* 65 (Fall 1980): 361–64.

Childers, Henry H. "Reminiscences of the Battle of Pleasant Hill." *Annals of Iowa.* Des Moines: Henry H. English, 1906.

Clark, Orton S. *The One Hundred and Sixteenth Regiment of New York Volunteers.* Buffalo: Printing House of Matthews and Warren, 1868.

Collins, Thomas Benton. "A Texan's Account of the Battle of Valverde." *Panhandle Plains Historical Review* 37 (1964): 33–35.

*The Color Bearer, Francis A. Clary.* New York: American Tract Society, 1864.

*Complete Roster of the Eighth Regiment New Hampshire Volunteers.* Concord, NH: Ira C. Evans, 1890.

Connecticut Adjutant General's Office. *Catalogue of Connecticut Volunteer Organizations (Infantry, Cavalry and Artillery,) in the Service of the United States, 1861–1865, with Additional Enlistments, Casualties, and Brief Summaries Showing the Operations and Service of the Several Regiments and Batteries.* Hartford, CT: Brown & Gross, 1869.

————. *Record of Service of Connecticut Men in the Army and Navy of the United States during the War of the Rebellion*. Hartford, CT: Case, Lockwood, Brainard, 1889.

Connor, Seymour V., ed. *Dear America: Some Letters of Orange Cicero and Mary America (Aikin) Connor*. Austin, TX: Jenkins Publishing Co., 1971.

Cory, Charles E. *The Soldiers of Kansas: The Sixth Kansas Cavalry and Its Commander: An Address by Charles E. Cory*. Topeka: Kansas Historical Society, 1910.

Coutts, John. "The Civil War Experiences of John Coutts." *Cedar County Historical Review* (July 1964): 1–30.

Craig, William J. *West of the Mississippi with Waller's 13th Texas Cavalry Battalion, CSA*. Comp. and ed. by Charles Spurlin. Hillsboro, TX: Hill Junior College Press, 1971.

Crandall, Warren D. *History of the Ram Fleet and the Mississippi Marine Brigade in the War for the Union on the Mississippi and Its Tributaries: The Story of the Ellets and Their Men*. St. Louis: Society of Survivors, 1907.

Crawford, Samuel J. *Kansas in the Sixties*. Chicago: McClurg, 1911.

Croffut, W. A., and John M. Morris. *The Military and Civil History of Connecticut during the War of 1861–1865*. New York: Ledyard Bill, 1869.

Crosley, George W. "Charge of the Light Brigade." In *War Sketches and Incidents. Military Order of the Loyal Legion of the United States*, IA, 1. Des Moines: Kenyon, 1893.

Curtis, Oscar H. *Proceedings of the Twenty-Sixth Annual Reunion of the 114th NY Regimental Association and Dedicatory Services at Winchester, Va., Oct. 19, 1898*. Washington: Conwell Printing, 1899.

Dana, C. A. *Recollections of the Civil War*. New York: D. Appleton and Co., 1898.

Debray, Xavier Blanchard. *A Sketch of the History of Debray's (26th) Regiment of Texas Cavalry*. Austin: Eugene von Boeckmann, 1884. Reprint, Waco: Village Press, 1961.

————. "A Sketch of Debray's Twenty-Sixth Regiment of Texas Cavalry." *Southern Historical Society Papers* 13 (1885): 153–65.

Dill, Samuel Phillips. *A Brief Sketch of the 173rd Regiment, N.Y.V.* Brooklyn, N.Y.: N.p., 1868.

————. *Journal of the Escape and Re-Capture of Samuel P. Dill, Late Capt. and Brevet Major 173d Regt. New York Vols*. Brooklyn: J. H. Broach and Brothers, 1867.

Dodge, James H. "Across the Plains with the Ninth Wisconsin Battery in 1862." War Paper 23. *Military Order of the Loyal Legion of the United States*. Washington, DC.

Dorsey, Sarah H. *Recollections of Henry Watkins Allen, Brigadier General Confederate State Army, Ex-Governor of Louisiana*. New York: M. Doolady, 1866.

Douglas, Henry Kyd. *I Rode with Stonewall*. Chapel Hill: Univ. of North Carolina Press, 1940.

Dow, Neal. *The Reminiscences of Neal Dow: Recollections of Eighty Years*. Portland, ME: Evening Express Co., 1898.

Driggs, George W. *Opening of the Mississippi: Or, Two Years Campaigning in the Southwest, a Record of the Campaigns, Sieges, Actions and Marches in Which the 8th Wisconsin Volunteers Have Participated, Together with Correspondence, by a Non-commissioned Officer*. Madison, WI: William J. Park and Co., 1864.

Duffy, Edward. *History of the 159th Regiment, N.Y.S.V., Comp. from the Diary of Edward Duffy*. New York: N.p., 1890.

Duncan, William. "The Army of the Tennessee under Major General O. O. Howard." *Glimpses of the Nation's Struggle. Order of the Loyal Legion of the United States,* MN, 4. St. Paul: Collins, 1898.

Dyer, Frederick H. *A Compendium of the War of the Rebellion.* 3 vols. Dayton, OH: Morningside, 1979.

Eddy, Thomas M. *The Patriotism of Illinois: A Record of the Civil and Military History of the State in the War for the Union With a History of the Campaigns in Which Illinois Soldiers Have Been Conspicuous.* 2 vols. Chicago: Clarke, 1866.

Edmonds, David C. *The Conduct of Federal Troops in Louisiana during the Invasions of 1863 and 1864: Official Report compiled from Sworn Testimony under the Direction of Governor Henry W. Allen, Shreveport, April, 1865.* Lafayette: Acadiana Press, 1988.

Edwards, Abial Hall. "Dear Friend Anna": The Civil War Letters of a Common Soldier from Maine. Orono: Univ. of Maine Press, 1992.

Edwards, John N. *Shelby and His Men; or, The War in the West.* Cincinnati: Miami Printing and Publishing Co., 1867.

"Ed Wright: Secretary of State." *Western Life-Boat and Journal of Biography, History and Geography* 1, pt. 1–3 (1873–74): 43–45.

Ely, John F. "First Year's Medical History of the Twenty-Fourth Iowa." *Military Order of the Loyal Legion of the United States,* IA, 1:105–14.

Engle, Francis E. *Worden's Battalion and Company E of the Fourteenth Wisconsin Veteran Volunteer Infantry: Paper Prepared for Reunion of Regiment, Fond Du Lac, June 8, 9 and 10, 1904.* Indianapolis: N.p., [1904].

Ewer, James K. *The Third Massachusetts Cavalry in the War for the Union.* Maplewood, MA: Historical Committee of the Regimental Association, 1903.

Fairbanks, Henry N. "The Red River Expedition of 1864." *Military Order of the Loyal Legion of the United States,* ME, 1:181–90.

Farley, Edwin. *Experiences of a Soldier, 1861–1865.* Paducah, KY: Billings Print Co., 1918.

Favell, Thomas R. *Civil War Years: Thomas Favell and the 8th Wis. Inf'ty.* Sarasota, FL: L. Favell, 1975.

Fearn, Francis, ed. *Diary of a Refugee.* New York: N.p., 1910.

Field, Charles D. *Three Years in the Saddles from 1861 to 1865: Memoirs of Charles D. Field; Thrilling Stories of the War in Camp and on the Field of Battle.* Goldfield, IL: N.p., 1898.

*First and Second Re-Unions of the Thirty Fifth Iowa Infantry, Held at Muscatine, Iowa.* Muscatine: Journal Printing Co., 1889–90.

Fitts, James Franklin. "In the Ranks at Cedar Creek." *Galaxy* 1 (1866): 534–43.

———. "A June Day at Port Hudson." *Galaxy* 2 (1866): 121–31.

———. "The Last Battle of Winchester." *Galaxy* 2 (1866): 322–32.

———. "Days with the Knapsack." *Galaxy* 2 (1866): 405–12.

———. "Mosby and His Men." *Galaxy* 2 (1866): 643–51.

———. "The Story of a Mutiny." *Galaxy* 10 (1870): 224–28.

Fitzpatrick, Mike. "Asa W. Hebbard of the 28th Infantry." *Military Images* 23 (July/Aug. 2001): 33–34.

Fletcher, Samuel H. *The History of Company A, Second Cavalry.* Chicago: N.p., 1912.

Flinn, Frank M. *Campaigning with Banks in Louisiana in '63 and '64 and with Sheridan in the Shenandoah Valley in '64 and '65.* Lynn, MA: Thomas. P. Nichols, 1887.

Ford, Orrin B. *Biography of O. B. Ford, "Written by Himself."* Yale, OK: Yale Record Print, 191– [no specific date].

Fordyce, Dr. Benjamin A. *Dr. Benjamin A. Fordyce Echoes: From the Letters of a Civil War Surgeon.* Edited by Lydia P. Hecht. Sarasota, FL: Bayou Publishing, 1996.

Fowler, Philemon Halstead. *Memorials of William Fowler.* New York: Anson D. F. Randolph and Co., 1875.

Freemantle, Arthur Lyon. *The Fremantle Diary: Being the Journal of Lieutenant Colonel James Arthur Lyon Fremantle, Coldstream Guards, on His Three Months in the Southern States.* Edited by Walter Lord. Boston: Little, Brown and Co., 1954.

French, Frank F. *The Lost Detachment.* Humboldt, IA: N.p., 1907.

Geer, John James. *Beyond the Lines, or, a Yankee Prisoner Loose in Dixie.* Philadelphia: J. W. Daughaday, 1863.

Gerard, Clinton W. *A Diary, The Eighty-Third Ohio Vol. Inf. in the War, 1862–1865.* Cincinnati, OH: N.p., 1889.

Giesecke, Julius. "The Diary of Julius Giesecke, 1861–1862." Translated by Oscar Haas. *Texas Military History* 3 (Winter 1963): 228–42 (pt. 1); (Spring 1963): 27–54 (pt. 2).

Gilpin, Ebenezer N. "The Last Campaign: Cavalryman's Journal." *Journal of the U.S. Cavalry Association* 18 (1908): 617–75.

Gordon, Seth C. "Reminiscences of the Civil War from a Surgeon's Point of View." *Military Order of the Loyal Legion of the United States*, ME, 1:129–44.

Gould, John Mead. *The Civil War Journals of John Mead Gould, 1861–1866.* Baltimore: Butternut and Blue, 1997.

———. *Directory of the First-Tenth-Twenty Ninth Maine Regiment Association, Compiled for the Use of the Association.* Portland, ME: Stephen Berry, Printer, 1889.

———. *History of the First-Tenth-Twenty-Ninth Maine Regiment, in Service of the United States, from May 3, 1861, to June 21, 1866.* Portland, ME: Stephen Berry, 1871.

*Grand Army of the Republic Department of New York. Lafayette Post No. 140. Proceedings of the Grand Army of the Republic Lafayette Post No. 140 in Memory of Senior Vice Commander Samuel N. Benjamin . . . Whose Death Occurred at Governor's Island, New York Harbor, on the Fifteenth Day of May, 1886.* New York: Trow's Printing & Bookbinding Co., 1886.

Grant, U.S. *Personal Memoirs of U. S. Grant.* New York: Da Capo, 1982.

Graves, Harrison A. *Andrew Jackson Potter, the Fighting Parson of the Texan Frontier.* Nashville: Southern Methodist Publishing House, 1881, 1889.

Greene, J. Harvey. *Letters to My Wife: A Civil War Diary from the Western Front.* Apollo, PA: Closson Press, 1995.

———. *Reminiscences of the War Bivouacs, Marches, Skirmishes and Battles. Extracts from Letters Written Home from 1861 to 1865.* Medina, OH: Gazette Printing, 1886.

Griggs, George W. *Opening of the Mississippi; or, Two Years' Campaigning in the South-West.* Madison, WI: William J. Park and Co., 1864.

Grisamore, Silas. *Reminiscences of Uncle Silas: A History of the Eighteenth Louisiana Infantry Regiment.* Edited by Arthur W. Bergeron Jr. Baton Rouge, LA: Le Comite des Archives de la Louisiane, 1981. Reprint ed. titled *The Civil War Reminiscences of Major Silas T. Grisamore, CSA.* Baton Rouge: Louisiana State Univ. Press, 1993.

Guernsey, Alfred H., and Henry M. Alden, eds. *Harper's Pictorial History of the Civil War.* Chicago: Puritan Press, 1866.

Gunby, A. A. *Life and Services of David French Boyd.* Baton Rouge: Louisiana State Univ. Press, 1904.

Hall, Charles Badger. "Notes on the Red River Campaign of 1864." *Military Order of the Loyal Legion of the United States,* ME, 4:264–81.

Hamersly, Thomas H. S., comp. and ed. *Complete Army Register.* New York: By the author, 1880.

Hanabaugh, David H. *History of the One Hundred and Twenty-eighth Regiment, New York Volunteers.* Poughkeepsie, NY: Press of the Enterprise Publishing Co., 1894.

Hancock, John. *The Fourteenth Wisconsin, Corinth and Shiloh, 1862–1895: Paper on the Battle of Shiloh.* Indianapolis, IN: F. E. Engle, 1895.

Hander, Christian Wilhelm. "Excerpts from the Hander Diary." Translated and edited by Leonard B. Plummer. *Journal of Mississippi History* 26 (May 1964): 141–49.

Hanna, Ebenezer. "The Journal of Ebenezer Hanna." Edited by Martin H. Hall. *Password* 3 (Jan. 1958): 14–29.

Harrell, J. M. "Arkansas." In *Confederate Military History.* Vol. 10. Atlanta: Confederate Publishing Co., 1899.

Hartlerode, Lawrence. *Out of a Rebel Prison during the War, Thrilling Account of the Hairbreadth Escapes and Life and Death Struggles of Private Harderode of the 46th Indiana.* Winamac, IN: J. J. Gorrell, 1895.

Haskin, William Lawrence. *The History of the First Regiment of Artillery, from Its Organization in 1821, to January 1st, 1876.* Portland, ME: B. Thurston and Co., 1879.

Hawes, Levi Lindley. "Personal Experiences of a Union Veteran." *Historical Leaves* (Somerville Historical Society) 4 (1905): 25–37, 49–62.

Heartsill, W. W. *Fourteen Hundred and 91 Days in the Confederate Army: A Journal Kept by W.W. Heartsill for Four Years, One Month, and One Day or, Camp Life; Day by Day, of the W. P. Lane Rangers from April 19th, 1861 to May 20th, 1865.* Edited by Bell Irvin Wiley. Wilmington, NC: Broadfoot Publishing Co., 1992.

Heimstreet, Edward Burton. *The History of Old Abe, the War Eagle and a Condensed Record of the Eighth Wisconsin Infantry, Better Known as the Eagle Regiment.* Lake Mills, WI: By the author, 1933.

Hesseltine, Francis S. "Amusing the Enemy." *Military Order of the Loyal Legion of the United States,* MA, 1:27–44.

Hinkley, Julian W. *A Narrative of Service with the Third Wisconsin Infantry.* Madison: Wisconsin Historical Commission, 1912.

———. "Some Experiences of a Veteran in the Rear." In *Glimpses of the Nation's Struggle. Military Order of the Loyal Legion of the United States,* MN, 4:112–23. St. Paul, MN: Collins, 1898.

*An Historical Sketch of the 56th Ohio Volunteer Infantry during the Great Civil War.* Columbus, OH: N.p., 1899.

*History of the Forty-Sixth Regiment Indiana Volunteer Infantry.* Compiled by the committee. Logansport, IN: Wilson Humphreys, 1888.

*An Historical Sketch of the 162d Regiment N.Y. Vol. Infantry (3d Metropolitan Guard), 19th Army Corps, 1862–1865.* Albany, NY: Weed, Parsons, and Co., printers, 1867.

*History and Roster One Hundred and Thirtieth Illinois.* Greenville, IL: Advocate Print, 1892.

*History of the Second Battalion, Duryee Zouaves, One Hundred and Sixty Fifth Regt., New York Volunteer Infantry.* New York: Peter de Baun & Co., 1904.

Hoadley, John C. *Memorial of Henry Sanford Gansevoort, Captain Fifth Artillery, and Lieutenant-Colonel by Brevet, U.S.A.; Colonel Thirteenth New York State Volunteer Cavalry, and Brigadier General of Volunteers by Brevet.* Boston: Franklin Press, 1875.

Hoag, Levi L. "The Civil War Diary of Levi L. Hoag." Edited by Edwin C. Bearss. *Annals of Iowa* 39 (Winter 1968): 168–93.

Hobard, Ella E. G. *The Soldier's Gift. The Dangers and Temptations of Army Life.* Chicago: Tribune Press, 1863.

Hoey, George. *The 165th New York Volunteers.* N.p., 1890.

———. *The 165th New York Volunteers, Written by George Hoey, and Read by James F. Ferguson, on Decoration Day, May 30th, 1890, at Tottenville, Staten Island.* N.p., n.d.

Hoffman, Wickham. *Camp, Court and Siege, A Narrative of Personal Adventure and Observation during Two Wars 1861–1865, 1870–1871.* New York: Harper and Brothers, 1877.

Homans, John. "The Red River Expedition." In *The Mississippi Valley, Tennessee, Georgia, Alabama, 1861–1864.* Vol. 7, *Papers of the Military Historical Society of Massachusetts.* Boston: Military Historical Society of Massachusetts, 1910.

Hopkins, Alphonse Alva. *The Life of Clinton Bowen Fisk, with a Brief Sketch of John A. Brooks.* New York: Funk & Wagnalls, 1888.

Howe, M. A. DeWolfe, ed. *Home Letters of General Sherman.* New York: Charles Scribner's Sons, 1909.

Hubbard, Lucius Frederick. "Civil War Papers." *Collections of the Minnesota Historical Society* 12 (1908): 531–638.

Hubbard, Thomas Hamlin. *The Lost Cause, Delivered to the Commandery of the State of New York, Military Order of the Loyal Legion of the United States.* N.p., 1912.

Hughes, John C. *A Soldier's Dream of Home: The Civil War Letters of John C. Hughes to His Wife, Harriet.* Ft. Worth, TX: Arcadia-Clark, 1996.

Illinois Military and Naval Department. *Report of the Adjutant General of the State of Illinois.* 8 vols. Springfield, IL: Phillips, 1901.

Illinois 10th Cavalry Regiment. *Proceedings of the Annual Reunion of the Society of the Illinois 10th Cavalry Regiment Held at Springfield, Illinois, September 24, 1895.* Springfield, IL: N.p., 1895.

———. *Roster of the Survivors of the 10th Illinois Cavalry and Proceedings of the Society of the 10th Illinois Cavalry, October 16th, 1894.* Springfield, IL: N.p., 1894.

Indiana Adjutant General's Office. *Report of the Indiana Adjutant General's Office for 1861–1865*. Vol. 2. Indianapolis: Samuel M. Douglass, 1866.

Ingersoll, Lurton D. *Iowa and the Rebellion*. Philadelphia: Lippincott, 1867.

Iowa Adjutant General's Office. *Roster and Records of Iowa Soldiers in the War of the Rebellion Together with Historical Sketches of Volunteer Organizations, 1861–1865*. Des Moines, IA: E. H. English, 1908.

———. *35th Infantry Regiment First and Second Reunions of the Thirty-fifth Iowa Infantry Held at Muscatine, Iowa*. Muscatine, IA: Journal Printing Co., 1889–90.

Irwin, Richard B. *History of the Nineteenth Army Corps*. Baton Rouge: Elliott's Book Shop Press, 1985.

Jackson, Isaac. "Some of the Boys." *The Civil War Letters of Isaac Jackson, 1862–1865*. Edited by Joseph Orville Jackson. Carbondale: Southern Illinois Univ. Press, 1960.

Jarratt, J. A. *Reminiscences of a Great Struggle Told by Heroes of the Confederacy*. Mansfield, LA: By the author, 1907.

Jenkins, Wilton A. "A Leaf from Army Life. Military Essays and Recollections." *Military Order of the Loyal Legion of the United States*, IL, 3:437–45. Chicago: Dial Press, 1899.

Jeter, Katherine Brash, ed. *A Man and His Boat: The Civil War Career and Correspondence of Lt. Jonathan H. Carter, CSN*. Lafayette: Univ. of Southwestern Louisiana, 1996.

Johansson, Jane Harris, and David H. Johansson. "Two Lost Battle Reports: Horace Randal's and Joseph L. Brent's Reports of the Battles of Mansfield and Pleasant Hill, 8 and 9 April 1864." *Military History of the Southwest* 23, no. 2 (Fall 1993): 149–67.

Johnson, Charles Beneulyn. *Muskets and Medicine; or, Army Life in the Sixties*. Philadelphia: F. A. Davis Co., 1917.

Johnson, Robert U., and Clarence C. Buel, ed. *Battles and Leaders of the Civil War*. 4 vols. Secaucus, N.J.: Castle, 1986.

Johnston, Joseph E. *Narrative of Military Operations during the Civil War*. New York: D. Appleton and Co., 1874.

Jones, James P., and Edward F. Keuchel. *Civil War Maine: A Diary of the Red River Expedition, 1864*. Washington: History and Museum Division, Headquarters, U.S. Marine Corps, 1975.

Jones, S. C. *Reminiscences of the 22nd Iowa Infantry Giving Its Organization, Marches, Skirmishes, Battles, and Sieges, As Taken from the Diary of Lieutenant S.C. Jones of Company A*. Iowa City: Camp Pope Bookshop, 1993.

Jones, William E. *The Military History of the One Hundred & Sixty First New-York Volunteers, Infantry, from August 15th, 1862, to October 17th, 1865*. N.p.: Bath, Hull and Barnes, printers, 1865.

Kansas Adjutant General's Office. *Official Military History of Kansas Regiments during the War for the Suppression of the Great Rebellion*. Leavenworth, KS: W. S. Burke, 1870.

Kennedy, John. *Diary of John Kennedy*. Copied by Ruth Genevieve Hanneman. Rossville, MI: N.p., 1959.

Lane, Walter P. *The Adventures and Recollections of General Walter P. Lane, a San Jacinto Veteran*. Marshall, TX: Jenkins Publishing Co., 1970.

Lines, Charles B. *Memorial of Edward C. D. Lines, Late Captain of Co. C, 2d Reg't Kansas Cavalry.* New Haven, CT: Tuttle, Morehouse and Taylor, 1867.

Long, Byford E. *Captain B. E. Long Diary and History of Co. E, 67th Regiment.* N.p, n.d.

Longley, Charles L. "Champion's Hill." *Military Order of the Loyal Legion of the United States,* IA, 56:208–14. Wendell, NC: Broadfoot, 1992.

———. "The Twenty-Fourth Iowa Volunteers." *Annals of Iowa,* ser. 3, vol. 1 (1894): 445–54, 553–65; vol. 2 (1895): 44–56.

Lossing, Benson J. *Memoir of Lieut-Col. John T. Greble of the United States Army.* Philadelphia: Privately printed, 1870.

Lothrup, Charles H. *A History of the First Regiment Iowa Cavalry Veteran Volunteers, from Its Organization in 1861 to Its Muster Out of the United States Service in 1866.* Lyons, IA: Beers & Eaton, 1890.

Love, William D. *Wisconsin in the War of the Rebellion.* Chicago: Church and Goodman, 1866.

Lubbock, Francis R. *Six Decades in Texas.* Austin: Ben C. Jones and Co., 1900.

Lucas, Charles Alexander. "A Soldier's Letters from the Field." *Iowa Historical Record.* Vols. 16–28. Des Moines: Iowa Historical Society.

Lufkin, Edwin B. *History of the Thirteenth Maine Regiment, From Its Organization in 1861 to Its Muster-Out in 1865.* Brighton, ME: H. A. Shorey and Son, 1898.

Magdeburg, Frederick H. "William T. Sherman." War Papers. *Military Order of the Loyal Legion of the United States,* WI, vol. 2:1–51. Milwaukee: Burdick, Armitage and Allen, 1898.

———. "Worden's Battalion." Paper read at the First Annual Reunion of the 14th Wisconsin Veteran Voluntary Infantry, Fond Du Lac, Wisconsin, Wednesday and Thursday, June 16–17, 1886.

Mahan, Alfred Thayer. *The Gulf and Inland Waters.* New York: Charles Scribner's Sons, 1883.

Mahan, D. H. *A Treatise on Field Fortifications Containing Instructions on the Methods of Laying Out, Constructing, Defending, and Attacking Intrenchments, with the General Outline Also of the Arrangement, the Attack, and Defense of Permanent Fortifications.* New York: John Wiley, 1863.

Maine Adjutant General's Office. *Annual Report of Maine Adjutant General's Office for the Years 1864 and 1865.* Augusta, ME: Stevens and Sayward, 1866.

*Manual of the 116th Regiment, New York State Volunteers.* Buffalo, NY: Lockwood and Company's Steam Press, n.d.

Marshall, Thomas B. *History of the Eighty-Third Ohio Volunteer Infantry, the Greyhound Regiment.* Cincinnati: Eighty-Third Ohio Volunteer Infantry Association, 1913.

Martin, N. B. "Letters of a Union Officer: L. F. Hubbard and the Civil War." *Minnesota History* 35, no. 7 (Sept. 1957): 313–19.

Maryland Commission on the Publication of the Histories of the Maryland Volunteers during the Civil War. *History and Roster of the Maryland Volunteers, War of 1861-5.* 2 vols. Silver Spring, MD: Family Line Publications, 1987.

Massachusetts Adjutant General's Office. *Massachusetts Soldiers, Sailors and Marines in the Great Civil War.* Vols. 4–6. Norwood, MA: Norwood Press, 1931.

Maury, D. H. "Sketch of General Richard Taylor." *Southern Historical Society Papers* 7 (1879): 343–45.

McCall, D. *Three Years in the Service, A Record of the Doings of the 11th Reg. Missouri Vols.* 2nd ed. Springfield: Johnson and Bradford, 1864.

McCann, Thomas H. *The Campaigns of the Civil War in the United States of America, 1861–1865.* Hoboken, NJ: Hudson Observer Job Print, 1915.

McClellan, George B. *McClellan's Own Story.* New York: C. L. Webster and Co., 1887.

McCormick, Andrew W. "Battles and Campaigns in Arkansas." *Sketches of War History. Military Order of the Loyal Legion of the United States,* OH, 6. Cincinnati: Monfort, 1908.

———. "Sixteen Months a Prisoner of War." *Sketches of War History. Military Order of the Loyal Legion of the United States,* OH, 5. Cincinnati: Robert Clarke, 1903.

McCulloch, John Scouller. *Reminiscences of Life in the Army and as a Prisoner of War.* N.p., n.d.

McGregor, Frank Ross. *Dearest Susie: A Civil War Infantryman's Letters to His Sweetheart.* Edited by Carl E. Hatch. New York: Exposition Press, 1971.

Mechling, William T. "William T. Mechling's Journal of the Red River Campaign, April–May 10, 1864." Edited by Alwyn Barr. *Texana* 1 (Fall 1963): 363.

*A Memorial to Brevet Brigadier General Lewis Benedict, Colonel of 162d Regiment N.Y.V.I., Who Fell in Battle at Pleasant Hill, La., April 9, 1864.* Albany, NY: J. Munsell, 1866.

Merwin, J. W. *Roster and Monograph, 161st Reg't. N.Y.S. Volunteer Infantry, Rebellion 1861–1865.* Elmira, NY: Gazette Printing, 1903.

Meyer, John. "John Meyer: Grocer, Newton, Iowa." *The Western Life-Boat and Journal of Biography, History and Geography* 1, pt. 6 (1863–74): 205–6.

Miles, Selim C. *The Eagle of the Regiment, A Complete History of That Famous Bird, "Old Abe," the War Eagle, with Thrilling Battle Scenes and Incidents of Fighting Joe Mowers' "Invincible" Second Brigade.* Stetsonville, WI: War Eagle Book Association, 1894.

*Military Order of the Loyal Legion of the United States (MOLLUS).* 70 vols. Wilmington, NC: Broadfoot, 1995.

Miller, Francis T., ed. *The Photographic History of the Civil War.* 10 vols. New York: Review of Reviews, 1911.

Minnesota Board of Commissioners on Publication of History of Minnesota in the Civil and Indian Wars. *Minnesota in the Civil and Indian Wars.* 3 vols. St. Paul, MN: Pioneer Press, 1890.

Missouri Adjutant General's Office. *Annual Report of the Missouri Adjutant General's Office for 1864.* Jefferson City, MO: W. A. Curry, 1865.

———. *Annual Report of the Missouri Adjutant General's Office for 1865.* Jefferson City, MO: Emory S. Foster, 1866.

Moat, Louis S., ed. *Frank Leslie's Illustrated History of the Civil War.* New York: Fairfax Press, 1977.

Moore, Frank, ed. *The Rebellion Record: A Diary of American Events.* New York: Putnam (vols. 1–6) and Van Nostrand (vols. 7–12), 1868.

Moore, William R. "Our Red River Expedition." Broadside poem.

Musser, Charles O. *Soldier Boy: The Civil War Letters of Charles O. Musser, 29th Iowa.* Edited by Barry Popchock. Iowa City: Univ. of Iowa Press, 1995.

New Hampshire Adjutant General's Office. *Revised Register of Soldiers and Sailors of the Rebellion, 1861–1866.* Concord, NH: Ira C. Evans, 1895.

New York Adjutant General's Office. *Annual Report of the New York Adjutant General's Office for the Year 1894.* No. 4. Albany, NY: J. B. Lyon, 1895.

———. *Annual Report of the New York Adjutant General's Office for the Year 1897.* No. 15. Albany, NY: Wynkoop, Hallenbeck, Crawford, 1898.

———. *Annual Report of the New York Adjutant General's Office for the Year 1901.* No. 31. Albany, NY: J. B. Lyon, 1902.

———. *Annual Report of the New York Adjutant General's Office for the Year 1903.* No. 37. Albany, NY: Oliver Quayle, 1904.

———. *Annual Report of the New York Adjutant General's Office for the Year 1904.* No. 39. Albany, NY: Brandow, 1905.

———. *Annual Report of the New York Adjutant General's Office for the Year 1904.* No. 40. Albany, NY: Brandow, 1905.

Newsome, Edmund. *Experience in the War of the Rebellion.* Carbondale, IL: By the author, 1880.

Newton, James K. *Wisconsin Boy in Dixie: Civil War Letters of James K. Newton.* Edited by Stephen E. Ambrose. Madison: Univ. of Wisconsin Press, 1995.

New York Volunteer Infantry. *Album of the Second Battalion, Duryee Zoaves, One Hundred and Sixty Fifth Regt.* New York: n.p., 1906.

Nicolay, John G., and John Hay. *Abraham Lincoln, A History.* New York: Century Co., 1909.

Noel, Theophilus. *Autobiography and Reminiscences of Theophilus Noel.* Chicago: Theophilus Noel Co. Print, 1904.

———. *A Campaign from Santa Fe to the Mississippi Being a History from Its First Organization to the Present Time, Its Campaigns in New Mexico, Arizona, Texas, Louisiana, and Arkansas, in the Years of 1861-2-3-4.* Shreveport, LA: Shreveport News, 1865.

*Official Report to the Conduct of Federal Troops in Western Louisiana, during the Invasions of 1863 and 1864, Compiled from Sworn Testimony under Direction of Governor Henry Watkins Allen.* Shreveport: State of Louisiana (C.S.A.), 1865.

Ohio Roster Commission. *Official Roster of the Soldiers of the State of Ohio in the War of the Rebellion.* 11 vols. Akron: Werner Printing & Manufacturing Co, 1887.

Olmstead, Frederick L. *A Journey through Texas.* New York: Dix, Edwards and Co., 1857.

Olney, Warren. "'Shiloh' as Seen by a Private Soldier." War Papers. *Military Order of the Loyal Legion of the United States,* CA, Paper 5.

One Hundred and sixty-second Infantry Regiment Association. *An Historical Sketch of the One Hundred and sixty-second Regiment New York Volunteer Infantry in the War of the Rebellion.* Albany, NY: Weed and Parsons, 1867.

———. *165th Infantry Regiment History of the Second Battalion Duryee Zouaves, One Hundred and Sixty-fifth Regiment New York Volunteer Infantry, Mustered in the United States Service at Camp Washington, Staten Island, N.Y.* New York: n.p., 1905.

O'Pry, Maude Hearn. *Chronicles of Shreveport and Caddo Parish.* Shreveport, LA: Times Publishing Co., 1928.

Page, Thomas Manning. *Bohemian Life; or, Autobiography of a Tramp.* San Francisco: J. Dewing and Co., 1884.

Paris, Compte de (Louis Philippe Albert d'Orléans). *History of the Civil War in America.* 4 vols. Philadelphia: Porter and Coates, 1875–88.

Parkhurst, Charles H. *Incidents of Cavalry Service in Louisiana.* Providence: Rhode Island Soldiers and Sailors Historical Society, 1879.

———. *Incidents of Cavalry Service in Louisiana. Personal Narratives.* Rhode Island Soldiers and Sailors Historical Society. Ser. 1, no. 7. Providence: Rhode Island Soldiers and Sailors Historical Society, 1879.

Parks, George. *The Civil War Letters of Private George Parks, Company C, 24th New York Cavalry Volunteers: With Additional Commentary on the Civil War Experiences of Private Francis Overfield, 116th New York Infantry Volunteers and Landsman Joseph J. Overfield, United States Navy.* Buffalo, NY: Gallagher Printing, 1992.

Peck, Lewis M. "History of the One Hundred and Seventy-Third New York Volunteers, Fourth Metropolitan Brigade." *Brooklyn Advance* 11 (1884): 4–11.

Pellet, Elias P. *History of the 114ᵗʰ Regiment, New York State Volunteers.* Norwich, NY: Telegraph and Chronicle Press Print, 1866.

Petty, A. W. M. *A History of the Third Missouri Cavalry: From Its Organization at Palmyra, Missouri, 1861 Up to November Sixth, 1864: With an Appendix and Recapitulation.* Albany, MO: Century Reprints, 1997.

Phillips, Ulrich Bonnell, ed. *The Correspondence of Robert Toombs, Alexander H. Stephens, and Howell Cobb.* New York: Da Capo Press, 1970.

Phisterer, Frederick, comp. *New York in the War of the Rebellion, 1861–1865.* Vol. 5. Albany, NY: Weed and Parsons, 1890.

Pitts, Florison D. "The Civil War Diary of Florison D. Pitts." Edited by Leo M. Kaiser. *Mid-America* 40 (Jan. 1958): 22–63.

Porter, David Dixon. *Incidents and Anecdotes of the Civil War.* New York: Appleton, 1885.

———. *Naval History of the Civil War.* Secaucus, NJ: Castle, 1984.

Porter, John C. *Texans in Gray: A Regimental History of the 18th Texas Infantry, Walker's Texas Division in the Civil War.* Edited by James Henry Davis. Hughes Springs, TX: Heritage Oak Press, 1993.

Porter, V. Mott. *A History of Battery "A" of St. Louis: With an Account of the Early Artillery Companies from Which It Is Descended. A Paper Read before the Society, Feb. 11, 1904.* St. Louis: Society, 1905.

Post, Lydia, ed. *Soldier's Letters from Camp, Battlefield and Prison.* New York: Bruce and Huntington, 1865.

Potter, Edward N. *Sergeant Potter's War in the West: Featuring Sgt. Edward N. Potter, His Squad and the Men of Company D, 29th Wisconsin Volunteer Infantry.* Oregon, WI: R. N. Larsen, n. d.

Potts, Gregg, and Kevin Hardy Jr. "Letters of a Union Chaplain at Mansfield, 1864." *North Louisiana Historical Association Journal* 16, nos. 2–3 (1985): 69–77.

Powers, George W. "Bitter and Sweet." *Bivouac* 3 (1885): 342–45.

———. *The Story of the Thirty Eighth Regiment of Massachusetts Volunteers*. Cambridge, MA: Dakin and Metcalf, 1866.

*Prison Life in Texas: An Account of the Capture, and Imprisonment of a Portion of the 46th Regiment, Indiana Veteran Volunteers, in Texas*. Logansport, IN: Journal Office, 1865.

*Proceedings of the First Re-Union of the One Hundred and Sixteenth New York Volunteers, May 21, 1873*. Buffalo: Printing House of Matthews and Warren, 1873.

Quiner, E. B. *The Military History of Wisconsin*. Chicago: Clarke, 1866.

Rabb, Virgil Sullivan. "'Bully for Flournoy's Regiment, We Are Some Punkins, You'll Bet': The Civil War Letters of Virgil Sullivan Rabb, Captain, Company 'I,' Sixteenth Texas Infantry, C.S.A." Pt. 1. Edited by Thomas W. Cutrer. *Military History of the Southwest* 19, no. 2 (Fall 1989): 161–90.

———. "'Bully for Flournoy's Regiment, We Are Some Punkins, You'll Bet': The Civil War Letters of Virgil Sullivan Rabb, Captain, Company 'I,' Sixteenth Texas Infantry, C.S.A." Pt. 2. Edited by Thomas W. Cutrer. *Military History of the Southwest* 20, no. 1 (Spring 1990): 61–96.

Ray, D. M. *Roster of 16th Texas Cavalry (Dismounted), C.S.A.* Whitewright, TX: By the author, 1907.

"The Red River Expedition." *Military Order of the Loyal Legion of the United States*, MN, 2:267–79.

Reed, David W. *Campaigns and Battles of the Twelfth Regiment, Iowa Veteran Volunteer Infantry from Organization, September 1861 to Muster-out, January 20, 1866*. Evanston, IL: n.p., 1903.

Reid, John B. *Civil War Letters of John B. Reid*. Greenville, IL: Bond County Historical Society, 1991.

Reid, Whitelaw. *Ohio in the War: Her Statesmen, Her Generals and Soldiers*. Vol. 2. Cincinnati: Wilstach, Baldwin, 1872.

*Report of the Proceedings of the 29th Wisconsin Infantry Association Annual Reunion of the 29th Wisconsin Infantry, Held at Madison, Wisconsin, 1890–1895*. Vols. 8–14. N.p., 1898–99.

*Reunion of the 2nd Illinois Cavalry Volunteers: Held at St. Louis, Mo., Sept. 28, 1887*. Lancaster, OH: Printed at the Boys' Industrial School, 1888.

*Reunion of the Twenty-Third Regiment Wisconsin Infantry Volunteers at Madison, Wisconsin, 1898, 1907, 1912*. N.p., n.d.

Rhode Island Adjutant General's Office. *Names of Officers, Soldiers and Seamen in Rhode Island Regiments . . . Who Lost Their Lives in the Defense of Their Country in the Suppression of the Late Rebellion*. Providence: Providence Press, 1869.

———. *Official Register of Rhode Island Officers and Soldiers Who Served in the United States Army and Navy, from 1861 to 1866*. Providence: General Assembly, 1866.

Rigby, Alfred A. *Union Soldier's Diary*. N.p.: Tortoise Press, n.d.

Rodenbough, Theo. F., and William L. Haskin, eds. *The Army of the United States*. New York: Maynard, Merrill, 1896.

Rogers, James B. *War Pictures: Experiences and Observations of a Chaplain in the U.S. Army, in the War of the Southern Rebellion.* Chicago: Church and Goodman, 1863.

Rose, Victor M. *Ross' Texas Brigade.* Louisville, KY: Courier-Journal, 1881.

*Roster of the 165th Regiment, N.Y. Vols. 2d Duryee Zouaves, September 1861–September 1865.* N.p., 1903.

*Roster of the Survivors of the Twenty Third Regiment Wisconsin Volunteer Infantry.* Neehah, WI: Neenah, Blair and Huie, Printers, 1889.

*Roster of the Survivors and Widows of Deceased Comrades of Ninety- Sixth Regiment Ohio Volunteers, and Post Office Addresses.* Cardington, OH: N.p., 1888.

Rothrock, James H. *Proceedings of the Iowa State Bar Association's Annual Meeting* 5 (1899): 160–63.

Scott, Joe M. *Four Years' Service in the Southern Army.* Fayetteville, AR: Washington County Historical Society, 1992.

Scott, John. *Story of the Thirty Second Iowa Infantry Volunteers.* Nevada, IA: By the author, 1896.

Scott, Livingston. "A Soldier Writes His Congressman: The Civil War Letters of Livingston Scott to Thomas A. Jenckes." Edited by Frank F. White Jr. *Rhode Island History* 18 (Oct. 1959): 97–114 (pt. 1); 19 (Jan. 1960): 13–25 (pt. 2).

Scott, Reuben B. *The History of the 67th Regiment Indiana Infantry.* Bedford, IN: Herald Book and Job Print, 1892.

——. *The History of the 67th Regiment of Indiana Volunteer Infantry . . . From the Manuscript Prepared by the Late Chaplain John J. Hight.* Princeton, IN: N.p., 1895.

Scott, Robert Graham. *Memoirs and Poetic Sketches.* Camden, MO: Reveille Print., 191– (no specific date).

Selfridge, Thomas O. *What Finer Tradition: The Memoirs of Thomas O. Selfridge, Jr., Rear Admiral U.S.N.* Columbia: Univ. of South Carolina Press, 1987.

Sherman, William T. *Memoirs of General W. T. Sherman Written by Himself.* 2 vols. New York: D. Appleton and Co., 1875.

——. *Report of Major General William T. Sherman.* Millwood, NY: Kraus Reprint Co., 1977.

Shorey, Henry Augustus. *The Story of the Maine Fifteenth: Being a Brief Narrative of the More Important Events in the History of the Fifteenth Maine Regiment, Together with a Complete Roster of the Regiment.* Bridgton, ME: Press of the Bridgton News, 1890.

Shumway, Francis. *Francis #3138: The Civil War Letters of Francis (Frank) Shumway, Company F, Eighth Regiment, Wisconsin Volunteers, 1861–1862.* La Crosse, WI: R. W. Harris, 1995.

Simmons, John. "The Confederate Letters of John Simmons." Edited by Jon Harrison. *Chronicles of Smith County, Texas* 14 (Summer 1975): 25–57.

Simmons, John T. *History of the Twenty Eighth Iowa Volunteer Infantry, from the Date of Enlistment Down to January 1st, 1865.* Washington: William H. Moore, 1865.

Sliger, J. E. "How General Taylor Fought the Battle of Mansfield, LA." *Confederate Veteran* 31 (Dec. 1923): 456–58.

Smith, George G. *Leaves from a Soldier's Diary: The Personal Record of Lieutenant . . . , Co. C, 1st Louisiana Regiment Infantry Volunteers (White) during the War of the Rebellion; Also a Partial History of the Operations of the Army and Navy in the Department of the Gulf from the Capture of New Orleans to the Close of the War.* Putnam, CT: G. G. Smith, 1906.

Smith, Thaddeus L. "The Twenty-Fourth Iowa Volunteers." *Annals of Iowa,* ser. 3, vol. 1 (1893): 15–37, 111–28, 180–96.

Smith, Walter G. *Life and Letters of T. Kilby Smith.* New York: G. P. Putnam's Sons, 1898.

Sobieski, John. *The Life Story and Personal Reminiscences of Col. John Sobieski.* Los Angeles: L. G. Sobieski, 1900.

*Society of the 28th Wisconsin Volunteer Infantry Reunion. Proceedings of the Annual Reunion Society of the 28th Wisconsin Volunteer Infantry.* Various publishers, 1882–83, 1885, 1888–91, 1893, 1898, 1900–1915, 1918.

*Souvenir 116th Reg't. New York Vol. Infantry, Twenty-Fifth Anniversary of Muster Into the U.S. Service.* Buffalo: Hass and Klein, Printers, 1887.

Sperry, Andrew F. *History of the 33d Iowa Infantry Volunteer Regiment.* Des Moines: Mills and Co., 1866. Reprint, Fayetteville, AR: Univ. of Arkansas Press, 1999.

Sprague, Homer B. *History of the 13th Infantry Regiment of Connecticut Volunteers, during the Great Rebellion.* Hartford, CT: Case, Lockwood, 1867.

———. *Lights and Shadows in Confederate Prisons.* New York: Putnam's, 1915.

Stanton, Edward F., and William Quensell. "Civil War Diaries of Edwin F. Stanton, U.S.A., and William Quensell, C.S.A. 'Yank and Reb' under One Cover." Edited by Edgar E. Lackner. *East Texas Historical Journal* 18, no. 2 (1980): 25–59.

Stanyan, John Minot. *A History of the Eighth Regiment of New Hampshire Volunteers, Including Its Service as Infantry, Second N.H. Cavalry, and Veteran Battalion in the Civil War of 1861–1865.* Concord, NH: Ira C. Evans, 1892.

Starr, Frank. "New Mexico Campaign Letters of Frank Starr, 1861–1862." Edited by David B. Gracy II. *Texas Military History* 4 (Fall 1964): 169–88.

Stevenson, B. F. *Letters from the Army, 1862–1864.* Cincinnati: N.p., 1886.

Stevenson, John D. "Pope's Virginia Campaign." War Papers and Personal Reminiscences. *Military Order of the Loyal Legion of the United States,* MO. St. Louis: Becktold, 1892.

Stoker, William Elisha. "The War Letters of a Texas Conscript in Arkansas." Edited by Robert W. Glover. *Arkansas Historical Quarterly* 20 (Winter 1961): 355–87.

Stone, Edwin W. *Rhode Island in the Rebellion.* Providence: G. H. Whitney, 1865.

Stone, Kate. *Brokenburn: The Journal of Kate Stone, 1861–1868.* Baton Rouge: Louisiana State Univ. Press, 1955.

*The Story of the Thirty-eighth Regiment of Massachusetts Volunteers.* Cambridge, MA: Dakin & Metcalf, 1866.

Stuart, Addison. *Iowa Colonels and Regiments.* Des Moines: Mills, 1865.

Sutton, Aaron T. *Prisoner of the Rebels in Texas: The Civil War Narrative of Aaron T. Sutton, Corporal, 83rd Ohio Volunteer Infantry.* Edited by David G. Maclean. Decatur, IN: American Books, 1978.

Swiggett, Samuel A. *The Bright Side of Prison Life: Experiences in Prison and Out, of an Involuntary Sojourner in Rebeldom.* Baltimore, MD: Fleet, McGinley, 1897.

Taylor, Charles H. *The North in War Time.* Boston: N.p., 1912.

Taylor, Richard. *Destruction and Reconstruction: Personal Experiences in the Civil War.* New York: Da Capo, 1995.

Thompson, Seymour D. *Recollections with the Third Iowa Regiment.* Cincinnati: By the author, 1864.

Thorndyke, Rachel. *Sherman and the Sherman Letters: Correspondence between General Sherman and Senator Sherman from 1837 to 1891.* New York: Da Capo, 1969.

Tiemann, William F. *The 159th Regiment Infantry, New York State Volunteers, in the War of the Rebellion, 1862–1865.* Brooklyn: By the author, 1891.

Tupper, James B. T. Civil War Memories, Occupation of New Orleans by the 31st Massachusetts Regiment and the Forces Under Command of Gen. Butler, May 1, 1862, Personal Reminiscences. Paper read before the Burnside Post, G.A.R., Washington, DC, May 9, 1917.

Union Soldiers and Sailors Monument Association. *The Union Regiments of Kentucky.* Louisville, KY: Courier-Journal, 1879.

*"Univ. Recruits," Company C, 12th Iowa Infantry.* Evanston, IL.: N.p., 1903.

U.S. Adjutant-General's Office. *Alphabetical Index of the 162d New York Volunteer Infantry, Being an Abstract of the Field and Staff and Company Rolls.* Washington: Government Printing Office, 1889.

Vail, Joe R. *Joe Vail's Civil War: And, Some Vail Family Genealogy.* Sparta, WI: Angelo Books, 1989.

Van Alstyne, Lawrence. *Diary of an Enlisted Man.* New Haven, CT: Tuttle, Morehouse and Taylor, 1910.

Van Dyke, Ben. "Ben Van Dyke's Escape from the Hospital at Pleasant Hill, Louisiana." *Annals of Iowa.* Des Moines: Henry H. English, 1906.

Vermont Adjutant and Inspector General's Office. *Revised Roster of Vermont Volunteers Who Served in the Army and Navy of the United States during the War of the Rebellion, 1861–1865.* Montpelier, VT: Watchman, 1892.

Waite, Otis F. R. *Vermont in the Great Rebellion: Containing Historical and Biographical Sketches.* Claremont, NH: Tracy, Chase, 1869.

Way, Frederick, Jr., ed. *Way's Packet Directory, 1848–1994.* Athens: Ohio Univ. Press, 1994.

Wells, Carol, ed. *Civil War, Reconstruction and Redemption on Red River: The Memoirs of Dosia Williams Moore.* Ruston, LA: McGinty Publications, 1990.

Whipple, Henry P. *The Diary of a Private Soldier.* Waterloo, WI: N.p., 1906.

Whitcomb, Caroline E. *History of the Second Massachusetts Battery of Light Artillery, 1861–1865.* Concord, NH, 1912.

Whitman, William W. S. *Maine in the War for the Union: A History of the Part Borne by Maine Troops in Suppression of the American Rebellion.* Lexington, ME: Nelson Dingley, 1865.

Wiley, Bell Irvin, ed. *Fourteen Hundred and 91 Days in the Confederate Army: A Journal Kept by W.W. Heartsill for Four Years, One Month and One Day or Camplife; Day-by-Day, of the W. P. Lane Rangers from April 19th, 1861 to May 20th, 1865.* Wilmington, NC: Broadfoot Publishing, 1992.

Willard, Van R. *With the 3rd Wisconsin Badgers: The Living Experience of the Civil War through the Journals of Van R. Willard.* Edited by Stephen Ambrose. Mechanicsburg, PA: Stackpole, 1999.

Williams, E. Cort. "Recollections of the Red River Expedition." In *Sketches of War History, 1861–1865, Papers Read before the Ohio Commandery of the Military Order of the Loyal Legion of the United States 1886–1888.* Cincinnati: Robert Clarke and Co., 1888.

Williams, Enoch Pearson. *A Quaker Goes to War against Slavery: The Limited Diary of Enoch Pearson Williams, Company H 8th Iowa Infantry.* N.p., n.d.

Williams, John Melvin. *"The Eagle Regiment," 8th Wis. Inf'ty Vols., A Sketch of Its Marches, Battles and Campaigns, from 1861 to 1865.* Belleville, WI: Recorder Print, 1890.

Williams, Thomas J. *An Historical Sketch of the 56th Ohio Volunteer Infantry.* Columbus, OH: Lawrence Press, 1899.

Wiley, William. *The Civil War Diary of a Common Soldier: William Wiley of the 77th Illinois Infantry.* Edited by Terrence J. Winschel. Baton Rouge: Louisiana State Univ. Press, 2001.

Wisconsin Adjutant General's Office. *History of the Third Regiment of Wisconsin Veteran Volunteer Infantry, 1861–1865.* Madison: Democrat Printing Co., 1891.

———. *Roster of Wisconsin Volunteers, War of the Rebellion, 1861–1865.* 2 vols. Madison: Democrat Printing, 1866.

———. "Some Experiences of a Veteran in the Rear." In *Glimpses of the Nation's Struggle. Military Order of the Loyal Legion of the United States,* MN, 4:112–23. St. Paul, MN: Collins, 1898.

———. *23rd Infantry Regiment. Roster of the Survivors of the Twenty-third Regiment, Wisconsin Volunteer Infantry.* Neehah, WI: Blair & Huie, 1889.

———. "William T. Sherman." *War Papers. Military Order of the Loyal Legion of the United States,* WI, 2. Milwaukee: Burdick, Armitage & Allen, 1898.

Woods, Joseph T. *Services of the Ninety-sixth Ohio Volunteers.* Toledo, OH: Blade Printing and Paper Co., 1874.

# *Secondary Sources*

## Published Secondary Sources

Abernethy, Byron R. *Private Elisha Stockwell, Jr. Sees the Civil War.* Norman: Univ. of Oklahoma Press, 1985.

Acker, Henry J. *Gulf Spy.* Tall Timbers, MD: Headquarters Press, 1961.

Ackerman, William K. *Historical Sketch of the Illinois Central Railroad.* Chicago: Fergus Printing Co., 1890.

Adams, Herbert. "Neal Dow of Maine: Enemy of Rebels and Rum Lovers." *Civil War Times Illustrated* 25 (Mar. 1986): 46–51.

Alexander, William Lee. "An Appraisal of the 1862 New Mexico Campaign: A Confederate Officer's Letter to Nacogdoches." Edited by Martin Hardwick Hall. *New Mexico Historical Review* 52 (Oct. 1976): 329–35.

Allen, Desmond W. *First Arkansas Union Infantry.* Conway: Arkansas Research, 1987.

———. *Third Arkansas Union Cavalry.* Conway: Arkansas Research, 1987.

Ambrose, Stephen E. *Halleck: Lincoln's Chief of Staff.* Baton Rouge: Louisiana State Univ. Press, 1962.

Anders, Curt. *Disaster in Damp Sand: The Red River Expedition.* Carmel, IN: Guild Press of Indiana, 1997.

Anderson, Charles G. *Confederate General William R. "Dirty Neck Bill" Scurry, 1821–1864.* Snyder, TX: Snyder Publishing Co., 1999.

Anderson, John Q., ed. *Campaigning with Parsons' Texas Brigade, CSA: The War Journals and Letters of the Four Orr Brothers, 12th Texas Cavalry Regiment.* Hillsboro, TX: Hill Junior College Press, 1967.

Andrews, J. Cutler. *The North Reports the Civil War.* Pittsburgh: Univ. of Pittsburgh Press, 1983.

Arceneaux, William. *Acadian General: Alfred Mouton and the Civil War.* Lafayette: Center for Louisiana Studies, Univ. of Southwestern Louisiana, 1981.

Arey, Frank. "A Deserter From the 15th Texas Infantry (Confederate) and His Stolen Horse, ca. December 1862." *Military Collector and Historian* 53 (Fall 2001): 135.

Ayers, Thomas. *Dark and Bloody Ground: The Battle of Mansfield and the Forgotten Civil War in Louisiana.* Dallas: Taylor Publishing Co., 2001.

Badeau, Adam. *Military History of Ulysses S. Grant.* 3 vols. New York: D. Appleton and Co., 1868–81.

Bailey, Anne J. *Between the Enemy and Texas: Parson's Texas Cavalry in the Civil War.* Fort Worth: Texas Christian Univ. Press, 1989.

———. "Chasing Banks Out of Louisiana: Parsons' Texas Cavalry in the Red River Campaign." *Civil War Regiments* 3, no. 1 (1993): 212–35.

———. *Texans in the Confederate Cavalry.* Fort Worth: Ryan Place Publications, 1995.

Bankston, Mary L. B. *Camp-Fire Stories of the Mississippi Valley Campaign.* New Orleans: L. Graham Co. Publishers, 1914.

Baringer, William Eldon. *Lincoln's Rise to Power.* St. Clair Shores, MI: Scholarly Press, 1971.

Barr, Alwyn. "Confederate Artillery in Western Louisiana, 1864." *Louisiana History* 5, no. 1 (1964): 53–73.

———. "Polignac's Texas Brigade." *Texas Gulf Coast Historical Association* 8 (Nov. 1964): 1–72.

———. *Polignac's Texas Brigade.* College Station: Texas A & M Univ. Press, 1998.

———. "Texan Losses in the Red River Campaign, 1864." *Texas Military History* 3 (Summer 1963): 103–13.

Bates, Samuel P. *History of the Pennsylvania Volunteers, 1861–5.* Vol. 2. Wilmington, NC: Broadfoot, 1993.

Bearss, Edwin C. *Steele's Retreat from Camden and the Battle of Jenkins Ferry.* Little Rock: Eagle Press of Little Rock, 1990.

Bearss, Edwin C., and Willie Tunnard. *A Southern Record: The Story of the 3rd Louisiana Infantry, C.S.A.* Dayton, OH: Morningside Bookshop, 1988.

Belisle, John G. *History of Sabine Parish Louisiana.* Many, LA: Sabine Banner Press, 1912.

Bergeron, Arthur W., Jr. *The Civil War Reminiscences of Major Silas T. Grisamore C.S.A.* Baton Rouge: Louisiana State Univ. Press, 1993.

———. "A Colonel Gains His Wreath: Henry Gray's Louisiana Brigade at the Battle of Mansfield, April 8, 1864." *Civil War Regiments* 4, no. 2 (1994): 1–25.

———. "General Richard Taylor as a Military Commander." *Louisiana History* 23 (Winter 1982): 35–47.

———. *A Guide to Confederate Military Units, 1861–1865.* Baton Rouge: Louisiana State Univ. Press, 1989.Billias, George A. "Maine Lumbermen Rescue the Red River Fleet." *New England Social Studies* 16, no. 1 (1958): 5–8.

Billings, George A. "Maine Lumbermen Rescue the Red River Fleet." *New England Social Studies Bulletin* 16, no. 1 (1958): 5–8.

Blanton, DeAnne, and Lauren M. Cook. *They Fought Like Demons: Women Soldiers in the American Civil War.* Baton Rouge: Louisiana State Univ. Press, 2002.

Booth, Andrew B. *Records of Louisiana Confederate Soldiers and Louisiana Confederate Commands.* 3 vols. Spartanburg, SC: Reprint Company, 1984.

Borritt, Gabor, ed. *The Lincoln Enigma: The Changing Faces of an American Icon.* New York: Oxford Univ. Press, 2001.

Bounds, Steve, and Curtis Milbourn. "The Battle of Mansfield." *North and South* 6, no. 2 (Feb. 2003): 26–40.

Bradford, James C., ed. *Captains of the Old Steam Navy: Makers of the American Naval Tradition, 1840–1880.* Annapolis: Naval Institute Press, 1986.

Brock, Eric, and Gary D. Joiner. *Red River Steamboats.* Charleston: Arcadia, 1999.

Brooksher, William Riley. *War along the Bayous: The 1864 Red River Campaign in Louisiana.* Washington: Brassey's, 1998.

Burgess, Lauren Cook. "The Private Lyons Wakeman—A Soldier with a Secret." *Civil War Magazine* 53 (Oct 1995): 63–64.

Burrage, Henry Sweetser. *Thomas Hamlin Hubbard, Bvt. Brigadier General U.S. Vols.* Portland, ME: n.p., 1923.

Byrne, Frank L. "A General behind Bars: Neal Dow in Libby Prison." *Civil War History* 8 (June 1962): 164–83.

Cade, Edward W. *A Texas Surgeon in the CSA.* Edited by John Q. Anderson. Tuscaloosa, AL.: Confederate Publishing Co., 1957.

Calore, Paul. *Naval Campaigns of the Civil War.* Jefferson, NC: McFarland & Co., 2002.

Cameron, Alexander. "Alexander Cameron in the Louisiana Campaign, 1863–1865." Edited by J. S. Duncan. *Military History of Texas and the Southwest* 12, no. 4 (1975): 245–71 (pt. 1); 13, no. 1 (1976): 37–57 (pt. 2).

———. "A Soldier's Fare Is Rough: Letters from A. Cameron in the Indian Territory, Arkansas Campaign, 1862–1864." Edited by J. S. Duncan. *Military History of Texas and the Southwest* 12, no. 1 (1975): 39–61.

Campbell, Randolph B., and Donald K. Pickens. "Fannie. 'My Dear Husband: A Texas Slave's Love Letters, 1862.'" *Journal of Negro History* 65 (Fall 1980): 361–64.

Canney, Donald L. *Lincoln's Navy: The Ships, Men and Organizations, 1861–1865.* Annapolis, MD: Naval Institute Press, 1998.

———. *The Old Steam Navy: The Ironclads, 1842–1885.* Annapolis, MD: Naval Institute Press, 1993.

Cardin, Clifton D. *Bossier Parish History: The First 150 Years. 1843, 1993.* Shreveport, LA: Aero Press, 1993.

Casdorph, Paul D. *Prince John Magruder: His Life and Campaigns.* New York: John Wiley & Sons, 1996.

Castell, Albert. *General Sterling Price and the Civil War in the West.* Baton Rouge: Louisiana State Univ. Press, 1968.

Christ, Mark K., ed. *Rugged and Sublime: The Civil War in Arkansas.* Fayetteville: Univ. of Arkansas Press, 1994.

Collins, R. M. *Chapters from the Unwritten History of the War between the States, or, The Incidents in the Life of a Confederate Soldier in Camp, on the March, in the Great Battles, and in Prison.* Dayton, OH: Morningside, 1982.

Commager, Henry Steele. *The Blue and the Grey: The Story of the Civil War as Told by the Participants.* 2 vols. Indianapolis: N.p., 1950.

*Confederate Military History, Extended Edition.* Vols. 12–15. Wilmington, NC: Broadfoot, 1988–89.

Connor, Mary America, and Orange Cicero Connor. *Dear America: Some Letters of Orange Cicero and Mary America (Aikin) Connor.* Edited by Seymour V. Connor. Austin: Jenkins Publishing Co., 1971.

Coombe, Jack D. *Thunder along the Mississippi: The River Battles That Split the Confederacy.* New York: Bantam, 1996.

Crary, Catherine S., ed. *Dear Belle: Letters From a Cadet and Officer to His Sweetheart, 1858–1865.* Middletown, CT: Wesleyan Univ. Press, 1965.

Craven, Avery. *The Coming of the Civil War.* Chicago: Univ. of Chicago Press, 1962.

Crousse, Nellis, M. *LeMoyne D'Iberville: Soldier of New France.* Baton Rouge: Louisiana State Univ. Press, 2001.

Crute, Joseph H., Jr. *Units of the Confederate States Army.* Midlothian, VA: Derwent Books, 1987.

Czech, Kenneth P. "The Much-Traveled 5th Minnesota Fought Sioux Warriors and Confederate Butternuts in Six States and 34 Battles." *America's Civil War* 10 (Nov. 1997): 18, 22, 24, 78.

Davis, James H., John C. Porter, and William C. Ogletree. *Texans in Gray: The 18th Texas Infantry in the Civil War.* Hughes Springs, TX: Heritage Oak Press, 1993.

*DeSoto Parish History: Sesquicentennial Edition, 1843–1993.* Mansfield, LA: DeSoto Parish Historical Society, 1995.

Dimitry, John. "Louisiana." *Confederate Military History.* Vol. 10. Atlanta: N.p., 1899.

Division of Engineers. *Red River and Tributaries, Louisiana, Arkansas, Oklahoma, Texas. Interim Review of Reports with Respect to Improvement of Navigation (1945).* Vicksburg, MS: Vicksburg District, U.S. Army Corps of Engineers.

Dollar, Susan E. "The Red River Campaign, Natchitoches Parish, Louisiana: A Case of Equal Opportunity Destruction." *Louisiana History* 43, no. 4 (2002): 411–32.

Dufour, Charles L. *The Night the War Was Lost*. Garden City, NY: Doubleday, 1960.

Duncan, J. S. "Alexander Cameron in the Louisiana Campaign, 1863–1865." *Military History of Texas and the Southwest* 12, no. 4 (1975): 245–71.

———. "A Soldiers Fare Is Rough: Letters from A. Cameron in the Indian Territory, Arkansas Campaign, 1862–1864." *Military History of Texas and the Southwest* 12, no. 1 (1975): 39–61.

Dunnavent, R. Blake. *Brown Water Warfare: The U.S. Navy in Riverine Warfare and the Emergence of a Tactical Doctrine, 1775–1970*. Gainesville: Univ. of Florida Press, 2003.

Ellis, Volney. "'A Experience in Soldier's Life': The Civil War Letters of Volney Ellis, Adjutant, Twelfth Texas Infantry, Walker's Texas Division, C. S.A." Edited by Thomas Cutrer. *Military History of the Southwest* 20, no. 2 (Fall 1992): 109–72.

Estaville, Lawrence E., Jr. *Confederate Neckties: Louisiana Railroads in the Civil War*. Ruston, LA: McGinty Publications, 1989.

Faulk, Odie B. "Confederate Hero at Val Verde." *New Mexico Historical Review* 38, no. 4 (1963): 300–311.

Femly, Bradford K., and John C. Grady. *Suffering to Silence: Twenty-ninth Texas Cavalry, CSA: Regimental History*. Quanch, TX: Nortex, 1975.

Fitzhugh, Lester N. *Texas Batteries, Battalions, Regiments, Commanders and Field Officers, Confederate States Army, 1861–1865*. Midlothian, TX: Mirror Press, 1959.

———. "Texas Forces in the Red River Campaign." *Texas Military History* 3 (Spring 1963): 15–22.

Fitzpatrick, Mike. "Old Abe, the War Eagle of the 8th Infantry." *Military Images* 23 (July/Aug. 2001): 19–20.

Fogel, Robert William, and Stanley L. Engerman. *Time on the Cross: The Economics of American Negro Slavery*. New York: W. W. Norton & Co., 1989.

Foner, Eric. *Reconstruction: America's Unfinished Revolution, 1863–1877*. New York: Harper & Row, 1988.

Foote, Shelby. *The Civil War: A Narrative*. Vol. 1: *Fort Sumter to Perryville*. New York: Random House, 1958.

Fordyce, Benjamin A. *Echoes from the Letters of a Civil War Surgeon*. Longboat Key, FL: Bayou Publishing, 1994.

Forsyth, Michael J. *The Red River Campaign of 1864 and the Loss by the Confederacy of the Civil War*. Jefferson, NC: McFarland & Co., 2002.

Fowler, Donald M. "'Mules Won't Do!' The Troubles of a Downsville Soldier in the Civil War, 1864–1865." *North Louisiana Historical Association Journal* 14, no. 2–3 (1983): 61–81.

Frankignoul, Daniel. *Prince Camille de Polignac Major General ,C.S.A "The Lafayette of the South."* Brussels: Confederate Historical Association of Belgium, 1999.

Freehling, William W. *The South vs. The South: How Anti-Confederate Southerners Shaped the Course of the Civil War*. New York: Oxford Univ. Press, 1999.

Freeman, Douglas Southall. *R. E. Lee: A Biography*. 4 vols. New York: Charles Scribner's Sons, 1934–35.

Fry, Alice L. *Kansas and Kansans in the Civil War: First through the Thirteenth Volunteer Regiment*. Kansas City, KS: Crossed Lines Research, 1996.

Gallaway, B. P. *The Ragged Rebel: A Common Soldier in W. H. Parsons' Texas Cavalry, 1861–1865.* Austin: Univ. of Texas Press, 1988.

———. "A Texas Farm Boy Enlists in the 12th Cavalry." *Texas Military History* 8, no. 2 (1970): 87–95.

Gibbons, Tony. *Warships and Naval Battles of the Civil War.* New York: W. H. Smith, 1989.

Gibson, Charles Dana, and E. Kay Gibson. *The Army's Navy Series.* Vol. 2, *Assault and Logistics: Union Army Coastal and River Operations, 1861–1866.* Camden, ME: Ensign Press, 1995.

———. *Dictionary of Transports and Combatant Vessels Steam and Sail, Employed by the Union Army, 1861–1868.* Camden, ME: Ensign Press, 1995.

Gienapp, William E. *Abraham Lincoln and Civil War America: A Biography.* New York: Oxford Univ. Press, 2002.

———. *This Fiery Trial: The Speeches and Writings of Abraham Lincoln.* New York: Oxford Univ. Press, 2002.

Gladstone, William A. *United States Colored Troops, 1863–1867.* Gettysburg, PA: Thomas Publications, 1990.

Glatthaar, Joseph T. *Forged in Battle: The Civil War Alliance of Black Soldiers and White Officers.* New York: Free Press, 1990.

———. *Partners in Command—The Relationship between Leaders in the Civil War.* New York: Free Press, 1994.

Gosnell, H. Allen. *Guns of the Western Waters: The Story of River Gunboats in the Civil War.* Baton Rouge: Louisiana State Univ. Press, 1949.

Grabeau, Warren E. *Ninety-Eight Days: A Geographer's View of the Vicksburg Campaign.* Knoxville: Univ. of Tennessee Press, 2000.

Greene, Jack. *Ironclads at War: The Origin and Development of the Armored Warship, 1854–1891.* Conshohocken, PA: Combined Books, 1998.

Gute, Fredricka Doll, and Katherine Brash Jeter. *Historical Profile of Shreveport: 1850.* Shreveport: Shreveport Committee of the National Society of the Colonial Dames of America in the State of Louisiana, 1982.

Guttman, Jon. "'Old Abe' Goes to War." *America's Civil War* 3 (Nov. 1990): 26–33.

Hagerman, Edward. *The American Civil War and the Origins of Modern Warfare: Ideas, Organizations and Field Command.* Bloomington: Indiana Univ. Press, 1992.

Hale, Douglas. "One Man's War: Captain Joseph H. Bruton, 1861–1865." *East Texas Historical Journal* 20, no. 2 (1982): 28–45.

Hall, Martin Hardwick. *The Confederate Army of New Mexico.* Austin, TX: Presidial Press, 1978.

Halsell, Willie D. *Indiana Military History.* N.p., 1947.

Hamilton, James Allen. "The Civil War Diary of James Allen Hamilton." Edited by Alwyn Barr. *Texana* 2 (Summer 1964): 132–45.

Hander, Christian Wilhelm. "Excerpts from the Hander Diary." Translated and edited by Leonard B. Plummer. *Journal of Mississippi History* 36 (May 1964): 141–49.

Hannan, Laurence. "An Iowa Private in the Civil War." Edited by George Hanrahan. *Palimpsest* 58 (Nov./Dec. 1977): 182–91.

Harrington, Fred Harvey. *Fighting Politician, Major General N.P. Banks*. Philadelphia: Univ. of Pennsylvania Press, 1948.

Hasskarl, Robert A. *Waul's Texas Legion, 1862–1865*. Ada, OK: By the author, 1985.

Hearn, Chester G. *Admiral David Dixon Porter: The Civil War Years*. Annapolis, MD: Naval Institute Press, 1996.

———. *Ellet's Brigade: The Strangest Outfit of All*. Baton Rouge: Louisiana State Univ. Press, 2000.

Henderson, Harry McCorry. "26th Texas Cavalry." In *Texas in the Confederacy*, pp. 106–112. San Antonio: Naylor, 1955.

Hewitt, Lawrence Lee. *Port Hudson: Confederate Bastion on the Mississippi*. Baton Rouge: Louisiana State Univ. Press, 1987.

Hicken, Victor. *Illinois in the Civil War*. Urbana: Univ. of Illinois Press, 1991.

Hoehling, A. A. *Damn the Torpedoes! Naval Incidents of the Civil War*. Winston-Salem, NC: John F. Blair, 1989.

Hollandsworth, James G., Jr. *The Louisiana Native Guards: The Black Military Experience during the Civil War*. Baton Rouge: Louisiana State Univ. Press, 1995.

———. *Pretense of Glory: The Life of General Nathaniel P. Banks*. Baton Rouge: Louisiana State Univ. Press, 1998.

Howard, William F. "Col. Lewis Benedict: The Forgotten Hero of Pleasant Hill." *The Kepi* 3 (Apr./May 1985): 13–17, 31.

Huffstodt, Jim. *Hard Dying Men: The Story of General W.H.L. Wallace, General T.E.G. Ransom, and Their "Old Eleventh": Illinois Infantry in the American Civil War (1861–1865)*. Bowie, MD: Heritage Books, 1991.

Hummel, Jeffrey Rogers. *Emancipating Slaves, Enslaving Free Men: A History of the American Civil War*. Chicago: Open Court, 1996.

Ingrisamo, Michael N., Jr. *An Artilleryman's War: Gus Day and the 2nd United States Artillery*. Shippensburg, PA: White Mane, 1998.

Johansson, Jane Harris, and David H. Johansson. "Two Lost Battle Reports: Horace Randal's and Joseph L. Brent's Reports of the Battles of Mansfield and Pleasant Hill, 8 and 9 April 1864." *Military History of the Southwest* 23, no. 2 (Fall 1993): 149–67.

Johansson, M. Jane. *A History of the 28th Texas Cavalry 1862–1865*. Fayetteville: Univ. of Arkansas Press, 1998.

Johnson, Curt, ed. "We Cleared Their Way": Battery C, 2nd U.S. Artillery Firing Canister. *Civil War Times Illustrated* 32 (Mar./Apr. 1993): 20, 22.

Johnson, Ludwell H. *Red River Campaign: Politics and Cotton in the Civil War*. Kent, OH: Kent State Univ. Press, 1993.

Joiner, Gary D. *40 Archaeological Sites in the Red River Campaign* (1997). Archives of the Division of Archaeology, State of Louisiana, Baton Rouge.

———. "I Will Fight Banks If He Has a Million Men." *DeSoto Plume* 37, no. 3 (Spring 2002): 2–10.

———. *One Damn Blunder from Beginning to End: The Red River Campaign of 1864*. Wilmington, DE: Scholarly Resources, 2003.

Joiner, Gary D., and Stephen R. James. "Phase I Cultural Resources Investigation: Harrah's Entertainment Project, City of Shreveport, Caddo Parish, Louisiana." Archives of the Division of Archaeology, State of Louisiana, Baton Rouge, 1997.

Joiner, Gary D., and Charles E. Vetter. "The Union Naval Expedition on the Red River, March 12–May 22, 1864." *Civil War Regiments* 4, no. 2 (1994): 26–67.

Jones, Michael. "Hero from the Bayou: Alfred Mouton." *Civil War Times Illustrated* 22, no. 9 (Jan. 1984): 32–37.

Jones, Michael D. "Private Burton Marchbanks." *Military Images Magazine* 11 (Mar./Apr. 1990): 11.

Jones, Michael E. "18th Louisiana Infantry: Acadians in Gray." *Military Images Magazine* 7 (May/June 1986): 5–7.

Jones, Terry L. *Historical Dictionary of the Civil War.* 2 vols. Lantham, MD: Scarecrow Press, 2002.

Jones, Virgil Carrington. *The Civil War at Sea, July 1863–November, 1865: The Final Effort.* 3 vols. New York: Holt Rinehart and Winston, 1962.

Kakuske, Louis F. "The Kakuske Diary." *Civil War Times Illustrated* 15 (July 1976): 36–43.

Keen, Newton A. *Living and Fighting with the Texas 6th Cavalry.* Gaithersburg, MD: Butternut, 1986.

Kerby, Robert L. *Kirby Smith's Confederacy: The Trans-Mississippi South, 1863–1865.* Tuscaloosa: Univ. of Alabama Press, 1972.

Kinard, Jeff. *Lafayette of the South: Prince Camille de Polignac and the American Civil War.* College Station: Texas A & M Univ. Press, 2001.

King, Wilburn H. *With the 18th Texas Infantry: The Autobiography of Wilburn Hill King.* Edited by L. David Norris. Hillsboro, TX: Hill Junior College Press, 1996.

Kraczorowski, Robert J. *The Politics of Judicial Interpretation: The Federal Courts, Department of Justice and Civil Rights, 1866–1876.* New York: Oceana Publications, 1985.

Krick, Robert K. *Stonewall Jackson at Cedar Mountain.* Chapel Hill: Univ. of North Carolina Press, 1990.

Labadie, Paul G. "The Farm Boys in the 96th Ohio Regiment Found Themselves Knee-Deep in Alligators in Louisiana." *America's Civil War* (Sept. 1992): 16, 18, 20, 71–72, 74.

Lale, Max S. "For Lack of a Nail." *East Texas Historical Journal* 30, no. 1 (1992): 34–43.

———. "New Light on the Battle of Mansfield." *East Texas Historical Journal* 25, no. 2 (1987): 34–41.

Leonard, Elizabeth D. *All the Daring of the Soldier: Women in the Civil War Armies.* New York: Penguin Books, 1999.

Leuschner, Charles A. *The Civil War Diary of Charles A. Leuschner.* Edited by Charles D. Spurlin. Austin, Texas: Eakin Press, 1992.

Lewis, Lloyd. *Captain Sam Grant.* Boston: Little, Brown, and Co., 1950.

Lindemann, Georgianne. "Monarch of the Skies: 'Old Abe' The Union War Eagle." *Civil War Times Illustrated* 23, no. 9 (1985): 34–39.

Loop, Charles. "I Was There." *Civil War* 9 (Jan./Feb. 1991): 11, 59–60.

Lowe, Richard. *Walker's Texas Division, C.S.A.: Greyhounds of the Trans-Mississippi.* Baton Rouge: Louisiana State Univ. Press, 2004.

Louisiana Division of Archaeology. Submissions for the National Register of Historic Places for Forts Randolph and Buhlow. Archives of the Division of Archaeology, State of Louisiana, Baton Rouge.

Luraghi, Raimondo. *A History of the Confederate Navy.* Annapolis: Naval Institute Press, 1996.

Lyon, Bellie L. "Christian Soldier." *Palimpsest* 25 (1944): 50–64.

Lyon, William Penn. *Reminiscences of the Civil War.* San Jose, CA: Press of Muirson and Wright, 1907.

Mahin, Dean B. *One War at a Time: The International Dimensions of the American Civil War.* Washington, DC: Brassey's, 2000.

Manakee, Harold R. *Maryland in the Civil War.* Baltimore: Maryland Historical Society, 1961.

Manchester, Albert. 'Although Not as Illustrious as Some Regiments, the 30th Maine Played Its Own Small Part in Union Victory.' *America's Civil War* (Sept. 1991): 16, 70–71.

Martin, David. "The Red River Campaign: The Ill-Fated Western Expedition of Nathaniel P. Banks, 7 March to 20 May, 1864." *Strategy and Tactics,* no. 106 (1986): 11–20.

Matthews, James T. "A Time for Desperate Valor: The Confederate Attack on Fort Butler, Louisiana, 1863." *Military History of the West* 26, no. 1 (1996): 23–34.

Matthews, Richard. "Up Another River: Fourteen Days on the St. Johns." *Pennsylvania Folklife* 37, no. 3 (1988): 112–17.

May, Robert E. *The Southern Dream of A Caribbean Empire, 1854–1861.* Gainesville: Univ. Press of Florida, 2002.

McConn, Bob. "History of Company B, 47th Illinois Volunteer Infantry." Illinois in the Civil War Web site: http://www.illinoiscivilwar.org/cw47-histb.html.

McElfresh, Earl B. *Maps and Mapmakers of the Civil War.* New York: Harry N. Abrams, 1999.

McGowen, Stanley Sidney. "Augustus Buchel: A Forgotten Texas Patriot." *Military History of the West* 25, no. 1 (Spring 1995): 1–21.

———. *Horse Sweat and Powder Smoke: The First Texas Cavalry in the Civil War.* College Station: Texas A & M Univ. Press, 1999.

McLain, David. *The Civil War Letters of Private David McLain, Co. C, 8th Wisconsin Vol.* N.p.: M. M. McLain, 1976.

McWhiney, Grady. *Cracker Culture: Celtic Ways in the Old South.* Tuscaloosa: Univ. of Alabama Press, 1988.

———. "The South's Celtic Heritage." *North Louisiana Historical Journal* 24, no. 4 (Fall 1993): 135–43.

Meed, Douglas V. *Texas Wanderlust: The Adventures of Dutch Wurzbach.* College Station: Texas A & M Univ. Press, 1997.

Melia, Tamara Moser. *"Damn the Torpedoes": A Short History of U.S. Naval Mine Countermeasures, 1777–1991.* Washington, DC: Naval Historical Center, 1991.

Meyer, Steve. *Iowa Valor: A Compilation of Civil War Combat Experiences from Soldiers of the State Distinguished as Most Patriotic of the Patriotic.* Garrison, IA: Meyer Publishing Co., 1994.

Milbourn, Curtis. "Fighting for Time." *North and South* 5, no. 4 (May 2002): 68–76.

Miller, Bud. *Full Measure of Devotion: The Columbia Companies of the One Hundred and Twenty-eighth New York, A Narrative.* Chatham Center, NY: N.p., 1977.

Miller, Jud L. *Two Boys in Blue, George and John U.: The Civil War Experiences of George Dugan and John U. Miller.* Milo, IA: J. L. Miller, 1992.

Miller, R. Russell. "Some New Notes on 'Old Abe'—The Battle Eagle." *Military Collector and Historian* 15, no. 4 (1963): 109–13.

Mills, Gary B. *The Forgotten People: Cane River's Creoles of Color.* Baton Rouge: Louisiana State Univ. Press, 1977.

———. *Of Men and Rivers: The Story of the Vicksburg District* (1978). Vicksburg, MS: Vicksburg District, U.S. Army Corps of Engineers.

Mitchell, Joseph B. *The Badge of Honor: Letters from Civil War Medal of Honor Winners.* Shippensburg, PA: White Mane, 1997.

Musicant, Ivan. *Divided Waters: The Naval History of the Civil War.* New York: Harper Collins, 1995.

Neverman, Maurice J. *"I Just Got Talked Into It."* Watertown, WI: Pacesetter Prompt Printing, 1993.

Nichols, James L. *The Confederate Quartermaster in the Trans-Mississippi.* Austin: Univ. of Texas Press, 1964.

Noll, Arthur Howard. *General Kirby-Smith.* Sewanee: Univ. of the South, 1907.

Norris, L. David, James C. Millican, and Odie B. Faulk. *William H. Emory: Soldier-Scientist.* Tucson: Univ. of Arizona Press, 1998.

Oakes, James. *The Ruling Class: A History of American Slaveholders.* New York: W. W. Norton, 1998.

Oates, Stephen B. *Confederate Cavalry West of the River.* Austin: Univ. of Texas Press, 1961.

O'Flaherty, Daniel. *General Jo Shelby: Undefeated Rebel.* Chapel Hill: Univ. of North Carolina Press, 1954.

O'Pry, Maude. *Chronicles of Shreveport and Caddo Parish.* Shreveport, LA: Journal Printing Co., 1928.

Osborne, Seward R. "A Modest Hero." *Military Images Magazine* 9 (July/Aug. 1987): 14–15.

———. *The Saga of the "Mountain Legion": (156th N.Y. Vols.) in the Civil War.* Hightstown, NJ: Longstreet House, 1994.

Page, Dave. *Ships vs. Shore: Civil War Engagements along Southern Shores and Rivers.* Nashville, TN: Rutledge Hill Press, 1994.

Parks, Joseph Howard. *General Edmund Kirby Smith, C.S.A.* Baton Rouge: Louisiana State Univ. Press, 1954.

Parrish, T. Michael. *Richard Taylor: Soldier Prince of Dixie.* Chapel Hill: Univ. of North Carolina Press, 1992.

Pearson, Charles. "Historical Survey and Assessment of Waterborne Commerce and Transportation and an Inventory of Underwater Cultural Resources on the Red River." Archives of the Division of Archaeology, State of Louisiana, Baton Rouge, 1995.

Perkins, John D. *Daniel's Battery: The 9th Texas Field Battery.* Hillsboro, TX: Hill College Press, 1998.

Perry, Milton F. *Infernal Machines: The Story of Confederate Submarine and Mine Warfare.* Baton Rouge: Louisiana State Univ. Press, 1965.

Peticolas, Alfred Brown. *Rebels on the Rio Grande: The Civil War Journal of A. B. Peticolas.* Edited by Don E. Alberts. Albuquerque: Univ. of New Mexico Press, 1984.

Petrie, Donald A. *The Prize Game: Lawful Looting on the High Seas in the Days of Fighting Sail.* Annapolis, MD: Naval Institute Press, 1999.

Petty, Elijah Parsons. *Journey to Pleasant Hill: The Civil War Letters of Captain Elijah P. Petty, Walker's Division, C.S.A.* Edited by Norman D. Brown. San Antonio: Univ. of Texas Institute of Culture, 1982.

Phillips, Jennifer. "The Fine Line: A Study of the Definition of Partisan Ranger, Guerrilla and Jayhawker as Seen in North Louisiana during the Civil War." *North Louisiana Historical Journal* 27, no. 4 (Fall 1996).

Pierson, Marshall Samuel. "The Diary and Memoirs of Marshall Samuel Pierson, Company C, 17th Reg., Texas Cavalry, 1862–1865." Edited by Norman C. Delaney. *Military History of Texas and the Southwest* 13, no. 3 (1976): 28–38.

Plank, Will. *Banners and Bugles: A Record of Ulster County, New York and the Mid-Hudson Region in the Civil War.* Marlborough, NY: Centennial Press, 1972.

Plummer, Alonzo. *Confederate Victory at Mansfield Including Federal Advance and Retreat to Natchitoches.* Shreveport, LA: Kate Beard Chapter No. 397, United Daughters of the Confederacy, 1964.

Plummer, Mark A. *Frontier Governor: Samuel J. Crawford of Kansas.* Lawrence: Univ. of Kansas Press, 1971.

Polignac, Camille. "Polignac's Diary—Part 1." *Civil War Times Illustrated* 19 (Aug. 1980): 14–18; 19 (Oct. 1980): 34–41.

Ponder, Jerry. *Major General John S. Marmaduke, C.S.A.* Mason, TX: Ponder Books, 1999.

———. *The 9th Missouri Infantry Regiment, C.S.A. and the 12th Missouri Regiment, C.S.A.* Ozark, MO: Dogwood Printing, 1996.

Powers, Norman. *The Civil War Letters of Norman Powers of Fox Lake, Dodge Co., Wisconsin: And Other Related Family Letters.* Transcribed by Jackie Selden Riley. Long Beach, CA: J. S. Riley, 1982.

Ragan, Mark K. *Union and Confederate Submarine Warfare in the Civil War.* Mason City, IA: Savas, 1999.

Reed, Rowena. *Combined Operations in the Civil War.* Lincoln: Univ. of Nebraska Press, 1978.

Richard, Joseph L. *28th Thomas' Regiment Louisiana Infantry, CSA: A Brief History and Roster.* Kenner, LA: By the author, 1998.

Ringle, Dennis J. *Life in Mr. Lincoln's Navy.* Annapolis, MD: Naval Institute Press, 1999.

Robinson, Michael. *Gunboats, Low Water, and Yankee Ingenuity: A History of Bailey's Dam.* Baton Rouge: FPHC, 1991.

Rosholt, Malcolm, and Margaret Rosholt. *The Story of Old Abe.* Rosholt, WI: Rosholt House, 1987.

Rushing, Anthony C. *Ranks of Honor: A Regimental History of the 11th Arkansas Infantry Regiment and Poe's Cavalry Battalion, C.S.A., 1861–1865.* Little Rock: Eagle Press, 1990.

Sample, Wilton Wade. "A View of the Battle of Mansfield, From the Diary of Captain Felix Pierre Poche." *North Louisiana Historical Association Journal* 2, no. 1 (1970): 10–20.

Sauers, Richard A. *Advance the Colors: Pennsylvania Civil War Battle Flags.* Vol. 1. Harrisonburg, PA: Capitol Preservation Commission, 1987.

Savas, Theodore P. "A Death at Mansfield: Col. James Hamilton Beard and the Consolidated Crescent Regiment." *Civil War Regiments* 4, no. 2 (1994): 68–103.

Sayers, Brian. *On Valor's Side: Tom Green and the Battles for Early Texas.* Hemphill, TX: Dogwood Press, 1999.

Schafer, Louis S. *Confederate Underwater Warfare: An Illustrated History.* Jefferson, NC: McFarland and Co., 1996.

Schlay, Cora R. "Alexandria in the Civil War." *Four Louisiana Civil War Stories.* Baton Rouge: Louisiana Civil War Centennial Commission, 1961.

Schmidt, Lewis G. *A Civil War History of the 47th Regiment of Pennsylvania Veteran Volunteers: The Wrong Place at the Wrong Time.* Allentown, PA: L. G. Schmidt, 1986.

Schnetzer, Wayne H., comp. *Men of the Tenth: A Roster of the Tenth Missouri Infantry, Confederate States of America.* Independence, MO: Two Trails, 1997.

———, comp. *Men of the Eleventh: A Roster of the Eleventh Missouri Infantry, Confederate States of America.* Independence, MO: N.p., 1997.

Seale, Richard. "Pine Hills and Plantations: Some Social and Economic Views of the Civil War in Natchitoches Parish." *North Louisiana Historical Association Journal* 25, no. 4 (Fall 1994): 107–32.

Shannon, George W., Jr. "Cultural Resources Survey of the Port of Shreveport-Bossier, Caddo and Bossier Parishes, Louisiana, Unpublished Report for the Caddo/Bossier Port Commission." Archives of the Division of Archaeology, State of Louisiana, Baton Rouge, 1996.

Sifakis, Stewart. *Compendium of the Confederacy: Florida and Arkansas.* New York: Facts on File, 1992.

———. *Compendium of the Confederate Armies: Louisiana.* New York: Facts on File, 1995.

———. *Compendium of the Confederate Armies Kentucky, Maryland, Missouri, the Confederate Units and the Indian Units.* New York: Facts on File, 1995.

———. *Compendium of the Confederate Armies: Texas.* New York: Facts on File, 1995.

———. *Who Was Who in the Confederacy.* New York: Facts on File, 1988.

———. *Who Was Who in the Union.* New York: Facts on File, 1988.

Silverstone, Paul H. *Warships of the Civil War Navies.* Annapolis, MD: Naval Institute Press, 1989.

Simmons, John. "The Confederate Letters of John Simmons." Edited by Jon Harrison. *Chronicles of Smith County, Texas* 14 (Summer 1975): 25–57.

Simon, John Y. *Grant and Halleck: Contrasts in Command.* Milwaukee: Marquette Univ. Press, 1996.

Simson, Jay W. *Naval Strategies of the Civil War: Confederate Innovations and Federal Opportunism.* Nashville: Cumberland House, 2001.

Slagle, Jay. *Ironclad Captain: Seth Ledyard Phelps and the U.S. Navy, 1841–1864.* Annapolis: Naval Institute Press, 1996.

Smith, Jean Edward. *Grant.* New York: Simon & Schuster, 2001.

Smith, Steven D., and George J. Castille III. *Bailey's Dam*. Baton Rouge: Department of Culture Recreation and Tourism, Louisiana Archaeological Survey and Antiquities Commission, Anthropological Study No. 8 (1986).

Snell, Mark A. *From First to Last: The Life of Major General William B. Franklin*. New York: Fordham Univ. Press, 2002.

Soman, Jean Powers, and Frank L. Byrne, eds. *A Jewish Colonel in the Civil War: Marcus M. Spiegel of the Ohio Volunteers*. Lincoln: Univ. of Nebraska Press, 1985.

Spencer, John. *Terrell's Texas Cavalry*. Burnet, TX: Eakin Press, 1982.

Stephens, Robert W. *August Buchel, Texas Soldier of Fortune*. Dallas: n.p., 1970.

Spicer, Ron, and Roger D. Stureke. "The 165th New York Volunteer Infantry Regiment, 1863." *Military Collector and Historian* 20, no.2 (1968): 49–51.

Stampp, Kenneth. *The Peculiar Institution: Slavery in the Antebellum South*. New York: Alfred A. Knopf, 1956.

State of Louisiana Department of Culture, Recreation and Tourism, Division of Archaeology. Site Form 16CD246. Baton Rouge, n.d.

Steers, Ed., ed. "Garrison Duty in Alexandria: The Red River Campaign Letters of Lt. Charles W. Kennedy, 156th New York Volunteer Infantry." *Civil War Regiments* 4, no. 2 (1994): 104–17.

Stoker, William Elisha. "The War Letters of a Texas Conscript in Arkansas." Edited by Robert W. Glove. *Arkansas Historical Quarterly* 20 (Winter 1961): 355–87.

Suderow, Bryce, ed. "'The World Never Witnesses Such Fights': A Southern Officer Tells of the War in Louisiana." *Civil War Times Illustrated* 24 (Sept. 1985): 20–25.

Sullivan, Steven. "Some of the Boys." *Military Images* 14, no. 5 (Mar. 1993): 14.

Sutton, John M. "Gray's 28th Louisiana Infantry, Confederate States of America." *North Louisiana Historical Journal* 29, no. 4 (Fall 1998): 113–34.

Tap, Bruce. *Over Lincoln's Shoulder: The Committee on the Conduct of the War*. Lawrence: Univ. Press of Kansas, 1998.

Taylor, John M. "Good Soldier Thompson: Albert Thompson Marches 2,300 Miles to Victory." *Manuscripts* 34, no. 3 (1982): 185–92.

Temple, Wayne Calhoun. *A Chaplain in the 11th Missouri Infantry*. Harrowgate, TN: Lincoln Memorial Univ. Press, 1962.

"Time Lapse." *Civil War Times Illustrated* 27 (Feb. 1989): 50.

Todd, Maria P. "'Old Abe,' War Eagle of the 8th Wisconsin." *Military Collector and Historian* 4 (1952): 72–73.

Trice, James Chesley. "No Descendants to Honor Them." *Arkansas Historical Quarterly* 10 (1951): 85–88.

Trudeau, Noah Andre. *Like Men of War: Black Troops in the Civil War 1862–1865*. Edison, NJ: Castle Books, 2002.

Tucker, Spencer C. *Andrew Foote: Civil War Admiral on Western Waters*. Annapolis, MD: Naval Institute Press, 2000.

Turner, Martha Anne. *Richard Bennett Hubbard: An American Life*. Austin: Shoal Creek, 1979.

"Unpublished After-Action Reports from the Red River Campaign." *Civil War Regiments* 4, no. 2 (1994): 132–34.

U.S. Navy Department, Naval History Division. *Civil War Naval Chronology 1861–1865.* Washington, DC: U.S. Government Printing Office, 1971.

——. *Dictionary of American Fighting Ships.* Vol. 2. Washington, DC: U.S. Government Printing Office, 1963.

Vandiver, Frank E. *Ploughshares into Swords: Josiah Gorgas and Confederate Ordnance.* College Station: Texas A & M Univ. Press, 2002.

"A Veteran of 33 Battles." *Civil War Times Illustrated* 32 (May–June 1993): 74.

Vetter, Charles Edmund. *Sherman: Merchant of Terror, Advocate of Peace.* Gretna, LA: Pelican, 1992.

Voorhis, Aurelius Lyman. *The Life and Times of Aurelius Lyman Voorhis.* Edited by Jerry Voorhis Sr. New York: Vantage Press, 1976.

Warner, Ezra J. *Generals in Blue: Lives of the Union Commanders.* Baton Rouge: Louisiana State Univ. Press, 1993.

——. *Generals in Gray: Lives of the Confederate Commanders.* Baton Rouge: Louisiana State Univ. Press, 1993.

Weddle, Robert S. *Plow-Horse Cavalry: The Caney Creek Boys of the Thirty-Fourth Texas.* Austin: Madrona Press, 1974.

West, Richard S., Jr. *The Second Admiral: A Life of David Dixon Porter.* New York: Coward McCann, 1937.

Whittington, G. P. "Rapides Parish, Louisiana—A History." *Louisiana Historical Quarterly* 18 (1935): 26–28.

Wight, Levi, Lamoni Wight, and Sophia Wight. *The Reminiscences and Civil War Letters of Levi Lamoni Wight: Life in a Mormon Splinter Colony on the Texas Frontier.* Edited by David Bitton. Salt Lake City: Univ. of Utah Press, 1970.

Williams, John C. "'The Fire of Hatred': A Rebel Remembers the Red River Campaign." *Civil War Times Illustrated* 17 (Jan. 1979): 20–31.

Williams, T. Harry. *Lincoln and the Radicals.* Madison: Univ. of Wisconsin Press, 1941.

——, ed. *Military Analysis of the Civil War: An Anthology by the Editors of Military Affairs.* Millwood, NY: KTO Press, 1977.

Winschel, Terrence J. "To Rescue Gibraltar: John G. Walker's Texas Division and the Relief of Fortress Vicksburg." *Civil War Regiments* 3, no. 3 (1993): 33–58.

Winters, John D. *The Civil War in Louisiana.* Baton Rouge: Louisiana State Univ. Press, 1963.

Winters, William. *The Musick of the Mocking Birds, the Roar of the Cannon.* Lincoln: Univ. of Nebraska Press, 1999.

Wright, Marcus J. *Arkansas in the War, 1861–1865.* Batesville, AR: Independence County Historical Society, 1963.

——, comp. *Texas in the War, 1861–1865.* Edited by Harold B. Simpson. Hillsboro, TX: Hill Junior College Press, 1965.

Zeitlin, Richard H. *Old Abe the War Eagle: A True Story of the Civil War and Reconstruction.* Madison: State Historical Society of Wisconsin, 1986.

——. *The Eighth Regiment, 1861–1865.* Racine, WI: Racine County Historical Society, 1984.

# Dissertations and Theses

Bailey, Georgianne. "Between the Enemy and Texas: Parson's Texas Cavalry in the Civil War." Master's thesis, Texas Christian Univ., 1987.

Bailey, Lelia. "The Life and Public Career of O. M. Roberts, 1815–1883." Ph.D. diss., Univ. of Texas, 1932.

Bergeron, Arthur W., Jr. "General Richard Taylor: A Study in Command." Master's thesis, Louisiana State Univ., 1972.

Johansson, M. Jane Harris. "Peculiar Honor: A History of the 28th Texas Cavalry (Dismounted), Walker's Texas Division, 1862–1865." Ph.D. diss., Univ. of North Texas, 1993.

Kimble, Harvey Harold. "A History of the 24th Iowa Infantry, 1862–1865." Master's thesis, Western Illinois Univ., 1974.

Kinard, Jeff Sowers. "Lafayette of the South: Prince Camille de Polignac and the American Civil War." Ph.D. diss., Texas Christian Univ., 1997.

McGowen, Stanley Sidney. "Horse Sweat and Powdersmoke: The 1st Texas Cavalry in the Civil War." Ph.D. diss., Texas Christian Univ., 1997.

———. "The Lineage and History of the 1st Regiment of Texas Cavalry in the Civil War." Master's thesis, Tarleton State Univ., 1993.

Miller, Robert E. "Missouri Secessionist General Mosby M. Parsons." Master's thesis, Univ. of Missouri, St. Louis, 1982.

Morris, Curtis Brooks. "The Life of Edward Clark: A War-Time Governor of Texas." Master's thesis, Stephen F. Austin State Univ., 1954.

Perkins, John Drummond. "Daniel's Battery: A Narrative History and Socio-Economic Study of the Ninth Texas Field Battery." Master's thesis, Univ. of North Texas, 1995.

Prushankin, Jeffery Scott. "A Crisis in Command: Richard Taylor and Edmund Kirby Smith in Confederate Louisiana during the Red River Campaign." Master's thesis, Villanova Univ., 1996.

Sanders, Raymond Wesley. "Men of Peoria in the Civil War." Master's thesis, Illinois State Normal Univ., 1960.

Schmidt, Peter C. "A Historical Study of the Fifth Minnesota Infantry Regiment in the Civil War." Master's thesis, Mankato State College, 1963.

Snyder, Perry Anderson. "Shreveport, Louisiana, during the Civil War and Reconstruction." Ph.D. diss., Florida State Univ., Tallahassee, 1979.

# INDEX

**Through the Howling Wilderness** was designed and typeset on a Macintosh computer system using InDesign software. The body text is set in 10/12 Minion and display type is set in Belwe. This book was designed and typeset by Stephanie Thompson and manufactured by Thomson-Shore, Inc.